Remarkable WOMEN

Remarkable WISDOM

A DAYBOOK OF REFLECTIONS

SISTER MARY FRANCIS GANGLOFF, O.S.F.

ST. ANTHONY MESSENGER PRESS

Cincinnati, Ohio

Scripture citations are taken from the *New Revised Standard Version Bible*, copyright ©1989 by the Division if Christian Education of the National Council of Churches of Christ in the U.S.A. and used by permission.

We are grateful for permission to quote material printed by the following publishers:

Reprinted by permission of Pinnacle Books, excerpts from *The Quotable Woman from Eve to 1799*, by Elaine Partnow, copyright © 1985. Reprinted by permission of the author, excerpts from *Give Her This Day: A Daybook of Women's Words*, by Lois Stiles Edgerly, copyright © 1990. Reprinted by permission of Pinnacle Books, excerpts from *The Quotable Woman 1800-On*, by Elaine Partnow, copyright © 1978. Reprinted by permission of Caillech Press, excerpts from *And Then She Said: Quotations by Women for Every Occasion*, by J.D. Zahniser, copyright © 1989. Reprinted by permission of the author, excerpts from *Quotable Saints*, by Ronda De Sola Chervin, copyright © 1992. Reprinted by permission of Running Press, excerpts from *The Quotable Woman*, copyright © 1991. Reprinted by permission of Williamson Music, "God Bless America," copyright ©1938, ©1939, ©1965, ©1966 by Irving Berlin. Reprinted by permission of The Stonesong Press, excerpts from *The New York Public Library Book of Twentieth-Century American Quotations*, Stephen Donadio, Joan Smith, Susan Mesner and Rebecca Davison eds., copyright © 1992 by Stonesong Press Inc. and the New York Public Library. Reprinted by permission of Houghton Mifflin Co., excerpts from *Through a Window: My Thirty Years With the Chimpanzees of Gombe*, by Jane Goodall, copyright © 1990, by Soko Publications, Ltd. Reprinted by permission of Pinnacle Books, Inc., excerpts from *The Quotable Woman: 1900- the Present*, by Elaine Partnow, copyright © 1977. Reprinted by permission of Peter Pauper Press, excerpts from *Women*, by Evelyn Beilenson, copyright © 1991. Reprinted by permission of Tan Books and Publishers, excerpts from *Modern Saints: Their Lives and Faces*, by Ann Ball, copyright © 1990. Reprinted by permission of Franciscan Press, excerpts from *Lives of the Saints: Daily Readings*, by Augustine Kalberer, O.S.B., copyright © 1983. Reprinted by permission of Armitage Watkins, Inc., *A Matter of Eternity: Selections From the Writings of Dorothy L. Sayers*, by Rosamond Kent Sprague, copyright ©1973. Reprinted by permission of the Estate of Robert N. Linscott, Emily Dickinson's "Bring Me the Sunset in a Cup," from *Selected Poems and Letters of Emily Dickinson*, copyright © 1959.

Cover and interior design by Constance Wolfer

ISBN 0-86716-352-6

Published by St. Anthony Messenger Press

www.AmericanCatholic.org

Printed in the U.S.A.

DEDICATION

This book is dedicated to:

Mom and Dad
Ruth and Tony

Ruth Anna Bookmiller Gangloff Zimmer
and Anthony Bernard Gangloff

my loving parents
whose very lives taught me that
women are remarkable and wise

ACKNOWLEDGEMENTS

This book comes from a lifelong interest in knowing prayerful women of strength and courage, reading about the wisdom and vision of women from many cultures, and a lived experience of relationships with remarkable women who held a strong sense of Jesus as Friend with women in the Gospels and beyond.

From my childhood years I thank :

- my parents—Ruth and Tony—for affirming that women are wonderful and resourceful, intelligent and creative and quite capable of deep spirituality;
- my sister and brothers—Joanne, John and George who have always been supportive of my interests and projects;
- my relatives and friends who modeled for me all that women can be.

From my school years I thank:

- many teachers and educators and parish priests who affirmed my interest in women's studies from grade school through high school and into college;
- Girl Scout leaders, neighborhood mothers, Franciscan friars, and other mentors including the children in my life who deepened my sense of life's windows which offer glimpses of God and views of women who flourished in wise and remarkable ways on their journeys to God.

In a special way, I thank:

- the remarkable women in my Franciscan community who have fostered the growth of this book by the ways in which they were still enough to see God's presence, generous enough to love tenderly, informed enough to act justly, and wise enough to walk humbly this good earth with God as Creator, with Jesus as Brother and Friend, and with Holy Spirit as Holy Wisdom.

Specific to this book, I wish to express my gratitude to a number of friends from whom I received encouragement, critique and suggestions, typing and computer assistance, helpful conversations, financial help, and spiritual reassurance... as the project spread over many years:

- Williamsville Franciscan Sisters—all of them, and especially: Sister Joanne Gangloff, Sister Margaret Toohill, Sister Margaret Therese Toohill, Sister Bea Leising, Sister Marie Louise Thompson, Sister Leona Marx, Sister Maureen Ann Muller, Sister Anne Hoyer, Sister Marian Rose Mansius, Sister Joan Hupp, Sister Virginia Balk, Sister Julie Uhrich, Sister Patricia Burkard, Sister Grace Marie Korn, Sister Mary David Gloekler, Sister Marie McTarnaghan, Sister Mary Dolores Cook, Sister Ann Helene Koenig, Sister Eleanor Galucki, Sister Marie Canice Geyer, Sister Mary Louise Lopez, Sister Kathleen Marie Huntz, Sister Dolores Wittmann, Sister Carmelita Rodriguez, Sister Catherine Meiler, Sister Dorothy Smith,

- And many others: Msgr. David Lee, Father Paul Priester, Msgr. Alan Zielinski, M. Dolores Lee, Victoria Gangloff, Esther Rae, Carol Riniolo, Grace Joly, Anne Marie O'Connor, Roberta Mure, Cathy Palz, Gretchen Lee, Claire Rung, Paula DeAngelis, Agnes Walsh, Rita Leising Staebell, Mary Dyster, Marianne Bookmiller Cody, Shannon Bowling, Wendy Gorski Kidder, Keith Kidder, Ray Stoklosa, Nancy Kelchin, Joanne Basta, Margaret Buckley, Susan Harper, Kathleen Carroll and Lisa Biedenbach.

CONTENTS

PREFACE

As a reader, you may choose to use this book in a number of different ways. You might wish to read the entry for each day on the day—taking a full year to make it round the 365 days—meditating on the message and praying and perhaps even sharing it in teaching, preaching, or conversation.

You might select key dates for yourself—your birthday, family birthdays and anniversaries, and see what women share those dates and what wisdom they offer.

You might go through and select women familiar to you already—and then come back and consider those not so familiar.

You might be looking for a particular woman or theme for some reason—and find it here.

However you choose to reflectively read and pray this book, my wish and prayer is that these remarkable women will bring to you and yours the blessings of wisdom they have brought to me.

Sister Fran Gangloff, O.S.F.
June 2001

 *January 1*

MARY, MOTHER OF GOD

Wife, mother, homemaker, disciple • Israel • 1st century

SCRIPTURE THEME

Motherhood

"But Mary treasured all these words and pondered them in her heart."
   — Luke 2:19

QUOTATION

"God could not be everywhere and therefore he made mothers."
   — Jewish proverb, A Book of Days, *page 293*

THE MOTHERHOOD OF THE VIRGIN MARY has remained a celebrated mystery throughout Christian history. For hundreds of years, the Eastern Rites celebrated the feast of Theotokos (meaning "Mother of God," one of Mary's titles), while the Western Rites celebrated the feast of the Maternity of Mary. In 1969, the two agreed on a calendar revision making January 1 the feast of the Mother of God.

All lands and cultures, and every human life, have experienced motherhood. The songs of twenty centuries sing its praises. All of us have known the love of a mother (even if it was from someone other than our birth mothers) and the joy of mothering another creature—a child, a sick friend, a pet or a plant.

Mary, the Mother of God, symbolizes all that is ideal about motherhood. Her selfless devotion is reassuring. Her courage through dishonor, poverty and the unspeakable pain of losing a child is inspirational. And her loving presence, available to Jesus through his triumphs and his pain, reminds us of mothers who walked us through the park, read us stories and nursed us through heartaches. She is honored in symphonies and great works of art, but nowhere more than in those of us who try to bring the compassion of motherhood to our small charges.

REFLECTIONS

- Pray for your mother.
- Many works of art, music, literature and Scripture honor the Mother of God and mothers in general. Choose a favorite of these works, and reflect on why you like it so much.

- How have your memories of your mother or grandmother shaped how you feel about mothers and motherhood?

PRAYER

O God,
  We praise you for Theotokos,
  Mother of God,
  Your mother and our mother.

Mother of God,
  Theotokos,
  We pray for world peace.
  Through your intercession,
  Mother of God,
  Bring us the peace of a comforting mother
  To spread throughout our families
  And from there to all the lands of the world.
  Amen.

 *January 2*

BETSY ROSS

Legendary maker of first U.S. flag • U.S. • 1752–1836

SCRIPTURE THEME

Love of country

"Give therefore to the emperor the things that are the emperor's."
  — *Matthew 22:21*

QUOTATION

"A nation thrills, a nation bleeds,
A nation follows where it leads,
And every [one] is proud to yield
His life upon a crimson field
For Betsy's battle flag."
  — *Minna Irving,* The Quotable Woman: From Eve to 1799, *page 98*

BETSY IS REMEMBERED IN LEGEND for designing and sewing the first flag of the United States. As the story goes, she suggested a design to George

Washington who then drew a rough sketch with pencil. It is believed that George selected six-pointed stars, but Betsy convinced him to have five-pointed ones (because they could be cut with a single snip of the scissors). She did the stitching in her back parlor, and the Continental Congress adopted the flag in June 1777.

Betsy was born Elizabeth Griscom on January 1, 1752, in Philadelphia. Her family called her by the shorter "Betsy" and gave her a Quaker education. When she married John Ross, an Episcopalian upholsterer, in 1773, the Quakers disowned her because of her husband's religious beliefs. When John died in 1776, Betsy took over the upholstery business.

In 1777, Betsy married Joseph Ashburn, and after he died in 1782 in a British prison, Betsy married John Claypoole in 1783. She continued the upholstery business until 1827, when she turned it over to her daughter.

Betsy died January 30, 1836. The house in Philadelphia where it is thought she made the flag was marked as a historic site in 1887.

It is impossible to verify the legend of Betsy Ross and her flag making. Some sources say that she was a real person and an upholsterer but that she did not make the first flag or any flag. However it may have started, though, Betsy's story is firmly part of the American legend.

REFLECTIONS

- How do you feel about the American flag? Does it stir in you feelings of pride? Sadness? Indifference?
- What is your sense of patriotism? What would you do for your country? What would you refuse?
- For whom in your life is the flag most significant? How have their experiences colored their views?

PRAYER

We praise you, O God,
For women
Whose craft of quiet hours
Brings beauty
And meaning into our lives.
Amen.

January 3

ZINTKALA NUNI

Native American massacre survivor • U.S. • 1890–1920

SCRIPTURE THEME

Birds

"Look at the birds of the air; they neither sow nor reap nor gather into barns, and yet your heavenly Father feeds them. Are you not of more value than they?"
— Matthew 6:26

QUOTATION

"This is one lost bird and she's going to go home and rest near her parents."
— Renee Sansom-Flood, The Buffalo News, July 14, 1991

ON THE KILLING FIELDS OF WOUNDED KNEE, SOUTH DAKOTA, on January 3, 1891, one infant was found alive beneath her mother's body. The child was only a few months old, a member of the Lakota, called Sioux by the whites. The battle, which raged from December 29, 1890, through January 3, 1891, claimed the lives of two hundred Native Americans.

The young survivor was found by Brigadier General Leonard Colby, who adopted her and called her Marguerite. When the baby was found, she had on a small buckskin cap, which was decorated with bright bead-work of the American flag. Clara Colby, the general's wife, did all she could to help their adopted child.

Lost Bird's adopted father treated her as a "living curio" of the massacre. Her life was haunted by the stories of her origins. Although she returned to South Dakota several times in search of her family, she never found any members.

As part of Buffalo Bill's Wild West Show, Lost Bird rode horses and traveled around the country, doing vaudeville and small parts in silent films. She suffered physical and sexual abuse, according to a contemporary biographer, Renee Sansom-Flood. Marguerite died at twenty-nine and was buried in California.

Sansom-Flood, a former social worker on American Indian reservations, spent eight years researching the life of Lost Bird and locating her burial place. Arrangements were made to relocate her grave to the site of the mass grave at Wounded Knee, where her mother was buried at the time of the massacre.

The present-day spiritual leaders of the Lakota purified the gravesite with burnt sage and conducted the graveside ceremony in Lakota and English. They also planted small cherry trees, symbolic of life. Lost Bird's soul was set free to be reunited with the spirit of her people.

REFLECTIONS

- Read more about Wounded Knee and the Trail of Tears. Or learn more about Lakota spirituality at your local library.
- Have you thought about where (and whether) you will be buried? Do you feel strongly about what is done with your body after your death?
- Visit the grave site of someone dear to you. When do you most miss this person? How is the deceased person even more present to you now?

PRAYER

In visiting cemeteries
May we call to mind
The lives of all buried there
And pray to God
That their spirits and souls
Be set free
To be reunited
With the spirits and souls
Of their loved ones.
Amen.

 *January 4*

ELIZABETH ANN SETON

Wife, mother, founder of Sisters of Charity and parochial school system in U.S. · U.S. · 1774–1821

SCRIPTURE THEME

Good neighbors

"'Love your neighbor as yourself.' Love does no wrong to a neighbor, therefore, love is the fulfilling of the law."

— *Romans 13:9-10*

QUOTATION

"Through piety and gratitude we come to the deepest recess of peace and true contentment."

— *Elizabeth Seton,* The Last Word, *page 19*

ELIZABETH ANN BAYLEY WAS BORN IN NEW YORK CITY to a wealthy family. At twenty, she married William Seton and soon became the mother of five children. By the early 1800's, William Seton had lost his wealth when his shipping business failed. His health declined from worry, and he died in 1803. Elizabeth was not quite thirty.

Shortly after the birth of their fifth child, the Setons went to Italy for the sake of William's health. After William died in Italy, a local family, the Filicchis, included Elizabeth in their prayers and visits to Catholic churches. After much study and prayer, Elizabeth left her Episcopal roots to convert to Catholicism—and lost the friendship of many relatives and friends as a result.

In 1809, Elizabeth established a small religious community in Emmitsburg, Maryland. The sisters cared for poor children—including Elizabeth's own. These Sisters of Charity were the first congregation of religious women in the United States.

With her community, Elizabeth established a school in Baltimore. Mother Seton and seventeen companions devoted themselves to education, assuring the growth of the parochial school system in the United States. Mother Seton wrote textbooks, worked among the poor and the sick, and trained her sisters for teaching.

Her community grew. Some of the sisters were sent to open an orphanage in Philadelphia in 1814, followed by one in New York City in 1817.

Elizabeth died on January 4, 1821. She was canonized in 1975, the first American-born saint. Her body lies enshrined in Emmitsburg, at the motherhouse of the American Sisters of Charity.

REFLECTIONS

- If you are ever in the vicinity of Gettysburg, Pennsylvania, go to the next town of Emmitsburg, Maryland, to the Shrine of Saint Elizabeth Ann Seton. There are several buildings, a museum and a cemetery to visit. Nearby is the small chapel on the hillside where she used to go to pray.

- If you have an opportunity to visit the national Women's Hall of Fame at Seneca Falls, New York, look for the display on Elizabeth Ann Seton.

- Elizabeth was a wife, mother, widow, teacher and religious founder. How many roles do you have right now?

PRAYER

> May we learn, O God,
> To ask your help in filling
> All our roles.
> Remind us to include everyone,
> Even members of our own family,
> In our works of mercy.
> Amen.

January 5

OLYMPIA BROWN

Universalist minister • U.S. • 1835-1926

SCRIPTURE THEME

Ministry

"You are my sheep, the sheep of my pasture and I am your God, says the Lord GOD."
— *Ezekiel 34:31*

QUOTATION

"It was the first time I heard a woman preach and the sense of victory lifted me up."
— *Olympia Brown,* Remember the Ladies, *page 13*

BORN JANUARY 5, 1835, on a Michigan frontier farm, Olympia journeyed to Massachusetts for her education at Mount Holyoke Female Seminary. After a year, she transferred to Antioch College in Ohio and graduated in 1860.

During her college years, Olympia met Antoinette Brown Blackwell, the Congregationalist minister. When Olympia decided to pursue a similar path, she entered the theological school at St. Lawrence University and was ordained in 1863 by the Northern Universalist Association. Her first parish was in Weymouth, Massachusetts.

Olympia's interest in social reform and women's suffrage brought her into contact with Susan B. Anthony and Lucy Stone and several suffrage organizations of the times. In 1873, Olympia became a pastor in Bridgeport, Connecticut. There she met John Henry Willis. They were married later that year. Olympia continued to use her maiden name.

Their first daughter was born in 1876. In 1878, the family moved to Racine, Wisconsin, where their second child was born. Her husband became part owner of the *Racine Times,* while Olympia served as pastor and expanded her suffrage activities.

In 1887, Olympia resigned her pastorate to work full-time for the suffrage cause. In her later years, Olympia used her daughter's home in Baltimore as a base of operation for her speaking tours. It was at her daughter's home on such a visit that Olympia died in 1926.

REFLECTIONS

- How do you feel about families in which both parents work? Do you think it is a fulfilling alternative? A necessary evil? Selfish ambition?

- What would you be willing to give up in order to pursue a cause you considered important? What causes do you consider of vital importance? Why?

PRAYER

In our ministering, mothering,
Lecturing, campaigning,
May we imitate you, God,
For the well-being
Of our little families
And for our global family.
Amen.

 *January 6*

CATHERINE OF ARAGON

Wife, mother, queen • England • 1485–1536

SCRIPTURE THEME

Crown, persecution

"Blessed are those who are persecuted for righteousness' sake, for theirs is the kingdom of heaven."

— *Matthew 5:10*

QUOTATION

"They tell me nothing but lies here, and they think they can break my spirit. But I believe what I choose and say nothing. I am not so simple as I seem."

— *Catherine in a letter to King Ferdinand of Spain (1508),* The Quotable Woman: From Eve to 1799, *page 83*

CATHERINE'S PARENTS WERE KING FERDINAND V AND ISABELLA OF SPAIN. Catherine was engaged to Arthur, the eldest son of King Henry VII of England. When Arthur died, Catherine was persuaded to remain in England and marry Arthur's brother, Henry, who became Henry VIII at the death of his father.

As a devout Catholic and a member of the Third Order of Saint Francis, Catherine attended daily Mass and lived a virtuous life. She was devoted to the education of her children, five of whom died young. Only Mary survived.

Catherine suffered greatly when Henry turned his affection to another woman, Anne Boleyn. Henry wanted to divorce Catherine and marry his mistress. When the Catholic Church refused its consent, Henry broke with it, and founded his own church, plunging the country into centuries of religious wars and persecution.

Catherine insisted on a decision from the pope rather than the English court. But the papacy, fearful of the political repercussions, delayed for several years and Henry, impatient for a male heir, married Anne Boleyn secretly. In 1534, the papal authorities declared the marriage valid and Catherine stuck by this.

Catherine removed herself to a secluded place and lived out her days deprived of her children and her church because of the persecution wrought by Henry VIII. She died January 6, 1536.

REFLECTIONS

- When have you held to your faith in the midst of persecution? Have you ever been asked to defend your beliefs or faith? How did you feel?
- Watch the PBS series *The Wives of Henry VIII,* available on video.
- Have you ever found yourself in honest disagreement with the teachings of your faith tradition? How did you handle the discrepancy?

PRAYER

We praise you, O God,
For those with faith enough
To pursue what is right
And to endure what is wrong.
Give us the strength in faith
To lead noble lives.
Amen.

ZORA NEALE HURSTON

Writer • U.S. • 1901–1960

SCRIPTURE THEME

Hometown

"When he came to Nazareth, where he had been brought up, he went to the synagogue on the sabbath day, as was his custom."
— Luke 4:16

QUOTATION

"Mama exhorted her children at every opportunity to 'jump at de sun.' We might not land on the sun, but at least we would get off the ground."
— Zora Neale Hurston, And Then She Said, *page 4*

PRAISED FOR HER USE OF DIALECT AND FOLKLORE, Zora based her fiction on her personal experience. Born in Eatonville, Florida, on January 7, 1901, she drifted from relative to relative after the death of her mother in 1910. She worked domestic jobs to support her two years at Morgan College in Baltimore. She enrolled at Howard University until a scholarship allowed her to attend Barnard College. In 1928, a fellowship allowed her to go south to collect folklore.

During this time, Zora wrote short stories, some of which were published. Her first novel, *Jonah's Gourd Vine,* was published in 1934. Her second, *Their Eyes Were Watching God,* received high praise and is considered her best novel. Her third, *Seraph on the Suwanee,* reveals the struggle of a southern white woman in a rural setting.

Zora made the most of the culture and setting of her hometown, thoroughly integrating the folklore and native dialect into all her work. She died January 28, 1960.

REFLECTIONS

- Read *Drenched in Light*, Zora Neale Hurston's early biographical story.
- Are you proud of your hometown? Do you celebrate its unique traditions?
- Recall some of the local folklore that intrigued you as a child—haunted houses, historic places, famous names. How did these stories shape your imagination?

PRAYER

May we praise you, O God,
In every dialect and language
Of all the peoples.
May we celebrate
The wealth of our diversity
And proudly represent
Our heritage.
May our eyes
Ever be watching God.
Amen.

 *January 8*

EMILY BALCH

Economist, social reformer • U.S. • 1867–1961

SCRIPTURE THEME

Peace, refugees

"The LORD is a stronghold for the oppressed, a stronghold in times of trouble."
  — Psalm 9:9

QUOTATION

"When I sailed on the Noordam, in April [1915], with the forty-two other American delegates to the International Congress of Women at The Hague, it looked doubtful to me, as it did to others, how valuable the meeting could be made.... What stands out most strongly among all my impressions of those thrilling and strained days at The Hague is the sense of the wonder of the beautiful spirit of the brave, self-controlled women who dare ridicule and every sort of difficulty to express a passionate human sympathy, not inconsistent with patriotism, but transcending it."
  — Emily Balch, Give Her This Day, *page 10*

BORN NEAR BOSTON ON JANUARY 8, 1867, Emily attended Bryn Mawr College and was in its first graduating class in 1889. After studying in Paris, Berlin and Chicago, Emily trained in social work, including work at a settlement house in Boston. She began teaching at Wellesley College and in 1913 was named a professor of political and social science. Still interested in settlement houses, she worked with Jane Addams's Hull House in Chicago. She also served on commissions and promoted industrial education, child welfare reforms and immigration concerns.

Since Emily was a member of the Society of Friends (the Quakers), the issue of peace was especially important to her. In 1915, she attended the International Congress of Women at The Hague and became ever more committed to what was then the unpopular cause of peace. By 1918, Wellesley dismissed Emily for her views. She turned her energies to helping Jane Addams begin the Women's International League for Peace and Freedom (WILPF) in Zurich. Emily served as secretary of the group from 1919 to 1922, and again in 1934 to 1935.

In 1926–1927, Emily served on a commission to study conditions in Haiti and was the principal author of the report, *Occupied Haiti*. This work hastened the withdrawal of U.S. forces from Haiti. In 1946, she was recognized for her peace efforts as she shared the Nobel Peace Prize with John R. Mott. She gave her share of the money to WILPF.

Emily wrote several books on social topics and, in 1941, published a book of verse titled *The Miracle of Living*. She died January 9, 1961, one day after her ninety-fourth birthday.

REFLECTIONS

- Find a list of Nobel Prize winners. In which category are women best represented? Does this surprise you?
- How have you worked to foster the cause of peace?
- Are there refugees, immigrants or itinerant workers in your area? Is your attitude toward them one of sympathy or disdain? Could you imagine a day in their shoes?

PRAYER

With peace, O God,
Bless our world and homes,
As we praise you for peacemakers
And pray to know our part in peace works.
Amen.

January 9

JOAN BAEZ

Folk singer, political activist • U.S. • 1941—

SCRIPTURE THEME

Singing, nonviolence

"And I heard a voice from heaven like the sound of many waters and like the sound of loud thunder; the voice I heard was like the sound of harpists playing on their harps, and they sing a new song before the throne...".

— *Revelation 14:2-3*

QUOTATION

"You don't get to choose how you're going to die. Or when. You can decide how you're going to live. Now."

— *Joan Baez,* The Quotable Woman: 1800-On, *page 24*

JOAN WAS BORN JANUARY 9, 1941, on Staten Island, New York City, to Quaker parents. Her family moved through different cities of the eastern United States, eventually settling in Boston. After spending some time at Boston University, Joan began singing in local coffeehouses.

People liked her direct and simple style with folk songs, ballads and the guitar. She sang at the 1959 and 1960 Newport Folk Festivals. Her first album was named simply *Joan Baez*.

Joan began singing protest songs as well as old English ballads and country music. She went on concert tours in the United States, Europe and Japan. Her involvement in the civil rights activities in the early 1960's and her opposition to the Vietnam War in the later 1960's firmed up her commitment to nonviolence. She used her music as a vehicle to promote nonviolent opposition to injustice and war.

Both Joan and her mother (also named Joan) were imprisoned in Santa Rita prison in October 1967 and again later that year for involvement in demonstrations of support for young men who refused to be drafted into the army. Joan met her future husband, David Harris, during her prison stay.

In March 1968, Joan and David were married. After the birth of their son Gabriel (Gabe), there were serious tensions and conflicts and an eventual separation. Gabe moved back and forth between his parents.

Since 1974, Joan has served on the advisory council of Amnesty International. She helped to found the International Human Rights

Commission of 1979. She opened the Live Aid concert to benefit Ethiopian famine victims on July 13, 1985, singing "Amazing Grace." In 1987, her book was published and became a national best-seller. *A Voice to Sing With* reveals Joan's personal ideals and values as well as her public life.

REFLECTIONS

- Listen to recordings of some of Joan Baez's music. How do artists and musicians promote the cause of social justice and reform?

- Joan's mother went to Somalia at age sixty-nine as a volunteer nurse at a relief camp in a Moslem world. She tells her story in *One Bowl of Porridge*. When have you used age or infirmity as an excuse when you might have helped?

- What social justice issues have you learned from your mother, and she from you?

PRAYER

We lift our voices, O God,
In songs and hymns to praise you
And encourage one another.
Amen.

 *January 10*

LAURA INGALLS WILDER

Pioneer woman, writer · U.S. · 1867–1957

SCRIPTURE THEME

Courage

"Be strong and courageous; for you shall put this people in possession of the land that I swore to their ancestors to give them. Only be strong and very courageous…".

— *Joshua 1:6-7*

QUOTATION

"'Did little girls have to be as good as that?' Laura asked, and Ma said: 'It was harder for little girls. Because they had to behave like little ladies all the time, not

only on Sundays. Little girls could never slide downhill, like boys. Little girls had to sit in the house and stitch on samplers.'"

— *Laura Ingalls Wilder,* The Quotable Woman: 1800-On, *page 128*

WHEN LAURA AND HER HUSBAND, MANLY, built their home at Rocky Ridge near Mansfield, Missouri, Laura wanted windows and lots of them, especially in her kitchen, so she could look out as she prepared food and enjoy the great outdoors which she loved.

Laura was born February 7, 1867, in a little log cabin in the big woods near Lake Pepin, Wisconsin. (Today, there's a historical marker, a rebuilt log house and a museum about Laura and her family at Pepin.)

Laura's "Pa" (as she fondly called her father) had "restless feet" (as he called them), and the family moved around by covered wagon to find better land for crops during the era of homesteading. When she had grown, her daughter, Rose, encouraged her to write. Laura had a lot of practice at creating word pictures. When she was a young girl, her sister, Mary, was blinded by diphtheria and depended on Laura's vivid descriptions. Laura wrote the stories of all these "little houses" into books for children. The first one, *Little House in the Big Woods,* was published in 1932 when Laura was sixty-five.

In addition to the Little House books, Laura's diary of the trip from Dakota to Missouri in 1894, as well as her letters back home to Manly during her 1915 trip to San Francisco to visit Rose and the World's Fair, were published into books. The diary and letter format was retained for *On the Way Home* and *West From Home.*

Laura died in 1957, a few days past her ninetieth birthday.

REFLECTIONS

- Laura began publishing books at age sixty-five. What are your plans for your senior years and retirement?
- Pa had favorite nicknames for Laura—"Half-Pint," "Little Half-Pint of Cider Half Drunk Up." Laura also loved Pa's fiddle music and stories. What are your most fond memories of your father?
- If you have never done so, read a book from the Little House series or share it with a child.

PRAYER

Be our strength and courage, O God,
   As we face the frontiers of our times.
   Let our vision and experience

Light the path for others.
Amen.

I thank you, God,
For the women in my life
Who have windows in their minds
And prayers in their hearts.
Amen.

January 11

ALICE PAUL

Feminist, lawyer • *U.S.* • *1885-1977*

SCRIPTURE THEME

Single-mindedness

"Blessed are the pure in heart, for they will see God."

— *Matthew 5:8*

QUOTATION

"I always feel the movement is a sort of mosaic. Each of us puts in one little stone, and then you get a great mosaic at the end."

— *Alice Paul*, And Then She Said, *page 48*

FOR ALICE PAUL, THROWING BRICKS THROUGH THE WINDOWS of public buildings became her expression of rebellion. She was living in England at the time, in tune with the logic of British women who used this militant tactic as evidence that their spirits and souls were alive.

When back in the United States and questioned about the Christian nature of window smashing, Alice said that she saw no particular sanctity in a twenty-five-cent windowpane. Like the British who considered windows public property and broke only one or two at a time to make their point, Alice defended her stance of violence against property.

This violence, minor though it was, did not sit well with the Quakers, of whom Alice was a member. Alice graduated from a Friends school, studied philanthropy and worked with Quakers at settlement houses. She won a fellowship to a Quaker center in England, and there she grew in sympathy for the suffrage movement (and the window-smashing technique).

Alice was a woman ahead of her time and grew impatient with the pace of Quaker women's activities. In her singleness of purpose, Alice devoted herself to the passage of women's suffrage—the Nineteenth Amendment—in the United States. She developed a strategy of asking those women who had the vote in the western states to vote against certain candidates. Alice led demonstrations against President Woodrow Wilson, goading him to obtain passage of the amendment.

Credit must go to Alice Paul for her leadership in peaceful protests, acceptance of prison terms and nonviolence toward persons in the struggle for women's rights.

With the ratification of the Nineteenth Amendment on August 26, 1920, Alice Paul celebrated and then moved on to the Equal Rights Amendment. She earned several law degrees in her efforts to gain acceptance and to secure federal legislation that would protect the rights of working women. From 1923 to 1972, Alice and her colleagues lobbied for this amendment at every session of Congress.

Often criticized and challenged by the Society of Friends who saw social issues as interconnected, Alice pursued her single-minded cause. While other Quaker women put their efforts into peace work and racial justice, Alice insisted that these would be secured when women had equal access to power.

Alice was many decades ahead of her time and did not always fit the image of a model Quaker woman, but throughout her life, she considered herself a Quaker and valued her Quaker heritage.

REFLECTIONS

- The Quaker tradition offers great diversity and variety for its members in a unity of openness to God's Holy Spirit. Is this also true of your religious tradition?
- What cause would keep you returning to Congress to lobby for fifty years?
- Write a letter, make a phone call, send a contribution or volunteer your talents for your favorite cause.

PRAYER

May we remember to use wisely
The right to vote
For the good of peoples
And for the peace of our world.
Amen.

 *January 12*

AGATHA CHRISTIE

Mystery novelist · England · 1890–1976

SCRIPTURE THEME

Love of Christ

*"Set me as a seal upon your heart
as a seal upon your arm;
for love is strong as death,
passion fierce as the grave."*

— *Song of Solomon 8:6*

QUOTATION

"It is completely unimportant. That is why it is so interesting."

— *Agatha Christie,* The Quotable Woman: 1800-On, *page 223*

THE AGATHA CHRISTIE LEGEND was celebrated in centenary in September 1990, the hundredth anniversary of the birth of Agatha Mary Clarissa Miller. Probably the greatest writer of detective fiction, Agatha was certainly prolific and popular in what she wrote.

In her youth, Agatha wrote poetry and studied singing and music. She trained in pharmacy and served as a nurse. Her accomplishments affirm that women have intelligence, imagination and a sense of responsibility. Her accurate knowledge of poisons along with her ingenuity informed many of the crimes in her stories.

She married Archie Christie in 1914, and they had a daughter in 1919. Agatha pursued her career of writing. In 1924, they made a world tour. In 1928, Archie and Agatha divorced. In 1930, Agatha married again.

Hercule Poirot and Miss Marple, characters created by Agatha, live in the pages of her fiction. So, too, do a number of other memorable sleuths and characters. *Murder on the Orient Express* brought the famous train to vivid life, offering flights of imagination through Europe and the Near East to Baghdad.

Agatha was also able to do script writing, making her mystery novels into movies. And secretly, she wrote six books, sometimes described as romantic novels, under the name of Mary Westmacott. They were the books she always wanted to write about the thoughts and feelings of women.

Agatha wrote for radio, performing in some of the productions herself. And she wrote plays by the dozens, many of which were made into movies and TV films (mostly after her death). At seventy-five, Agatha wrote her autobiography. She died in 1976, on January 12.

REFLECTIONS

- Agatha kept by her bedside her mother's copy of Thomas à Kempis's *The Imitation of Christ* in which she had written this passage from Romans: "Who shall separate us from the love of Christ?" What special mementos keep you mindful of God's care in your life?
- Agatha's gift of writing had worldwide influence—from the convalescing person who reads a mystery to the crowds who see a movie or dinner theater in nearly every country of the world. How have you reached out to others with your gifts?

PRAYER

May we keep by our bedsides
The memory of a mother's faith,
The remembrance of a mother's love,
The treasure of a mother's hope.
Amen.

 *January 13*

SARAH CALDWELL

Opera producer, director and conductor • *U.S.* • *1928—*

SCRIPTURE THEME

Music

"I will sing to the LORD as long as I live;
I will sing praise to my God while I have being."
— *Psalm 104:33*

QUOTATION

"We must continuously discipline ourselves to remember how it felt the first moment."
— *Sarah Caldwell,* The Quotable Woman: 1800-On, *page 376*

SARAH WAS BORN JANUARY 13, 1928, and lived in Missouri and Arkansas as a child. She was gifted in music and gave public violin recitals by the time she was ten. She completed high school at fourteen, attended local colleges and then moved to Boston to enroll in the New England Conservatory of Music.

She chose opera over symphony orchestra and went to work as assistant to Boris Goldovsky in the New England Opera Theater. In 1946, Sarah's first production on her own, Ralph Vaughan Williams's *Riders to the Sea*, attracted good reviews. She spent several summers as instructor at the Berkshire Music Center at Tanglewood. From 1952 to 1957, she headed the opera workshop at Boston University.

In 1957, Sarah organized the Boston Opera Group and helped it establish a fine reputation with both new and traditional productions. Sarah understood opera as both musical and visual and was skilled in theatrical productions.

As conductor, she was also gifted. In 1975, she conducted the New York Philharmonic Orchestra. In 1976, she became the first woman to conduct at the Metropolitan Opera in New York City. In 1983, she began a new role as artistic director of Israel's New Opera Company. Sarah is world renowned as a conductor and opera producer.

REFLECTIONS

- Check your local music scene for women in musical leadership roles. How does their musical interpretation speak to you?
- Attend an opera or rent a video of one. Do you find the staging reinforces the power of the music? How does this compare with a movie version of a favorite book?

PRAYER

May we be women of wisdom
Speaking our voices in truth,
Lifting our voices in praise,
Sharing our voices in love.
May the actions of our lives truly reflect
The music in our souls.
Amen.

January 14

MACRINA THE ELDER

Mother and grandmother in saintly family • Cappadocia • 3rd century

SCRIPTURE THEME

Grandmother

"Honor your father and your mother, so that your days may be long in the land that the LORD your God is giving you."

— *Exodus 20:12*

QUOTATION

"Words make a noise, but example thunders."

— *Latin maxim,* The One Year Book of Saints, *page 22*

MACRINA, A NATIVE OF THIRD-CENTURY CAPPADOCIA, now eastern Turkey, was born about the time of the death of Saint Gregory the Wonderworker who Christianized the area. Her family absorbed the faith of Gregory, and Macrina grew up with a strong sense of religious conviction. Macrina read the writings of Gregory and treasured the inspiration they were for her.

During the persecution of Emperor Galerius in the fourth century, Macrina and her husband fled to the wooded hills and stayed there for seven years, often hungry and in need. During a later persecution, their property was seized. Their faith kept them going during these trials and persecutions.

Macrina became the grandmother of several saints—Basil, Gregory of Nyssa and Macrina the Younger. As children, they learned of the Christian faith and grew to adulthood nurtured in Christian discipline.

Macrina, called the Elder to distinguish her from her granddaughter, died at Neo-Caesarea about the year 340.

REFLECTIONS

- If you are a grandmother, what aspects of faith have you treasured and handed on? As a grandchild, what faith heritage comes from each of your grandparents and from your parents?

- Macrina grew spiritually from the writings of Gregory. Who are your favorite spiritual authors? Have you shared them with others?

- Pray for faith strong enough to endure whatever trials, tribulations and persecutions you will meet in life.

PRAYER

For our ancestral grandmothers
And spiritual teachers,
We thank you, O God.
Amen.

 *January 15*

JANE TAPSUBEI CREIDER

Woman in cross cultures • Kenya and Canada • 1946—

SCRIPTURE THEME

Home

"Those who love me will keep my word, and my Father will love them, and we will come to them and make our home with them."

— *John 14:23*

QUOTATION

"The only thing she was permitted to do was look through a window."

— *Jane Tapsubei Creider,* Two Lives, *page 73*

JANE'S BIRTH DATE, JANUARY 15, is contrived. When she was born among the Nandi people of East Africa, children were born at home and no one wrote down or remembered the date. When Jane found she needed a birth certificate, she and her father guessed at the year and made up the month and day. The Nandi people were much like the Masai in that they kept cattle and formed nomadic tribes always in search of pastures. Jane's spirit name was Chepituny Tapsubei, but because her mother's family had been converted to Christianity by missionaries, Jane also had a Christian name and spent some time at a mission school. Because her parents split up, Jane's childhood was split between mother and father.

In her autobiography, *Two Lives: My Spirit and I,* Jane describes her years on her grandmother's farm living in a thatched hut, and tells of initiation ceremonies and customs. In some cases, when a girl was spoken for as to marriage and initiated and engaged, she was then locked up until the time of the formal ceremony, sometimes for three or four years.

"The only thing she was permitted to do was look through a window," Jane wrote. "The 'window' itself was only a little peephole not much bigger than an eye."

Jane put off marriage and wandered in search of her mother and meaning for her life. In her book, Jane tells of her jobs as baby-sitter and nursery school worker, of her efforts at further education, of her experiences with missionaries and shopkeepers, and of her relationships with children and other adults.

Jane was able to move to Canada in the autumn of 1972, at the age of twenty-six, and pursued a career as a writer and clay sculpture artist. Her first son, Colin, was born in 1977. In 1980, the family returned to Africa for an extended family visit. Her interracial marriage and other experiences have made Jane "color-blind" and able to make close friends with people from any tribe or culture.

REFLECTIONS

- Reflect on times when you "hated" someone. Why did you feel this way? Did your feelings change? Why?
- Jane writes, "I was sure that God had never intended that some of his disciples sleep in luxury hotels while others suffered from mosquitoes" (*Two Lives*, The Woman's Press Limited, 1986, page 117). Are you ever struck by the incongruities between the lives of the poor and the lives of the rich?
- Volunteer to work in a soup kitchen or a shelter for homeless people.

PRAYER

May we find
In a mothering God
Meaning for our lives.
Amen.

 *January 16*

SAINT PRISCILLA

Early Christian • Rome • 1st century

SCRIPTURE THEME

Name of Priscilla

"There he found a Jew named Aquila, a native of Pontus, who had recently come from Italy with his wife Priscilla…".

— Acts 18:3

QUOTATION

"I am the daughter of the Church."

— Saint Teresa of Avila, Quotable Saints, *page 87*

HISTORY SAYS THAT PRISCILLA LIVED IN ROME in a villa near the catacombs. Tradition says that she offered hospitality to Saint Peter who made his Roman headquarters near her home.

Priscilla was the wife of Manius Acilius Glabrio and the mother of the senator Pudens. The papal headquarters near the catacombs bears Priscilla's name to this day.

REFLECTIONS

- Another first-century Priscilla was the wife of Aquila. This Jewish couple worked as tentmakers in Rome after they were banished from their homeland by Claudius. When they settled in Corinth, they welcomed Saint Paul into their home. Later, they returned to Rome, and it is believed that they were martyred there. Both were canonized as saints, and their feast is observed on July 8. What makes a married couple holy?

- What is your sense of hospitality? Does prayer play a part?

PRAYER

May we find our home in God,
As the marsh hen finds her nest,
And grow in willingness
To share our home and provisions
With friends and guests
And may we be mindful in prayer and deed
Of the needs of the homeless,

For God provides even the smallest bird
With food and shelter.
Amen.

January 17

ANNE BRONTË

Novelist · England · 1820–1849

SCRIPTURE THEME

Poetry

*"O Lord, open my lips,
and my mouth will declare your praise."*

— *Psalm 51:15*

QUOTATION

"There is always a 'but' in this imperfect world."

— *Anne Brontë,* The Beacon Book of Quotations for Women, *page 109*

THE YOUNGEST OF THE THREE BRONTË SISTERS, Anne was born January 17, 1820. Anne received almost no formal education. She and her sisters, Charlotte and Emily, wrote collaboratively as children and developed their imaginations to an artistic degree. As adults, they developed more individual styles of writing.

Anne is the one who saw more of the world outside the Brontë household at Haworth. It was Anne who spent five years as governess in the north country. There, she gained knowledge of the social life of well-to-do people, especially of their children—all from the perspective of governess.

Some of Anne's poetry was included in the 1846 publication of poems by Currer, Ellis and Acton Bell, the Brontë sisters' pseudonyms. Anne's poetry conveys her love of nature, her religious sensibilities and her love unfulfilled.

The writings of all three sisters were very popular and successful. During the winter of 1846–1847, Anne wrote *Agnes Grey*, which was published with Emily's *Wuthering Heights*.

Agnes Grey is semiautobiographical. Anne portrays with authenticity the manners of the early Victorian era as well as a sense of choice and self-dependence for females. In 1849, she wrote the melodramatic *Tenant of Wildfell Hall*.

Anne's health, always poor, grew worse following Emily's death in

December 1848. Anne died in May of the following year, at age twenty-nine.

REFLECTIONS

- Do you have sisters and brothers? How are their talents and interests different from your own?
- Have you ever felt overshadowed by a talented relative, fellow student or coworker? How can you use your gifts without devaluing the gifts of others?
- Read *Agnes Grey.*

PRAYER

For those who are left out,
Who are overshadowed by others,
We pray to you, God,
That their talents and gifts
May also receive recognition.
Amen.

January 18

MARY ANN LONG

Child who died of cancer • U.S. • 1946–1959

SCRIPTURE THEME

Sick child

"Why do you make a commotion and weep? The child is not dead but sleeping."
— Mark 5:38

QUOTATIONS

"You mean we make it so bright and cheerful here that everyone will know what it'll be like in Heaven?"

— Mary Ann Long, Modern Saints, *page 408*

MARY ANN LONG, BORN IN 1946, was diagnosed with incurable cancer at the age of three and a half. Her family was poor, her mother was ill, and the hospital would no longer keep her. A decision was made to send

Mary Ann to a home run by the Dominican sisters in Atlanta, at least until her mother could regain her health.

Though she had never seen nuns before, Mary Ann adjusted well. Almost immediately, she took an interest in other cancer patients and found little ways to cheer their days.

Mary Ann had to have an eye removed because of cancer. But despite her own suffering, her inner joy was evident—something more than the usual goodness of innocent childhood. Mary Ann's parents decided to have her baptized Catholic. The sisters instructed her in religious practices and prepared her early for her first Holy Communion when she was five and Confirmation when she was six.

Mary Ann went home to her parents and her Louisville, Kentucky, home for a while when she was six and again when she was eight, but for the most part, she lived at Our Lady of Perpetual Help Home with the sisters and other poor cancer patients. Mary Ann's sister, Sue, came to spend summers, and the two girls became interested in "playing nun." Sue also decided to become a Catholic.

Mary Ann did many thoughtful services for the other patients, often inviting them to pray with her. When a baby, Stephanie, came to the home with cancer, eleven-year-old Mary Ann became like a little mother to her. By her twelfth year, Mary Ann's health was much worse. She was allowed to become a Third Order Dominican, receiving a Dominican scapular and the name of Sister Loretta Dorothy.

During the night of January 18, 1959, Mary Ann died in her sleep. In her twelve years, she had joyfully lived the will of God.

REFLECTIONS

- When the Dominican sisters decided to write a biography of Mary Ann Long, they asked Flannery O'Connor to write the introduction. Find and read *A Memoir of Mary Ann* by the Dominican nuns (New York: Farrar, Strauss and Co., 1961).

- Do you know a family whose child has a serious illness? Pray and think about how you could help bring comfort, strength and faith to that child or family.

PRAYER

Bless all children, O God,
Especially those suffering
From incurable diseases,
And bring them the inner joy
Of your presence.
Amen.

January 19

OVETA CULP HOBBY

First commander of Women's Army Corps • U.S. • 1905–1995

SCRIPTURE THEME

Military

"Wisdom is better than weapons of war."

— Proverbs 9:18

QUOTATION

"Nothing gives me so widened a view of things as listening to a five-year-old tell about his school doings."

— *Oveta Culp Hobby*, Famous American Women, *page 220*

OVETA'S CHILDHOOD EDUCATION came from listening to visitors in her father's law office and reading the *Congressional Record* as much as it did from any schooling. Born January 19, 1905, in Texas, Oveta was fifteen when her father was elected to the state House of Representatives and moved to the capital of Austin. And she followed closely the sessions that discussed the League of Nations and the Women's Suffrage Amendment. Oveta was fifteen when women got the vote. She finished high school and one year of college and then served as parliamentarian for the Texas House of Representatives.

She worked for the *Houston Post* and married the publisher, William Hobby. Their creative partnership flourished, both in the newspaper world and in the home.

In 1941, Oveta went to Washington, D.C., to set up a Women's Interest Section of the War Department's Bureau of Public Relations. She assembled a staff of women reporters. She also spoke before House and Senate committees on behalf of an auxiliary corps of women for the army. At age thirty-six, she became the first commander of the Women's Army Auxiliary Corps (WAAC). She worked tirelessly building the nation's first women's army. She kept in touch with her children and husband by telephone calls every evening.

The corps' name was eventually changed to WAC, and Oveta became Colonel Hobby, with ever-expanding duties and demands as supervisor of WAC. In 1945, Oveta was awarded the Distinguished Service Medal, the first ever given to a woman. And then she returned to the *Houston Post*.

She served on the U.S. delegation to the United Nations Conference on Freedom of Information and the Press. In 1953, she was sworn in as director of the Department of Health, Education and Welfare, the second U.S. woman to hold a Cabinet position. She extended Social Security benefits and improved health care services.

Back in Texas after 1955, Oveta continued her cultural and civic interests. The library in the new college in her hometown of Killeen, Texas, is named the Oveta Culp Hobby Library.

REFLECTIONS

- Do you have any military experience? Do you know a woman who does?
- Do you know which current Cabinet members are women? How can you draw inspiration from them?
- Are you involved in civic and cultural affairs? Do you think it is important that women assume the responsibility of leadership roles?

PRAYER

For all the women in the military, we pray,
That their roles may be of service
And that they may always be treated
With equality and respect.
Amen.

January 20

SAINT AGNES

Virgin, martyr • Rome • 3rd century

SCRIPTURE THEME

Lamb of God

"*The next day he saw Jesus coming toward him and declared, 'Here is the Lamb of God who takes away the sin of the world!'*"

— *John 1:29*

QUOTATION

"*Christ made my soul beautiful with the jewels of grace and virtue. I belong to Him whom the angels serve.*"

— *Saint Agnes*, Quotable Saints, *page 74*

AGNES AND HER PARENTS practiced their Christian religion secretly as long as they were able. In the third century, the Roman emperors were intent on destroying Christianity and Christians.

A particular suitor desired Agnes in marriage. When she refused, he had her imprisoned, thinking she would choose him over torture. But Agnes took her stand against worship of pagan gods and against men who tried to take her by force.

Agnes was martyred in Rome around the year 300. *The Depositio Martyrum* of 354 records her feast. About the same time, Constantina, the daughter of Constantine, erected a basilica over her grave. Saint Ambrose praises her in his *De Virginibus* treatise and also in a hymn. Judentius and Saint Jerome also wrote about her. Because her name is close to the Latin for *lamb* (*agnus*), she is often pictured with a lamb or symbolized by one. She is the patron of young Christian womanhood.

It became the custom in England for girls to make special cakes on the Eve of Saint Agnes. At bedtime, the girls would walk upstairs backward with the cakes, put them under their pillows and pray that Saint Agnes would send them dreams of fine men to marry.

REFLECTIONS

- Do you know a woman who has refused a suitor because of his religious beliefs? Do you find this admirable? Foolish?

- Agnes, just as many other women martyrs, was very young at her death. Do you find that your youthful idealism has faded with the years? Or do you feel grateful that you have learned better than to follow your heart so passionately?

- Do you think that a woman's virginity is given too much emphasis? Too little?

PRAYER

For all young girls
That they may grow
In the gospel value of chastity,
That the sexually abused
May be healed with grace,
That those who are looking
May find suitable husbands,
For all these we pray,
Lamb of God, hear us.
Amen.

January 21

ANNA WHITE

Shaker eldress, writer • *U.S.* • *1831–1910*

SCRIPTURE THEME

Motherhood of God

"Can a woman forget her nursing child,
or show no compassion for the child of her womb?
Even these may forget,
Yet I will not forget you."

— *Isaiah 49:15*

QUOTATION

"By its existence, the Peace Movement denies that governments know best; it stands for a different order of priorities: the human race comes first."

— *Martha Gellhorn,* The New York Public Library Book of Twentieth Century American Quotations, *page 414*

BORN OF QUAKER PARENTS ON JANUARY 21, 1831, Anna was educated at a Quaker boarding school in Poughkeepsie, New York. At eighteen, she began to work with her father. It was on their travels together that she came to know the Shakers. She felt drawn to the Shaker music and worship.

Before her nineteenth birthday, despite family disappointment, Anna joined the Shaker community at New Lebanon. She lived with the North family section and was tutored by Shaker leaders including Ruth Landon. She rose to a leadership position in the community, becoming associate eldress for the care of the girls in 1865. She became first eldress of the North family section in 1887 and remained so until her death.

Anna had a keen social conscience and was concerned especially about international disarmament and peace efforts, as well as women's rights.

Anna compiled two books of her favorite Shaker hymns. She also wrote some of her own. She collaborated with another Shaker woman, Leila S. Taylor, to publish a history of the Shaker movement. Near the end of her life, Anna wrote *The Motherhood of God,* a book that described her sense of God as mother.

In her later years, she lived quietly. She died in New Lebanon on December 16, 1910, at age seventy-nine.

REFLECTIONS

- Are you familiar with the style of Shaker furniture? What do you admire about it?
- Have you ever considered converting from one religion to another? Did the influence of family and friends affect your ultimate decision?
- What role does music play in your religious practice?

PRAYER

We praise you, God,
For all the simple gifts
That are part of our lives
Because of the Shaker tradition
Of true simplicity.
Amen.

 *January 22*

HELEN ALVARÉ

Pro-life activist · U.S. · 20th century

SCRIPTURE THEME

Choose life

"See, I have set before you today life and prosperity, death and adversity.... Choose life so that you and your descendants may live."
— *Deuteronomy 30:15-19*

QUOTATION

"Once you say, 'Abortion is such a complex problem, we'll never settle it,' you've given up the ship. What's complex are the situations women find themselves in where abortion appears to be an out."
— *Helen Alvaré, St. Anthony Messenger, January 1992, page 33*

IN OCTOBER 1990, HELEN TOOK UP THE POSITION of Director of Planning and Information for Pro-Life Activities at the National Conference of Catholic Bishops (NCCB). In this role, she acted as the national spokesperson for the U.S. Catholic bishops on the topic of abortion in print media as well as radio and television. Helen also handled the relationship of the NCCB with outside public affairs consultants in policy, programming and financial areas.

Born in the early 1960's, Helen was the youngest of five children. Her father, Louis, was a native Cuban; her mother, Rosemary, an Irish American. From them, Helen inherited a love for prayer and books, a respect for life and devotion to Mary.

Helen attended St. Catherine of Siena grade school and Villa Maria Academy, both in Philadelphia. Over the years, Helen developed a keen interest in the Virgin Mary, especially the deep faith of this human woman. She graduated summa cum laude from Villanova University with a bachelor's degree in economics in 1981. She received her law degree in 1984 from Cornell University. In 1989, Helen received her master's in systematic theology from Catholic University and began work on her doctorate in the same field. She interrupted her doctoral work in 1990 to take on her post at the NCCB, which she held for ten years. In July, 2000, Helen took a position as professor at the Catholic University of America's Columbus School of Law.

Helen has also worked as a litigation associate for a Philadelphia law firm and as an attorney in the Office of General Counsel for the United States Catholic Conference (USCC). In this role, Helen coauthored several briefs in major abortion cases, as well as euthanasia cases, maternal-fetal conflict cases and First Amendment cases.

REFLECTIONS

- Helen has a bumper sticker on her small truck: "Real Feminists Don't Kill Babies." Do you have strong feelings about the abortion issue? What personal experiences have helped to shape your opinions?

- What are your views on child care and maternal leave? Do you believe that our culture gives mothers the support they need? How can you be more supportive of a mother you know?

- What progress has been made in the workplace toward equality for women? What yet remains to be accomplished?

PRAYER

For every woman, we pray,
    That she may support life
    In her values, her decisions,
    Her teachings, her examples,
    Her witness, her choices.
    Amen.

In our efforts to respect life,
> May we absorb the Spanish tradition
> Of welcoming children as gifts
> And of valuing family life.
> We ask your blessing, O God,
> On all children and families.
> Amen.

 *January 23*

MARY WARD

Apostolic worker • England • 1585–1645

SCRIPTURE THEME

Prophet

"There was also a prophet, Anna…. She never left the temple but worshiped there with fasting and prayer night and day."

— *Luke 2:6*

QUOTATION

"Fervor is not placed in feelings but in will to do well, which women may have as well as men. There is no such difference between men and women that women may not do great things as we have seen by example of many saints who have done great things."

— *Mary Ward*, The Quotable Woman: From Eve to 1799, *page 136*

BORN IN YORKSHIRE, ENGLAND, IN 1585, Mary became associated with a religious community in her twenties. She founded an organization of lay-women who were subject to the pope rather than to the local bishop. The women worked especially for the education of women. English Catholic leaders asked the pope to dissolve the group on the grounds that women's temperaments made them unsuitable for pastoral work.

In 1629, the congregation founded by Mary Ward was suppressed. Mary was excommunicated as a heretic when she continued with her work. When death was near, she was refused the sacraments. Five decades after Mary's death, the suppression was lifted.

REFLECTIONS

- How much has our world grown in its understanding about the ability of women to serve? Are there still roles that people feel are more appropriate for men than women?

- Some consider Mary Ward a prophet before her time. Others consider her a disobedient heretic. What is your opinion?

- Do others see you as an original thinker, or are you content to follow the crowd? When has your temperament kept you from achieving something important? When have the misguided opinions of others done so?

PRAYER

In setbacks, in rejections,
May we pause a while,
And sit quietly with you, God,
And reassess where we're going
And listen again to your plan
For the pattern of our lives.
Amen.

 *January 24*

MARIA TALLCHIEF

Dancer • U.S. • 1925—

SCRIPTURE THEME

Dance

"You have turned my mourning into dancing;
you have taken off my sackcloth
and clothed me with joy."

— *Psalm 30:11*

QUOTATION

"Marriage and dancing are both very important, but it is better to take them one at a time."

— *Maria Tallchief,* Maria Tallchief, *page 32*

BORN JANUARY 24, 1925, IN FAIRFAX, OKLAHOMA, Maria Tallchief of the Osage people was named Elizabeth Marie and called Betty Marie. Dancing fascinated Betty Marie, both the ceremonial dances of the Osage and the ballet lessons to which her mother took her.

A discovery of oil on the Osage reservation provided good income for the family, and they moved to Los Angeles when Betty Marie was eight. By the time she was twelve, Betty Marie felt really divided between dancing and music. At fifteen, with a great Russian ballet teacher, she felt drawn even more to the dance. At seventeen, she went to New York and joined the Ballet Russe Company. She agreed to use Maria as a stage name but insisted on keeping her family name of Tallchief.

At twenty-one, Maria married George Balanchine, choreographer at Ballet Russe. In France, Maria danced with the Paris Opéra Ballet, and the people loved her. With her husband's choreography and her own sense of music, Maria danced beautifully in ballet after ballet.

She loved her work, but her life was almost entirely work. She wanted children, but her husband preferred total devotion to ballet. Their marriage lasted just six years. Eventually, she married an engineer in Chicago and became the mother of Elise Maria. She continued to work part-time as a guest ballerina. In 1980, she founded the Chicago City Ballet and served as its artistic director through 1987. Then she retired from the stage and devoted herself to family and home.

Her hometown and people honored her at a special Native American ceremony and made her a princess of the Osage.

REFLECTIONS

- What role does dancing play in your life? Do you find it liberating? Embarrassing?
- When have you felt pulled apart by two valuable options? How did you resolve the tension?

PRAYER

O Lord,
May we ever
Move in the rhythm of your love.
Amen.

January 25

CORAZON AQUINO
Political leader • Philippines • 1933—

SCRIPTURE THEME

Courage

"So we do not lose heart…. For this slight momentary affliction is preparing us for an eternal weight of glory beyond all measure."

— *2 Corinthians 4:16-17*

QUOTATION

"Faith is not simply a patience which passively suffers until the storm is past. Rather, it is a spirit which bears things—with resignation, yes, but above all with blazing, serene hope."

— *Corazon Aquino,* The Picture Life of Corazon Aquino, *page 39*

CORAZON WAS BORN ON JANUARY 25, 1933, about fifty miles north of Manila in the Philippines. She grew up on a fifteen-thousand-acre sugarcane plantation. When she was nine, the Japanese invaded Manila, and things changed for everyone.

In 1945, she came to the United States and attended schools in Philadelphia and New York City. Like most Filipinos, Corazon was Catholic and was educated as such. When she returned to the Philippines, she studied law and soon married a politician-journalist, (Benigno) Ninoy Aquino.

When President Marcos declared the Philippines under martial law, Ninoy was seized and imprisoned. This left Corazon responsible for their five children. When Ninoy suffered a heart attack in 1980, he was sent to the United States for surgery. The Aquino family made its home in Boston. Ninoy decided to return to the Philippines in 1983; he was assassinated as he arrived. Corazon became active in the opposition party, and when a tainted election in 1986 left Marcos in power, the influence of the Church and the might of the military helped Corazon become president of the Philippines.

Corazon Aquino faced many problems but made some progress with human rights. Rumored and attempted coups made her presidency difficult. The ratification of the Philippine constitution in February 1987 affirmed her as the people's choice.

In 1992, when the presidential election was held again in the Philippines, Corazon decided not to seek another term, choosing instead to spend more time with her family.

REFLECTIONS

- What is the role of women in government? How many women have risen to political prominence on the coattails of their husbands? How do you feel about this?
- Cardinal Jaime Sin of the Philippines offered strong Church support of Corazon, especially through the Catholic radio network. Do you think the religious establishment should try to influence politics? Why or why not?

PRAYER

Strengthen us, O God of freedom,
To work for human rights in every place
Where they are suppressed or denied.
Amen.

 *January 26*

MARIA VON TRAPP

Mother of a family of singers • Austria and U.S. • 1905–1987

SCRIPTURE THEME

Music

"David took the lyre and played it with his hand, and Saul would be relieved and feel better."

— 1 Samuel 16:23

QUOTATION

"He was the right husband for me and the relationship was every bit as romantic as the movie and play made it out to be."

— *Maria von Trapp*, Los Angeles Times, *March 30, 1987*

THE 1959 BROADWAY MUSICAL *The Sound of Music* brought to popular audiences the story of Maria von Trapp and her musical family. The stage play won six Tony Awards. The film version by the same name became an Academy Award winner.

The story of the young novice who chose the love of a man and his children over religious vows charmed its way into the hearts of audiences. And the real von Trapp family traveled about performing its music.

Maria was born January 26, 1905, in Austria. As an orphan, she became the ward of a man who was both socialist and anti-Catholic. By age eighteen, she had converted to Catholicism and entered a Benedictine convent as a candidate for the novitiate. The mother superior, sensing twenty-year-old Maria's uncertainty about a religious vocation, sent her to widower Baron George von Trapp's household as a teacher for his seven children. In time, she fell in love with the baron and his children. Eventually, she married him and joined the family.

The Trapp Family Singers, trained in Renaissance and Baroque music, sang throughout Austria and Europe until the Nazi invasion forced them to flee to the United States. *The Sound of Music* tells the story of Maria's life from her time in the convent until she and her family fled the Nazis.

The family set up housekeeping in an Austrian-style house in Vermont and continued to do singing tours until 1955. Maria organized a relief effort in the 1940's for Austrians left destitute by World War II. She began in 1955 to lecture and write about her faith and her family. On March 28, 1987, Maria died after surgery. She was eighty-two.

REFLECTIONS

- Watch a video of *The Sound of Music* or a local school's production of it.
- What values do you admire in Maria's life?
- Although she had long considered life as a Benedictine sister, Maria eventually chose to join a ready-made family with seven children. When have you found yourself making a life-changing decision? How do you feel about your decision in retrospect?

PRAYER

We thank you, O God,
For those who make music
In their hearts,
With their voices,
And on their instruments.
Amen.

January 27

ANGELA MERICI

Founder of the Ursulines • Italy • 1474–1540

SCRIPTURE THEME

Teacher

*"They were astounded at his teaching, for he taught them as one having author-
ity, and not as the scribes."*

— *Mark 1:22*

QUOTATION

*"If according to times and needs you should be obliged to make fresh rules, do it
with prudence and good advice."*

— *Angela Merici,* The One Year Book of Saints, *page 35*

ANGELA WAS BORN IN 1474 at Desenzano on the shore of Lake Garda in
Venice, Italy. At an early age, she was left an orphan. With a brother and
a sister, she was raised by her uncle.

She became a Franciscan tertiary and taught catechism to children in
her village. In 1516, she was asked to teach children in Brescia. She
organized an association of young women into the Company of Saint
Ursula, dedicated to teaching and good works.

Angela was the originator of the idea of a secular institute. The group
lived in their own homes, coming together for prayer and devoting
themselves to ministry. They took no vows and wore lay clothes but dedicated themselves to living the evangelical counsels privately.

Church authorities were unsure about mobile and unenclosed religious, and the group did not become a formal religious congregation
until after Angela's death.

Angela died January 27, 1540. The people of Brescia immediately
revered her as a saint. She was beatified in 1768 and canonized in 1807.
The Ursulines spread worldwide and still observe each year their founding date of November 25, 1535.

A convent school for girls, the first in North America, was established
in 1639 in Quebec by the Ursulines under the leadership of Blessed Marie
of the Incarnation.

REFLECTIONS

• What is your impression of nuns who teach? Do you have any personal experience of this?

- Do you belong to any group that devotes itself to good works? Have you ever received help from such a group?

PRAYER

As Angela prayed,
"Into Thy hands, I commend my Spirit,"
May we also pray
In the face of death,
"Into your hands, O God,
We commend our spirits."
Amen.

 *January 28*

CHRISTA MCAULIFFE

Astronaut, teacher, mother • *U.S.* • *1948–1986*

SCRIPTURE THEME

The stars, the heavens

"If I ascend to heaven, you are there."

— *Psalm 139:8*

QUOTATION

"I liken what I'm going to do to the women who pioneered the West in...wagons. They didn't have a camera; they described things in vivid detail, in word pictures."

— *Christa McAuliffe*, People, *August 5, 1985*

JANUARY 28, 1986: A few minutes before noon, the news came that the *Challenger* space shuttle had exploded in the first few moments of flight. The news stunned the nation, much as the news of the assassination of President John F. Kennedy had done. But this time, schoolchildren were much more involved. On board the *Challenger* was Christa McAuliffe, a teacher. And her class, as well as classes everywhere, had been primed with science lessons about this space flight and were planning to watch lessons from space that Christa would teach aboard the *Challenger*.

Christa, born September 2, 1948, was the first ordinary citizen to be selected for the NASA program of space flight. Her five months of intensive training at the Johnson Space Center in Houston received wide publicity as a model for the future of space flight. Public interest ran very high as the January launch was delayed because of weather conditions. When the *Challenger* finally lifted off and then exploded, television viewers around the world saw it happening and sorrowfully watched the slow-motion video replayed for several days thereafter. That giant fireball trailing across the sky in its downward plunge remains etched in many memories.

Sadly, Christa's husband Steven and their two children, Caroline and Scott, were among those who witnessed the tragedy.

Reflections

- What are your memories of the *Challenger* explosion?
- Modern technology brings the details of tragedy into everyone's lives. How does this affect people, family life, children, you personally?
- What risks are reasonable in the cause of exploration, discovery and progress?

Prayer

For those who died in the *Challenger* explosion,
For their families and friends,
For their students and coworkers, we pray,
That all may find strength to live
In the memory of their service
In the space research program.
Amen.

 *January 29*

Elizabeth of Toro

African princess · Uganda · 20th century

Scripture Theme

Ancestors

*"I said, 'Let days speak,
and many years teach wisdom.'"*

— Job 32:7

QUOTATION

"Defiantly, I resolved that if I could play a part in saving our civilization from within Uganda, I would try."

— *Elizabeth*, Elizabeth of Toro, *page 118*

"I HAVE NEVER CELEBRATED BIRTHDAYS," Elizabeth states in her autobiography. For her, the African concept of time and life extends in both directions before conception and beyond death. This is her expression of the universal African concept of spiritual identification with ancestors.

Elizabeth was born in the kingdom of Toro (in Uganda) and named Bagaaya, an African name of strong and fearless women with a heritage of temporal and spiritual well-being for all the people. Daughter of Queen Kuzia Byanjeru and King George Matthew Kamurasi Rukiiki III, this East African princess (Batebe) was trained in the rituals and traditions of Toro and educated as a Christian in England. She graduated from Cambridge University, served at the English bar and returned to Uganda as its first woman lawyer. Indeed, she was the first woman lawyer in all of East Africa.

January 29, 1924, marked the coronation of her father as King of Toro, and its annual observance was the focal family and national celebration.

In 1965, the King died, and Elizabeth's brother, Patrick, was crowned. But Milton Obote's coup d'etat unleashed a dictatorship and a reign of terror. Elizabeth escaped to England where her years as an actress and fashion model made her a celebrity. When Obote was overthrown, General Idi Amin invited Elizabeth back to Uganda as Ambassador at Large and Minister of Foreign Affairs. She returned to her native land in 1971 and was most successful as a roving diplomat and foreign minister.

In 1974, Elizabeth led a delegation from her country to the United Nations, where she made a brilliant appearance as a woman of international understanding.

Amin turned against her and, in February 1975, she was forced to flee to Kenya where President Kenyatta gave her asylum and a home with his daughter, Margaret. After Amin's fall, Elizabeth returned to Uganda and married Wilbur Nyabongo, and together they worked for the liberation of Uganda. She wrote her autobiography, *African Princess*, and served as ambassador to the United States.

REFLECTIONS

- Elizabeth studied at Cambridge with Germaine Greer and considered her a friend. Do you recognize in your life the influence of high school or college friends? Do you still keep in touch with them?

- In her autobiography, Elizabeth describes the January 29 celebration in great detail. What are the key celebrations in your family—the preparations, observances and lasting meaning? What role do you play in preserving these traditions?

- Elizabeth acted in two films, *Things Fall Apart* and *No Longer at Ease*, based on books by Nigerian author Chinua Achebe. If you can, see one of these films.

PRAYER

Let us pray for those women
Who are imprisoned
Or held under house arrest
When they seek true freedom
For themselves and their countries,
That they may wait in hope
For deliverance and peace.
Amen.

 *January 30*

ELLA CARA DELORIA

Preserver of Native American culture • U.S. • 1888–1971

SCRIPTURE THEME

The good in one's native place
"He makes me lie down in green pastures;
he leads me beside still waters;
he restores my soul."
— *Psalm 23:2-3*

QUOTATION

"To have something given away in one's name was the greatest compliment one could have. It was better than to receive."
— *Ella Deloria, Waterlily, page 77*

ELLA WAS BORN A DAKOTA SIOUX at the Yankton Reservation. She studied at Oberlin College and Columbia University. Interested in the language and culture of the Dakota people, she did extensive research. Her scholarship and work proved most valuable to students of Native American life.

Ella was just as devoted to her family. She lived with her sister, Mary Sully, who was an artist. Together they published *Speaking of Indians* (1944), with text by Ella and illustrations by Mary.

From 1955 to 1958, Ella served as director of the Wakpala mission schools, which had been founded by her father in the 1880's. Ella also was assistant director of the University of South Dakota Museum. Ella continued her devotion and study of Dakota culture well into her seventies. Never did she have more than a meager income, but her work helped preserve the Native American culture of the Dakotas. Ella died at age eighty-three on February 12, 1971.

REFLECTIONS

- See if your library has a copy of any of Ella Deloria's books: *Waterlily, Dakota Texts, Dakota Grammar* and *Speaking of Indians*. Read one that interests you.

- What do you know of Native American culture? Do you think there are still Native Americans living much as they did before the European colonization?

PRAYER

We praise and thank you, O Great Spirit,
For the spiritual values in Native American cultures,
And we pray to be open and receptive
To learning and sharing these gifts of spirit.
Amen.

 *January 31*

SAINT MARCELLA

Noblewoman, widow · *Rome* · *325–410*

SCRIPTURE THEME

Widows

"Let your widows trust in me."

— *Jeremiah 49:11*

QUOTATION

"In three different ways, woman can fulfill the mission of motherliness: in marriage, in the practice of a profession which values human development...and under the veil as the Spouse of Christ."

— *Saint Theresa Benedicta,* Quotable Saints, *page 135*

MARCELLA WAS OF THE NOBLE CLASS in fourth-century Rome. After the death of her husband at an early age, Marcella turned her home into a place of retreat for women. She also offered hospitality to Saint Jerome for three years. He, in turn, guided her in reading and studying the Bible.

Jerome also encouraged Marcella to prayer and almsgiving. Though she had given her wealth to those in need, she was scourged by the Goths during the sacking of Rome—they believed she had hidden her wealth. From the effects of the cruel treatment, Marcella died in 410.

REFLECTIONS

- Reflect on the way Marcella learned and studied the Bible. Is the Bible central to your spirituality? Why?
- Who has guided you in prayer or good works? How has your life changed because of that influence?
- How are your money and possessions of service to people in need?

PRAYER

As Marcella studied the Scriptures
Under the guidance of Jerome
And practiced prayer and almsgiving,
May we, too, find
In the words of Scripture
Inspiration for prayer and good deeds.
Amen.

 *February 1*

BRIGID OF KILDARE

Founder of nunnery in Kildare • Ireland • 4th and 5th centuries

SCRIPTURE THEME

Compassion

"Finally, all of you, have unity of spirit, sympathy, love for one another, a tender heart, and a humble mind."

— 1 Peter 3:8

QUOTATION

"What is mine is theirs."

— Brigid, Lives of the Saints, *page 41*

BRIGID IS CLEARLY THE MOST POPULAR female saint in Ireland. Though much of what was written about her in the centuries after her death around 523 is mixed with folklore, her personality comes across as strong and happy with compassion and charity. The miracles and anecdotes attributed to her tell of her response to the physical and spiritual needs of her neighbors.

There is factual evidence that she founded a community of dedicated women at Kildare, where she served as abbess. The nuns wore habits of white homespun. Brigid used a chariot to go from Kildare on her errands of mercy.

Brigid has many names and titles: Mary of Gael, Queen of the South, Prophetess of Christ, and Bride. And many places bear her name: Bride's Peak in the Himalayas, Bride's Island off the shore of Japan, St. Bride's Bay in Wales. Many churches are called St. Bride's.

It is said that the word *bride* (or *bridgets*) as used in the English language came from the custom among the Knights of Chivalry of referring to the girls they married as their "brides." The nickname "Bridie" came from this word.

Brigid is the patron of all women born on Irish soil or of Irish descent.

REFLECTIONS

- You may enjoy reading more about Brigid's "miracles," such as changing bath water into beer or her cows giving milk three times a day.
- You might also enjoy reading more about the survival of her cloak and shoes and of her phase as a nun-cowgirl.

- The legend of Brigid's fire combines Christian and pagan elements. If you wish, look for more information.

PRAYER

May we tend the fire of love
As Brigid did tend the fire day after day after day—
So our hearts may grow
In courage, compassion, and good cheer.
Amen.

 *February 2*

ELIZABETH LANGE

Religious founder · Cuba and U.S. · d. 1889

SCRIPTURE THEME

Vision of peace, providence

*"Depart from evil, and do good;
seek peace, and pursue it."*

— *Psalm 34:14*

QUOTATION

*"Come quickly, come quickly, my neighbor.
The Savior of the World is just born.
Haste my neighbor, run my neighbor."*

— *a Christmas carol from a tale Elizabeth often told*, Mother Mary Elizabeth Lange: Life of Love and Service, *page 29*

THE FIRST RELIGIOUS CONGREGATION for women of African heritage to educate and evangelize Americans of African descent was founded by Mother Elizabeth Lange in 1829. Over a century and a half later, the Oblate Sisters of Providence staff twenty-three missions. Their membership, while still predominantly black, includes women of many nationalities and races.

Elizabeth was born in Cuba of San Domingian refugee parents. It is believed that Elizabeth traveled alone to the United States around 1817 and eventually settled in Baltimore where many French-speaking San Domingian refugees made new homes. About the same time, Sulpician fathers fleeing the French Revolution came to Baltimore.

James Joubert, a soldier, had fled France for San Domingo in 1777. In 1804, he fled to Baltimore, where he entered the Sulpician seminary and was ordained a priest.

Elizabeth Lange and a friend, Marie Balas, had been holding school for black children in Elizabeth's home. When Father Joubert became interested in the education of black children, he was put in touch with Elizabeth. They worked together to establish a teaching congregation of women religious.

Elizabeth became Sister Mary and Marie Balas became Sister Mary Frances. Two others joined them. The Oblates of Providence were officially founded July 2, 1829. The community, with Mother Lange in charge, found racial prejudice in the neighborhood and city and in the Church. Some objected to black women being allowed to wear a religious habit.

Some of the clergy and people of Baltimore were not supportive of the sisters. They felt that women of color were meant to be servants (and slaves), not religious, and that their children should not be educated.

Mother Lange took up kitchen work at the seminary to help support the community and school during hard times. Some members left; Sister Mary Frances Balas died. In 1845, hearing of their troubles, Father John Neumann (later bishop and saint) sent a Redemptorist to help the sisters, and things improved. In 1860, a Jesuit was sent to direct the sisters.

Housing problems and continued prejudice plagued the sisters during the Civil War era. Mother Lange carried on, even sending sisters to schools in New Orleans and Philadelphia. Some of the schools failed due to lack of funds and diocesan support and to continued prejudice and harassment.

In 1879, the fiftieth year of the Oblates, the Josephite fathers came to the assistance of the sisters. Mother Lange also celebrated her fiftieth anniversary.

In 1889, after several years of ill health, Mother Lange died on February 3. The process of her canonization was begun in April 1991.

REFLECTIONS

- Keep in mind that Elizabeth Lange's community of black women was set up in a slaveholding state before the Civil War. How do you resist injustices in your culture?

- Who are today's refugees, and how are they treated in your area?

- How do racism and sexism affect women, children and minorities in your neighborhood? Your household?

PRAYER

We praise you, O God,
For the wonderful heritage
Of Africa and African descendants.
As we look
To the future of religious life,
We pray for a vision
That is more inclusive
Of people of other colors,
In the spirit of Elizabeth Lange.
Amen.

 *February 3*

ELIZABETH BLACKWELL

Physician • England and U.S. • 1821–1910

SCRIPTURE THEME

Healing

"A cheerful heart is a good medicine,
but a downcast spirit dries up the bones."

— *Proverbs 17:22*

QUOTATION

"For what is done or learned by one class of women becomes, by virtue of their common womanhood, the property of all women."

— *Elizabeth Blackwell,* The Quotable Woman: 1800-On, *page 45*

BORN IN ENGLAND ON FEBRUARY 3, 1821, Elizabeth was well educated by private tutors and grew up in a cultured, prosperous family. When Elizabeth was eleven, her family came to know William Lloyd Garrison and became active in the abolitionist movement.

Elizabeth and her two sisters opened a school, and for several years, Elizabeth taught there. She also began to study medicine with a private tutor. Medical schools rejected her until Geneva Medical College accepted her. She was shunned by most of the male students and by most of the townspeople as she pursued her studies.

In January 1849, she became the first U.S. woman to graduate from medical school. She ranked first in her class. She was the first woman to become a doctor of medicine in modern times.

After becoming a naturalized American citizen, she went to Europe for further education. She studied midwifery in Paris and had hoped to study surgery. An eye disease left her blind in one eye, and she had to abandon her dream of becoming a surgeon.

In 1851, she returned to New York City where both her private practice and public acceptance were slow in developing. When she opened a small dispensary in a slum district, two other doctors, both women—one of them her sister Emily—came to help. In 1857, the dispensary was greatly enlarged and became the New York Infirmary for Women and Children.

Elizabeth devoted some time to writing and lecturing. She helped train nurses for the Civil War hospitals. In consultation with Florence Nightingale, Elizabeth was able to open the Women's Medical College at the New York Infirmary.

Elizabeth moved back to England in 1869 where, two years later, she helped to organize the National Health Society. For several years, she was professor of gynecology at the London School of Medicine for Women. She wrote several books, including *The Religion of Health* (1871) and *Pioneer Work in Opening the Medical Profession to Women* (1895). She died May 31, 1910.

REFLECTIONS

- How much rejection might you endure in order to pursue a special calling or dream?
- What other doors need to be opened to women in the medical profession? In other professions?

PRAYER

In gratitude for brave women
Who paved the way for us
As pioneers and as pathfinders,
As patrons and as employers,
As inspiration and as teachers,
We say, "Thank you," God.
Amen.

February 4

MANCHE MASEMULA

Martyr • South Africa • 1913–1928

SCRIPTURE THEME

Faith

"According to your faith let it be done to you."
— *Matthew 9:29*

QUOTATION

"Our real work is prayer. What good is the cold iron of our frantic little efforts unless first we heat it in the furnace of our prayer? Only heat will diffuse heat."
— *Mother Maribel*, Simpson's Contemporary Quotations, *page 191*

MANCHE BECAME A MARTYR AT THE AGE OF FIFTEEN. The calendar of the Anglican Church of the Province of South Africa commemorates her martyrdom on February 4.

Born in 1913 near Praetoria, Manche grew up in a village where animism was practiced. This primitive form of religion holds that the natural world is inhabited by and controlled by spirits. At fourteen, Manche witnessed the sacrificial death of her young cousin as an offering to the spirits of the weather.

The first person she happened upon after this frightful experience was the Christian priest in the village. He coaxed her into telling him about the evil spirits, and he told her about the great, good Spirit. Manche became a regular visitor to the Christian mission. She longed for Baptism, but she knew that would anger her family and village.

When Manche fell ill, her own village and family beat her for accepting medicine from the mission doctor rather than their witch doctor. Her family demanded that Manche give up her belief in the Christian God. When she refused, they beat her to death. When they tried to bury her, their tools struck stone. In fear, the family and villagers sent for the Christian priest. Because the priest was away, an elderly Christian gentleman came and buried Manche.

REFLECTIONS

- At what age did you claim or reject your religious heritage? When should children be allowed to make such decisions?

- When has someone outside your family helped you to see a better way of doing something? What was your family's reaction?

PRAYER

To you,
O great and good Spirit,
I have made a promise
And I cannot go back
On that promise.
Amen.

February 5

SAINT AGATHA

Early martyr • Sicily (Italy) • 3rd century

SCRIPTURE THEME

Fire

"I baptize you with water for repentance, but one who is more powerful than I is coming after me; I am not worthy to carry his sandals. He will baptize you with the Holy Spirit and fire."

— *Matthew 3:11*

QUOTATION

*"Christ, Who is the Ultimate Fire
Who will burn away the cold in the heart of Man."*

— *Edith Stillwell,* Harper Religious and Inspirational Quotation Companion, *page 186*

BOTH PALERMO AND CATANIA CLAIM to be the birthplace of Agatha. Not much is known except that she died as a virgin martyr, probably in the third century. Legends abound, but none can be independently verified.

Her name is included in the martyrologies of the early Church, the calendar of Carthage and the Canon of the Mass.

Sicilians invoked her help against the eruptions of Mount Etna; by extension, her prayers are asked in protection from fires.

In some parts of Europe, bread, candles and fruit are blessed in her honor. In Germany, Agatha is the patron of Alpine nurses and guides. Sicilians have a great day of merrymaking on her feast.

REFLECTIONS

- The process of canonization can sometimes take centuries. How do you recognize saints and holy women living among us today?
- What women in your life have been called "saints"? How have they shaped your choices?

PRAYER

In union with your suffering, Jesus,
 I offer my suffering—
 All the aches and pains and wounds—
 And I unite my headaches
 With your crowned head of thorns.
 Amen.

February 6

MARY TERESA BONZEL

Virgin, Third Order Franciscan • England • 1830–1905

SCRIPTURE THEME

Love of neighbor

"Bear one another's burdens, and in this way you will fulfill the law of Christ."
 — Galatians 6:2

QUOTATION

"To become all to all."
 — *motto of Mary Teresa's life*, The Poverello's Round Table, *page 76*

WORKS OF MERCY UNITED WITH PERPETUAL ADORATION summarize the life of Mary Teresa. She was born September 17, 1830, in Olpe in southern Westphalia. Mary Teresa joined the Third Order for laity before her twentieth birthday. She longed for convent life, but a heart ailment and her mother's opposition frustrated her plans.

Yet, in 1860, Mary Teresa and eight other young women received the habit, and in due time, they founded a new congregation called the Poor Franciscans of Perpetual Adoration. The sisters devoted themselves to perpetual adoration before the Blessed Sacrament and to the education of youth and the care of the sick and poor. Their membership increased, and they established convents in the Old World and the New World.

Mother Mary Teresa never refused charity to anyone in need. The sisters of her congregation and the poor at her doorstep received generously all she had. Mary Teresa died February 6, 1905.

REFLECTIONS

- What is the motto of your life? How often do you remind yourself to pursue its ideals?
- When have you rejected someone's plea for help and regretted it? When have you responded and regretted it?

PRAYER

We adore you, O Christ,
    And we bless you
    In your presence.
    Amen.

Let us kneel in awe
    Before the presence of God
    And adore and praise and give thanks.
    Let us remain in sorrow
    Before the presence of God
    And beg forgiveness
    For times when we forget
    Or neglect this gift of love.
    Let us leave
    The presence of God
    With renewed strength and peace
    And take Jesus to those in need.
    Amen.

February 7

JESSICA POWERS

Mystic, poet • U.S. • 1905–1988

SCRIPTURE THEME

Mercy of God

"The steadfast love of the LORD never ceases,
his mercies never come to an end."

> — *Lamentations 3:22*

QUOTATION

"I think: if I would lift this window now and pause to listen, leaning on this sill, I might hear, for my heart's full consolation, the whip-poor-wills on some Wisconsin hill."

> — *Jessica Powers, in "Escape,"* The Selected Poetry of Jessica Powers, *page 102*

"...[T]HE JESSICA POWERS STORY was also a window onto a fertile, vibrant period of Catholic intellectual and artistic life." So writes Dolores Lecky in "Notes on a Poet's Life," in the fall 1990 issue of *Spiritual Life*. Dolores completed a portrait-biography of Jessica Powers, known in her Carmelite convent as Sister Miriam of the Holy Spirit.

Born February 7, 1905, in Mauston, Wisconsin, to John and Delia Powers, Jessica was educated at rural schools. She attended Marquette University in Milwaukee, enrolling in the school for journalism because the liberal arts school did not accept women at the time—1922.

Jessica's father died when she was thirteen, and her mother died seven years later. She lived on the family farm until 1936. After her two brothers married, Jessica moved to New York City where she lived with the Pegis family and joined the Catholic Poetry Society of America.

Jessica had published some poems in local papers while still in Wisconsin. In 1939, her first volume of poetry, *The Lantern Burns*, was published.

In 1941, Jessica entered a Carmelite convent in Milwaukee. She continued to write poetry, and several volumes were published. She also served three terms as prioress. In 1988, she approved the manuscript of selected poetry as selected and edited by Regina Siegfried and Robert Morneau. The volume, published as *Selected Poetry of Jessica Powers* (1989), contains a chronology of her life as well as a bibliography of primary works and secondary sources of Jessica's poetry.

In gathering material for the biography, Dolores visited and interviewed Jessica several times during 1986-1988. Jessica died August 18, 1988.

REFLECTIONS

- Jessica was woman, Catholic, American, Celtic, nun, poet, farmer. With which of these facets do you most connect?

- In describing her role as biographer of Jessica, Dolores speaks of creating a portrait in the style of the sixteenth-century Dutch school. Dolores writes: "There's a window in the foreground of this painting, and through it one can see Cat Tail Valley. I think there's a sparrow on the windowsill. There's a table under the window, catching the daylight." What do you expect a biographer to do? How have the gifts of writers made their subjects more real to you than your own experience of them?

PRAYER

May the birds on our windowsills
Speak to us of your presence, O God.
Amen.

February 8

JOSEPHINE BAKHITA

Religious • Sudan and Italy • 1869–1947

SCRIPTURE THEME

Freedom of the children of God

"For you were called to freedom, brothers and sisters; only do not use your freedom as an opportunity for self-indulgence."

— *Galatians 5:13*

QUOTATION

"Be good, love God, pray for the pagans."

— *Josephine Bakhita,* Faces of Holiness, *page 442*

BORN IN SOUTHERN SUDAN OF CENTRAL AFRICA about 1869, Josephine was named Bakhita ("the Lucky One") by the Arab slave traders who took her from her family and village when she was about nine years old. When she and another young slave girl tried to escape, they were treed by a lion. They spent a whole night in the tree until the lion left in the morning. They met up with another slave trader, and Josephine was bought and sold several times. Her last owner was an Italian vice-consul who took her to Italy. The kindly officer and his wife provided for Josephine and placed their daughter, Mimmina, and Josephine at a convent for instruction in the Catholic faith. Josephine was Muslim, but she immediately felt at home in the convent.

When the time came for her to go home, she announced that she intended to stay. After discussion over whether she was still the property of the vice-consul's family, the authorities decided that she was a free woman since slavery was illegal in Italy.

Josephine was baptized when she was about twenty-one, and she joined the Daughters of Charity of Canossa. Though she would have liked to return to Africa and work among her own people, she was sent on lecture tours all around Italy to speak on African missions.

Because of her dark skin, she was called "Madre Moretta"—"Mother Negress." She spent over fifty years as a Canossian sister and was noted for being always happy, cheerful and kind.

She died February 8, 1947. A marble monument was erected over her grave by the people of the town of Schio, near the Italian Alps. And in the Cathedral of Obeid, in Sudan, a wall painting shows Mother Bakhita standing beside Our Lady, Queen of Africa.

The Vatican decree of her heroic virtue was issued December 1, 1978. Pope John Paul II beatified her on May 17, 1992, and canonized her on October 1, 2000.

REFLECTIONS

- Have you ever had to adjust to a new cultural setting? What sort of changes were most difficult?

- Do you know someone who is always cheerful? How does this attitude affect you? How can you be more cheerful?

PRAYER

We bless your names, O God,
For you are Allah.
Amen.

February 9

MARGARET GAFFNEY HAUGHERY

Businesswoman, philanthropist • Ireland and U.S. • 1813–1882

SCRIPTURE THEME

Bread for the poor

"Eat, that you may have strength when you go on your way."

— *1 Samuel 28:22*

QUOTATION

"...[T]he substance of her life was charity, the spirit of it, truth, the strength of it, religion, the end peace—then fame and immortality."

— *said of Margaret at the dedication ceremony for a statue of her,* The History of American Catholic Women, *page 61*

KNOWN AS THE "BREAD WOMAN OF NEW ORLEANS" because of her generosity to those in need, Margaret was a master of business.

She was born in Ireland in 1813 and brought by her parents to America in 1818. She received no schooling. When her parents died of yellow fever, nine-year-old Margaret went to live with neighbors and worked as a domestic. In 1835, she married and moved to New Orleans. When her husband died a year later, Margaret took work as a laundress.

With money she earned as a laundress, Margaret bought two cows and started a dairy. She peddled milk and also gave it to those in need. Despite her generosity, or more likely because of it, her dairy prospered. By 1840, she had forty cows and a thriving business.

Her generosity helped establish and provide for orphan asylums and an industrial school for girls. She personally nursed the sick during a yellow fever epidemic. In time, she acquired a bakery, the first in the South to use steam. She sold the dairy business and concentrated on the bakery business. She is credited with the idea of packaging crackers for sale.

Margaret's business acumen enabled her to be ever more generous with personal philanthropies as well as institutional ones. During the Civil War, she reached out to families of soldiers.

Most of her generous help was unknown to the public during her lifetime. At the time of her death on February 9, 1882, Margaret left an estate of almost a half-million dollars to charitable institutions.

Two years later, a statue to honor her memory was unveiled in

Margaret Haughery Park in New Orleans. This statue is believed to be the first in the United States to honor a woman.

REFLECTIONS

- What public statues of women have you seen in your area or on your travels? Whom did they depict? Is it helpful to have such public examples of great women?

- What women do you know who are successful in business? How do they use their creative and enterprising approaches to the tasks at hand?

PRAYER

You are the Bread of Life, O God.
Give us strength enough to share with others,
That we may nourish other lives
As you nourish our own.
Amen.

 *February 10*

SAINT SCHOLASTICA

Benedictine nun • Italy • 5th century

SCRIPTURE THEME

Brother, sister, family

"Where you go, I will go;
  where you lodge, I will lodge;
your people shall be my people,
  and your God my God.
Where you die, I will die—
  there will I be buried."

— *Ruth 1:16*

QUOTATION

"Please do not leave me tonight, brother; let us keep talking about the joys of heaven until morning."

— *Scholastica, Lives of the Saints, page 53*

Scholastica was born about 480 at Nursia, the sister and possibly the twin of Saint Benedict. She dedicated herself to God at an early age and probably continued to live at her parents' house. Later, she lived near Monte Cassino, but it is not clear whether she lived alone or in a community.

Some sources say that she did live in a nunnery and was the first Benedictine nun and the prioress of her convent. At any rate, she and Benedict used to meet at a house near his monastery once a year.

The now-famous story about Scholastica is that on one visit, she begged Benedict to stay longer. When he refused, she prayed and a heavy rain and thunderstorm prevented him from leaving. This was their last visit; Scholastica died three days later. Benedict had her buried in a tomb he himself prepared. The *Dialogues of St. Gregory the Great* recorded for posterity the memory of this brother-sister pair of saints. Scholastica is the patron of Benedictine nunneries.

REFLECTIONS

- The relationship of Benedict and Scholastica exemplifies the masculine and feminine aspects of a balanced, whole human spirituality. What have you learned from men in your life that has helped you to become a more whole person? What have you taught them?

- What examples and influences have you received from your own sisters and brothers?

PRAYER

We thank you, O God,
For brothers and sisters
With whom we share
The joys of knowing you.
Amen.

February 11

BARBARA HARRIS

Episcopal Church bishop • U.S. • 1930—

SCRIPTURE THEME

Church leadership

"Keep watch over yourselves and over all the flock, of which the Holy Spirit has made you overseers, to shepherd the church of God."

— Acts 20:28

QUOTATION

"A fresh wind is indeed blowing.... To some the changes are refreshing breezes. For others, they are as fearsome as a hurricane."

— *Barbara Harris,* Contemporary Newsmakers, *1989*

WHEN BARBARA HARRIS, FEMALE, BLACK AND DIVORCED, was consecrated as bishop in the Episcopal Church in February 1989, controversy and talk of schism was stirred up. Barbara, with a background in politics and business rather than seminary training, has established herself as a writer and preacher with strong opinions.

Barbara was ordained a deacon of the Episcopal Church in 1979 and a priest in 1980. She served in Philadelphia as priest and as chaplain at a prison. She also served as writer, editor and publisher of *The Witness*, a church journal, and as executive editor of the Episcopal Church Publishing Company.

Born in 1930 in Philadelphia, Barbara was always active in lay ministry in her church while pursuing her business career. She married in 1960 and divorced in 1965, with no children.

In the late 1970's, she moved toward priesthood and full-time ministry in her church. When the Episcopal Church as a national body approved the election of Barbara as assistant (suffragan) bishop of the Episcopal Diocese of Massachusetts in September 1988, the church also voted for approval of her consecration.

The window thus opened by these changes stirred the controversy. While some spoke out in opposition to the ordination and consecration of any woman, others spoke out against this particular woman because of her lack of academic and seminary training and her leftist politics.

Barbara, meanwhile, seemed to thrive on the ambiguity. She had not asked to be bishop but rather was elected to that position. She sought solidarity with other clergywomen and simply tried to defuse the objections.

Because of the intense controversy in the worldwide Anglican Church, Barbara even received death threats. Recognizing that there were theological and emotional problems on both sides of the issue, she continued to work for reconciliation.

Barbara continues to serve in Boston, as suffragan bishop of the Episcopal Diocese of Massachusetts while retaining some ties to her friends and ministry in Philadelphia.

REFLECTIONS

- What role do you feel women should play in religious organizations? Are you called to play such a role?

- Do you feel that women are valued as equals in your faith tradition? How does this affect your "loyalty" to your church? How do you feel about women whose anger over such issues prompts them to abandon their churches? What about those who stay with their churches and work and pray for changes from within?

PRAYER

Strengthen us, O God,
To face the challenges
And changes in the days ahead.
Amen.

 *February 12*

FANNY CROSBY

Hymn writer • U.S. • 1820–1915

SCRIPTURE THEME

Hymns

"Day and night without ceasing they sing,
'Holy, holy, holy,
the Lord God the Almighty,
who was and is and is to come.'"

— *Revelation 4:8*

QUOTATION

"As he touched my head and looked into my face he remarked, 'And here is a poetess; give her every possible encouragement. Read the best books to her, and teach her to appreciate the finest there is in poetry. You will hear from this young lady some day.' This was as music to my soul. I had waited long for someone to encourage me to adhere to what I already felt was to be my lifework, hymn-writing."

— Fanny Crosby, Give Her This Day, *page 91*

ONE OF AMERICA'S MOST POPULAR CHURCH HYMN WRITERS was born as Frances Jane Crosby on March 24, 1820, near New York City. Fanny, as she was known, was blinded at six weeks of age because of an incompetent doctor. Before her first birthday, Fanny's father died.

At fifteen, Fanny attended the New York Institution for the Blind in New York City and was encouraged in her writing of verse. When she graduated in 1843, Fanny joined the school as a teacher. Her poems were published: one volume in 1844, a second in 1851, a third in 1858.

Also in 1844, Fanny appeared before a joint session of the U.S. Congress as an example of what a blind person can learn to do.

In 1858, Fanny married Alexander van Alstyne, who also was blind. Over the next several decades, Fanny wrote the words and verses in collaboration with several hymn writers, many of them well known. Also, some of her poems were set to music. Some of her work was done under a pseudonym.

Fanny's hymns, which number in the several thousands, became very popular, especially with the Methodists. She lived into her nineties and wrote two autobiographical volumes. She died at Bridgeport, Connecticut, on February 12, 1915.

REFLECTIONS

• What is your experience of blindness? Have you or someone you know dealt with limitations in vision? What sort of adaptations are necessary?

• What are your favorite hymns? Do you know much about their authors? Do you listen to them outside of church services?

• Have you ever known someone whose disability did not seem to disable the person in any way? Do you react to your own aches and illnesses with the same courage and cheer?

PRAYER

Let us sing songs, hymns, and spiritual canticles

To our God and to encourage one another.
Jesus, Gentle Savior,
We pray for that "Blessed Assurance"
That is to be found
Near you and near your cross.
Amen.

 *February 13*

CATHERINE DE RICCI

Dominican tertiary, mystic · Italy · 16th century

SCRIPTURE THEME

The Passion of Christ

"My God, my God, why have you forsaken me?"
— *Matthew 27:46*

QUOTATION

"The Way of the Cross is the Way of Light."
— *Medieval proverb,* The Harper Religious and Inspirational Quotation Companion, *page 123*

CATHERINE WAS BORN AT FLORENCE IN 1522 and became a Dominican nun at Prato in Tuscany. She was noted for her balanced personality and good sense. She had a wide circle of friends and cared for the sick with compassion and competence. She was an able administrator and served as prioress.

Catherine also received mystical graces, among them "spiritual visits" by bilocation (being in two places at the same time) of Saint Philip Neri and Saint Mary Magdalen de Pazzi; the stigmata (bearing the same wounds on the hands, feet and side as Christ); and for twelve years a certain ecstasy of Christ's Passion from Thursday noon until Friday at 4 P.M. This last phenomenon caused people to want to see her. The disruptions by visitors to the convent became so great that the sisters prayed for the ecstasies to stop.

A poem written by Catherine was incorporated into the Dominican Liturgy. She gave spiritual advice in person and in charming letters. After a long illness, she died February 2, 1590, and was canonized in 1747.

REFLECTIONS

- Naldini did a portrait of Catherine with a book in her hand and a winsome expression on her face. Perhaps you can find a copy to look at. What are your thoughts as you reflect on her expression?
- How do you feel about the visionaries of Medjugorje?
- Catherine was connected with the Savonarola reforms. You may wish to read more about this in Church history.

PRAYER

Gift us, O God,
With balance and good sense
In our daily lives.
Amen.

February 14

JOAN OF VALOIS

Wife, founder of convent · *France* · *1464–1505*

SCRIPTURE THEME

Annulment

"Therefore what God has joined together, let no one separate."

— *Mark 10:9*

QUOTATION

"O Virgin most charitable, fill our hearts with charity, with love, and with God's grace. Mother of Mercy, under this dear title the Church invokes you, have pity on us, oppressed beneath the weight of our sins and afflictions. Look on us, in your maternal pity, that your mercy may lead you to help us in our needs."

— *Joan of Valois, in "The Ten Virtues of Our Lady,"* Prayer Book of the Saints, *page 120*

BORN APRIL 23, 1464, Joan was the princess-daughter of King Louis XI and Charlotte of Savoy. While the regal couple had hoped for a son, they saw a political asset in a marriageable daughter and betrothed the newborn to two-year-old Louis, Duke of Orleans.

Joan was placed in the care of a childless elderly couple. A spinal disease affected Joan's growth and posture, and Louis did not want to marry her, but at the king's command, Louis did so. The marriage took place in 1476. Joan was twelve and Louis fourteen.

Louis was away from the castle most of the time, and when forced by the king to be at the castle, Louis ignored Joan. Meanwhile, Joan prayed and tried to win her husband by loyalty and kindness. When Louis fell ill with smallpox, Joan stayed with him until he recovered.

At the death of her father the king, Joan's brother, Charles, became king. Louis was imprisoned for conspiracy against the new king. Joan arranged better living quarters for him, even selling her jewelry to pay for his needs. Joan's pleas saved Louis from execution. After his release from prison, Louis treated Joan with courtesy and respect.

At the death of Charles, Louis became King Louis XII and Joan the queen. One of his first acts was to seek an annulment of his marriage so he could marry Anne of Brittany.

Joan believed their marriage was true and valid. The Holy See after many months of question and investigation declared the marriage null and void because of the undue force put on Louis. Her husband obtained this decree of nullity of marriage after twenty-two years. Joan had never known of the king's threats to Louis at the time of the marriage.

Louis made Joan the duchess in the principality of Berry, and for a time, Joan grieved her misfortune. But, in time, she took a personal interest in the government of the city. She organized charities, selected good administrators, provided funds for the university and for scholars, and personally cared for the indigent. During a plague, she doubled her efforts, her prayers and her care of the sick.

Joan tried to correct abuses in regard to the cloister enclosure rules, which were being ignored at the local Benedictine convent. In a series of discussions, Joan influenced the community toward greater religious fervor.

In 1501, Joan fulfilled a childhood dream to found a contemplative religious order honoring the Annunciation. She professed vows in the Annonciades Order in 1504. Shortly thereafter, in 1505, she died.

An old gardener, previously employed by Joan, was cured of his paralysis as Joan's casket was carried to the church for her funeral. Canonized in 1950, Joan of Valois is honored on February 14.

REFLECTIONS

- Joan is a patron saint for those affected by broken marriages. Were you the child or partner of a broken marriage? How can you heal those wounds?

- Learn more about the ministry of marriage counselors and marriage tribunal officials. Do you have the skills and experience to counsel someone in marital difficulties?

- When were you able to overcome disappointment and disillusionment? Did prayer play a part?

PRAYER

Bless, O God, all who suffer
From problems with their marriages
And guide them into right decisions.
Amen.

 *February 15*

SUSAN B. ANTHONY
Social reformer • U.S. • 1820–1906

SCRIPTURE THEME

Self-reliance, perseverance

*"She looks well to the ways of her household,
and does not eat the bread of idleness."*
— *Proverbs 31:27*

QUOTATION

"...[A]nd I shall earnestly and persistently continue to urge all women to the practical recognition of the old Revolutionary maxim, 'Resistance to tyranny is obedience to God.'"
— *Susan B. Anthony,* The Last Word, *page 26*

BORN IN 1820, SUSAN WAS THE SECOND DAUGHTER of a farmer and cotton mill owner and his wife. When the cotton mill failed and Susan's father refused to buy cotton produced by slaves, the family learned the pain involved in living by principles.

Susan became a schoolteacher and formed a temperance society. She also managed the family farm. When she was not allowed to speak at male temperance meetings, she became active in women's rights movements. Though she did not attend the first Women's Rights Convention in 1848, she did attend in 1852. Susan became a friend to other leading feminists, especially Elizabeth Blackwell and Margaret Fuller.

In 1868, after the Civil War, Susan began her own newspaper called *Revolution*. Though the paper failed after two years, her name had become known. On lecture tours all over the United States, she drew crowds. She spoke against slavery and for equal voting rights and equal pay for women.

In 1872, she illegally registered and cast a vote in the presidential election. She was arrested, convicted and fined but refused to pay. With Elizabeth Cady Stanton, Susan began in 1880 to write *A History of Woman Suffrage*. Susan and her sister lived out their last years in Rochester, New York, and their home is preserved as a historical place. Susan died in 1906, fourteen years before women got the right to vote. She is buried in Mount Hope Cemetery in Rochester, New York.

REFLECTIONS

- Susan B. Anthony is honored on the $1 coin, first minted in 1979. Do you feel this was an appropriate tribute? How do you feel about the other figures represented on our currency?

- Susan was often demanding, impatient and intense in campaigning for women's labor and civil rights. What issues do you feel intensely about?

- Is breaking the law ever justified? What social norms are you willing to challenge to support a cause important to you?

PRAYER

May we ever be obedient to you, O God,
In the ways we choose to resist tyranny
And promote human rights.
May we dedicate our skills
To champion those causes
That speak with clarity
To our hearts and minds.
Amen.

February 16

PHILIPPA MARERI

Virgin, hermit, founder, Second Order Franciscan • Italy • d. 1236

SCRIPTURE THEME

Godliness, wisdom, peace

"And the peace of God, which surpasses all understanding, will guard your hearts and your minds in Christ Jesus."

— *Philippians 4:7*

QUOTATION

"I already have a spouse, the noblest and the greatest, our Lord Jesus Christ."

— *Philippa,* The Poverello's Round Table, *page 97*

PHILIPPA WAS BORN IN THE MARERI ANCESTRAL CASTLE near Rieti, Italy, toward the end of the twelfth century. She was educated, becoming proficient in Latin and taking great pleasure in reading Holy Scripture.

Saint Francis of Assisi sometimes visited the Mareri family near the valley where he had established several convents. Philippa was impressed with his holiness and simplicity of life.

Philippa refused offers of marriage, cut off her hair and withdrew to a nearby cave. Later, her brother provided a convent for her and her companions, where they took up and lived the Rule of Saint Clare. Many young women from the nobility joined them, and the convent flourished.

Philippa died February 16, 1236.

REFLECTIONS

- Do you feel it is acceptable for a woman to decide against marriage? In what ways is this a difficult choice?

- How have our views toward single women changed over the years? Why are more women marrying later or not at all?

PRAYER

We find great joy, O God,
In reflecting on your truths
Found in the Holy Scripture.
Amen.

 *February 17*

BESS STREETER ALDRICH

Writer • U.S. • 1881–1954

SCRIPTURE THEME

Affirmation of life, wholesomeness

"I will rejoice in doing good to them, and I will plant them in this land in faithfulness, with all my heart and all my soul."

— *Jeremiah 32:41*

QUOTATION

"Because I was born at the tag end of a large family I never experienced any of the pioneer hardships of which I wrote, for by that time my parents were living in a growing town with its (for the time) conveniences."

— *Bess Streeter Aldrich*, Twentieth Century Authors, *page 16*

BESS STREETER WAS BORN FEBRUARY 17, 1881, in Cedar Rapids, Iowa, where her grandparents had settled in frontier days. Bess completed Teachers' College in 1901 and taught for six years. She also wrote stories for children and magazine articles for teachers' magazines. In 1907, she married Charles Aldrich, and they had four children. When her husband died suddenly in 1925, Bess supported her children and herself by her writing.

Bess became the book editor of the *Christian Herald* in 1930. In 1935, she received an honorary doctorate of literature.

A love of the natural world, especially the prairies of Iowa and Nebraska, provides settings in the novels Bess wrote. Her first novel, *The Rim of the Prairie*, tells the story of a farm girl living near a small town.

A Lantern in Her Hand, one of her best books, bases much of its narrative on her family history. This very popular novel remained a bestseller for years and provided the income she needed for her family.

A White Bird Flying, Miss Bishop, Spring Came On Forever and other novels came from Bess's pen through the 1930's and 1940's. She used realistic backgrounds with fine characterizations. Her writing affirms life and gives her readers optimism. The novels of Bess Streeter Aldrich are genuinely wholesome.

Bess died August 3, 1954. She was elected to the Nebraska Hall of Fame in 1973.

REFLECTIONS

- How does your view of the natural world affirm life and God to you?
- Do you like to spend time outdoors? How can you make this a more prayerful time?
- What is your definition of "wholesome"? In what ways do you strive to make your environment more positive and healthful?

PRAYER

We thank you, O God,
For writers who affirm life values
And offer us optimism.
Amen.

February 18

NARCISSA WHITMAN

Pioneer missionary · U.S. · 1808–1847

SCRIPTURE THEME

Pioneer missions

"This continued for two years, so that all the residents of Asia, both Jews and Greeks, heard the word of the Lord."

— Acts 19:10

QUOTATION

"Again I can speak of the goodness and mercy of the Lord to us in an especial manner. On the evening of my birthday, March 14th, we received the gift of a little daughter—a treasure invaluable. During the winter my health was good, so I was able to do my work."

— Narcissa Whitman, Give Her This Day, page 81

ON FEBRUARY 18, 1836, Narcissa and her husband, Marcus, a missionary-physician, set out from New York State to cross the Rocky Mountains and Columbia River. That same year, the Whitmans and a few other missionaries established a Presbyterian mission in the Pacific Northwest.

The letters written and the diaries kept by Narcissa offer a rich and varied account of the missionary experience among the Native

Americans of the area. Whitman College in Walla Walla, Washington, serves as a museum and archives for the mission records, including what Narcissa wrote.

Born March 14, 1808, in Prattsburg, New York, Narcissa Prentiss was the third of nine children. At eleven, Narcissa made a confession of faith during a church revival and turned her sights toward church service. Her formal education was at Emma Willard's Female Seminary at Troy and at the Ben Franklin Academy at Prattsburg. For a time, Narcissa and her sister ran a kindergarten.

When Marcus Whitman felt a missionary calling, he wanted Narcissa to accompany him. They were married on February 17, 1836, in Angelica, New York, and set out the very next day for the long trip to the West. Narcissa's diary gives details of the dangers and difficulties as well as their trust in Divine Providence.

The small party of missionaries crossed the Continental Divide on July 4, 1836, and by fall settled into the Waiilaptu Mission. Narcissa began a school where she taught American Indian children. On the day before her twenty-ninth birthday, Narcissa gave birth to her daughter, Alice Clarissa. The child accidentally drowned when she was two. The Whitmans took in native children in need of homes as well as the seven children of a pioneer family when the parents died.

On November 29, 1847, Narcissa and Marcus and several children who made their home with them were massacred in a raid. They are buried near the Washington-Oregon state line.

REFLECTIONS

- When have you opened your home to children other than your own? In what ways did the experience enrich your life?
- Reflect upon the difficulties of pioneer life. What difficulties are you enduring to bring about a better way of life for future generations?

PRAYER

How beautiful
Upon the prairie
And the frontiers
Are the feet of women
Who bring good tidings
And words of peace.
Amen.

February 19

CARSON MCCULLERS
Novelist • U.S. • 1917–1967

SCRIPTURE THEME

Outcast

"Father, I have sinned against heaven and before you; I am no longer worthy to be called your son; treat me like one of your hired hands."
— Luke 15:19

QUOTATION

"People are never so free with themselves and so recklessly glad as when there is some possibility of commotion or calamity ahead."
— *Carson McCullers, in* The Ballad of The Sad Café, Sunbeams, *page 136*

CARSON HAD, IN EDITH SITWELL'S PHRASE, "a great poet's eye." And Carson chose to see and write about the anguish of the outcast and the misfit, the disabled, the homosexual and the adolescent.

Born February 19, 1917, in Georgia, Carson set out at thirteen to become a concert pianist. On her way to New York City and the Juilliard School of Music, all her money (which had been obtained by selling the family jewelry) was stolen on the subway.

Carson turned to doing odd jobs by day and studying creative writing at night. *The Heart Is a Lonely Hunter,* written when she was twenty-three, established her reputation as a talented writer.

Carson became connected with the Artist Colony at Saratoga, New York, and remained associated with it for the rest of her life. Though ill health and alcoholism shortened her career, Carson continued writing creatively. She died at age fifty, in 1967.

REFLECTIONS

- Read *The Ballad of The Sad Café* and other titles by Carson McCullers.
- How do you express your compassion for the outcasts of society? Can you genuinely empathize with the downtrodden, or do you simply pity them?
- When have your plans been thwarted by tragedy, only to be turned to something more wonderful? Are you grateful for the turn of events, or do you still wonder what might have been?

PRAYER

Reach out with us and through us, O God,
To the people who are marginal and outcast in our society.
Amen.

February 20

JACINTA MARTO

Child visionary of Fatima • Portugal • 1910–1920

SCRIPTURE THEME

Children, simplicity

"Let the little children come to me; do not stop them; for it is to such as these that the kingdom of God belongs."

— *Mark 10:14*

QUOTATION

"My Jesus, I love you."

— *Jacinta's frequent prayer,* Saints in the Making, *page 103*

BORN IN A HAMLET BELONGING TO THE PARISH OF FATIMA in central Portugal, Jacinta had an ordinary childhood. Jacinta, her brother Francisco and their cousin Lucia dos Santos were the three children to whom Our Lady of Fatima appeared in 1917.

Jacinta has been described as a lively, outgoing child, sensitive to the beauties of nature, music and religious devotion. The children spent their days pasturing sheep and praying the rosary in the fields.

In 1916, the children had apparitions of an angel of peace. In 1917, on May 13, they experienced their first apparition of a beautiful lady at the Cova da Iria. She reappeared each month through October. The children began to pray the rosary with more devotion.

Church and town officials cross-examined the children and generally gave them a difficult time. The children continued to pray and offered their sufferings as sacrifice.

In October 1918, Jacinta and Francisco took sick with influenza. Both children suffered their ailments with a sense of God's plan. Francisco died April 4, 1919; Jacinta less than a year later, on February 20, 1920. Lucia had further visions related to the five First Saturdays and the consecration of Russia to her Immaculate Heart.

The lives of Francisco and Jacinta have been presented to the Church for examination and consideration for the beatification and canonization process. The historical and cultural context of their visions, as well as their young ages, limits the language and images, but the holiness of their lives remains an inspiration.

REFLECTIONS

- Marian apparitions have been reported around the world—Lourdes, Knock, Guadalupe, Medjugorje. What is your opinion of such visions?

- Millions were inspired by the messages of Fatima to pray the rosary for the conversion of Russia. Do you believe their prayers have been answered?

- Pray the rosary. The rosary is prayed by saying an Our Father and ten Hail Marys while meditating on one of the fifteen mysteries of Mary's life with Jesus.

PRAYER

Let us pray in honor of Our Lady of Fatima:
"Jesus, Mary, Joseph,
I love you,
Save souls."
Amen.

We pray with Jacinta:
"My Jesus, I love you."
Amen.

 *February 21*

ANAÏS NIN

Artist, novelist • France and U.S. • 1903–1977

SCRIPTURE THEME

Water

"Those who drink of the water that I will give them will never be thirsty. The water that I will give will become in them a spring of water gushing up to eternal life."
— *John 4:14*

QUOTATION

"I wanted to write in a personal way, very close to experience, and what I felt to be the difference between what a woman has to say and what a man has to say."

— Anaïs Nin, Anaïs Nin Observed, *page 44*

ANAÏS NIN WAS BORN FEBRUARY 21, 1903, in Paris, France. As a child, she was nurtured by the Catholic mysteries. Many of her early journal entries are religious.

She kept voluminous journals, which have a "feminine sensitivity." She was eleven when her father abandoned the family. Anaïs kept her journal as an endless letter to him. As an adult, she lived in Paris and in New York City with many intimate friends among the artists and writers.

Her inner life was nourished by art, music, poetry, writing. "The great concern of my diaries," she says, "is with the psychic life—the life of the soul, of the spirit, the concern with human values" (Snyder, page 92). Her published *Diaries* began to appear in 1966. They brought consolation and hope to many who read them, especially women.

REFLECTIONS

- How does the personal life of an artist, for better or for worse, affect the values of her art as a vehicle of truth?
- Do you believe there is a difference in the work of male and female artists? Can you define it?

PRAYER

We praise you, O God,
For men and women
And the differences between them.
May we learn to appreciate those differences
And cherish the similarities.
Amen.

February 22

MERIDEL LE SUEUR

Artistic writer · U.S. · 1900–1996

SCRIPTURE THEME

Annunciation

"The angel said to her, 'Do not be afraid, Mary, for you have found favor with God.'"

— Luke 1:30

QUOTATION

"The history of an oppressed people is hidden in the lies and the agreed-upon myths of its conquerors."

— Meridel Le Sueur, And Then She Said, *page 22*

OFTEN CALLED THE "VOICE OF THE PRAIRIE," Meridel Le Sueur was born February 22, 1900, in Iowa. Her life and work began and remained rooted in Midwestern culture. Her father was a socialist lawyer; her mother was an active feminist.

Meridel associated with artists of the radical left. As she produced poetry and prose, journalism, philosophy and history, she developed a revolutionary aesthetic form and style of writing to convey her content.

One of her finest short stories, titled "Annunciation," integrates poetry and prose as an expectant mother speaks to her unborn child. This literary reflection celebrates the creative force of women.

American cultural myths and folklore offered Meridel material for several children's books on heroes such as Abraham Lincoln and Nancy Hanks Lincoln. *Sparrow Hawk* (1950) tells a cross-cultural story about an American Indian and a white boy.

Meridel's interest in and sympathy with women's experiences and Native American philosophy form and inform much of what she wrote. Rhythms and patterns from these sources determine her style. Meridel's poems in *Rites of Ancient Ripening* unite the rhythms of women's voices and the communal experience of women with Native American songs, tales and images. Many of Meridel's stories tell of life in the Midwest; among these stories are *Women on the Breadlines* and *Women Are Hungry*. In a story of the life of her parents called *Crusaders*, Meridel tells of her pioneer grandmother and feminist mother. In historical books for children, Meridel writes with concern for her native Midwest and the survival, despite all odds, of its people.

REFLECTIONS

- In what way is the history of women like the history of an oppressed people? How is our history defined by those who "conquered" us in the past?
- What do you feel is "the creative force of women"? Reflect on the ways in which this force is expressed in women's lives.

PRAYER

O God, may we hear your voice
In the prairie winds of our lives.
Amen.

February 23

EMMA HART WILLARD

Teacher • U.S. • 1787–1870

SCRIPTURE THEME

Teaching

"Day after day I was with you in the temple teaching."
— Mark 14:49

QUOTATION

"What if the good we undertake be for the distant and the future? When our souls are free, no longer bound to a clod that gravitates to the earth, these things will be neither distant or future."
— Emma Hart Willard, The Quotable Woman: From Eve to 1799, *page 401*

EMMA WAS THE SIXTEENTH OF SEVENTEEN CHILDREN raised in a New England home where books were highly treasured. Emma studied at the Berlin Academy in her hometown and taught there. Beyond that she was largely self-taught.

She married in 1809 and learned much from her physician husband's medical books. Though she studied the appropriate curriculum of Middlebury College, she was not allowed to attend classes or receive a degree. This fired her determination to work for formal women's education.

She opened the Middlebury Female Seminary in 1814 and offered a wide variety of subjects to women. In 1819, Emma presented to the governor of New York her plan for quality education, her "Plan for Improving Female Education." Her school offered courses of serious study equivalent to the best men's high schools.

Somehow, she found time to write several textbooks. Her history texts were exceptional and offered a popular moral tone, born of her Episcopal faith. At the invitation of Troy, New York, Emma was put in charge of the first women's college. Many influential teachers graduated from Troy Female Seminary.

Her first husband died in 1825. When she entered into a second marriage in 1838, she had the foresight to draw up a prenuptial contract that protected her schools as well as her income and property. This proved prudent, as her second husband had problems with gambling.

Emma did not participate in women's rights activities, but she supported those who did. She felt that she pleaded the cause of her sex in her own way by promoting equal opportunities for women who were teachers. Emma died April 15, 1870.

REFLECTIONS

- Recall your education. Was it equal to that given to boys or men?
- What do you think of schools segregated by sex? Do they give women a better chance to participate?
- How do you contribute to the betterment of women's education?

PRAYER

We thank you, O God,
For all those
Who have been our educators
Over the years.
Amen.

February 24

IDA LEWIS

Lighthouse keeper • *U.S.* • *1842–1911*

SCRIPTURE THEME

Light in the darkness

"The light shines in the darkness, and the darkness did not overcome it."

— *John 1:4*

QUOTATION

"The supreme gift, after light, is scale."

— Helen Frankenthaler, The New York Public Library Book of Twentieth Century American Quotations, *page 64*

IDAWALLEY ZORADIA LEWIS, ALWAYS CALLED IDA, was born February 25, 1842, in Newport, Rhode Island. When she was fifteen, the family moved to the island Lime Rock in Newport Harbor, where her father became the lighthouse keeper.

When her father suffered a disability, Ida took over much of his work, including the rowing of the boat to get the children to school on the mainland. Ida rescued several people who were in trouble at sea. One of these rescues caught the attention of a New York reporter, and the story of Ida Lewis was soon told throughout the nation. Lime Rock celebrated her glory, and she was given a boat named *Rescue* and a boathouse.

She married a fisherman in 1870, but when the marriage didn't work out, Ida resumed her maiden name and her duties at the lighthouse. She continued rescue work right into her sixties. She died October 24, 1911.

REFLECTIONS

• People who live near seacoasts (as well as visitors) often find a special beauty in lighthouses. Take a good look at one—in real life or in art or photography. What has served as a lighthouse in your life, setting boundaries, protecting you from danger?

• Think of and pray for those who make their living protecting and rescuing others.

PRAYER

You, O Eternal Light,
Are the beacon of hope

On the sea of life.
Amen.

February 25

MARIA KOLBE

Mother, secular Franciscan • Poland • 1870–1946

SCRIPTURE THEME

Suffering and death of son

"He was his mother's only son, and she was a widow.... When the Lord saw her, he had compassion for her."

— *Luke 7:12-13*

QUOTATION

"Vehemently and with conviction I begged, as a mother who really loves her children, for Maximilian the strong love of martyrs: A love stronger than death— love that allows one to face death with joy. I listen with a torn heart to an inner voice that whispers, 'Above natural love, one must place the love of God, and the desire for eternal happiness for those we love.'"

— *Maria Kolbe,* Mothers of the Saints, *page 16*

MARIA DABROWSKA WAS BORN IN RUSSIAN-OCCUPIED POLAND on February 25, 1870. Her parents were weavers when weaving was still a cottage industry. Maria loved God and religion and dreamed of being a nun, but that was not possible in a land and time when Russia suppressed the Catholic Church.

She married Julius Kolbe in 1891, and in time, they had five sons. Julius and Maria became secular Franciscans. Maria was a good friend to other women, serving as a midwife with compassion and sensitivity.

Though the Kolbe family lived in tough economic times, three of the five brothers studied for the priesthood after being smuggled into Austrian Poland.

By mutual agreement, Maria went to live at a convent, and Julius at a monastery. The two oldest sons were received as Franciscan friars in 1910. The oldest was given the name Valerian and the second Maximilian. Later, the third one became known as Alphonse. When the oldest left the Franciscans and married, Maria was unable to accept his decision. For years, she remained unhappy about his decision and struggled to come to acceptance.

The family was separated by World War I; Julius was captured and hung. In 1918, Maximilian was ordained, and both Maximilian and Alphonse were involved in publishing the *Knight of the Immaculate,* a magazine promoting Marian devotion. This apostolate under the leadership of Maximilian grew to a city of seven hundred friars and the largest publishing house in Poland.

In 1938, the friars added a radio broadcast. Father Maximilian Kolbe became a major force of public opinion against the Nazis. With the invasion of Poland, Maximilian was arrested, sent to various prisons, and eventually to Auschwitz. During these years, Maria lived at a Felician convent, doing errands and odd jobs, with time for prayer and befriending the postulants and novices.

Maria received only one letter from Auschwitz in which Maximilian told her not to worry. Only after the war did she learn the details that when ten prisoners were selected to die, Maximilian volunteered to take the place of one who had a family. He died in August 1941. (Pope John Paul II canonized Saint Maximilian Kolbe in October 1982.)

Maria's youngest two sons had died as children. Alphonse had died in 1930 of appendicitis. Now all that was left to Maria was her eldest, and the relationship was strained because he did not live up to her dream for him.

Valerian tried to comfort his sorrowing mother by writing several letters. Some say that it was the first miracle of Saint Maximilian Kolbe that Maria and Valerian were at long last reconciled. And then he, too, was arrested for his underground resistance work and sent to a concentration camp where he died just before the end of the war.

Maria lived out her last years in prayer and peace with the Felician sisters. She died on March 17, 1946.

REFLECTIONS

- Maria taught her children to read and write and pray. Who taught you these things? To whom will you pass them on?
- Have you lived up to your mother's expectations? Do you have expectations that others feel obligated to live up to?

PRAYER

We pray, dear God, for mothers everywhere
    Who see their children suffer and die,
    That they may have strength

To stand with faith and love
At the cross of Jesus crucified.
Amen.

We thank you, O Mother-God,
For your mother love
When we are in danger and trouble.
Amen.

 *February 26*

ANNE LINE

Martyr · England · d. 1601

SCRIPTURE THEME

Hospitality

"Do not neglect to show hospitality to strangers, for by doing that some have entertained angels without knowing it."

— *Hebrews 13:2*

QUOTATION

"I am sentenced to die for harbouring a Catholic priest; and so far am I from repenting for having so done that I wish, with all my soul, that where I have entertained one, I could have entertained a thousand."

— *Anne Line, to the crowd gathered to watch her execution,* Lives of the Saints, *page 73*

ANNE WAS CANONIZED IN 1970 as one of the Forty Martyrs of England and Wales. She was martyred in 1601 for harboring priests in her home.

Anne was the daughter of a Protestant English gentleman. When Anne and her brother became Catholic, their father disinherited both of them.

When she was nineteen, Anne married Roger Line, also a convert to Catholicism. After his death in 1594, Anne devoted her life to the service of persecuted Catholics. Despite ill health, she took care of a house of refuge for the clergy. With the help of Jesuit priests, Anne continued to hide priests and hold hidden Masses.

After suspicious neighbors reported her to the authorities, Anne was arrested and imprisoned. Because of illness, Anne was brought to court in a chair. She was found guilty on the circumstantial evidence of an altar set up in her home and small crowds of people coming and going.

Anne spent her last days in prison peacefully and prayerfully. She was hanged from gallows on February 27, 1601.

REFLECTIONS

- Do you harbor refugees of any kind because of faith?
- Religious wars and persecutions have created countless tragedies but also many saints. Do you feel that you could be heroic under such difficult circumstances? Under ordinary circumstances?

PRAYER

In your martyrs, O God,
May we find models of suffering
For the sake of love.
Amen.

February 27

JULIA WARD HOWE

Poet, writer, social reformer • U.S. • 1819–1910

SCRIPTURE THEME

Poetry

"*Honor the* LORD *with your substance and with the first fruits of all your produce.*"

    — *Proverbs 3:9*

QUOTATION

"*In the beauty of the lilies*
Christ was born across the sea,
With a glory in His bosom
That transfigures you and me:
As He died to make men holy,
Let us die to make men free..."

    — *Julia Ward Howe, in "The Battle Hymn of the Republic,"* The Quotable Woman: 1800-On, *page 39*

BORN IN NEW YORK CITY ON MAY 27, 1819, Julia received an excellent education in languages and literature. She continued learning by teaching herself German and studying the German philosophers. She channeled her emotions into the writing of religious poetry.

In 1843, Julia married Samuel Gridly Howe, the director of the Perkins Institute for the Blind. They had six children.

Though her husband disapproved, Julia wrote and published poetry anonymously. Her primary poetic form became that of verses to commemorate or celebrate a famous person or significant event. Her most famous and best-remembered poem is "The Battle Hymn of the Republic," which first appeared in *The Atlantic Monthly* in February 1862, during the Civil War.

Julia also wrote for an abolitionist paper. Her belief in women's intellectual and spiritual equality with men pervaded her articles, lectures and sermons, many of which she devoted to the cause of women's suffrage.

Probably, Julia's major contribution is how she rallied women into cooperative actions on behalf of better education and working conditions for women, and even a better sense of cooperative power in the family unit.

Julia died October 17, 1910.

REFLECTIONS

- If long before 1900 Julia and others believed in women's spiritual and intellectual equality with men, why are we still struggling with this understanding and its practical implications?

- Read or sing the words of "The Battle Hymn." How do you feel about the warrior tone of the poem? Was the hymn more appropriate in the 1860's than it is today?

PRAYER

May our eyes see your glory, Lord,
In the windows of our churches,
In the windows of our homes,
In the windows of our schools and offices,
Wherever you come as the Lord of truth.
Amen. Hallelujah! Amen.

February 28

MARY LYON

Educator, college founder • U.S. • 1797–1849

SCRIPTURE THEME

Teacher

"And the Lord's servant must not be quarrelsome but kindly to everyone, an apt teacher, patient, correcting opponents with gentleness."

— *2 Timothy 2:24*

QUOTATION

"Its grand object [Mount Holyoke Female Seminary] is to furnish the greatest possible number of female teachers, of high literary qualifications, and of benevolent, self-denying zeal."

— *Mary Lyon,* The Quotable Woman: From Eve to 1799, *page 444*

BORN FEBRUARY 28, 1797, Mary had a home life that meant homespun clothing from flax grown, spun, and woven at home; shoes from calves raised on the farm; food from the produce grown in the garden and animals raised in the pasture. Mary's father died when she was six, and her mother remarried when Mary was thirteen. For the next four years, Mary kept house for her brother, and then she went out on her own as a teacher.

She studied at Ashfield and Amherst academies where she worked as a servant to help pay her way. When lack of finances caused her to drop out, the Ashfield academy made arrangements for a scholarship. Mary's eagerness for women's education led her to teaching and administration of local academies.

On November 8, 1837, she founded Mount Holyoke Seminary, where she served as president. At times, she accepted household goods in place of fees so poor girls could receive an education. Later known as Mount Holyoke College, the school was renowned for its high intellectual and moral standards. Mary rejoiced to see the graduates go off and serve as teachers and missionaries. She spent twelve happy years there before her health failed her.

Mary died March 5, 1849, at age fifty-two, and was buried on the grounds of the college. She was elected to the American Hall of Fame in 1905.

REFLECTIONS

- Recall your own education. How did it prepare you to be of service?
- Mary's belief in the love of God and God's goodness prompted her to regard all with great dignity. What is your attitude about the worthiness of persons, time and small things?

PRAYER

May we reverence each person, O God,
    Because you give each one dignity of life.
    Amen.

We pray that education
    May make each woman
    "A handmaid to the Gospel
    And an efficient auxiliary
    In the great task
    Of renovating the world."
    Amen.

— *Mary Lyon*, Remember the Ladies, *page 47*

 *March 1*

AGNES OF BOHEMIA

Poor Clare nun • Czechoslovakia • d. 1282

SCRIPTURE THEME

Humility

"For all who exalt themselves will be humbled, and those who humble themselves will be exalted."

— *Luke 14:11*

QUOTATION

"...that, like another Rachel, you always remember your resolution and be conscious of your beginning."

— *Clare in a letter to Agnes,* Clare of Assisi: Early Documents, *page 40*

AGNES WAS A CONTEMPORARY OF SAINT CLARE OF ASSISI. In fact, four of Clare's letters to Agnes survive and are treasured and studied as writings of Clare.

Agnes was a princess, the daughter of the King of Bohemia, and a first cousin of Saint Elizabeth of Hungary. She had many suitors, including Emperor Frederick II, but she declined them all, preferring to single-mindedly serve God. The aristocracy and nobility were so impressed with her attitude that dozens followed her to the convent and other wealthy ladies provided for Poor Clare foundations.

Agnes came to know the spirituality of Clare from the Franciscans Minor who preached in Prague. (Present-day Czechoslovakia was then known as Bohemia.) Inspired by the Franciscan values of poverty and simplicity, she founded the Hospital of St. Francis at Prague. She also founded a Poor Clare monastery, the first north of the Alps, and entered it herself on Pentecost day in 1234. She professed solemn vows of chastity, poverty and obedience and was encouraged in the spiritual life by letters from Saint Clare. Though the two never met, they had a wonderful spiritual friendship that lasted for twenty years.

Agnes lived as a cloistered Poor Clare nun for forty-five years. At the pope's request, she served as abbess. She died March 6, 1282. She was canonized on November 12, 1989.

REFLECTIONS

- Do you have a spiritual friendship with a faraway person? If so, nurture it with letters and phone calls. If not, is there someone with whom you could cultivate such a friendship?

· What is your attitude toward the wealthy and privileged? Do you believe in the concept of noblesse oblige?

PRAYER

We rejoice in you, O God,
And in the spiritual friendships
That enrich our lives.
Amen.

March 2

KAREN CARPENTER

Singer · U.S. · 1950–1983

SCRIPTURE THEME

Singing

*"I will proclaim your name to my brothers and sisters,
in the midst of the congregation I will praise you."*

— *Hebrews 2:12*

QUOTATION

"This was a fresh voice that came out of this really fresh, wonderful girl."

— *Burt Bacharach about Karen Carpenter,* Too Young to Die, *page 271*

HER SONGS LIVE ON INTO OUR TIME, but Karen died in 1983, just a month before her thirty-third birthday. The official cause was "cardiac arrest," but the underlying reason was never stated. Karen suffered from anorexia nervosa—an eating disorder—as early as 1975.

Born March 2, 1950, in New Haven, Connecticut, Karen and her brother, Richard, made a pop-rock combination. Karen played drums while Richard did the arrangements. Both sang, and in 1970, the two received the Grammy Award for best contemporary vocal performance by a group. In the seventies and eighties, they had five gold singles and five gold albums to their credit.

By the mid-1970's, Karen was in poor health. A concert tour of the Orient and of Europe had to be canceled while she struggled to control her dieting binges and recover from the ill effects of serious weight loss. In 1980, Karen married Thomas Burris, a real estate developer; they separated a year later. Many close to Karen thought she had recovered from her ailment and were surprised at her sudden death on February 4, 1983.

REFLECTIONS

- Reflect on food, fasting, feasting, dieting, fat. Are any of these a problem in your life?
- Some have said food is a particularly feminine issue because it's often the one thing over which women have some control. Do you agree?

PRAYER

Provider of food,
We praise and thank you
For your gifts of nourishment.
May we wisely use your gifts
For our body
And share your gifts
With all our human family.
Amen.

March 3

KATHARINE DREXEL

Religious founder · U.S. · 1858–1955

SCRIPTURE THEME

Sharing, beneficence

"Happy are those who consider the poor,
The LORD delivers them in the day of trouble."

— *Psalm 41:1*

QUOTATION

"To be the mother and servant of the Indian and Negro races according to the rule of the Sisters of the Blessed Sacrament, and not to undertake any work which would lead to the neglect or abandonment of the Indian and Colored races."

— *one of Katharine's vows,* Modern Saints, *page 461*

BORN INTO A WEALTHY FAMILY in Philadelphia on November 26, 1858, Katharine Mary Drexel lost her mother only one month later. Katharine's father, an international banker, remarried, and her deeply religious family provided home and education for Katharine. The Drexels were generous with their wealth and regularly aided the poor. Mrs. Drexel arranged for twelve-year-old Katharine and her sister to teach Sunday school to the children of the workmen.

Katharine made her social debut in Philadelphia in 1879 and took part in the social whirl expected of her. When she felt a growing attraction to religious life, her spiritual director advised her to write a list of reasons for and against. Katharine always felt a special devotion to the Blessed Sacrament, and she developed a love for Native Americans and those of African descent—usually called "Indians" and "Coloreds" in those days.

During a trip to Europe with her sisters, Katharine had a private audience with Pope Leo XIII. Katharine begged him to send more missionaries for the American Indians. The pope suggested that Katharine consider becoming a missionary.

The Drexel sisters devoted a good part of their inheritance and time to Native Americans and Blacks, especially for their education. Katharine asked the U.S. hierarchy to establish a bureau for "colored and Indian Missions." After her two sisters married, Katharine was challenged by a bishop, who was also a friend, to found a new congregation who would serve the needs of American Indians and Blacks.

She made her novitiate with the Pittsburgh Sisters of Mercy. In 1891, she founded a new congregation, the Sisters of the Blessed Sacrament for Indians and Colored People. She used the old Drexel summer home for her first convent.

Katharine Drexel endowed St. Augustine Seminary in Bay St. Louis, Mississippi, out of her inheritance. The seminary library houses a collection of works dealing with the experiences of Catholics of color.

Requests for her sisters came from the South and Southwest, and off they went establishing missions with schools. In 1915, Mother Drexel founded the first U.S. Catholic institution of higher learning for African Americans—Xavier University in New Orleans. By 1935, she had founded forty-nine missions. In her frequent letters to each, she included checks to assist their missionary work. Also in 1935, she suffered a heart attack, but she kept up her interest in all her missions.

During her later years, Katharine was an invalid and spent her time in prayer. She died March 3, 1955, at age ninety-six. The work of her sisters carries on her spirit. On October 1, 2000, Pope John Paul II canonized her. More than 2,000 pilgrims from the Philadelphia area attended.

REFLECTIONS

- Katharine was appalled at the plight of Native Americans as she read about it in Helen Hunt Jackson's *A Century of Dishonor*. Read this book, or *Ramona* by the same author.

- Katharine gave up seven million dollars when she embraced religious life, and this made the headlines of the country's newspapers. What have you left behind to follow God's call to you?

PRAYER

Keep us mindful, O God,
Of the human needs and rights
Of all peoples,
Especially those
Who are outwardly different
From us.
Amen.

 *March 4*

MIRIAM MAKEBA

Singer, activist • South Africa, U.S., Guinea • 1934—

SCRIPTURE THEME

Oppression, freedom

"Thus says the LORD, the God of Israel, 'Let my people go…'."

— *Exodus 5:1*

QUOTATION

"It was the Superior Being who gave me a voice to sing with, but it was my mother and grandmother who gave me my first words to sing."

— *Miriam Makeba*, Sangoma

MIRIAM'S VOICE SPEAKS OUT AGAINST APARTHEID. Miriam's voice sings out of her South African culture. The recording of *Sangoma* in the late 1980's brings to life Miriam's spirit of song and the wisdom of her ancestors. People all over the world call her "Mama Africa."

Miriam, born on March 4, 1934, in Johannesburg, South Africa, was imprisoned as an infant with her mother—jailed for trying to support her family by illegally brewing beer. Miriam's gift of singing brought her recognition and invitations. She performed in a 1958 documentary named *Come Back to Africa*. She met Harry Belafonte who became her mentor and promoted her career. He also encouraged her to speak out against apartheid. Miriam's single "Pata, Pata" was a hit in the United States. She became the "empress of African song" in the United States in the 1960's, and was the first African to gain an international following.

Miriam was exiled from South Africa because of her political views. When she wished to return to South Africa in 1960 at the death of her mother, Miriam learned that her passport had been revoked. She married Stokely Carmichael, a militant Black leader, in the late 1960's. For several years, her concerts were canceled and her records boycotted in Great Britain and the United States.

She settled in Guinea, and in 1975 was appointed the Guinea delegate to the United Nations. In memory of her daughter, Bongi, who died after giving birth, Miriam founded a maternity hospital in Guinea and continues to provide medical equipment and supplies. When Miriam performed with Paul Simon's *Graceland* tour in 1987, she enjoyed a great comeback. In 1988, she published her autobiography, *Makeba: My Story*, and a new album of songs, *Sangoma*. These songs, based on African tribal chants, were taught to Miriam by her mother, who was a *sangoma*, or healer. In 1990, Miriam toured the United States with Harry Belafonte. Their concerts were well acclaimed.

REFLECTIONS

- Do you have a *sangoma*, or healer, in your life?
- Have you ever faced living away from home, in some kind of exile?
- Spiritual contact with ancestors is important in African spirituality. How are your ancestors present in your family traditions and in your personal spirituality?

PRAYER

May the songs of our homeland
   Remind us of you, O God,
   For in you all find a home.
   Amen.

Maria Solares

Chumash American Indian traditionalist leader · *U.S.* · *1842–1923*

Scripture Theme

Missionary

"Remember your leaders, those who spoke the word of God to you; consider the outcome of their way of life, and imitate their faith."

— *Hebrews 13:7*

Quotation

"Somewhere, and I can't find where, I read about an Eskimo hunter who asked the local missionary priest, 'If I do not know about God and sin, would I go to hell?' 'No,' said the priest, 'not if you do not know.' 'Then why,' asked the Eskimo earnestly, 'did you tell me?'"

— *Annie Dillard,* Sunbeams, *page 155*

MARIA WAS BORN IN 1842 IN ALAXULAPU, a Chumash village in southern California. Her father, a descendent of Chumash chiefs, served as an American Indian mayor (*alcaldes*) at Mission Santa Ynez. Her mother was a descendent of the inland Chumash and of the Yokuts. And so, along with the Catholicism of the mission, Maria grew up learning the languages and cultures of her Native American ancestors.

When the mission was secularized, Maria and her family, as well as all the native peoples associated with the mission, suffered from great poverty and deprivation. As both Americans and Mexicans expanded their control of California, the natives were pushed out.

In three marriages, Maria bore three children who lived to adulthood. Her third marriage to Manuel Solares brought Maria into the special religious ceremonies (*antap*) of Chumash.

As a doctor and midwife on the Santa Ynez Reservation, Maria became familiar to not only the American Indians, but also the Mexicans and Whites. She treated the patients other doctors refused to see.

Able to balance her native religion with the Catholic religion, Maria became godmother to many of the American Indian and Mexican babies at their Baptisms. Her knowledge of the Chumash religion and culture was preserved in a Smithsonian Institution study done by John Peabody Harrington. During Maria's later years, she and Harrington collaborated on a large collection of narratives about Chumash beliefs.

Maria died March 6, 1923, on the Santa Ynez Reservation. Today, Maria's descendents recognize her as the preserver of their Chumash religion and culture.

REFLECTIONS

- Look for and read *December's Child* by Thomas Blackburn. Maria's contributions make up more than half the book.
- Reflect on the joys and trials of balancing two or more religions and cultures. Do you think it is valid to combine aspects of several different religions in one's own spirituality?
- Much is being published on Native American religion. Do you find peace in these practices?

PRAYER

Through the intercession of Mary,
Mother of all refugees,
We pray for those whose work
For the benefit of refugee peoples.
We pray that refugees may find safe haven
At home and work
And respect for their native spirituality
Through the efforts of people like Maria Solares,
Also called "Maria Isidore del Refugio."
Amen.

March 6

LOUISA MAY ALCOTT

Novelist · U.S. · 1832–1888

SCRIPTURE THEME

Imagination, dreams, visions

"God gave knowledge and skill in every aspect of literature and wisdom; Daniel also had insight into all visions and dreams."

— Daniel 1:17

QUOTATION

"I like to help women help themselves, as that is, in my opinion, the best way to

settle the woman question. Whatever we can do and do well we have a right to, and I don't think any one will deny us."

— *Louisa May Alcott,* And Then She Said..., *page 57*

BORN ON NOVEMBER 29, 1832, Louisa was well educated by her transcendentalist father. She loved drama and had a keen awareness of the sensational in everyday life. Her jobs as teacher, seamstress, maid and companion provided a wealth of raw materials for her later writing.

The portrayal of real life in *Hospital Sketches* based on her experience as a Civil War nurse convinced Louisa that success lay in realistic more than highly imaginative stories. *Little Women,* with the everyday events and small crises of Jo, Meg, Beth and Amy, became immediately popular and was translated into more than thirty languages. The warmth of life in this family carried over into Louisa's subsequent books *Little Men* and *Jo's Boys.* Some of the daughters in these later books pursue careers as a doctor, an artist and an actress—and this is in books of the 1870's and 1880's.

Eight Cousins and *Rose in Bloom,* delightful books with memorable personalities, offered Louisa a vehicle for poking fun at the values of Victorian society.

Louisa suffered ill health during her last years and died March 6, 1888, in Boston, a few days after her father's death.

REFLECTIONS

- Did you read any of Louisa's books when you were a child? What do you remember of them?
- Read one of her books or some of her letters and journals. Check with your local library for what's available.
- As a child, Louisa kept an "imagination notebook." What do you write down for yourself to keep, reread and remember?

PRAYER

Forgive us, loving God,
For times when we have kept
Women from doing
What lies in their power
And rights to do.
Amen.

 *March 7*

Saints Perpetua and Felicity

Martyrs • Carthage (North Africa) • d. 203

Scripture Theme

Martyrs

"Those who find their life will lose it, and those who lose their life for my sake will find it."

— *Matthew 10:39*

Quotation

"Continue firm in the faith, love one another, and be not offended at our sufferings."

— *Perpetua,* The Quotable Woman: From Eve to 1799, *page 22*

PERPETUA, A YOUNG MARRIED WOMAN WITH A BABY, and Felicity, a slave girl, were martyred in 203 at Carthage along with four male companions, one of whom was the husband of Perpetua. These young Christians refused to abandon or deny their faith. They refused to worship the pagan gods, and they were imprisoned, tortured and finally martyred.

The piece of writing known as *The Passion of Saints Perpetua and Felicity*, written partly by Perpetua and partly by another of the Carthage martyrs named Saturus, and then completed by a third writer after 203, offers one of the most inspiring and authentic accounts of the early martyrs. It is interesting to note that the writings preserved from the third century pay more attention to the two women than to the four men.

In her writing, Perpetua described the visions of the ladder to heaven she had after her Baptism. She tells, too, of her concern for her elderly father, who did not understand her Christianity, and of her concern for her baby.

When Perpetua, Felicity and the others were arrested and condemned to death, their faith and prayer encouraged each other. Felicity gave birth to her daughter while in prison. Both her baby and Perpetua's were sent to be raised by friends.

Of the crowds of spectators who watched the violent deaths by wild beasts in the amphitheater of Carthage, some reveled in the spectacle; others were converted. According to an old adage: "The blood of martyrs is the seed of faith."

REFLECTIONS

- Read part of *The Passion of Saints Perpetua and Felicity.*
- Look in art history books for the Ravenna mosaics of the sixth century and the fourteenth-century altar frontal piece of Barcelona, both of which depict Perpetua.
- Do you have children in your care? Who will assume your role when you can no longer be a caregiver?

PRAYER

For mothers
Who must entrust their children
To the care of others,
We pray, O God,
And in a special way
We pray for mothers
Who chose adoption rather than abortion
For an unexpected baby.
Amen.

May the blood of your martyrs, O God,
Be the seed of our faith,
In contemporary times
As well as ancient times.
Amen.

March 8

INTERNATIONAL WOMEN'S DAY

SCRIPTURE THEME

Globe

*"Who shut in the sea with doors
when it burst out from the womb?—
when I made the clouds its garment,
and thick darkness its swaddling band."*

   — *Job 38:8-9*

QUOTATION

"It will be a great day when our schools get all the money they need and the air

force has to hold a bake sale to buy a bomber."

— *Women's International League of Peace and Freedom,* The New York Public Library
Book of Twentieth Century American Quotations, *page 415*

THE OBSERVANCE OF THIS DAY is said to have originated in an 1857 demonstration and march in New York City on the part of garment and textile workers.

In 1910, an international conference of women in Helsinki, Finland, decided that March 8 should be observed each year to commemorate the demonstration and to honor working women. In 1960, Clara Zetkin (1857–1933) was credited with initiating Women's Day.

In China and in the former Union of Soviet Socialist Republics, March 8 is observed as a national holiday, and working women are presented with gifts and flowers. The organization of United Nations systems also observes the day.

The week of March 8 is Universal Women's Week. The International Society of Friendship and Good Will promotes the value of women of all ages, all classes, all cultures, and calls for honoring outstanding women in every field of human endeavor.

REFLECTIONS

- Find out how International Women's Day and Universal Women's Week are observed in your area at local colleges, libraries and churches.

- If you could name a woman to the Universal Hall of Fame, who would it be? Why?

- Reflect on the work you do. How does it build upon and honor the work of other women?

PRAYER

"Let us raise our voice in unison
And cry out with one heart, one breath,
'We are Humanity.'
We are bound,
Heart to heart,
Mind to mind,
By our shared destiny.
We are as one body,
Living, breathing upon this earth.
Our needs are one...
But we shall rise up
As a mighty, swelling tide

Of compassion and understanding
That shall encompass the earth."

— *Proclamation of Peace, International Society of Friendship and Good Will*

 *March 9*

FRANCES OF ROME

Wife, mother, widow, religious founder • *Rome (Italy)* • *1384–1440*

SCRIPTURE THEME

Guardian angel

"Are not all angels spirits in the divine service, sent to serve for the sake of those who are to inherit salvation?"

— *Hebrews 1:14*

QUOTATION

"She must sometimes leave God at the altar to find him in her housework."

— *Frances,* Lives of the Saints, *page 87*

FRANCES WAS BORN IN 1384 of a pious and well-off family. Though she desired to become a nun, she was married at thirteen to Lorenzo Ponziano. They lived in the same house with Lorenzo's brother and sister-in-law, Vanozza.

The two young women shared some of the same values and soon were bringing aid to the poor of Rome, especially those made sick by plagues and wars.

At sixteen, Frances had her first of six children. She devoted herself to the care of the children and the household while continuing her concern for the poor in her area. Two of her children died young.

In 1425, Frances founded a society of devout women who lived by the Benedictine way of life but without the vows of religion. These Roman women who cared for the poor were known as Oblates of Mary (later Oblates of Tor di Specchi). After her husband died and her children were on their own, Frances joined this community as a simple novice, never moving beyond this stage to solemn vows. She never took vows and is honored now as a holy widow. It is said that in their forty years of marriage, Frances and her husband never quarreled.

During her later years, Frances experienced visions and revelations.

For several years, she had a continuous vision of her guardian angel. She died in 1440 and was buried in a church at Rome now called Santa Francesca Romana. Her home *(Pallazo Ponziano)* became and remains a center of pilgrimages.

REFLECTIONS

- Consider with gratitude other women with whom you have shared your values and activities.
- Reflect on the traditional role of women in child care and household care. Do you find this role confining? Undervalued? Fulfilling?
- Frances combined a sense of mystical prayer with a sense of social responsibility. How does your prayer life move you to consider others?

PRAYER

Let us prayerfully repeat the words
Of this Benedictine saint, Francesca di Roma:
"It is most laudable
In a married woman
To be devout…
[But] sometimes
She must leave God at the altar
To find him in housekeeping."
Amen.

 *March 10*

HARRIET TUBMAN

Former slave, abolitionist • U.S. • 1821–1913

SCRIPTURE THEME

Freedom

"I am the LORD your God, who brought you out of the land of Egypt, out of the house of slavery."

— Exodus 20:2

QUOTATION

"When I found I had crossed dat line, I looked at my hands to see if I was de same

pusson. There was such a glory ober ebery ting; de sun came like gold through the trees and ober the fields and I felt like I was in Heaben."

— *Harriet Tubman,* The Quotable Woman: 1800–On, *page 30*

BORN A SLAVE IN MARYLAND IN 1821, Harriet was called "Hattie" or "Hat" by her family. By age eight, she was pressed into domestic service, but her already rebellious spirit brought her into disfavor. She was sent to the fields to work and gained great strength in doing so. Working with the hymn-singing slaves, she also gained spiritual strength. Her father taught her survival skills in the outdoors.

Through the "grapevine telegraph," that is, the word-of-mouth network of slaves, Harriet learned of freedom via the Underground Railroad in the North and set her heart to gaining that freedom.

At age thirteen, Harriet was struck in the head by an overseer and suffered all her life from that injury.

When the owner of the plantation died and there were rumors that the slaves would be sold to the deep South, Harriet started out on her escape route. With stations at various Quaker homes, Harriet was able to make her way from Baltimore to Philadelphia. She obtained work in the city, but not being satisfied with only her own freedom, she returned time and time again to help her relatives and friends escape along the dangerous route. In all, she made nineteen trips helping more than three hundred fugitives escape to northern states or Canada.

When Harriet was able to bring her parents north, she settled them in Auburn, New York, and devoted her time to lecturing on abolition and women's rights.

During the Civil War, Harriet served as nurse, cook and spy. Harriet married Nelson Davies in 1869. Together they founded schools for free Blacks and helped with the teaching. Harriet also established in Auburn a home for elderly Blacks.

Named "the Moses of her people," Harriet eventually received a $20-a-month pension for her Civil War service. She died March 10, 1913, and is buried at Auburn.

REFLECTIONS

- Read a biography of Harriet Tubman: *Harriet Tubman, the Moses of Her People* by Sarah Bradford; *Harriet Tubman* by E. Conrad; or *Freedom Train: The Story of Harriet Tubman* by Dorothy Sterling.

- Harriet had a $40,000 bounty on her head for assisting slaves to escape, but she kept on with her risky role as conductor in the Underground Railroad. What would inspire you to incur so great a risk?

PRAYER

Give us the courage,
O great conductor and guide,
To assist others over and over again
In their journeys to freedom,
In their passages from enslavement
To promised lands.
Amen.

 *March 11*

EDITH ELIZABETH LOWRY

Ecumenist, worker for migrants · U.S. · 1897–1970

SCRIPTURE THEME

Migrant worker

"Since there will never cease to be some in need on the earth, I therefore command you, 'Open your hand to the poor and needy neighbor in the land.'"
— *Deuteronomy 15:11*

QUOTATION

"Go to the most abandoned of this world and the next."
— *Blessed Eugénia Smet,* Quotable Saints, *page 124*

BORN MARCH 23, 1897, IN NEW JERSEY, Edith joined the Baptist religion of her parents. After graduation from Wellesley College in 1920, she worked as a staff member for mission work in the Presbyterian Church.

In 1926, she began work in an interdenominational ministry to migrant workers and served as director of this ministry for several decades. During the Great Depression, she brought teachers, nurses and social workers to the migrants and raised the consciousness of the general public to the needs of the migrants.

For many years, Edith served as executive secretary for the Council of Women for Home Missions, an early national ecumenical group. For a short time, she served as its president. During these same years, she wrote pamphlets on the migrants and spoke on the National Radio Pulpit, the first woman to do so.

During the 1940's, Edith continued her concern for the migrants and helped establish day care for working parents. When the Home Mission Council merged with other groups to form the National Council of Churches, Edith became the first secretary of the new group's Board of Home Missions. She reached out to the migrants in more remote areas.

After her retirement, Edith lived out her years on a quiet farm in Vermont. She died March 11, 1970.

REFLECTIONS

- Look for Edith's pamphlets at a public library: *Migrants of the Crop: They Starve That We Might Live* and *Tales of Americans on Trek.*
- Are there migrant workers in your area? What spiritual and social, physical and educational services are provided for them? Is there some way you can help?
- Do you get involved in ecumenical prayer or programs in your area? Why or why not?

PRAYER

O God, you are God for all peoples
In many religious experiences.
May we build on what unites us
And work for the well-being
Of all human beings.
Amen.

March 12

GIRL SCOUT DAY

Founded in the U.S. in 1912

SCRIPTURE THEME

"Be prepared" (Girl Scout motto)

*"Go to the ant...
Without having any chief
or officer or ruler,
it prepares its food in summer,
and gathers its sustenance in harvest."*

— *Proverbs 6:6-8*

QUOTATION

"I will do my best: To be honest, To be fair, To help where I am needed, To be cheerful, To be friendly and considerate, To be a sister to every Girl Scout, To respect authority, To use resources wisely, To protect and improve the world around me, To show respect for myself and others through my words and actions."

— *Girl Scout Law*

ON MARCH 12, 1912, IN SAVANNAH, GEORGIA, Juliette Gordon Low held the first Girl Guides meeting in her home. She soon changed the name to Girl Scouts. When the group was incorporated in 1915, Juliette became the first president.

The idea grew out of the Girl Guides started in England in 1907 and in Canada in 1910. In 1920, Olave Baden-Powell, wife of Robert Baden-Powell (who founded Boy Scouts in 1907) called the first international conference of Girl Guides. Members from fifteen countries met in Great Britain. Over the decades, Girl Scouting has grown to eight million girls and leaders on every continent.

The U.S. Congress issued a charter to the Girl Scouts of the U.S. in 1950. In 1984, Daisy Girl Scouting was introduced for five-year-olds; this grouping is named for Juliette Gordon Low whose nickname was Daisy. Other age groupings include Brownie Scouts for six- to eight-year-olds, Junior Girl Scouts for nine- to eleven-year-olds, Cadette Girl Scouts for twelve- to fourteen-year-olds, and Senior Girl Scouts for fourteen- to seventeen-year-olds.

The Juliette Low World Friendship Fund helps finance international exchange visits and helps promote global understanding through language training and other experiences.

REFLECTIONS

- What do you think about organizations that admit only girls? What about those that admit only boys?
- Do you think the Girl Scout Law and motto provide valid ideals for young women? Why?

PRAYER

For Girl Scouts
Everywhere in the world,
We pray
That God may bless
And guide their efforts

In international peace
And lasting friendships.
Amen.

March 13

EVIE HONE

Artist, maker of stained-glass windows · Ireland · 1894–1955

SCRIPTURE THEME

Stained glass

"Light is sweet, and it is pleasant for the eyes to see the sun."

— *Ecclesiastes 11:7*

QUOTATION

"People are like stained-glass windows. They sparkle and shine when the sun is out, but when the darkness sets in, their true beauty is revealed only if there is light within."

— *Elizabeth Kübler-Ross,* Sunbeams, *page 7*

A DEEPLY RELIGIOUS NATURE INSPIRED EVIE to develop her artistic talents into the making of stained-glass windows for churches.

Born April 22, 1894, in Dublin, Evie suffered from poliomyelitis as a child and was left a semi-invalid by the disease. Her determination to be an artist led her to study in London and Paris with her devoted friend Maimie Jellett. Both young artists studied and worked under Lhote and Gleizes. Evie worked with abstract painting before turning to stained glass. Maimie painted large wall murals.

One of Evie's best-known works was *My Four Green Fields*. She produced over 150 stained-glass panels, including five windows for the Jesuit College at Tullaberg and a large Last Supper–Crucifixion window at Eton College.

Evie assisted Maimie Jellett in founding the Irish Exhibition of Living Art in 1943. Despite ill health, Evie worked at her art until her death on March 13, 1955, at age sixty.

REFLECTIONS

· Take a fresh look at the stained glass in your church or other churches. What sort of devotion does it inspire? What sort of devotion did it require?

- Spend some time watching the world through a window. Is the experience different than simply going outside? How so?
- Cultivate a craft or hobby that will allow you to bring beauty of your own design into the world.

PRAYER

In the multicolored light of stained glass,
May we marvel at the variety
Of God's peoples, God's colors, God's love.
Amen.

March 14

LUCY BEAMAN HOBBS TAYLOR

Dentist, reformer • U.S. • 1833–1910

SCRIPTURE THEME

Perseverance

"Therefore take up the whole armor of God, so that you may be able to withstand on that evil day, and having done everything, to stand firm."

— *Ephesians 6:13*

QUOTATION

"You must do the thing you think you cannot do."

— *Eleanor Roosevelt*, Quotable Women

THE FIRST WOMAN TO BECOME A CERTIFIED DENTIST, Lucy began her career as a schoolteacher. She was born March 14, 1833, probably in Franklin County of New York and graduated in 1849 from Franklin Academy in Malone, New York.

After some years of teaching, Lucy took up the study of medicine and dentistry with a private tutor. She was refused admission to medical colleges because she was a woman. Though Lucy was apprenticed to a dentist graduate of the Ohio College of Dental Surgery, the dental college refused her admission.

So she set up practice on her own, was later elected to the Iowa State Dental Society and was sent as a delegate to the national dental convention. In 1865, the dental college did admit her. When she graduated in 1866, she became the first American woman to receive a degree in dentistry. In 1867, Lucy married James M. Taylor and she instructed him in dentistry. They settled in Kansas and developed their practice of dental care.

When her husband died in 1886, Lucy retired from most of the dental practice. She lived well into her seventies, dying October 3, 1910.

REFLECTIONS

- Have you ever been treated by a female doctor or dentist? Do you have a preference for male or female health-care workers? Why?
- What skills or knowledge have you taught to a man? How did it feel? How was it received?

PRAYER

For those women who work hard
To make their dreams come true
Especially in areas just opening to women,
We pray for their concerns.
Amen.

March 15

LOUISE DE MARILLAC

Religious founder • France • 1591–1660

SCRIPTURE THEME

Care of infants

"When she could hide him no longer she got a papyrus basket for him, and plastered it with bitumen and pitch; she put the child in it and placed it among the reeds on the bank of the river. His sister stood at a distance, to see what would happen to him."

— *Exodus 2:3-4*

QUOTATION

"Be diligent in serving the poor. Love the poor, honor them, my children, as you would honor Christ himself."

— *Louise de Marillac,* Lives of the Saints, *page 94*

Louise was declared patron of social workers in 1960 by Pope John XXIII. Her compassion, concern and care for the poor make her an apt patron for all those devoted to contemporary social work.

Born in 1591 as the illegitimate daughter of a French nobleman, Louise received a good education and upbringing. She was a child when her mother died and only thirteen when her father died.

Though she wished to become a nun, on the advice of a priest she married Antony Le Gras. He was twenty-two years old. They had a son and a happy family life. When her husband fell ill, Louise cared for him until his death in 1625.

As a widow, Louise devoted herself to prayer and charitable works. In cooperation with Saint Vincent de Paul, Louise founded the Sisters of Charity. From 1633 until 1655, the Sisters of Charity took steps toward forming an institute of nuns. In 1655, Rome gave the approval.

Patients at the great Paris hospital of the Hotel-Dieu received care from the sisters. Children received care at a foundling home and in the classrooms staffed by the sisters.

Louise remained superior of the group until her death.

Louise always looked out for her son Michael and he was at her bedside when she died on March 15, 1660. It was 1920 when Louise was beatified and 1934 when she was canonized.

The Daughters of Charity developed a new form of religious life in leaving the cloister to serve the poor.

REFLECTIONS

- Are you or someone you know involved in social work? How much of this calling is religious in nature?

- How do you help the most desperate of your community? Is there more you could do?

PRAYER

For all infants born out of wedlock
That they may find deep love
And parental care
In those near to them,
We pray to God
Who is Mother and Father
To us all.
Amen.

March 16

CAROLINE HERSCHEL

Astronomer • Germany • 1750–1848

SCRIPTURE THEME

Astronomy, stars

"I will indeed bless you, and I will make your offspring as numerous as the stars of heaven and as the sand that is on the seashore."

— *Genesis 22:17*

QUOTATION

"Minding the heavens."

— Caroline Herschel in describing the fifty years she worked with her brother studying the sky, Remember the Ladies, *page 58*

BORN IN HANOVER, Caroline had a childhood that was caught between her father's interest in math, music and astronomy and her mother's concern for daily housekeeping. From the time she was seven through the age of ten, Caroline's father was away fighting a war and her mother's values held sway. With her father home, Caroline learned more philosophical things. After her father's death in 1767, Caroline moved to England, where her brother, William, continued her instruction in mathematics, bookkeeping, English and music.

When William first forced her to help him with astronomy experiments, Caroline had to give up her music. Later, she used her free time to search the sky on her own. Between 1786 and 1797, Caroline discovered eight comets. Her fame grew and she was given a salary by the king.

In 1788, William married Mary Pitts and Caroline lost her privileged position in her brother's life. She did grow to like her sister-in-law and continued to serve as William's astronomy assistant.

In 1797–1798, Caroline took up the arduous work of organizing the *Catalogue of Stars*. After William's death in 1822, Caroline moved back to Hanover, a move she regretted because it separated her from her brother's son John, also an astronomer. The two remained informed of each other's work by letter and occasional visits of John to Hanover.

Caroline compiled a new catalogue of nebulae and zones for John's work, and though the material was never published, Caroline was awarded a gold medal for it by the Astronomical Society in 1828.

Many scientists came to see Caroline, and she received several awards for her contribution to science. She lived to be ninety-seven and died January 9, 1848.

REFLECTIONS

- Caroline's accuracy and precision in observation balanced her brother's speculative and creative abstractions. When have you needed the help of another sort of personality in a work situation? What sort of difficulties were involved?

- Caroline was motivated by love for her brother to get involved in astronomy. Who or what inspired you to take up your current career?

- Consider your own early education. Were your parents biased in making decisions concerning it? Did they place a higher premium on having the boys in the family prepared to "make a living"?

PRAYER

Praised be you, O Creator,
For the stars of the skies
And for telescopes, which serve
As windows for "minding the heavens."
Amen.

March 17

CAMP FIRE DAY

Founded in 1910

SCRIPTURE THEME

"Give service" (Camp Fire slogan)

"When Jesus entered Peter's house, he saw his mother-in-law lying in bed with a fever; he touched her hand, and the fever left her, and she got up and began to serve him."

— Matthew 8:14-15

QUOTATION

"Worship God, Seek Beauty, Give Service, Pursue Knowledge, Be Trustworthy, Hold onto Health, Glorify Work, Be Happy."

— Camp Fire Law

CAMP FIRE GIRLS WAS FOUNDED MARCH 17, 1910, by Charlotte Velter Gulick and her husband, Luther Hasley Gulick, a doctor and leader in recreational programs for youth. The Gulicks had operated a family camp in Connecticut for a long time. In 1909, on Sebago Lake in Maine, they opened one of the first U.S. girls' camps, complete with swimming and canoeing. Luther was involved in the foundation of the Boy Scouts of America in 1910. When many asked for a similar program for girls, the Gulicks began the Camp Fire Girls program.

Over the years, Camp Fire Girls expanded beyond camping to include child care programs and social action work. In 1975, boys were admitted, and in 1979, the organization changed its name to Camp Fire, Inc.

The basic philosophy of Camp Fire, Inc., affirms that each person has special skills and a special personality to share with others.

REFLECTIONS

- Did you belong to Camp Fire Girls, Girl Scouts, 4-H or another similar group? How did your experiences shape the adult you have become?
- Reflect on how Camp Fire, Inc. came to change its name and include boys. Do you think Girl Scouts and Boy Scouts should include members of the opposite sex?
- Does the Camp Fire rule hold value for you? How is it different from basic Christian moral principles?

PRAYER

May all who gather
In circles around campfires
Be warmed by their flames
And affirmed by their light
And warmed and affirmed
By the campers gathered
Around the fires.
Amen.

March 18

LOUISA JAQUES

Religious • South Africa • 1901–1942

SCRIPTURE THEME

Rejection

"The stone that the builders rejected
has become the chief cornerstone."

— *Psalm 118:22*

QUOTATION

"*I saw the shadowy form of a woman coming into the room through the case-
ment as through a French window...and from time to time she turned her head
toward the window by which she had entered, as though someone were waiting
for her outside...*"

— *Louisa relates her vision of a nun in brown*, Revelations of Women Mystics, *page 130*

THIS WINDOW VISION OF A WOMAN came to Louisa at a time of disbelief and
doubt about God. The vision turned Louisa toward religion and the
Catholic faith. After her vision and search for faith, Louisa was baptized
on March 18, 1928, at age twenty-seven.

Louisa was born in South Africa in 1901. Her mother died in this childbirth. Her father took Louisa and her two sisters to Switzerland, where
an aunt raised them. Louisa worked as a governess in her twenties.

Louisa felt a strong call to religious life, but she was refused everywhere she asked because of poor health and no dowry. Finally accepted
in a teaching order, she was not allowed to take vows because she still
wanted to go to a contemplative convent.

She was allowed to join a Poor Clare convent but was forced to leave
because she objected to abusive rigidity. She went to Johannesburg,
South Africa, and tried to enter the Carmelites there. By the time permission came, Louisa had made up her mind to try the Carmelites in
Jerusalem. There she found her true home.

Her inner conversations with God became very frequent, and her notes
made a large collection. They were printed in 1942, the year of Louisa's
death, under the title *Soeur Marie de la Trinité*. In 1950 they were translated into English and published as *The Spiritual Legacy of Sister Mary of the
Holy Trinity, Poor Clare of Jerusalem*. This book was reprinted in 1954.

REFLECTIONS

- Rejection did not keep Louisa from continuing to try to do what she believed was God's will for her. How do you handle rejection?
- Do you keep a spiritual diary or journal? Does it help you to see how you have grown in wisdom over the years?

PRAYER

May we see your face, O God,
Ever ancient, ever new,
In the windows of our prayer.
Amen.

March 19

MARIA DE LA CABEZA

Wife of Saint Isidore · Spain · d. 1175

SCRIPTURE THEME

Marriage

"A capable wife who can find?
She is far more precious than jewels.
The heart of her husband trusts in her,
and he will have no lack of gain."

— *Proverbs 31:10-11*

QUOTATION

"Marriage is not just spiritual communion and passionate embraces; marriage is also three meals a day, sharing the workload and remembering to carry out the trash."

— *Dr. Joyce Brothers,* The Quotable Woman: 1800–On, *page 65*

AS A YOUNG WOMAN, Maria married Isidore who worked as a tiller of the fields for a wealthy landowner near Madrid. They had one son who died in childhood. Both Maria and Isidore were devout people who spent their days in prayer, labor and charity to the poor. After Isidore died in 1130, Maria lived several more years.

The relic of Maria's head (*cabeza*) is carried in procession in Spain during times of drought, in hopes her intercession will bring rain for the crops.

REFLECTIONS

- Do you become emotional at weddings? What is the source of your feelings?

- Pray for married couples you know. What sacrifices must married people make for the sake of their marriage? What are the rewards of their marriage?

- How do you feel about the traditional role of husband and wife? Are they simply outmoded cultural expectations or do you find them of value?

PRAYER

Remembering your goodness, O God,
In the lives of married saints,
We ask your blessings and love
On married couples in our times.
Amen.

March 20

MARGARET STRONG

Collector and museum procurator • U.S. • 1897–1971

SCRIPTURE THEME

Finding a treasure

"Or what woman having ten silver coins, if she loses one of them, does not light a lamp, sweep the house, and search carefully until she finds it?"

— *Luke 15:8*

QUOTATION

"From the time I was eight years old my father and mother would take me out of school and away we would go to foreign countries. I was allowed to carry a small bag to put my dolls and toys in, and to add anything I acquired on the trips. Consequently, my fondness for small objects grew."

— *Margaret Strong,* Margaret Woodbury Strong, Collector

BORN ON MARCH 20, 1897, as the only child of a well-to-do family with stock in the Eastman Kodak company, in the industrial-commercial prosperity of Rochester, New York, Margaret joined her parents in their world travels and began collecting toys and dolls at an early age. When at home, her parents also provided Margaret with abundant objects to study from rich and diverse cultures. Margaret had a special fondness for small objects and miniatures that fit into her bag.

Margaret's formal education was frequently interrupted by trips. Private tutors and family members as well as travel rounded out her studies. Margaret became accomplished at golf and making floral arrangements. She kept scrapbooks and diaries of her activities.

On September 20, 1920, Margaret married Homer Strong. Their daughter Barbara was born October 7, 1921. The family estate of thirty rooms offered Margaret plenty of space for her ever-growing collection. And Margaret began to develop her ideas for a museum of fascination.

Barbara died in 1946, at age thirty-five, and Homer died in 1958. Still owning stock in Kodak and with other financial assets, Margaret was unrestricted in her pursuit of collectible items. Her doll collection grew from 600 in 1969 to 27,000 by 1970. With toys and housewares, the collection grew to 500,000 objects.

In 1968, Margaret set up a museum corporation and her will provided for a perpetual endowment of the museum. Margaret died in 1971. The Strong Museum in downtown Rochester officially opened in 1982, with an emphasis on the American cultural ideas of 1820 to 1940.

REFLECTIONS

- Do you regularly visit museums? What kinds of things do you like to observe and learn in them?
- Are you a collector? How do you share your interests with others? Is your collection a reasonable use of your financial resources?
- Arrange to take a child to your favorite museum. How is the child's experience different from your own?

PRAYER

For those who collect and preserve
The artifacts of life
For others to appreciate
And learn from,
We thank you, God.
Amen.

March 21

PHYLLIS MCGINLEY

Poet, housewife • U.S. • 1905–1978

SCRIPTURE THEME

Contentment

"I have learned to be content with whatever I have."
　— *Philippians 4:11*

QUOTATION

"By hook, by crook, by hair of head,
By scruff of neck and seat of pants,
Our stubborn infants shall be led
Along the path of tolerance."
　— *Phyllis McGinley,* A Book of Days, *page 419*

HERE'S A PERFECTLY CONTENT SUBURBAN MOTHER and housewife. In her volume of essays, *The Province of the Heart* (1959), she sings the praises of the suburbs.

Phyllis was born March 21, 1905, and while pursuing a career as a teacher, she wrote poetry in her spare time. Her poems are light and witty; she seems to have avoided seriousness. In 1961, she won the Pulitzer Prize for her volume of collected poetry, *Three Times.* In this volume, some of her most charming poems are about saints and reformers. In her 1964 collection of essays, *Sixpence in Her Shoe,* Phyllis considers woman's role as wife and mother, which she called "woman's most honorable profession."

Her Catholic faith comes through clearly in *A Wreath of Christmas Legends* (1967) and *Saint-Watching* (1969), which shows the human side of the saints. Phyllis also wrote a number of children's books. She died February 22, 1978.

REFLECTIONS

- What do you think about suburban living? Is it a solution to the problems of urban living or an escape from them?

- What do you believe is a woman's "most honorable profession"? Would your mother agree?

PRAYER

May we find our peace and contentment
In you, O God, of our salvation.
Amen.

March 22

EQUAL RIGHTS AMENDMENT

SCRIPTURE THEME

Equality

"So God created humankind in his image,
in the image of God he created them;
male and female he created them."

— *Genesis 1:27*

QUOTATION

"Equality of rights under the law shall not be abridged by the United States or
by any State on account of sex."

— *The Equal Rights Amendment*

THE EQUAL RIGHTS AMENDMENT—the proposed Twenty-seventh
Amendment to the U.S. Constitution—was first introduced in Congress
in 1923. It fleshed out the basic equality and legal rights for women. The
amendment passed the House of Representatives in October 1971 and
passed the Senate on March 22, 1972.

By the end of 1973 the ERA had passed in thirty states, six states short
of the three-fifths requirement.

At the time, most major women's organizations supported the ratification of the ERA, though some, such as the National Council of Catholic
Women and STOP ERA led by Phyllis Schlafly, were opposed to it. There
were many arguments for the ERA, mainly to remove the burden of
English Common Law, which considers women chattel, and to give
women justice in all courts and to put the burden of proof on the government rather than on individual women.

Arguments against the ERA included objections about women being
subject to military service, changes in child custody laws, elimination of
alimony in divorce and removal of protective labor laws.

Ramifications of the proposed amendment on both sides abounded. In the end, not enough states ratified the proposed amendment, so it never went into effect.

Social discrimination against women continues to be a concern, with or without federal legislation.

REFLECTIONS

· If you were old enough to think about it in the 1970's, where did you stand on the proposed Equal Rights Amendment? What do you think of it now?

· Current supporters of the ERA have changed its language to include other groups of people. Do you consider the "common ground" approach a strength or a weakness?

· Can you respect a woman with a different perspective on this issue? What about a man?

PRAYER

Let us pray for greater justice
In women's issues,
For creative ways to make gains
In human rights
With and sometimes without
Government guarantees.
Amen.

March 23

FANNIE FARMER

Cooking expert, teacher · U.S. · 1857–1915

SCRIPTURE THEME

Cooking

"The kingdom of heaven is like yeast that a woman took and mixed in with three measures of flour until all of it was leavened."

— *Matthew 13:33*

QUOTATION

"Progress in civilization has been accompanied by progress in cookery."
— *Fannie Farmer,* The Quotable Woman, 1800–On, *page 98*

FANNIE WAS BORN IN BOSTON ON MARCH 23, 1857, and spent her childhood in Boston and Medford, Massachusetts. A paralytic stroke forced her to leave high school, and she never completed her formal education.

When she recovered somewhat from her illness, she was able to find work as a mother's helper. She was so good with food and cooking that her parents urged her to attend the Boston Cooking School. When she graduated at age thirty-two, she stayed on as assistant director. Five years later, she was in charge of the school. In 1902, she left and opened her own school—Miss Farmer's School of Cookery. She was invited to give lectures and write magazine columns.

Two of Fannie's lasting contributions are the standardization of level measurements in recipes and the 1896 *Boston Cooking School Cookbook*, which is still a best-seller in its modern form, *The Fannie Farmer Cookbook*.

Fannie's efforts were directed more to the housewife than to institutional cooks. Her intuitive sense of nutrition and diet forms an integral part of the many cookbooks she authored.

After her death on January 15, 1915, her cooking school continued for another thirty years.

REFLECTIONS

- Do you enjoy cooking? Do you find it a source of spiritual, as well as physical, nourishment?
- Does your family have favorite recipes? Have you thought of the cooks in your family who handed them down?

PRAYER

Bless us, O God,
And the gifts of food we receive
From your bounty
Through the cooking skills
Of our mothers, sisters,
Our wives, friends,
And others.
Amen.

 *March 24*

CATHERINE OF VADSTENA

Wife, religious • Sweden • d. 1381

SCRIPTURE THEME

Mother, daughter

"Do not withhold;
bring my sons from far away
*   and my daughters from the end of the earth—*
everyone who is called by my name."

— Isaiah 43:6-7

QUOTATION

"My mother is a poem I'll never be able to write
though everything I write is a poem to my mother."

— *Sharon Doubiago,* The Beacon Book of Quotations by Women, *page 217*

CATHERINE OF VADSTENA (OF SWEDEN) was the fourth and favorite daughter of Saint Bridget of Sweden. One of eight children, Catherine married at eighteen but always remained involved in her mother's religious activities, including a journey to the Holy Land.

After her husband's death, Catherine chose to not consider remarriage and devoted herself entirely to her mother's devotions and works of charity. When her mother died in Rome, Catherine had her body taken to Vadstena and buried at the monastery. Catherine then took up the task of completing the establishment of the Order of the Holy Savior (Bridgettines) started by her mother.

Catherine worked with Roman authorities for the approval of the order as well as for her mother's canonization. Catherine stayed in Rome for about five years and while there formed a close friendship with Saint Catherine of Siena. Catherine then returned to Vadstena, where after a painful illness, she died in 1381.

It is said that Catherine never spoke an unkind or impatient word and prayed that detraction and other sins of the tongue would never harm her community.

Her mother was canonized in 1391. Catherine was never formally canonized, but her name appears in the Roman Martyrology. Her feast day is observed in the Bridgettine Order and in Sweden.

REFLECTIONS

- Have you ever heard people claim that their mothers were saints? Do you think it would be difficult to live up to the expectations of such a mother? Or comforting to know of her unconditional love?

- What sort of values did your mother teach you? Do you see her in yourself at times?

PRAYER

For mothers and daughters,
We pray to you, God,
That the values and spiritual gifts
May pass from one generation
To the next
And enrich their lives.
Amen.

March 25

MARGARET CLITHEROW

Wife, martyr · *England* · *d. 1586*

SCRIPTURE THEME

Following

"Follow me."

   — *Matthew 4:19*

QUOTATION

"Having made no offense, I need no trial."

   — *Margaret Clitherow,* Lives of the Saints, *page 106*

MARGARET WAS BORN IN YORKSHIRE, ENGLAND, and became the wife of John Clitherow. Though John abandoned the Catholic faith of his ancestors for the state religion of England, Margaret converted to Catholicism after her marriage.

Margaret's home became a hiding place for priests who secretly offered Mass there when Mass in England was not allowed. Everyone in her household loved Margaret, and no one betrayed her harboring fugitive priests. Her husband's only complaint was that Margaret did not attend church with him, for which he was fined.

When the eldest son went to France to be educated, English authorities began asking questions and decided to search the house. When they found sacramental objects, Margaret was arrested, put on trial and condemned to death by pressing.

In pressing, the victim was placed under a door and rocks piled on until the person was crushed to death. Margaret died on March 25, 1586. Her dying prayer was: "Jesu, Jesu, Jesu, have mercy on me." She was only thirty years old.

The night before she died, Margaret sent her shoes and stockings to her twelve-year-old daughter, Agnes, indicating that Agnes should follow in her mother's footsteps.

REFLECTIONS

- Agnes became a nun at Louvain. Two of her brothers became priests. What faith heritage do you have from your mother?
- Find the words to the hymn "Faith of Our Fathers" and rethink them as "Faith of Our Mothers."
- Margaret prayed at the end for Queen Elizabeth's return to Catholicism. How do you feel about ecumenical efforts between Anglicans and Catholics?

PRAYER

"Jesu, Jesu, Jesu, have mercy on me."

— *prayer of Margaret,* The One Year Book of Saints, *page 92*

March 26

SANDRA DAY O'CONNOR

Supreme Court judge • U.S. • 1930—

SCRIPTURE THEME

Fairness, justice

*"The effect of righteousness will be peace,
and the result of righteousness,
quietness and trust forever."*

— *Isaiah 32:17*

QUOTATION

"Having family responsibilities and concerns just has to make you a more understanding person."

— *Sandra Day O'Connor,* Wit and Wisdom of Famous American Women, *page 51*

BORN IN EL PASO ON MARCH 26, 1930, Sandra grew up on a ranch on the border between Arizona and New Mexico. Sandra's mother was her teacher, with lesson plans coming in the mail. Later, Sandra lived with her grandmother while attending Radford School for girls. Sandra spent her summers back at the ranch.

Sandra loved horses and learned to ride at an early age. She enjoyed swimming at the ranch. She also learned to drive the truck and tractor, to brand cattle, mend fences and ride in roundups.

When Sandra graduated from Stanford University, she had completed all the courses she needed to be a lawyer. In 1950, she graduated cum laude from Stanford University in California with a bachelor of arts in economics, and later in 1952 with a bachelor of arts in law. As a woman, she had a hard time finding a job with a law firm. She worked as a deputy county attorney while her husband John Jay O'Connor III finished his law degree. Sandra and John both passed the Arizona bar exam in the fall of 1957. Then they both worked as lawyers in Germany. For five years, Sandra remained at home as full-time homemaker and mother to her three preschool sons.

In time, she worked as an assistant attorney general and became a state senator. She became judge for a county court, and then judge on the Arizona Court of Appeals. President Ronald Reagan asked her to serve as a United States Supreme Court justice and she was sworn in September 25, 1981.

REFLECTIONS

- Women are increasingly finding places in high offices. How are you inspired by the example of Sandra Day O'Connor and other prominent women? How do their positions change how you view your own?
- What childhood pleasures do you still treasure?
- Reflect on the conflicting demands and rewards of a woman who must juggle multiple roles. How do you handle challenges in balancing career and family responsibilities?

PRAYER

Teach us integrity of heart,

O Spirit of Wisdom,
In all the judgments and decisions we make.
Amen.

 *March 27*

SARAH VAUGHAN

Jazz vocalist · U.S. · 1924–1990

SCRIPTURE THEME

Music, jazz

*"Sing idle songs to the sound of the harp,
and like David improvise on instruments of music."*

— *Amos 6:5*

QUOTATION

"Music is our myth of the inner life."

— *Susanne Langer,* The New York Public Library Book of Twentieth Century
American Quotations, *page 61*

AN ONLY CHILD, SARAH WAS BORN IN NEW JERSEY to the Vaughan family on
March 27, 1924. Sarah joined her mother in the church choir and heard
her father play both piano and guitar. Piano and organ lessons began for
Sarah when she was eight. By her teens, Sarah was good at analyzing
music, especially voice parts. Her interest in jazz developed.

Some said of Sarah that she was the first jazz singer to have the voice
range of an opera singer. And it was the famed opera singer Leontyne
Price whom Sarah first admired. Sarah got her musical start in the church
choirs where she sang and also played piano and organ.

In 1942, at the age of eighteen, Sarah entered and won an amateur con-
test with her jazz style and found herself performing with Ella
Fitzgerald. In 1943, Earl "Fatha" Hines hired Sarah as a singer in the
Hines band, and her professional career began when she spent a year
touring with them. She developed her own singing style and special
touches, some of which came from listening to horns more than voices.

Sarah developed a reputation for being a bit "sassy" in her singing
style and in rapport with audiences. She loved stage and show and continued performing until her death of lung cancer in 1990.

REFLECTIONS

- As a child, did you belong to a church choir or school chorus? Did it lead you to a hobby or career in music?
- Who are your favorite singers? When do you find yourself most in need of their talents?

PRAYER

Let every form of music
And every kind of instrument
Make a joyful noise
Unto our God.
Amen.

March 28

VIRGINIA WOOLF

Novelist · England · 1882–1941

SCRIPTURE THEME

Whole world

"For God so loved the world that he gave his only Son, so that everyone who believes in him may not perish but may have eternal life."

— *John 3:16*

QUOTATION

"As a woman I have no country.... As a woman my country is the whole world."

— *Virginia Woolf*, And Then She Said, *page 56*

VIRGINIA WAS BORN JANUARY 25, 1882, in London, England. By the time she was twenty-two, Virginia had lost in death her mother, a stepsister, a brother and her father. In 1912, Virginia married Leonard Woolf.

Virginia was gifted with imagination and logical thought, though from the time of her mother's death, she suffered emotional imbalance and nervous breakdowns. Her husband was patient and helpful with her health needs and encouraged her creativity. Together they founded the Hobarth Press, at which most of her works were published.

Her first novel, *The Voyage Out*, was published in 1915. She wrote stories, novels, criticism, biography and other nonfiction, including *A Room of One's Own*, which pleads the cause of women's opportunities for achievement, and *Three Guineas*, which opposes war.

In her novels, especially *Mrs. Dalloway*, *To the Lighthouse* and *The Waves*, Virginia uses innovative techniques and allusive styles.

On March 28, 1941, depressed with her inability to concentrate, she drowned herself in the river near her Sussex home.

Volumes of her letters and diaries published since 1941 reveal some of her best writing and an interesting mind. She is regarded as one of the best novelists and critics of the twentieth century.

REFLECTIONS

- *A Room of One's Own* is a short treatise on the needs of women who are artists. Do you think women and men differ in what they need to be able to create?

- In her novels, Virginia stops time to show the importance of emotional experience. When have you had to take time to absorb the emotional impact of a situation? When have you not been able to take the time when you needed it?

PRAYER

God of hope, may we ever turn to you
In times of discouragement,
Depression, despair.
We pray to you, God,
That we may have
"Rooms of our own"—
Places where we may search
For truth and faith
And that we may see
The whole world
As our country.
Amen.

 *March 29*

PEARL BAILEY

Singer, U.N. delegate · *U.S.* · *1918–1990*

SCRIPTURE THEME

Truth

"If you continue in my word, you are truly my disciples; and you will know the truth, and the truth will make you free."

— *John 8:31-32*

QUOTATION

"You never find yourself until you face the truth."

— *Pearl Bailey,* The Quotable Woman: 1800–On, *page 36*

AT THE TIME OF PEARL BAILEY'S DEATH, Stan Irvin, her manager of twenty-five years, said, "Pearl Bailey was the mother of the world.... She was a very spiritual woman and she never recognized color. Her ideology was, 'we are humans'" (*The Buffalo News,* August 18, 1990).

Pearl Bailey considered herself a singer more than a performer of comedy, though she truly had a sense of humor. She is well remembered for her role as Dolly in a 1960's version of *Hello Dolly!*

In 1970, Pearl was named by President Nixon America's "ambassador of love" to the world. Her subsequent service as delegate to the United Nations under the administrations of Presidents Ford, Reagan and Bush earned for her great respect.

In her 1989 book of reminiscences, *Between You and Me,* Pearl tells of her visit to the Middle East and Persia: "The Middle Eastern people read eyes, not lips," she wrote. "That's the best way to read a man's soul."

Pearl wrote also of her travels to Russia and Africa and other places, as well as many other wonderful autobiographical accounts.

By 1988, Pearl was deeply involved in the cause of persons suffering with AIDS. She devotes a chapter to this topic in *Between You and Me.* She told the World Health Organization that she wanted to devote her life to fighting AIDS, and in December 1988, she participated in the Geneva Conference on AIDS. The text of her statement is part of the chapter in her book: "In some mind there is a key to open the door," she said. "Time is not on our side. God is.... We must keep searching until we find a cure for AIDS."

REFLECTIONS

- "The Middle Eastern people read eyes, not lips," Pearl Bailey wrote. How does this observation inform the tension and crises between some parts of the Arab world and the United States?

- What do you see as the essential spiritual values of Pearl's life?

PRAYER

We are grateful, O cosmic God,
For all those who serve as
"Ambassadors of love"
In our world.
May we always remember that
When time is not on our side,
God is!
Amen.

March 30

JESSE DONALDSON HODDER

Prison reformer, counselor of unwed mothers · U.S., Germany and Switzerland · 1867–1931

SCRIPTURE THEME

Prison reform

"The jailer called for lights, and rushing in, he fell down trembling before Paul and Silas. The he brought them outside and said, 'Sirs, what must I do to be saved?'"

— Acts 16:25

QUOTATION

"Darling, you'll never have a stepfather, don't worry—I promised both you and Olive that long ago and I never have broken a promise made to either you or her. Furthermore, your Daddy was my only love and no one has ever wanted to take his place nor have I ever seen anyone I would put in his place. God bless you, dear, and keep you pure and true to all your ideals..."

— Jesse Donaldson Hodder, Give Her This Day, *page 97*

IN HER WORK WITH UNWED MOTHERS, Jesse was motherly and compassionate. She promoted the ideas that the unwed mother should be helped to keep her child, and that the father should be sued for support though not forced into marriage—and this at a time when illegitimate children were usually institutionalized.

Born March 30, 1867, in Ohio, Jesse was raised by her grandmother after the death of her mother in 1869. Little else is known of Jesse's childhood.

At twenty-three, Jesse entered into a common-law marriage with Alfred Hodder and became the mother of two children. For some years, Jesse lived in Germany studying music and later lived with the children in Switzerland. Alfred abandoned her and married another. The oldest child Olive died and Jesse nearly committed suicide.

In 1906, Jesse returned to the United States and was helped by friends to obtain a position as housemother at an industrial school for girls and as a counselor for unwed mothers. In 1910, Jesse received an appointment as superintendent of the Massachusetts Prison and Reformatory for Women at Framingham. Jesse created a more homelike environment, got the legislature to remove the word *Prison* in 1911, and removed blocks from the window that faced a meadow. Jesse wanted the women to have windows to look out of and something of beauty to see out there.

She also updated the education and labor programs and improved the recreation. She improved individualistic treatment and the keeping of case records. Jesse's approach to penology was both maternal and scientific.

In 1921, Jesse toured European reformatories and prisons and in 1925, she was the only woman to serve as delegate to the International Prison Congress in London. Though she was designated to attend a similar conference in Prague in 1930, Jesse's illness kept her from going. She died at age sixty-four on November 19, 1931, from chronic myocarditis, at Framingham. There was an Episcopal funeral service for her. Her remains were cremated.

REFLECTIONS

- Can you have pity on those in prison? Does the nature of their crimes affect your ability to forgive them?
- How do you feel about unmarried women who choose to become mothers? How about those who unintentionally become mothers?
- What are your feelings on the death penalty? Are they carefully considered or perhaps merely inherited?

PRAYER

Direct us, O God,
To find ways to remove blocks and barriers
So that others may gain new views
Onto the fields and meadows of life.
Amen.

 *March 31*

HARRIET TALCOTT BUCKINGHAM

Pioneer, diarist • U.S. • 1832–1890

SCRIPTURE THEME

Diarist

"Many have undertaken to set down an orderly account of the events that have been fulfilled among us, just as they were handed on to us by those who from the beginning were eyewitnesses."

— *Luke 1:1-2*

QUOTATION

"The little girls and I sleep in one of the big covered ox wagons in which is a nice bed—really makes a cosy little low roofed room, it has a double cover—Mr. Smith has a coop fastened on behind the carriage which contains some fine white chickens—three hens and a rooster."

— *Harriet Talcott Buckingham,* Give Her This Day, *page 98*

BORN MARCH 31, 1832, IN OHIO, Harriet traveled by wagon train at age nineteen with her younger brother and an aunt and uncle. They settled in Oregon.

Beginning May 4, 1851, as they left Ohio, Harriet kept a detailed journal of her trip west. Once in Oregon, Harriet met Samuel A. Clarke, a businessman. They married and raised their four children in Portland, Oregon. Harriet died in 1890. Her husband went on to write a two-volume history of Oregon which he dedicated to her memory.

Harriet's daughter Sarah gave her mother's 1851 diary to the Oregon Historical Society.

REFLECTIONS

- Journal-keeping has been a favorite pastime for many women. Do you keep a journal? Why?
- What can we learn from diaries that other forms of literature cannot offer? Is this valuable?

PRAYER

Let us pray to our loving God
That each woman feel free
To express herself and her creativity
In the varied form she chooses —
Diaries, journals, letters,
Fine arts and practical arts,
Print media and electronic media,
Career and home,
And on and on.
Amen.

April 1

AGNES REPPLIER
Essayist • U.S. • 1855–1950

SCRIPTURE THEME

Essays, peace

"For learning about wisdom and instruction,
For understanding words on insight,
For gaining instruction in wise dealing,
Righteousness, justice, and equity."

— *Proverbs 1:2-3*

QUOTATION

"It is not what we learn in conversation that enriches us. It is the elation that comes of swift contact with tingling currents of thought."

— *Agnes Repplier,* The New York Public Library Book of Twentieth Century American Quotations, *page 288*

AGNES, BORN APRIL 1, 1855, IN PHILADELPHIA, was dismissed from two different schools for what they called "independent behavior." Her mother recited poetry to Agnes, and she loved to memorize and recite it in turn. With limited formal education, Agnes was ten before she learned to read. After that, she was largely self-educated through much reading and travel and residence in Europe. She especially enjoyed the French culture and country of her ancestors.

At sixteen, Agnes took up writing to help support her family. She developed a personal style enriched by her wit and knowledge. Some of her first essays were published in *Catholic World* and *The Atlantic Monthly*. Over the years, these essays were published in book form. As a devout Roman Catholic, Agnes approached her life and her writing with a strong sense of ethics. Among her specifically Catholic writings are the biography, *Mere Marie of the Ursulines*, and her autobiography, *In Our Convent Days*.

With a lifelong interest in the familiar essay, Agnes wrote of varied literary and social reform topics. She stood in opposition to any form of discrimination and admired the justice of the feminist cause.

Perhaps carrying her independent behavior through adulthood, Agnes never married. In time, she received honorary doctorates from the University of Pennsylvania, Yale, Columbia and Princeton. In 1911, she was awarded the Laetare Medal of Notre Dame University, and in 1935, the gold medal of the Academy of Arts and Letters.

At seventy, Agnes went to the Seville Exposition honoring Columbus. This was her last long journey. She died December 16, 1950, at age ninety-five.

REFLECTIONS

- Do you believe that formal education fails those of a more "independent" mind?
- If you had a hard time in school, what approaches to learning were helpful to you?

PRAYER

In reading the essays of Agnes,
May we come to know truth,
And to know you, O God,
Who is Truth for time and eternity.
Amen.

 *April 2*

MARY MAPES DODGE

Author of children's books • U.S. • 1830–1905

SCRIPTURE THEME

Children

"The wolf shall live with the lamb,
the leopard shall lie down with the kid;
the calf and the lion and the fatling together,
and a little child shall lead them."

— *Isaiah 11:6*

QUOTATION

"Life is a mystery as deep as ever death can be;
Yet oh, how sweet it is to us, this life we live and see!"

— *Mary Mapes Dodge,* Bartlett's Familiar Quotations, *page 740*

AMONG THE WORLD'S AUTHORS OF CHILDREN'S BOOKS, women outnumber men. One such woman is Mary Mapes Dodge. Born January 26, 1830, Mary Mapes married William Dodge in 1851. After her husband's death, Mary returned to the family farm where her father got her started on writing for his magazine, *The Working Farmer*.

Mary also made up stories to tell her two young sons. The Dutch sport of skating interested the boys. With the help of a nearby Dutch family for information, Mary wrote *Hans Brinker* (*The Silver Skates*), a best-seller in several countries, which has remained popular.

In 1865, Mary began editing a magazine called *Hearth and Home*. In 1873, she became the founding editor of *St. Nicholas*—widely considered the best children's magazine of all time.

Some of the best authors had their stories in *St. Nicholas*. Among them were "The Jungle Book" of Rudyard Kipling and "Little Lord Fauntleroy" of Frances Hodgson Burnett.

Mary died at age seventy-five on August 21, 1905. The magazine was still thriving at the time of her death.

REFLECTIONS

- Who are your favorite authors of children's books?
- Look for *St. Nicholas* magazine in shops of old editions, or ask for it at libraries.
- April 2 is International Children's Book Day. To celebrate, read *Hans Brinker* to a child.

PRAYER

Mother-Father God,
   guard and guide all children
   in their waking and in their sleeping.
   Amen.

An enormous thank-you, God,
   For all the wonderful books
   Written with children in mind —
   For all the stories and poems
   And fables and riddles
   And pictures and colors
   And wonderful authors
   Who tell children
   About your wide
   And wonderful world.
   Amen.

April 3

JANE GOODALL

Ethnologist • England and Kenya • 1934 —

SCRIPTURE THEME

Wilderness

"And the Spirit immediately drove him out into the wilderness."
  — Mark 1:12

QUOTATION

"There are many windows through which we can look out into the world search-ing for meaning. There are those opened up by science, their panes polished by a succession of brilliant, penetrating minds. Through these we can see ever fur-ther, ever more clearly, into areas that once lay beyond human knowledge. But there are other windows; windows that have been unshuttered by the logic of philosophers; windows through which the mystics seek their visions of the truth; windows from which the leaders of the great religions have peered. Most of us, when we ponder on the mystery of our existence, peer through but one of these windows onto the world. And even that one is often misted over by the breath of our finite humanity. We clear a tiny peephole and stare through. No wonder we are confused by the tiny fraction of a whole that we see."
  — *Jane Goodall, in* Through a Window, *page 10*

IN HER 1990 BOOK, *THROUGH A WINDOW,* Jane Goodall tells of her years at Gombe Stream observing chimps. It is Jane's belief that animal behavior helps educate people about human behavior.

Early in the book, Jane beautifully elaborates on how various modes of learning and knowledge serve as windows into the meaning of the created and uncreated world. As given in the quotation, she points to the windows of science and philosophy, of mysticism and spirituality, and to the windows on life as other forms of life look through them.

Considered the founding mother of ethnology (scientific study of ani-mal behavior in the wilds), Jane was born and grew up in England. Even as a child, she observed the natural world with great interest and dreamed of seeing African wildlife. By taking several odd jobs, Jane saved enough money by the time she was twenty-three to visit a friend in Kenya. In Kenya, Jane met the anthropologist Louis Leakey and served as his secretary. Leakey encouraged her to study chimpanzees.

Jane, accompanied by her mother, set up a field study on the Gombe Stream Reserve in Tanzania. The three-month study turned into six years, and Jane wrote her new knowledge into a book called *In the Shadow of Man* (1971), illustrated with photos by Hugo van Lawick. Jane married Hugo, and they had a son who grew up in "the bush."

Patience and acute observation enabled Jane to learn that chimps made primitive tools and eat meat, that they had a method of communication and games, and that they had a sense of society among themselves. Jane also wrote *Africa in My Blood* and *Reason for Hope: A Spiritual Journey*.

REFLECTIONS

- What have you observed about animal behavior as related to human behavior? Call to mind some of the animal images used to describe human behavior.
- There are several African naturalists you may wish to read about: Joy Adamson in *Born Free*, Dian Fossey in *Gorillas in the Mist*, Delia Owens in *Cry of the Kalahari*.
- The book about Jane's son, Grub, *The Bush Baby*, is quite delightful reading with many photos by Jane's husband, Hugo.

PRAYER

Through the windows of nature
  May we appreciate wildlife
  And the gifts of our environment
  And live in harmony with our planet.
  Amen.

 *April 4*

DOROTHEA DIX

Social reformer • U.S. • 1802–1887

SCRIPTURE THEME

Mental illness

"Those who are well have no need of a physician, but those who are sick."
  — *Matthew 9:12*

QUOTATION

"It is only the women whose eyes have been washed clear with tears who get the broad vision that makes them little sisters to all the world."

— Dorothea Dix, The Quotable Woman: 1800–1981, *page 114*

DOROTHEA WAS BORN APRIL 4, 1802, in an isolated area of Maine where her grandfather had sent her parents as newlyweds. Dorothea's mother was considered unstable, and her father was given to religious fanaticism and drink. As a child, Dorothea stitched together the pages of her father's religious tracts. When her father was off on preaching trips, Dorothea also cared for her invalid mother and two younger brothers. At twelve, she arrived at her grandmother's house in Boston and never explained why. At fourteen, she opened a "dame school" and taught the wonders of everyday life through stories. She later opened a school for poor children called The Hope. Dorothea joined the Unitarian Church and came to know the ideas of Dr. William Ellery Channing, who believed that government should ensure rights for all.

Ill health took her to England for an eighteen-month rest. While there, she learned of a modern mental hospital where books and music were provided. On her return to the States, she read books on the treatment of the insane and began to do the Sunday Bible readings for the women in one of the jails. Seeing the terrible conditions there, she began her reform efforts. She surveyed the care and lack of it for the mentally ill—in prisons, almshouses, workhouses, barns, sheds, stalls and outhouses throughout Massachusetts, and later of the entire country and parts of Canada. Her reports were ridiculed, but some state legislatures enacted laws for better mental hospitals. Gradually people sought her aid in obtaining better hospitals and better care.

During the Civil War, she served as superintendent for Army nurses on a volunteer basis, and though in her sixties worked as hard as anyone. Louisa May Alcott worked as a nurse under Dorothea. After the war, Dorothea returned to inspecting the asylums, where she turned mattresses and tasted soup to see that all was in good order. She retired in 1881 to the first of her 120 hospitals and asylums and died there July 18, 1887.

One of her last wishes was that a water fountain be erected in Boston on Milk Street. Her friend John Greenleaf Whittier saw that this was done.

REFLECTIONS

- Consider how Bible reading to inmates led Dorothea to vast social reform. What connections in your life come from Scripture, worship,

Church teachings and social responsibility in areas of economy, peace and human rights?

- Renita J. Weems in *Just a Sister Away* has Lot's wife write a letter to her daughters explaining her own mental and emotional instability. She asks their understanding and insists that she didn't so much look back as look around to get a glance at what she was leaving. Read this chapter, if you can.

- Pray about what the mentally ill ask of us as church, as Christians and as individuals.

- Do you find that more women than men are diagnosed or labeled as mentally or emotionally ill?

PRAYER

For mentally ill persons
And for those who provide care for them,
We pray to you, O God.
Amen.

 *April 5*

PANDITA RAMABAI

Social worker • India • 1858–1922

SCRIPTURE THEME

Search for faith

"What then did you go out to see? A prophet? Yes, I tell you, and more than a prophet."

— *Matthew 11:9*

QUOTATION

"I am the child of a man who had to suffer a great deal on account of advocating female education, and who was compelled to carry out his views amidst great opposition."

— *Pandita Ramabai*, Saints of the Twentieth Century, *page 51*

PANDITA WAS BORN IN 1858 IN INDIA. Brought up as Hindu, she benefited from her rebel father who taught her to read and speak Sanskrit at a time when girls were not taught these things. By the time she was twenty, Pandita was delivering lectures on female education, with frequent reference to the Hindu Scriptures. She hoped to improve the lot of wives in India by showing that some marriage traditions, such as wifely subservience, were foreign to Hindu doctrines.

Since their parents were dead, Pandita's brother accompanied her on her travels. In 1912, Pandita wrote a pamphlet called "A Testimony," in which she describes her life and travels in those early years. In 1878, Pandita returned to Calcutta and began to read the Christian Scriptures in Sanskrit. She married in 1880, but by 1882 was a widow with a baby daughter. Pandita continued her crusade for women's causes. When she met Anglican nuns in India, they advised her to pursue her education in England, which she did. While there, Pandita became impressed with the nuns' care of unwed mothers. She read more of the Christian Scriptures and came to believe in Christ as God. She was baptized September 29, 1883.

As she studied and traveled in England and in the United States, Pandita searched out the meaning of various religious sects. She tells how she met people in the High Church and the Low Church, the Baptist, Presbyterian, Methodist, Friend, Universalist, Unitarian, Jew, Roman Catholic and others, as well as Theosophist and Spiritualist, Christian Scientist and Mormon, and even people from occult religions. She made connections between many of these and the teachings of her native Hindu religion.

Pandita's searching and discoveries delayed her choosing a focused faith. Meanwhile, she wrote *The High-Caste Hindu Women* (1877) as part of a campaign to establish a home for child widows in Bombay. Back in India, Pandita continued to wear Indian dress and eat Indian food. She became a national figure and got involved in politics, pleading the cause of child widows and the emancipation of women.

In 1899, Pandita moved the home for child widows to Bombay, and it was at that same time that she gave her heart totally to Christ. She also began a farm at Kedgoon to help support the home. In the early 1900's, the program expanded to a boys' orphanage and a home for unwed mothers.

Pandita spent long hours in prayer. In 1905, she began going out to preach and evangelize. She learned Greek and Hebrew and was working on a translation of the Bible in Marathi when she died on April 5, 1922.

REFLECTIONS

· Does knowing more about other religions cause you to doubt your own faith? Does it deepen your faith?

• What services do women and children most need in your area?

PRAYER

We praise you God,
For women who devote their lives
To better conditions
For women and children.
Amen.

 *April 6*

POCAHONTAS

Peacemaker • U.S. • 1596–1617

SCRIPTURE THEME

Hearing God's voice

"They heard the sound of the LORD *God walking in the garden at the time of the evening breeze… [T]he* LORD *God called to the man, and said to him, 'Where are you?'"*

— *Genesis 3:8-9*

QUOTATION

"You promised my father [Chief Powhatan] that whatever was yours should be his, and that you and he would be all one. Being a stranger in our country, you called Powhatan father; and I for the same reason will now call you so."

— *Pocahontas to Captain John Smith,* The Quotable Woman: From Eve to 1799, *page 140*

POCAHONTAS, DAUGHTER OF CHIEF POWHATAN of the Algonquin confederacy of tribes in Virginia, lived from 1596 to 1617. Her personal name, Matoaka, meant "playful." In 1607, she saved the life of John Smith, the English settler, when her tribe captured him. Pocahontas helped to establish trade relations and prisoner exchanges with the English. After two years of tension, Pocahontas was captured by the English and held as ransom for goods and prisoners.

She remained at the English colony, was baptized a Christian as Rebecca, married John Rolfe and had a son. The marriage established a sense of peace between the Algonquins and the English settlers.

In 1616, Pocahontas visited England with her husband and baby. There she was presented at the court of James I. She longed to return home but died of pneumonia or tuberculosis just before the planned departure.

In her last weeks in England, she was visited by her first love, John Smith, whom she believed was dead from reports given her during her capture. Legends grew up around her "rescue for love" of John Smith. Novels and stories are based on this legend.

REFLECTIONS

- Consider the various names by which you are known. What do they mean to you?
- How do you feel about the renaming that happens with Baptism, marriage and other events?
- You may wish to read something historical or fictional about Pocahontas.

PRAYER

May we learn, O God, from Native American women,
The love and care of Mother Earth
And all the creatures of our planet.
Amen.

April 7

GABRIELA MISTRAL

Poet · Chile · 1889–1957

SCRIPTURE THEME

Reassurance

"Do not fear, for I have redeemed you;
I have called you by name, you are mine."
— Isaiah 43:1

QUOTATION

"Blushing, full of confusion, I talked with her about my worries and the fear in my body. I fell on her breast and all over again I became a little girl sobbing in

her arms at the terror of life."
    — *Gabriela Mistral,* The Quotable Woman: 1800–On, *page 217*

BORN APRIL 7, 1889, IN VICUNA, CHILE, Lucila Godoy Alcayaga adopted her pseudonym of Gabriela Mistral from the names of two poets: Gabriele D' Annuzio of Italy and Frederic Mistral of France. From 1912 to 1918, Gabriela taught high school and moved up to prominent positions in the Chilean school system. In 1922, she reorganized the rural schools of Mexico. From 1926 to 1939, she represented Chile at the League of Nations Committee on Acts and Letters. She also served as Chilean consul at Lisbon, Madrid, Nice and Los Angeles.

Gabriela's poetry gained international recognition and in 1945 she received the Nobel Prize in Literature, the first Latin American woman to do so. She is considered the founder of the modernist movement of Chilean poetry. Her poems speak of her love for children and for the downtrodden; her poetic style is religious, even mystic. Her poetry has been widely published and translated.

Her major works are *Sonnets of Death* (1914), *Desolation* (1922), *Tenderness* (1922, 1945), *Tala* (1938) and *Lagar* (1954).

Gabriela taught at the University of Puerto Rico as well as at Barnard, Middlebury and Vassar in the United States. She also served as delegate to the United Nations. She died January 10, 1957.

REFLECTIONS

- Try to read some of Gabriela's poetry in translation, or in Spanish if you know the language.
- Gabriela's poetry captures the national aspirations of her people and country. What poetry does this for your country or the nations of your ancestry?

PRAYER

May the mystical poetry we read,
O God of mystical love,
Show us windows onto eternity.
Amen.

April 8

JULIE BILLIART

Promoter of girls' education • France • 1751-1816

SCRIPTURE THEME

Gratitude

"Rejoice always, pray without ceasing, give thanks in all circumstances; for this is the will of God."

— *1 Thessalonians 5:16-18*

QUOTATION

"Since the good God gave me back my legs, surely He intended that I should use them."

— *Julie Billiart,* Modern Saints, *page 3*

MARIE ROSE JULIE BILLIART WAS BORN IN FRANCE IN 1751. From her very early years, Julie liked to play school, to be the teacher. When doing field work, she would teach Bible parables to the other workers during the lunch hour.

Her parish priest at Cuvilly taught Julie short mental prayers to help control her fiery temper. He also allowed her to make her First Communion at age nine when the usual age was thirteen. From overwork and nervous shock over an attempted murder on her father, Julie's health weakened. She spent twenty-two years as a total invalid, paralyzed and unable to move. Her cheerful acceptance of all this inspired those who knew her.

During the French Revolution, Julie offered her home as a hiding place for priests. The sixteen Carmelites who were guillotined during the revolution were Julie's friends. Five times, Julie had to flee to new locations for safety from those who hated her charity. This further weakened her health.

A vision came to Julie revealing that she was to establish a new institute devoted to educating the young. In 1794, with the Baroness de Bourbon, Julie founded the Sisters of Notre Dame de Namur. In 1804, through the prayers of a missionary priest, Julie regained enough strength to walk again. In 1805, Julie and her companions made their final profession of vows and Julie was elected as mother general.

From 1808 onward, Mother Julie had and used the gift of healing. She died on April 8, 1816, at the age of sixty-five. She was beatified in 1906 and canonized in 1969.

REFLECTIONS

- *Le bon Dieu,* meaning "the good God," is a common French expression and name for God. How have you experienced the goodness of God?
- When have you survived a dear friend? How has that experience shaped your view of your own life?

PRAYER

Le bon Dieu—the good God,
We praise you for your goodness.
Amen.

April 9

SACAJAWEA

Shoshone Indian guide · U.S. · 18th century

SCRIPTURE THEME

Guide, helper

"It is not good that the man should be alone; I will make him a helper as his partner."

— *Genesis 2:18*

QUOTATION

"Neither the word 'free' nor any corresponding term occurs in the root language, in the primal concept; there was never anything for the Indian to free himself from. His spirit was not seeking truth but holding on to truth. And his was the mind nourished by choice. Whatever he needed to know was sooner or later revealed to him. And that which he desired to know—the best way to achieve his maximum spiritual potential—was the only mystery he chose to investigate."

— *Ruth Beebe Hill,* Sunbeams, *page 96*

SACAJAWEA HAS BEEN HONORED in fictional writings and with monuments. A river, a peak and a mountain pass in Montana bear her name in honored memory, and a coin bearing her image has been minted.

For almost a century after the 1804–1805 expedition of Lewis and Clark, only the men were the heroes. Around 1900, suffragists claimed Sacajawea, the Native American wife of an interpreter on the expedition, as a heroine of that journey and a model for the suffragist cause.

Sacajawea, a Shoshone, was born around 1787 in Idaho. She was captured at ten by the Hidatsa people and lived in the Dakotas. A French trapper named Charbonneau "acquired," by purchase or by gambling, Sacajawea and another Shoshone woman and made both of them his wives.

When Lewis and Clark arrived in the Hidatsa villages in the winter of 1804–1805, they hired Charbonneau as interpreter. In the spring of 1805, they started toward the Rocky Mountains, taking Sacajawea and her two-month-old son with the expedition. It wasn't that Sacajawea knew the way, but, rather, that her presence with the White men calmed the various Native Americans they met. She also helped the explorers find edible roots and locate Shoshone horses for crossing the Continental Divide. Without Sacajawea's help, the men would have died from hostile natives or starvation. After the expedition, Sacajawea and her son moved to St. Louis. Clark later provided for the education of Sacajawea's son, Jean Baptiste Charbonneau.

In 1812, a Shoshone squaw died. It may have been Sacajawea or it may have been Charbonneau's other wife. In 1884, an old woman claiming to be Sacajawea died at Wind River Reservation in Wyoming. This uncertainty about Sacajawea's death has never been resolved.

REFLECTIONS

- There are more monuments in the United States to Sacajawea than to any other woman. Why do you think people began to honor this forgotten woman?

- When have you served as a guide or friend to someone in unfamiliar territory? How does it help to have companionship in difficult circumstances?

PRAYER

That the deep spirituality
And knowledge of Mother Earth
Of Native American women
May enrich our lives,
We humbly pray.
Amen.

April 10

CLARE BOOTH LUCE

Politician, diplomat, journalist · *U.S.* · *1903–1987*

SCRIPTURE THEME

Ambassador, messenger of goodwill and peace
"How beautiful upon the mountains
Are the feet of the messenger who announces peace."

— Isaiah 52:7

QUOTATION

"Censorship, like charity, should begin at home; but unlike charity, it should end there."

— *Clare Booth Luce,* Wit and Wisdom of Famous American Women, *page 35*

WELL-KNOWN FOR HER PLAY *THE WOMEN* (1936), Clare had a career that spanned politics and journalism, acting and playwriting. She was born April 10, 1903, in New York City, and educated there. She married in 1923, had one daughter and divorced by 1930.

Clare was an editor at *Vogue* magazine and managing editor at *Vanity Fair*. She wrote her first novel by 1933 and then turned to playwriting. In 1935, she married Henry Luce, publisher of the Time-Life group. She worked as a foreign correspondent for *Life* during World War II.

In 1943, she became the first woman elected to Congress from Connecticut. She delivered speeches during the 1944 presidential elections, including the national convention keynote address.

After her daughter's death in a car accident in 1944, Clare converted to Roman Catholicism. Her husband died in 1967.

In 1953, President Eisenhower appointed her ambassador to Italy; she was the first woman to hold a high diplomatic post. She was considered as an ambassador to Brazil in 1959, but no formal appointment ever came. It was feared that Clare's vehement anti-Communist views might jeopardize U.S. relations with Brazil and the other nations of South America.

Among other honors, she received the Hammarskjold Medal in 1960. She died in 1987.

REFLECTIONS

- What does it mean to be an ambassador to a foreign country? When have you served as an ambassador of sorts?

• Have you experienced a major conversion in your life as a result of an unexpected event or tragedy?

PRAYER

May we be, O God of Peace,
Ambassadors and messengers
Of your peace wherever we go.
Amen.

 *April 11*

GEMMA GALGANI

Suffering, stigmata • *Italy* • *1878–1903*

SCRIPTURE THEME

Rejection

"He was despised and rejected by others;
a man of suffering and acquainted with infirmity."

— Isaiah 53:3

QUOTATION

"There is neither cross nor sorrow, when we are tightly united to Jesus."

— *Gemma Galgani*, Modern Saints, *page 179*

GEMMA MEANS "GEM" IN ITALIAN. Gemma was born March 12, 1878, in Italy. When she was baptized, her mother was concerned that her daughter did not have a saint's name. A priest told her that the child might be a "gem in Paradise."

Her mother, who died when Gemma was quite young, taught her child about God and heaven and prayer. Gemma was a good student, but her frail health forced her to quit school. When her father died in 1897, Gemma and her brothers and sisters were left on their own.

When offers of marriage came for Gemma, she refused and turned even more to prayer. When serious illness confined her to bed, she remained courageous and cheerful. Gemma was miraculously cured.

In a vision, she was advised to become a nun. Though Gemma tried to enter the convent, she was rejected six times because of her health.

Mystical graces, ecstasies, prophecy and the stigmata came to Gemma during the years she lived at home and later with a family named Giannani. One of the graces was the visibility of her guardian angel, whom she often sent on errands to deliver letters or messages.

In 1903, Gemma learned that she had tuberculosis and moved to a small, isolated apartment. There she died on April 11. In 1917, Church authorities examined Gemma's life. She was beatified in 1933 and canonized in 1940. Gemma is buried at the Passionist monastery in her hometown of Lucca.

REFLECTIONS

- How do you handle rejection? When have you had to reject someone else? How did you soften the blow?

- Do you believe in guardian angels? What special graces have you received?

PRAYER

Jesus, Jesus,
Jesus, Jesus.
Hold us in your hand,
O Divine Jeweler,
As a precious gem,
Especially when we feel rejected.
Amen.

April 12

CLARA BARTON

Founder of American Red Cross · *U.S.* · *1821–1912*

SCRIPTURE THEME

Healing

"The prayer of faith will save the sick, and the Lord will raise them up; and anyone who has committed sins will be forgiven."

— James 5:15

QUOTATION

"When you were weak and I was strong, I toiled for you. Now you are strong

and I am weak. Because of my work for you I ask your aid. I ask the ballot for myself and my sex. As I stood by you, I pray you stand by me and mine."

— *Clara Barton*, Remember the Ladies, *page 213*

WHEN CLARA FOUNDED THE AMERICAN NATIONAL RED CROSS on May 21, 1881, she became its president and remained so until 1904. Born in Massachusetts on Christmas Day, 1821, Clarissa Harlowe Barton was educated at home. As the youngest of five children, she grew up as a quite shy, but independent and willful girl.

At age fifteen, Clara began her teaching career. She attended the Liberal Institute at Clinton, New York, for further training. She then turned her attention to establishing a free school in Bordertown, New Jersey. When it grew larger, the town fathers would not allow a woman to run it. Clara resigned from the school rather than work under a male principal.

For several years, Clara worked at the United States Patent Office and was probably the first regularly appointed civil servant. During the Civil War, Clara distributed supplies with mule teams to the battlefields, nursed wounded soldiers and set up searches for missing soldiers, all without pay.

After the war, she organized a program that searched for missing soldiers. She also traveled around the country telling about her Civil War work. Clara also wrote many pamphlets and books on the Red Cross.

It was in 1869, when she was in Europe for her health, that she learned about the International Red Cross recently formed in Geneva, Switzerland. Returning to the United States, she campaigned and lobbied for the acceptance of the Red Cross. She was sixty years old when the United States signed on.

Devoted entirely to the organization, Clara solicited contributions and worked the fields, as well. She jealously guarded the activities, so much so that her resignation was forced in 1904. She was eighty-three.

At age eighty-six, Clara wrote an autobiographical book, *The Story of My Childhood.* On April 12, 1912, she died in Glen Echo, Maryland.

REFLECTIONS

• Have you or someone you know received assistance from the Red Cross in a time of disaster or emergency? How important is this kind of assistance?

• Clara made several career changes in her life. Have you had to make changes in the past? Do you need to make any now?

- Clara's work brought some sense of humanity to the battlefield. What do you feel is an appropriate role for women in time of war?

PRAYER

God, we pray
To stand by others in need
And have others stand by us
When we are in need.
Amen.

April 13

EUDORA WELTY

Short story writer, novelist · *U.S.* · *1909–2001*

SCRIPTURE THEME

Time

"Be careful then how you live, not as unwise people but as wise, making the most of the time."
— *Ephesians 5:15-16*

QUOTATION

"All serious daring starts from within."
— *Eudora Welty*, The Quotable Woman: 1800–On, *page 19*

EUDORA WELTY WAS A THOROUGHLY SOUTHERN WRITER. She was born April 13, 1909, in Mississippi and grew up there. She attended Mississippi State College for Women. She earned her bachelor of arts from the University of Wisconsin and studied advertising at Columbia University. Returning to Mississippi, Eudora took various jobs with local newspapers and radio stations and the Works Progress Administration (WPA). In this job, she traveled around the state interviewing people for human-interest stories. On her own, she took photos of them. Both offer mid-1930's documentation of the Depression. While she worked where she could, she also kept at her fiction writing. *A Curtain of Green and Other Stories*, a volume of short stories, was published in 1941. Other collections followed, with a compilation of the stories from 1936 to 1966 appearing in the 1980 edition of *The Collected Stories of Eudora Welty*. Eudora portrayed lower-middle-class characters well. Her narrative and lyrical qualities of writing won her many coveted literary prizes and popularity with her readers. Her use of myth and of the grotesque in her handling of tensions between peoples in the South secures her position as a Southern writer.

Her first novel, *The Robber Bridegroom*, came out in 1942. Others followed, including *The Optimist's Daughter* in 1972. In her autobiography, *One Writer's Beginning*, Eudora ponders three developments in her life: listening, learning to see and finding a voice.

And while it's usually only dead people whose portraits are displayed at the National Portrait Gallery in Washington, D.C., Eudora's was hung there in 1988, when she was seventy-nine. She died July 23, 2001.

REFLECTIONS

- What images have stayed with you since childhood? How do they connect with your present lifestyle and work?
- Have you found your "voice" yet? Are you comfortable with your own views and opinions?

PRAYER

Thank you, O God,
For artistic people
Who show us
New ways of looking
At the human condition.
Amen.

 *April 14*

ANNE SULLIVAN

Teacher of Helen Keller · U.S. · 1866–1936

SCRIPTURE THEME

Teacher

*"She opens her hand to the poor,
and reaches out her hands to the needy."*

— *Proverbs 31:20*

QUOTATION

"It is a rare privilege to watch the birth, growth, and first feeble struggles of a living mind."

— *Anne Sullivan*, The Quotable Woman, 1800–On, *page 125*

BORN APRIL 14, 1866, NEAR SPRINGFIELD, MASSACHUSETTS, Anne was the oldest child of impoverished Irish immigrants. When her mother died, Anne was only eight. She tried to keep house for her father while relatives cared for the other four children. But Anne's poor eyesight from the eye disease called trachoma and her father's alcohol problem made life very hard. By age ten, Anne and her brother Jimmie were sent to a poorhouse at Tewksbury.

A Catholic priest arranged for Anne to have eye surgery at Lowell Hospital where she came to love the nuns who were her nurses. At fourteen, Anne was able to attend the Perkins Institute for the Blind in Boston.

Several operations later, Anne's eyes improved and she could see well enough to read. Because the lighting at the institute was minimal, she used to lean way out a window to get light by which to read. In 1886, at age twenty, she graduated from the Perkins Institute. She was ranked first in her class and gave the valedictory speech. In 1887, Anne went to be companion and teacher for seven-year-old Helen Keller who was both blind and deaf. For many difficult months, Anne struggled to reach Helen's mind. The day came when Helen realized that the words stood for things. "Teacher," as Helen called Anne, was then able to teach all kinds of things. Helen's awakening became known at the Perkins Institute and the institute director called Anne "the miracle worker." As the years went on, Anne accompanied Helen to Radcliffe College, reading the texts to her.

When Helen's book *The Story of My Life* appeared in 1903, it was as much a book about Anne as about Helen. In 1905, Anne married John Macy, the friend who had served as agent and editor for the book. Helen was included in the household of three. After nine years of marriage, John left. Annie and Helen got busy with lecture tours.

Helen continued to write books with Anne's help. Over time, however, Anne's eyes became worse and Helen had to rely on other help. Polly Thompson was hired as secretary.

In 1933, a book by Nella Brady came out: *Anne Sullivan Macy: The Story Behind Helen Keller*. Both teacher and pupil were becoming well-known to the general public. In her sixties, Anne traveled to Europe with Helen and Polly. She visited Ireland, the birthplace of her parents. As she neared seventy, her eyes failed altogether, and Helen taught Braille to her teacher.

On October 20, 1936, Anne died. She was just past her seventieth birthday. Helen was fifty-six.

REFLECTIONS

- Watch the play or film *The Miracle Worker*.
- What childhood experiences of your own have enabled you to teach another how to cope with particular difficulties or disabilities?
- When have you experienced an intense and intimate relationship, yet felt the need for a separate but linked life?

PRAYER

Divine Teacher,
We pray for all teachers
Who awaken and enliven
The inner lives of those
Under their instruction.
Amen.

April 15

CORRIE TEN BOOM

Advocate for Jews • Holland and U.S. • 1892–1983

SCRIPTURE THEME

Good deeds

"Show by your good life that your works are done with gentleness born of wisdom."

— *James 3:13*

QUOTATION

"If God sends us stony paths, he provides strong shoes."

— *Corrie Ten Boom,* Remember the Ladies, *page 255*

CORNELIA WAS BORN APRIL 15, 1892, the youngest child in the warm circle of the Ten Boom family. She often accompanied her father to the Naval Observatory in Amsterdam to get the exact time. Caspar Ten Boom was a watchmaker, well respected in town and elsewhere. He made Bible reading in the mornings and evenings part of the family routine.

Though somewhat mischievous as a child, Corrie graduated from school with a diploma in home economics and took a job as a governess. She taught catechism classes and gave Bible talks and eventually moved back home. With the death of her mother and the aunts who lived with the family, Corrie managed the house and later the bookkeeping in her father's watch shop. She learned the trade and became a licensed watchmaker in Holland, the first woman to do so. Corrie also organized clubs for girls and boys together where spiritual and social needs were met.

As the need arose, Corrie and her sister, Betsie, and father took unfortunate children into their home. When Germany invaded Holland and openly persecuted Jewish people, life dramatically changed. The Ten Booms began hiding Jews in their attic rooms and helping them to escape through underground connections.

On February 28, 1944, the Gestapo searched the house. The next day the Ten Boom family was brought for questioning and put in prison cells, Corrie into solitary confinement. Later, Corrie and Betsie were reunited in a move to another camp at Vught. They both made every effort to bring the Lord's word to other prisoners. Later the Ten Boom sisters were moved to Ravensbruck prison where they continued to pray and encourage the other prisoners with Bible verses.

The two sisters managed to stay together and dream about their hopes and visions of making a home for victims of war. Betsie, however, died at Ravensbruck. In the winter Corrie was released. She left her smuggled Bible behind with a trusted prisoner. After returning to her home in Holland, Corrie carried out Betsie's wish to provide a home with love and flowers for people harmed in spirit by the war. When a wealthy widow opened her home to the cause, Corrie was able to convert it into a rehabilitation center. Corrie traveled worldwide, telling her story, and seeking funds to maintain the home and its gardens.

Corrie wrote of hiding the Jews in *The Hiding Place* and of her missionary journeys in *Tramp for the Lord*. Both books became very popular. At eighty-five, she settled into a home of her own in the United States. She died on April 15, 1983—her ninety-first birthday. Her work continues through the Corrie Ten Boom Memorial Fund.

Reflections

- Corrie and her sister carried on the prison ministry of offering comfort and prayer. Is there room in your life for a letter or support for prison ministry?

- Corrie greatly loved and admired her father and wrote about him in her book titled *In My Father's House*. In what ways do you admire your father?

PRAYER

For all those who suffered
And still suffer from the Holocaust,
We beg your mercy, O God.
Amen.

April 16

SAINT BERNADETTE

Visionary of Lourdes • France • 1844–1879

SCRIPTURE THEME

Immaculate Conception

"A great portent appeared in heaven: a woman clothed with the sun, with the moon under her feet, and on her head a crown of twelve stars."

— *Revelation 12:1*

QUOTATION

"I do not promise you happiness in this world, but in the next."

— *Mary to Bernadette*, Modern Saints, *page 73*

WHEN BERNADETTE WAS CANONIZED, it was not so much the visionary of Lourdes who was acclaimed as holy as it was the nun who lived out a life of virtue at Nevers.

Born in 1844 to a poor miller and his wife near Lourdes, France, Bernadette was the oldest of four surviving children. Five died in infancy. Extreme poverty forced the family to live in one room of an abandoned jail. Bernadette had asthma and general ill health.

Bernadette was good with a needle and worked at mending and sewing. A family friend took Bernadette to her home with the promise of education but sent her to tend sheep instead. The woman did teach Bernadette some catechism. After two years, Bernadette returned home.

On February 11, 1858, when Bernadette was fourteen, a beautiful lady appeared to her. In subsequent visions, the Lady gave messages to Bernadette—some for the public and some private. The lady asked for a chapel at the grotto and for processions. She said: "I am the Immaculate Conception," when Bernadette asked the lady her name.

The dogma of the Immaculate Conception had been proclaimed by Pope Pius IX only four years earlier, in 1854.

Bernadette made her first Holy Communion in the same year as the apparitions. For the next eight years, Bernadette attended school. She eventually went to live with the nuns at Nevers, and became a member in 1866. Her name in religion was Sister Marie Bernarde.

She lived an ordinary life in the convent, enjoying telling funny stories and singing songs in her native dialect. She nursed the ill sisters in the infirmary and coped with her own poor health.

Bernadette remained deeply devoted to the Blessed Mother. She was very ill the last four months of her life. She died April 16, 1879, at the age of thirty-five and was buried on the convent grounds at Nevers.

Thirty years after her death, Bernadette's body remained uncorrupt, and even today her lovely features remain.

The Church canonized Bernadette on December 8, 1933.

REFLECTIONS

- What do you think of visions and personal revelation? Have you received any revelation that you could share?
- Do you know people who have visited Lourdes? Ask them about their experiences.

PRAYER

May we always sing:
"Ave, Ave, Ave, Maria."
Amen.

April 17

SOR JUANA INÉS DE LA CRUZ

Poet, intellectual, nun, feminist • Mexico • 1651–1695

SCRIPTURE THEME

Learning

*"By wisdom a house is built
and by understanding it is established."*

— *Proverbs 24:3*

QUOTATION

"God gives talent for sacred use and it is so unjust that not only women (considered inept) but also men (who, simply by being thus, consider themselves wise) are forbidden the interpretation of the Holy Scriptures if they are not erudite and virtuous."

— Sor Juana, The Last Word, *page 18*

BORN NEAR MEXICO CITY ON NOVEMBER 12, 1651, Juana was raised by her maternal grandparents. By fourteen, with a reputation for scholarship, she came to court as a lady-in-waiting.

She spent some time at a Carmelite convent and then entered the Order of Saint Jerome in order to have time and peace to pray and study. For several years, she read, studied and collected books until she had the largest library in North America. She also wrote, and her plays, poetry and prose evidence Aztec symbolism integrated with Greek and Christian symbolism. Juana's poetry speaks of mystic love in perceptive and sensuous words.

In a dispute in 1690 with the bishop of Puebla, she defended women's learning. What she wrote in reply to the bishop also reads as a biography of Juana's intellectual development.

Later in life, she sold her four thousand books and musical instruments, gave the money to the poor and turned to nursing the ill. She died while nursing during a plague epidemic on April 17, 1695. She was forty-three years old.

REFLECTIONS

- What reading and study do you pursue? Are you fond of books? What kinds of reading materials are your favorites?
- How do you feel about women's education and intellectual development?

PRAYER

For each of us, we pray to God,
That our talents, beauty,
Education, freedoms, possessions
May never stand in the way
Of our spiritual welfare.
Amen.

April 18

BARBARA ACARIE

Wife, Carmelite • France and Canada • d. 1618

SCRIPTURE THEME

Holiness in marriage

"Enjoy life with the wife whom you love."
  — *Ecclesiastes 9:9*

QUOTATION

"I am training them to do God's will."
  — *Barbara Acarie in regard to her children,* Lives of the Saints, *page 136*

BARBARA AVRILLOT, DAUGHTER OF A FRENCH GOVERNMENT OFFICIAL, was educated at a convent where her aunt was the superior. At seventeen, she married Peter Acarie, a young lawyer. Peter gave as much help as he could to English Catholics living in exile in France during the reign of Elizabeth I of England.

Barbara and Peter had six children. Their three daughters became nuns, and one son became a priest.

At one point, Peter was banished from Paris because of debts he accumulated in his work for the Catholic cause. Barbara defended him before the king and convinced the king to allow the Acarie family to return to Paris. In fact, the royal family was so impressed with Barbara that they supported her efforts to bring Carmelites to Paris. Barbara had visions of Saint Teresa, and this encouraged her to bring the Discalced Carmelites to France.

After her husband's death, Barbara entered the Carmelites. She lived as a simple lay sister at the Amiens convent where her daughter was prioress. She was known as Sister Mary of the Incarnation.

The last several years of her life were spent in obscurity and intense prayer. She had the gift of mystical prayer. She died on Easter Sunday in 1618.

REFLECTIONS

- Barbara was gifted with the graces of motherhood and mystical prayer. How does prayer help you in your vocation?

- Would you be willing to live in exile in a foreign country in order to keep the practice of your faith?

PRAYER

May we find you,
O God of our hearts,
In the most mundane tasks
In the most lowly persons,
And may you find us
Doing the mundane tasks
And dwelling with the lowly ones.
Amen.

April 19

LUCRETIA GARFIELD

Teacher, mother, First Lady • U.S. • 1832–1918

SCRIPTURE THEME

Hospitality

"My lord, if I find favor with you, do not pass by your servant. Let a little water be brought, and wash your feet, and rest yourselves under the tree. Let me bring a little bread that you may refresh yourselves…".

— Genesis 18:3–4

QUOTATION

"Held our first morning Reception for all the great roaring world. For two hours we took the hands of the passing crowd without a moment's intermission. Before the first hour was over I was aching in every joint, and thought how can I ever last through the next long sixty minutes. Before the crowd soon made me forget myself, and though nearly paralyzed, the last hour passed more quickly than the first."

— Lucretia Garfield, Give Her This Day, page 116

LUCRETIA'S FATHER INSISTED THAT SHE RECEIVE A GOOD EDUCATION. It was at Geauga Seminary that she met a teacher named James Garfield. They were mutually attracted to the classics and to each other. Their friendship grew while Lucretia pursued a teaching career and James became professor and then president of the college in Hiram, Ohio. After eight years, they married on November 11, 1858.

During the Civil War, James served in the Union Army. In 1863, he was elected to Congress. The Garfields had five children. During their first seventeen years in Washington, Lucretia learned the ins and outs of the political scene.

When James was elected as president and then inaugurated in March 1881, Lucretia (or Crete, as her husband called her), held high hopes for the nation's healing of war wounds. Lucretia planned, as First Lady, to restore the White House to its original beauty. Rather than hosting and entertaining, Lucretia devoted her time to research in the Library of Congress for documents on the White House decor. Later in 1881, a malaria epidemic in humid Washington, D.C., forced Lucretia to move her children to their summer home in New Jersey. Just as James was leaving to join her, an assassin's bullet injured him. He lingered for two months until his death on September 19, 1881.

Lucretia was left a widow with five children. She survived her husband by thirty-six years.

REFLECTIONS

- The role of first ladies has changed over the years. How do you feel about these changes? Do you think the office of First Lady is outdated?
- Do you know any widows? How have they redefined themselves since the passing of their husbands?

PRAYER

For all women
Who are called to serve
As assistants and associates
In the careers of others,
We pray that they may have
Fine tact and faultless taste.
Amen.

April 20

AGNES OF MONTEPULCIANO

Dominican abbess · *Italy* · *1268–1317*

SCRIPTURE THEME

Solitude

"A garden locked is my sister, my bride,
garden locked, a fountain sealed."

    —*Song of Songs: 4:12*

QUOTATION

"Have a solicitous care in regard to this child. By supernatural revelation I assure you that as Agnes, the Virgin and Martyr, is hailed by the faithful as Saint Agnes, so also shall this child illustrate the Church by the same name."

    —*a canonical visitor of Convent Del Sacco,* Lives of Dominican Saints, *page 192*

As a child, Agnes lived in prayer and solitude. She had a favorite secluded spot in her father's garden. As young as six years, she expressed the desire to enter a convent, and at age nine her parents allowed her to go the sisterhood called Del Sacco—of the sackcloth. She lived a life of prayer and silence, humility and obedience.

At age fourteen she was placed in charge of temporalities and provided for the sisters' needs with care and generosity. By age fifteen, she had helped establish a new convent in Proceno, and was appointed abbess.

Mystical and miraculous moments filled her days with apparitions, replenishment of bread and oil, and other heavenly favors.

Entreaties from the citizens of Montepulciano brought her back to her home city. In a vision, Agnes saw Saint Augustine, Saint Dominic and Saint Francis, each inviting her to their boat. She heard Dominic say, "The Lord has disposed that she should embark on my boat." Agnes set about building a church and a convent at Montepulciano and there she founded a new community with the Rule of St. Dominic.

Agnes's days continued with prayer and service in the community. She died April 20, 1317.

REFLECTIONS

- What spiritual experiences colored your childhood? How has your experience of the spiritual changed with maturity?

- How do you practice the virtues of humility and obedience?

PRAYER

May we find you, Lord,
In our silence and solitude,
In our love of prayer,
And our love of others.
Amen.

 *April 21*

CHARLOTTE BRONTË

Novelist, poet · England · 1816–1855

SCRIPTURE THEME

Writer

"O that my words were written down!
O that they were inscribed in a book!"

— *Job 19:23*

QUOTATION

"Life, believe, is not a dream
So dark as sages say;
Oft a little morning rain
Foretells a pleasant day."

— *Charlotte Brontë,* The Quotable Woman: 1800–1981, *page 31*

CHARLOTTE, BORN APRIL 21, 1816, received her early education at home and then later went to a boarding school for clergymen's daughters. Her mother died when she was five; Emily was three, and Anne was one. The girls were brought up by an aunt.

After boarding school, Charlotte was encouraged to read widely and to discuss freely. She talked world affairs with her father and folklore with the neighbors. All the children wrote poetry, drama and sagas for amusement.

Charlotte tried work as a teaching assistant and as a governess but disliked both. In 1846, she helped publish Emily's poems, and this initiated the flurry of literary activity in the Brontë household.

Charlotte's *Jane Eyre* in 1847 became an overnight success. The three sisters, who had written as Currer Bell, Ellis Bell and Acton Bell, revealed their true identities.

In 1848, Branwell (their brother) died, and in 1849, Emily and Anne both died. Charlotte, despite her shyness, continued to make an impact on literary circles. She married, and then during her pregnancy, she died March 31, 1855.

REFLECTIONS

· Is shyness a problem for you? How do you deal with it in others?

· When have you had a good experience that began in an ominous way? Of what significance are beginnings?

PRAYER

Let us call upon God,
Who is Author of Life,
To nurture in each of us
The giftedness,
The talents,
The fire
For building the world community
With inspiration and imagination.
Amen.

 *April 22*

QUEEN ISABELLA OF SPAIN

Queen · Spain · 1451–1504

SCRIPTURE THEME

Vision, insight

" 'O LORD, please open his eyes that he may see.' So the LORD opened the eyes of the servant and he saw; the mountain was full of horses and chariots of fire all around Elisha."

— *2 Kings 6:17*

QUOTATION

"Hear the Prayer of Thy servant, and show forth the truth, and manifest Thy will with Thy marvellous works: so that if my cause is not just, I may not be allowed to sin through ignorance, and if it is just, Thou give me wisdom and courage to sustain it with the aid of Thine arm."

— *Queen Isabella,* The Quotable Woman: Eve to 1799, *page 77*

BORN IN CASTILE (SPAIN) ON APRIL 22, 1451, Isabella managed to marry the man of her choice, namely Ferdinand, heir to the king of Aragon, and managed to unseat her brother Enrique, who incompetently ruled Castile. Thus, Isabella was the moving spirit behind the unification of Spain.

Isabella and Ferdinand, while working closely together, maintained their independence. In their efforts to achieve religious unity for Spain, Ferdinand and Isabella expelled the Muslim Moors and Jews from their borders, indicative of the religious intolerance of the time.

When Christopher Columbus sailed and eventually "discovered" America, it was Isabella who had the intuition and vision that gave spirit to the expedition. At first, Isabella agreed with her husband in the impracticality of funding Columbus and his project, then she decided to support Columbus with her own jewels.

Isabella had been raised by her mother to pray devoutly, to esteem religion and learning, and all her life she did this. At her death in 1504, her country regarded her as a saint.

REFLECTIONS

- It has been said that behind every successful man, there stands a woman. How do you feel about this saying? Could the converse be said of a successful woman? Could either be said of you?

- How might the world be different had Isabella and Columbus lacked vision? When have you pursued a vision that changed your world?

PRAYER

May we esteem religion and learning,
O God, Source of all knowledge,
As windows of knowledge about you.
Amen.

 *April 23*

SHIRLEY TEMPLE BLACK

Actress, diplomat • U.S. • 1928—

SCRIPTURE THEME

Joy, delight, entertainment

"Go your way, eat the fat and drink sweet wine and send portions of them to those for whom nothing is prepared, for this day is holy to our LORD; and do not be grieved, for the joy of the LORD is your strength."

— *Nehemiah 8:10*

QUOTATION

"People will remember that I lived, that I didn't just exist."

— *Shirley Temple Black,* Shirley Temple Black: Actress to Ambassador, *page 57*

SHIRLEY TEMPLE WAS BORN APRIL 23, 1928. Her parents, Gertrude and George, played classical and popular music on their radio for the new infant and Shirley loved it. She danced to it as soon as she walked.

By the mid-1930's, the youngster's curly hair and bright eyes were seen across America in films such as *Bright Eyes, Curly Top* and *Dimples.* Little girls received Shirley Temple dolls for Christmas 1934—or paper dolls, or coloring books, or records of "On the Good Ship Lollipop."

In 1935, Shirley was the first child actor to receive an Academy Award. The country was in an economic depression, and by her movies, Shirley helped to bring cheer to the people.

Shirley became a little "big shot" with a big ego and showers of special attention. She was sometimes paired with a Black character, Bill "Bojangles" Robinson being her favorite. The two became adept at and famous for their stair dances. As Shirley entered her teens and lost her cuteness, she was no longer America's little sweetheart.

Shirley married John Agar in 1945. Their daughter, Linda Susan, was born in 1948. In 1951, John and Shirley were divorced, and Shirley married Charles Black. He had never seen a Shirley Temple movie. Their children were Charles Jr. and Lori. The family struggled for privacy as the public always clamored after Shirley.

Shirley made some TV appearances and in 1958 filmed the TV series called *The Shirley Temple Storybook.*

In 1967, Shirley decided to run for Congress. She lost, but in 1970, President Richard Nixon named her a U.S. delegate to the United Nations. In 1971, she visited Egypt, and President Sadat told her that he was the first Arab leader to truly want peace.

An operation for breast cancer gave Shirley the motivation to inform other women about the disease.

In 1974, President Gerald Ford appointed her ambassador to Ghana. In Ghana, families are traced through the female line and women are very important to society. She left Ghana in 1976 when she was appointed Chief of Protocol for the White House in Washington.

Shirley and her husband returned to private life. Shirley continues to speak on social problems. In 1988, President Ronald Reagan appointed her ambassador to Czechoslovakia. Also in 1988, the first volume of her autobiography, *Child Star,* was published.

REFLECTIONS

- Shirley's young acting career was her mother's dream and Shirley loved it. In what ways did you live your mother's dreams? Your own?
- Shirley's childhood persona was very different from that of the woman she became. How has your personality changed since childhood? Are you pleased with the changes?

PRAYER

May our joys
Ever echo your presence
In our hearts, O God.
Amen.

April 24

EUPHRASIA PELLETIER
Religious founder • France • 1796-1868

SCRIPTURE THEME
Good Shepherd
"I am the good shepherd. The good shepherd lays down his life for the sheep."
— John 10:11

QUOTATION

"It is human to fall, but angelic to rise again."

— *Saint Euphrasia*, Quotable Saints, *page 198*

ROSE VIRGINIA PELLETIER WAS BORN IN 1796 on an island off the coast of Vendée. Her parents were refugees from the Vendée wars. At eighteen, she joined the Institute of Our Lady of Charity and Refuge at Tours. She was made superior at Tours in 1825 and soon after made a new foundation at Angers.

As Mother Euphrasia, she met with opposition as she tried to make changes in the congregation. She rode out the storm with determination and humility. In 1835, she received official approval for her new foundation, the Institute of the Good Shepherd at Angers. This congregation, like the one at Tours, does rescue work for women.

During her years, Euphrasia saw the congregation expand to 110 convents on four continents. Euphrasia died at Angers in 1868 and was canonized in 1940.

Today, there are some ten thousand Good Shepherd sisters.

REFLECTIONS

- Who provides for girls and women in need in your area? When have you been in need of such assistance?
- What sort of women need "rescuing"? Should there be similar services for men?

PRAYER

For refugees who must leave behind
Their homes and homeland,
We ask your blessing and guidance, O God.
Amen.

April 25

ANZAC DAY

Australia

SCRIPTURE THEME

Rape

"While no one else was in the house, she caught hold of his garment, saying, 'Lie with me!' But he left his garment in her hand and fled and ran outside."

— *Genesis 39:11-12*

QUOTATION

"In memory of all women of all countries raped in all wars."

— *banner of Women Against Rape*, Sisterhood Is Global, *page 65*

ANZAC DAY IN AUSTRALIA COMMEMORATES THE LIVES of the sixty thousand Australian and New Zealand men sacrificed in the 1914–1918 war. The Anzacs landed on the shores of Gallipoli on April 25, 1915, and made their contribution to that war.

Each year, on April 25, Australia celebrates this event with patriotic parades and wreaths laid on shrines. In the 1950's, Australians began to question this waste of lives for the benefit of the British Empire.

By 1975, women in Australia began to use Anzac Day as a time to protest against rape in war. When some women marched in the 1980 Anzac parade as Women Against Rape, they were arrested. This launched a campaign centering around Anzac Day for the forgotten victims of war: women.

In 1982, the women wore buttons that read: "Women Against Rape—Canberra, We're Marching Anzac Day 1982."

Ordinances that attempted to keep these women from marching in parades only served to increase publicity. This feminist perspective and symbolic meaning of who will or will not march on Anzac Day challenged the sexism and racism of a particular form of patriotism.

The Women Against Rape wished to promote their values with visibility and nonviolence. Anzac Day has become their obvious confrontation with the patriarchal system.

In her book *The Road From Coorain*, Jill Ker Conway tells of her change of worldview: "From my new perspective, the Anzac Day we celebrated with such respect, remembering the courage of Australian troops, had a different symbolic meaning."

REFLECTIONS

- Are any groups banned from your local patriotic parades? How do you feel about this?
- What is your response to those who accuse the victim in cases of rape? Is a woman ever partially responsible for being a victim to this crime?
- How is rape used to demoralize the enemy in wartime? Is all fair in war?

PRAYER

For all women who have suffered from rape,
We beg your healing and love, O God.
Amen.

April 26

CAROL BURNETT

Comic actress · U.S. · 1933 —

SCRIPTURE THEME

Laughter

*"Then our mouth was filled with laughter,
and our tongue with shouts of joy."*

— Psalm 126:2

QUOTATION

"The first time I forgot I was homely was the first time I heard an audience laugh."

— Carol Burnett, Carol Burnett: The Sound of Laughter, *page 18*

WHEN CAROL WAS STILL A LITTLE GIRL, she would open the window that looked out onto the neighbors' apartments and shout out a one-person radio show. Carol would act the parts of announcer and of guest singer. When one of the neighbors yelled out, "Turn that radio off," Carol was thrilled because her act had been convincing.

Born on April 26, 1933, in San Antonio, Texas, Carol was the daughter of Louise (called Lou) and Joseph (called Jody). Jody suffered from alcoholism and Carol was often left with Nanny, her grandmother, as Lou and Jody both struggled with drinking problems and a crumbling marriage. Nanny loved movies, so Carol got to see lots of movies in her growing-up years.

Carol enjoyed pretending and acting and dancing and writing. In college, she got into a theater arts program and her acting made people laugh. In 1954, she went to New York City and her "star" rose with the rise of TV in the 1950's. She appeared on the *Paul Winchell Show, Stanley* and the *Garry Moore Show*. In 1955, she married Don Saroyan.

Carol's appearance in *Once Upon a Mattress*, a musical comedy, filled the theater with the beauty of laughter and brought raves for Carol.

By 1960, both of Carol's parents had died and she and Don had separated. Carol put her whole self into her spirited singing and acting. She became the first lady of TV, surpassing Lucille Ball as the country's favorite comedy actress.

In 1963, Carol married Joe Hamilton. They had three daughters, and Carol loved being a mother. From 1967 to 1978, the *Carol Burnett Show* ran on TV, a total of 286 shows. A 1977 poll indicated that Carol was one of the world's twenty most-admired women.

REFLECTIONS

- What makes you laugh? What does this say about you?
- When is humor inappropriate? When is it most needed?
- Pray for the gift of humor and laughter.

PRAYER

We thank you, O God,
For all who help us laugh
Or make us smile.
Amen.

April 27

SAINT ZITA

Domestic servant • Italy • d. 1278

SCRIPTURE THEME

Steward of the household

"She is not afraid for her household when it snows,
for all her household are clothed in crimson."

— *Proverbs 31:21*

QUOTATION

"After ecstasy, the laundry."

— *Zen statement,* Women

ZITA WAS BORN ABOUT 1218 IN ITALY and entered domestic service at age twelve. She remained in this household of a well-off weaver for the rest of her life, performing her duties promptly and carefully.

Fellow servants disliked her for these qualities, and her employer disapproved of her lavish gifts to the poor. She left the house early each morning for Mass at the parish church and got up during the night to pray.

Zita felt that religious spirit required dutifulness. Her work was part of the way she lived her religion. Eventually her goodness won the favor of all and the weaver's family realized the treasure they had in her. In time, she was put in charge of the children, and then, in charge of the household.

Zita also made her rounds of prisons and hospitals and homes of the poor, bringing food and goodness. She was especially devoted to condemned criminals and often spent hours praying with them.

Zita died April 17, 1278, in the same town where she was born. In 1953, Pope Pius XII proclaimed her the patron of domestic workers.

REFLECTIONS

- Zita's work was a song of praise to God. Does your work mean more to you than a means of subsistence? Would you work if money were no issue?

- Read *The Quotidian Mysteries* by Kathleen Norris.

- Do you enjoy managing your household and possessions? Is it more than mere "housework"?

PRAYER

For all domestic workers,
We ask your generous blessings, O God.
Amen.

HARPER LEE

Novelist • U.S. • 1926 —

SCRIPTURE THEME

Practical justice
"She was devoted to good words and acts of charity."
— Acts 9:36

QUOTATION

"The one thing that doesn't abide by majority rule is a person's conscience."
— *Harper Lee*, The New York Public Library Book of Twentieth Century American Quotations, *page 105*

LEE'S CLAIM TO FAME IS BASED ON HER FIRST NOVEL and, to date, only book, *To Kill a Mockingbird.* The story of a Black man accused of raping a White woman as told by a six-year-old girl whose father serves as defense attorney held strong national meaning in 1960 when the book first appeared. And it is still a powerful work.

The novel received a Pulitzer Prize in 1961, the Brotherhood Award of the National Conference of Christians and Jews in 1961 and several other awards. In 1962, the book was adapted into a screenplay. The book has been translated into ten languages and made into large print and popular editions.

Harper was born April 28, 1926, in Alabama. She was the youngest of three children. The Lee family is related to the Confederate General Robert E. Lee. Her father, a lawyer, practiced law with Harper's older sister, Alice.

Harper studied law at the University of Alabama and spent a year at

Oxford University. During the 1950's, she worked as an airline reservation clerk. She left that job to devote herself to full-time writing.

REFLECTIONS

- Harper's novel recollected the joys and sorrows of children growing up. What were the joys and sorrows of your own childhood?
- Harper considers her training in law an excellent preparation for writing. What other disciplines have prepared you for the work you now do?

PRAYER

May the books
We choose to read
Speak to us of spiritual values
And encourage us toward
Social concerns and actions.
Amen.

April 29

CATHERINE OF SIENA

Dominican nun, doctor of the Church • Italy • 1347–1380

SCRIPTURE THEME

Prayer, work, good example

*"Seek good and not evil,
    that you may live....
Hate evil and love good,
    And establish justice in the gate."*

    — *Amos 5:14-15*

QUOTATION

"Knowledge in itself is good and perfect when a learned person is also good, honourable, and humble in life. But if knowledge be joined with a proud, dishonourable, and wicked life it is a poison...."

    — *Catherine,* The Quotable Woman: From Eve to 1799, *page 66*

CATHERINE WAS BORN IN ITALY IN 1347, the twenty-third (some sources say twenty-fifth) child of Lapa and Jacopa Benincasa. She grew up as a cheerful and intelligent person with religious devotion. Her father gave her a private room so she could meditate and pray.

At eighteen, she became a Dominican tertiary and spent three years in secluded prayer. Gradually, her contemplative ways grew into a more public apostolate. She dictated letters for the spiritual instruction and encouragement of those who gathered around her. She entered into public affairs such as the crusade against the Turks and the difficulties of the pope at Avignon and of the pope with the city of Florence.

Catherine's major written work, called *The Dialogue*, deals with religious and moral problems. It is considered an Italian classic.

Her personal faith and holiness remain her claim to sanctity. At twenty-eight, she received the stigmata. At age thirty-three, she died in Rome, in the year 1380, on April 29. She was canonized in 1451 and declared a doctor of the Church in 1970.

REFLECTIONS

- Catherine had a great influence for good in the people she met. How does your life influence others for good?
- Catherine, like most women of her time, never learned to write. She had to dictate her thoughts and words for others (men) to write down. How do you use writing in your everyday life? How would you be limited if you could not write?
- Catherine's activities flowed from her prayer. Do you pray about the plans and projects you have?

PRAYER

For those among us
Who are involved
In public affairs and church affairs,
We pray for holiness of life,
Integrity of character,
Strength of mind
And wisdom of heart.
Amen.

April 30

MARIE GUYART

Educator • France and Canada • 1599–1672

SCRIPTURE THEME

Incarnation

"And the Word became flesh and lived among us, and we have seen his glory, the glory as of a father's only son, full of grace and truth."

— John 1:14

QUOTATION

"My aversion was changed into a cordial love for all those persons toward whom I experienced feelings of aversion and bitterness."

— Marie Guyart, Lives of the Saints, *page 155*

MARIE GUYART WAS BORN AT TOURS IN 1599. Her father was a master baker. Marie was one of seven children. When she spoke to her parents at age fourteen about entering the convent, they thought she was too vivacious and arranged a marriage for her. At age seventeen, she was married to Claude Martin, and at age nineteen, she was widowed with a six-month-old son.

While she raised her son, she made her living by managing her brother-in-law's delivery business, which included the supervision of several dozen men.

At thirty-one, she entered the Ursuline Sisters of Tours. At thirty-nine, she left for Canada with six companions. On August 1, 1639, they arrived in Quebec, where Marie served as the first superior of the Ursuline convent.

They began a school for Native American and French girls. Marie worked on catechisms and dictionaries in the Iroquois and Algonquin tongues. It is estimated that she also wrote some 20,000 letters (in French), many to her son who became a Benedictine priest in France. He published about 220 of these, including the long newsy ones she wrote him.

At age fifty-four, Marie wrote an autobiography at the request of her spiritual director. After her death, her son wrote a biography of her, using much of her autobiographical writings. Marie was a mystic with the gift of writing; the Incarnate Word and the Trinity were her favorite images of God.

Marie died April 30, 1672.

REFLECTIONS

- Reflect on the mystery of the Incarnation. What does it mean to you that God became human? How does this ennoble you as a human being?
- When have you had a spiritual experience that changed the way you felt about others? Were its effects permanent? Temporary? Recurring?

PRAYER

We admire the bravery, O God,
Of women who leave their homelands
And serve you in new countries.
May we be brave
In combating prejudice and racism
And welcome into our worlds
Peoples of color.
Amen.

May 1

KATE SMITH
Singer • U.S. • 1907–1986

SCRIPTURE THEME
Singing
"Awake, awake, utter a song!"
  — Judges 5:12

QUOTATION
"God bless America,
Land that I love.
Stand beside her
And guide her
Through the night
With a light from above.
From the mountains,
To the prairies,
To the ocean white with foam.
God bless America,
My home, sweet home."
  — *words by Irving Berlin, made famous by Kate Smith*

WHEN KATE SMITH PERFORMED IRVING BERLIN'S "GOD BLESS AMERICA" in 1938, the composer gave her exclusive rights. She popularized it with her many performances. Later, because of its popularity, the song was released to other performers. But right up until her death, audiences wanted Kate to sing this song, which became a sort of unofficial national anthem.

Kate was born May 1, 1907. Her singing career began at four when she accompanied her parents to church and sang right out, though she sometimes held the hymnbook upside down. All through her growing-up years, she sang at school and church.

She spent some months in nursing training but quit to take up singing at Keith's Theater. She was in a two-year run on Broadway, on tour with a road company and back in New York.

She made her radio debut on May 1, 1931, with a fifteen-minute program called *The Kate Smith Hour*. Two years later, she was the highest-paid woman on network radio.

Several years and two films later, *The Kate Smith Hour* premiered on television and continued throughout the 1950's. Kate also entertained the troops during World War II and made frequent appearances in musical and variety shows. In the 1960's, she launched another television program, made her debut at Carnegie Hall and did guest appearances.

The Philadelphia Flyers hockey team attributed its success to playing the tape of Kate singing "God Bless America" at the opening of each of their games. Once they flew her in especially to sing at a playoff game (they won).

In 1976, Kate suffered a diabetic coma and brain damage. She did make a special appearance at the 1982 Emmy Awards ceremony to lead the singing of *God Bless America*. In the same year, Kate received from President Reagan the Presidential Medal of Freedom, the highest award given to U.S. civilians.

Kate died June 17, 1986, and is buried at Lake Placid, New York. Plans are under way to establish a Kate Smith museum there.

REFLECTIONS

- What is your preference for a national anthem? Do you feel it should contain reference to God?

- Who, in your opinion, should receive our nation's highest honor? Artists? Statesmen? Politicians?

PRAYER

Bless, O God, this America,
The land that I live in and love,
The land I call home.
Amen.

 *May 2*

MAY SARTON

Writer • Belgium and U.S. • 1912–1995

SCRIPTURE THEME

Home

"By wisdom a house is built,
and by understanding it is established;

by knowledge the rooms are filled
   with all precious and pleasant riches."
— *Proverbs 24:3-4*

QUOTATION

"After the mad beautiful racing is done,
To be still, to be silent, to stand by a window
Where time not motion changes light to shadow,
Is to be present at the birth of creation."
— *May Sarton, in* Journey Toward Poetry, *page 151*

BORN ON MAY 3, 1912, IN BELGIUM, Eléanore Marie "May" Sarton was the only child of George, a noted historian, and Mable, an artist. May trained for a career in theater, but in her twenties turned to writing and devoted her life to it. She became a naturalized U.S. citizen in 1924.

Recognized by some as the author who freed women to write honestly, May's work dealt with anger, love and homosexuality. Both her fiction and journals, which explore the life of the mind, are clear and candid. Motive, belief, thought, feeling and impulse—all are examined in her telling.

She used houses and their windows, rooms and gardens as symbols of the joys of solitude and nurturing of the spirit. Her conversational tone and contemplative comments on relationships and friendships have made her valued by many and especially beloved by other women who write.

Any women's bookstore has an entire shelf of May's poetry, fiction and journals. Though some of her earlier writing hinted at lesbianism, *The Education of Harriet Hatfield* treats the situation with openness and honesty. This tale of an older woman who opens a bookstore for women in a blue-collar neighborhood revolves around the stories of her visitors.

Describing the renovation of an old house in *Plant Dreaming*, May treats the establishment of roots and the nurturing of spirit. In *The House by the Sea*, she writes about the joys of productive solitude. She has also written poetry and fiction that cover a wide range of political and social issues.

On her seventieth birthday, a film called *World of Light: A Portrait of May Sarton* was produced. In it, May reveals her inner world. A book based on the script and titled *May Sarton: A Self-Portrait* was published in 1982. By that time, May had written eleven volumes of poetry, sixteen novels and six books of memories and journals; more works have been published since that time.

May suffered a stroke in her seventies. Her journal writings of those months were published in *After the Stroke*. Though she loved to travel and lecture extensively, she spent her last years as a recluse in her house by the sea in Maine. In 1992, her journal entries from previous months of living with illness were published as *Endgame*. May died July 16, 1995.

REFLECTIONS

- How do you feel about repression and expression of strong emotions and experiences such as anger, love, creativity, sexuality and power?
- How honest do you want people to be in life? In literature?
- What role in nurturing your own inner being does solitude play?

PRAYER

Grant us, each day, O Mother-God,
Enough play and foolishness to balance
The discipline and order of our lives,
Enough joy to balance
Our affliction and sorrow.
Amen.

 *May 3*

GOLDA MEIR

Stateswoman • Russia, U.S. and Israel • 1898–1978

SCRIPTURE THEME

The Jewish state

"Where is the child who has been born king of the Jews?"
— *Matthew 2:2*

QUOTATION

"The unexplainable, the ultimately unknowable...we call that something 'spirit'—the spirit of this people—which has no limitations and is indestructible. This spiritual strength is eternal. It is transmitted from generation to generation, almost unwittingly."
— *Golda Meir*, Women of Faith and Spirit, *page 62*

WHEN GOLDA MEIR WAS MINISTER OF LABOR in the newly formed nation of Israel, she had homes built for those in need, and she insisted that there be a window over every kitchen sink so women could keep their eyes on their children at play.

Golda's chosen last name, Meir, means "to give light," and she did this by giving windows and giving inspiration to Jews who sought a homeland.

Born on May 3, 1898, in the Russian city of Kiev, and persecuted as a Jew, Golda knew from her early years the fear of pogroms and the pain of poverty. In 1903, Golda's father left Russia for the United States with a plan to send for his wife and three daughters as soon as he could earn money for boat tickets. In 1906, Golda and her mother and sisters came to Milwaukee, Wisconsin, and joined her father.

They tried to settle in, but many Jews among them kept alive the Zionist hope for a Jewish homeland. Golda's sister Sheyna was among those who clung to that hope. Golda went to school, helped in her mother's store, organized clubs and began to give sidewalk talks straight from her heart.

In 1917, Golda married Morris Myerson. In 1921, they moved to Palestine, just after the Balfour Declaration, which said that the British government felt the Jews should have a homeland in Palestine. Golda and Morris worked hard to help establish the new Jewish community and to secure lands from the Arabs. Golda became a leader in labor efforts and human services.

Israel was declared a state on May 14, 1948. Golda signed the Declaration of Independence with tears of happiness in her eyes. She served as Israel's first ambassador to the Soviet Union, and then as minister of labor in Israel, and then as foreign minister. In 1969, Golda became Israel's prime minister.

Golda sought to help poor African nations and visited them. She worked for peace and met with Pope Paul VI as part of her efforts. She got caught up in the 1973 war of Egypt, Syria, Iraq and Jordan against Israel.

In 1974, at age seventy-six, Golda resigned from government activities. She died on December 8, 1978. Only after her death did it become general knowledge that she had suffered from leukemia for twelve years. Her autobiography, *My Life*, was published in 1975.

REFLECTIONS

- Jesus and his mother, his friends and disciples were all Jews. Do you have any friends of the Jewish faith?

- What do you know about the Arab-Israeli conflict? What is your view of those who endorse violence in the cause of religion?

PRAYER

Deepen in our hearts, O God,
  A sense of eternal spiritual strength
  So that we may pass it
  From generation to generation.
  Amen.

Let us pray for working mothers
  That they may balance somehow
  The needs of children and careers
  And find dedication in this tension
  Of divided loyalties.
  Amen.

May 4

MARY AGNES HALLAREN

Army officer • U.S. • 1907—

SCRIPTURE THEME

War and peace

"A time to love, and a time to hate;
a time for war, and a time for peace."

— *Ecclesiastes 3:8*

QUOTATION

"You can no more win a war than you can win an earthquake."

— *Eleanor Roosevelt, in a letter to Harry S Truman,* The Beacon Book of Quotations by Women, *page 339*

COLONEL HALLAREN, THE FIRST WOMAN TO RECEIVE A COMMISSION in the Regular Army of the United States, served as director of the Women's Army Corps (WAC) from 1947 to 1953. Mary Agnes, born in Lowell, Massachusetts, on May 4, 1907, trained to be a teacher. She enjoyed travel to Europe, the Near East and South America during breaks in the early years of her teaching career.

When the Women's Auxiliary Army Corps (WAAC) formed in 1942, Mary Agnes was among the first to join. A year later, as Captain Hallaren, she commanded the first battalion to go overseas. At this time, WAAC changed its title to WAC and became part of the Regular Army of the United States.

In March 1945, as Lieutenant Colonel Hallaren, she became director of all WAC enlistees serving in Europe. In 1946, she became deputy director of WAC; in 1947, she became director.

Mary Agnes retired from the army in 1960. She worked for a time as director of the Women in Community Service division of the United States Labor Department.

REFLECTIONS

- What do you think of women in military service? In combat duty?
- How do you feel about gays serving in the military?

PRAYER

We pray, O gracious God,
For women serving in the military,
That genuine concern
For peacemaking and peacekeeping
And respect and reverence for life
Be the guiding principles
In all the services they render.
Amen.

 *May 5*

NELLIE BLY

Journalist • U.S. • 1867–1922

SCRIPTURE THEME

Journey

"Then Moses ordered Israel to set out from the Red Sea, and they went into the wilderness."

— *Exodus 15:22*

QUOTATION

"I became the bitterest striker of them all."

— *Nellie Bly,* Stop the Presses, Nellie's Got a Scoop!, *page 30*

AROUND THE WORLD IN EIGHTY DAYS! Well, actually, she took 72 days, 6 hours and 11 minutes. The best known journalist of her day, Nellie achieved the high point of her career as she traveled alone around the world by steamer, train, rickshaw and other vehicles between November 1889 and January 1890. Her attempt to outdo Jules Verne's fictional hero, Phileas Fogg, was well publicized. Her resulting 1890 book was a huge success.

Elizabeth Cochran (she later added an *e* to the end) was born May 5, 1867, in Pennsylvania. With little formal schooling, she began her career as a reporter in Pittsburgh, where she used the pen name of Nellie Bly.

She made a good impression with her stories about working girls and slum life. In 1886 and 1887, Nellie traveled throughout Mexico sending back reports on conditions among the poor.

Moving to New York City in 1887, Nellie went to work at Joseph Pulitzer's *New York World*. Her ingenuity and concern led her to feign insanity and gain admittance to an insane asylum. Her published reports about conditions there precipitated investigations and reforms. She undertook other similar reportage in jails, sweatshops and legislatures.

After her "around the world" journey, she married Robert L. Seaman in 1895. She was twenty-eight; he was seventy-three. After his death in 1910, she spent some years running his business. In 1919, she resumed journalism. On January 27, 1922, she died in New York City at age fifty-four.

REFLECTIONS

- If you could travel around the world, what countries, places, people would you wish to see? Why?
- How do you keep up on current affairs? What sort of stories attract you?

PRAYER

O God, may our travels
Near and far
Be as windows into your heart,
Where we learn compassion
And concern for the poor.
Amen.

May 6

MAYA YING LIN

Designer of Vietnam Memorial • *U.S.* • *1959—*

SCRIPTURE THEME

Memory of war

"They shall beat their swords into plowshares,
and their spears into pruning hooks;
nation shall not lift up sword against nation,
neither shall they learn war any more."

— *Isaiah 2:4*

QUOTATION

"I'm trying to make people become involved with the piece on all levels, with the touch and sound of the water, with the words, with the memories."

— *Maya Ying Lin,* People, *November 20, 1989*

MAYA YING LIN WAS BORN OCTOBER 5, 1959, in Athens, Ohio. She was still an architect student, a senior at Yale, when her design was selected from fifteen hundred entries for a memorial honoring those who died in the Vietnam War. She won the competition on May 6, 1981.

Lin received harsh criticism for the stark design by those who wished for flags and statues. She was also racially attacked as a Chinese American. She became confused and embittered by all the negative publicity at the time. But in a few short years, the black granite walls engraved with the names of the dead women and men became the most popular landmark in Washington, D.C.

The pressures of criticism and the politics of public art forced Lin into reclusion. She vowed to never again accept any war memorial projects but finished her schooling and worked as an architect. She refused to become a celebrity.

In 1988, she accepted an invitation from a law center in Alabama to design a memorial for those who have died in the civil rights struggle. A favorite biblical passage of Reverend Martin Luther King, Jr., inspired her creation of a solid, twelve-foot granite disk with the events and figures of civil rights inscribed. A black granite wall stands behind with the Scripture quote "...until justice rolls down like water and righteousness like a mighty stream." Over both pieces a continuously flowing stream of water takes on patterns of concentric circles when visitors touch the inscription.

REFLECTIONS

- In order to be true to her art and herself, Lin withdrew from the role of celebrity. What have you had to do to be true to yourself?
- Visit the Vietnam Memorial or the Civil Rights Memorial if ever you have the opportunity.
- Why do you think the Vietnam Memorial has become so popular? What kind of memorials do you think are appropriate for the victims of war?

PRAYER

Let us be creative and devoted
    In the ways we remember our war dead;
    And let us pray for an end to all wars,
    Now and in the future.
    Amen.

For the nearly sixty thousand dead from the Vietnam War,
    And for all those who die in ongoing wars,
    We pray for their eternal rest,
    And we pray for peace in the hearts of those
    Who hold dear the memory of their lives.
    Amen.

 *May 7*

ANA MARIA "EUGENIA" CASTILLO RIVAS

Revolutionary leader · El Salvador · 1950–1981

SCRIPTURE THEME

Sacrifice

"No one has greater love than this, to lay down one's life for one's friends."
— John 15:13

QUOTATION

"Eugenia always lived for the future. That's the truth of it. Eugenia always lived

for the future and that's how she asked the rest of us to live."
— *said by Commander Isabel,* They Won't Take Me Alive, *page 75*

BORN IN SAN SALVADOR ON MAY 7, 1950, Ana Maria Castillo Rivas had a twin sister who died at birth. Ana's parents were devout Catholics and she and her two other sisters were educated at a convent school.

From the age of fifteen, Ana was greatly involved in service to others, especially the poor, the hungry and the illiterate. At nineteen, she spent a year in Guatemala working among the poor. She then studied social psychology and continued Catholic Action work. Ana joined the University Socialist Movement and by 1974 was an underground peasant organizer. As "Eugenia," she was regarded as a revolutionary pioneer committed to the struggle of the masses.

Eugenia and Javier, a fellow revolutionary, were married in the spring of 1977. They had to stay in hiding because of their political activities. During her pregnancy, Eugenia carried on her work of revolution as much as her health allowed. Ana Patricia was born in hiding on December 13, 1979.

On January 4, 1981, Eugenia handed over to Javier their daughter, only thirteen months old. On January 17, in charge of a dangerous operation, Eugenia and her three companions were trapped and caught by the enemy. All four were killed.

Eugenia is remembered as a woman with great organizational ability, a woman with a certain mysticism and moral strength. She made the sacrifices necessary as a resistance leader while maintaining love and peace as a wife, mother and comrade.

REFLECTIONS

- Read Eugenia's story in *They Won't Take Me Alive.*
- What do you value enough to risk your life for? To hand over your infant daughter to another to care for?
- Do you find it more difficult to accept the patriotic sacrifices of a woman than her male counterpart? What if she is the mother of small children?

PRAYER

As we serve the hungry,
The homeless, the hurting,
May we be mindful that whatsoever we do,
We do for Christ.
And when we are called on to sacrifice

Our time, our loves, our very lives,
Let us imitate Christ in generosity.
Amen.

May 8

JESSIE ANNETTE JACK HOOPER
Peace advocate · U.S. · 1865–1935

SCRIPTURE THEME

Peace

*"Glory to God in the highest heaven,
and on earth peace among those whom he favors!"*
— *Luke 2:14*

QUOTATION

"The world would have peace if the men of politics would follow the Gospels."
—*Saint Brigitta of Sweden*, Quotable Saints, *page 17*

BORN NOVEMBER 8, 1865, to a farm family in Iowa, Jessie Jack was sickly as a child. Also, her family suffered from business debts. Jessie, taught at home by a governess, spent several winters in the South for the sake of her health. Jessie studied at Colnan College in Des Moines and took private art lessons in Chicago.

On May 30, 1888, Jessie married Ben C. Hooper and settled in Oshkosh, Wisconsin. They had one daughter, Lorna. Jessie took up various civic projects, while Ben worked as a lawyer and was later in charge of a wholesale grocery firm. Among Jessie's accomplishments were the first kindergarten and the first visiting nurse programs in Oshkosh.

In 1893, Jessie heard Susan B. Anthony speak at the World Expo in Chicago. From that time, Jessie worked for women's suffrage.

Ben was also in favor of women's right to vote and had from the time of their marriage voted in alternate years for candidates of Jessie's choice. Ben supported Jessie's suffrage efforts, which soon extended beyond Wisconsin to Iowa, and then to the federal level with frequent trips to Washington, D.C. It was Jessie's work and lobbying efforts in Madison that made Wisconsin the first state to ratify the Nineteenth Amendment to the U.S. Constitution which gave women suffrage.

When Carrie Chapman Catt requested it, Jessie toured several western states to promote the ratification of the Nineteenth Amendment.

In 1920, Jessie was honored by the women of her state when they elected her as the first president of the Wisconsin League of Women Voters. In 1921, she took up committee work for the reduction of armaments. In her concern for world peace, Jessie ran as a candidate for a seat in the U.S. Senate. She was not elected.

In 1924, Jessie coordinated nine women's societies into peace efforts, which became the Conference on the Cause and Cure of War, with Carrie Chapman Catt as chairperson. Jessie devoted herself to speaking engagements, correspondences and securing of signatures for the promotion of world peace. She organized a drive to obtain 600,000 signatures on a disarmament petition campaign and was among those who presented peace petitions with eight million names to the League of Nations at Geneva in 1932.

With failing health, Jessie served as vice president of her husband's firm and fulfilled other commitments in Oshkosh while continuing to speak and travel for world peace. She died of cancer on May 8, 1935, in Oshkosh, six months before her seventieth birthday.

REFLECTIONS

- Reflect on how you use the right to vote to promote values in which you believe.
- Consider being active in the League of Women Voters, local peace groups or other civic groups.
- Speak with elderly women about their memories of women getting the vote.
- Ponder the response of men—as husbands, fathers, brothers and friends—to women and voting, including Jessie's husband, Ben, and the men in your own life.
- Take every opportunity to vote as an informed citizen.
- Pray about how you vote as an exercise of your faith.

PRAYER

Inspire us, Spirit of God,
To vote wisely and well
For candidates and legislation
That will promote human rights
And the well-being of all persons.
Amen.

May 9

CATHERINE OF BOLOGNA

Poor Clare abbess • Italy • 1413–1463

SCRIPTURE THEME

Artists

"All the skillful women spun with their hands, and brought what they had spun in blue and purple and crimson yarns and fine linen; all the women whose hearts moved them to use their skill spun the goats' hair."

— Exodus 35:25-26

QUOTATION

"Sometimes, [the devil] inspires souls with an inordinate zeal for a certain virtue or some special pious exercise, so that they will be motivated in its practice by passion; or again, he permits them to become discouraged so that they will neglect everything because they are wearied and disgusted. It is necessary to overcome that one snare as well as the other."

— Saint Catherine of Bologna, Quotable Saints, *page 206*

CATHERINE'S BIRTH WAS FORETOLD TO HER FATHER BY AN ANGEL who said that Catherine would be a light to the world. Catherine was born March 25, 1413, the feast of the Annunciation and light, at Bologna. She was educated at the court of the marquis of Este, friend of her father. Along with Margaret, the daughter of the marquis, Catherine learned foreign languages and the fine arts. She excelled at reading the works of the fathers of the Church.

At seventeen, she joined a group of pious women at Ferraro. They eventually became Poor Clares. Catherine worked at baking bread.

Catherine was asked to train novices, and she did so with a sense of practical spirituality. During this time, she wrote *The Seven Spiritual Weapons*, an important treatise that reveals the mystical qualities of her life. She also painted a number of miniatures and illustrations for the breviary prayer book.

After twenty-four years, her home city of Bologna requested Catherine to come and establish a Poor Clare convent there. With fifteen sisters and Catherine as abbess, the new convent was founded. Catherine was especially solicitous for the sick and related to all with wisdom, motherly love and peace.

Catherine died March 9, 1463, not quite fifty years old. At first, she was buried without a casket. When the nuns decided more than two weeks later to rebury her in a casket, they found that her body remained uncorrupt and gave off a sweet fragrance. The nuns arranged her body in a seated position, and those who wished to view her could see her through the cloister window. Later, a chapel was built, and the saint's body, robed in a costly garment given by Saint Charles Borromeo, remains seated on a throne under a crystal shrine. The body remains uncorrupt, but has turned black from the smoke of oil lamps and votive candles of five and a half centuries.

REFLECTIONS

- Catherine has been named patron of artists. Spend some time on an artistic hobby you have, or visit an art gallery.
- Several saints have remained uncorrupt after death. If interested, look for more information about Saint Cecilia, Saint Rita of Cascia, Saint Catherine of Genoa, Saint Angela Merici, Saint Lucy Filippini, Saint Catherine Labouré, Saint Bernadette.

PRAYER

O God of all creation,
We ask your blessing on the things we make.
May they be of service to you
And bring beauty to the world.
Amen.

 *May 10*

ELLA T. GRASSO

Politician • U.S. • 1918–1981

SCRIPTURE THEME

Wise speech

*"She opens her mouth with wisdom,
and the teaching of kindness is on her tongue."*

— *Proverbs 31:26*

QUOTATION

"I'm opposed to abortion because I happen to believe that life deserves the protection of society."

—Ella Grasso, The Quotable Woman: 1800–On, *page 357*

ELLA WAS BORN MAY 10, 1918, in Connecticut and educated at parochial and private schools. In 1940, she graduated with honor from Mount Holyoke College, and by 1942, she earned her master's degree.

She married Thomas A. Grasso in August 1942. In the war years, she worked as assistant director of research for the War Manpower Commission, Connecticut office.

Active in democratic politics, Ella was elected in 1952 to the state legislature, and reelected in 1954. From 1958 to 1970, she served three terms as Connecticut's secretary of state. In 1970 and 1972, she was elected to Congress.

In 1974, she campaigned for and won the governorship. Inaugurated in January 1975, she was the first woman to become governor on her own merits. (Previous women had done so by succeeding their husbands.) She managed to turn the state deficit into a surplus during her first term.

REFLECTIONS

- If you were governor, what would you want to do for your state?
- Have you considered serving in a public office? Do you think that politics can still be a noble calling?
- Try to follow the news on women serving in political offices. How well do they promote your interests?

PRAYER

Lord and God, ruler of all,
We pray for women who rule and lead
As governors and heads of state
In our country
And all the countries of our world.
Amen.

May 11

MARTHA GRAHAM

Dancer, choreographer • U.S. • 1893–1991

SCRIPTURE THEME

Dance

"A time to dance."

— *Ecclesiastes 3:4*

QUOTATION

"No artist is ahead of his time. He is his time...others are behind the times."

— *Martha Graham*, Remember the Ladies, *page 92*

BORN MAY 11, 1893, MARTHA GRAHAM BECAME THE EXEMPLAR of modern dance in its break from classical ballet. Martha learned at an early age from her father, a doctor, that bodily movements reveal the truth of the inner spirit. After training for dance, Martha found this to be true when she agreed to dance with the Greenwich Village Follies. She was dissatisfied with the standard theme and techniques.

As she developed her own style, she brought into being the modern dance. This departure from all previous forms was Martha's way of dancing, and it was what she taught her students. Her stage works and her school enriched each other.

Her interest in primitive dance forms took her to American Indians in New Mexico resulting in pieces that included "Primitive Canticles" and "Ceremonials."

Martha explored in dance the emotions of American pilgrims, colonists, Indians, witches, homesteaders, trailblazers and more. She became famous for her "Appalachian Spring," with the bride's gentle dancing, praying and loving to the music of Aaron Copland. In "Letter to the World," Martha portrayed the inner life of Emily Dickinson.

In 1950, Martha performed in "Judith: Choreographic Poem for Orchestra." Meanwhile, her school took in students from many countries, and performances were scheduled for many parts of the world.

More and more, Martha explored ways to interpret through dance the inner spirit. In "Clytemnestra," she danced the ideas that went through the mind of the character. Her dance company reveals Martha's genius in the art of dancing.

When Martha Graham died April 1, 1991, those who loved her praised her vivacity and expressiveness as well as her definition of modern dance as she danced it and taught it.

REFLECTIONS

- How do the movements of your body express your emotions? How do you see this in others?
- Go to a ballet with a new sense of the hard work and artistic beauty.

PRAYER

We dance our way into your presence, O Lord,
  And ask you, please, to dance with us
  As daffodils dance in spring breezes,
  As a bride and groom dance on their wedding night,
  As a father and mother dance on a day of joy.
  Amen.

We dance, O God, in rhythm with your love,
  Praising you with all creation!
  We dance, in step, with you, O God,
  And the rhythm of our world.
  Amen.

May 12

FLORENCE NIGHTINGALE

Nurse • Italy and England • 1820–1910

SCRIPTURE THEME

Lamp

"Indeed, you are my lamp, O LORD,
  the LORD lightens my darkness"
  — 2 Samuel 22:29

QUOTATION

"Life is a hard fight, a struggle, a wrestling with the principle of evil, hand to hand, foot to foot. Every inch of the way is disputed. The night is given us to take breath and to pray, to drink deep at the fountain of power. The day, to use the

strength which has been given us, to go forth to work with it till the evening."
— *Florence Nightingale,* The New Book of Christian Quotations, *page 145*

BORN ON MAY 12, 1820, of English parents traveling in Florence, Italy, Florence was taught Latin and Greek by her father, but also was taught to be a "lady of leisure." Florence, who felt she was called by God to be of service to others, resented a society in which women were not allowed to work. Her frustrations are well expressed in her book *Cassandra.*

Florence studied nursing books and became an expert on hospitals. Despite family opposition, she went to Germany for training and returned to London where she worked as a hospital superintendent.

In 1854, Florence organized a group of nurses to aid injured soldiers in the Crimean War. She toured the wards bringing words of comfort.

Though she wished to overhaul the Army medical system, Florence herself fell ill. Eventually, she published a thousand-page report. She continued her surveys and notes with the goal of improving medical treatment. From a sickbed, she set up a school of nursing.

It was her example that inspired Henri Dunant to found the International Red Cross. She especially promoted the principles of hygiene in all her work.

Eventually, Florence was reconciled with her family. In 1901, she lost her sight. In 1907, she became the first woman appointed to the Order of Merit by Queen Victoria. Florence died in 1910.

REFLECTIONS

- Does your career spring from a sense of mission and service?
- Reflect on nurses and doctors and aides who have brought you healing and comfort during illness.
- Have you ever pursued a goal despite strong family opposition?

PRAYER

For nurses and all who work in health care services
We ask your graces of patience and compassion,
O God, Divine Healer, we pray.
Amen.

 *May 13*

JULIAN OF NORWICH
Mystic · England · 14th century

SCRIPTURE THEME

Revelations

"Consider your own call, brothers and sisters: not many of you were wise by human standards, not many were powerful, not many were of noble birth. But God chose what is foolish in the world to shame the wise."

— *1 Corinthians 1:26-27*

QUOTATION

"As truly as God is our Father, so truly God is our Mother."

— Julian, *"A Book of Showings,"* The Norton Anthology of Literature by Women, page 16

JULIAN OF NORWICH'S CLASSIC BOOK of mystical and spiritual teaching was written in 1393, about twenty years after Julian had her mystical revelations, or "shewings." The book, called *Showings (Revelations of Divine Love)*, treats the Holy Trinity, the passion of Christ, and divine love, and is considered among the most sublime of the mystical writings of the fourteenth and fifteenth centuries. The book also lays claim to being the first written in English by a woman.

Julian was born about 1340 and became an anchoress (female hermit) who lived in a small room attached to the old church of St. Julian in the city of Norwich. She lived to an old age and died about 1420.

REFLECTIONS

- Do you know anyone who has chosen a life of solitude? When do you find solitude helpful? When do you least want to be alone?
- How do the images of father and mother relate to your image of God? Do you find one resonates more deeply?

PRAYER

We know you as Mother, O God,
In that you never forget us,
You never leave us orphans,

You carve us on your heart.
Amen.

May 14

SISTER MARY JOSEPH DEMPSEY
Surgical nurse at Mayo Clinic • U.S. • 1856–1939

SCRIPTURE THEME

Healing
"Then Jesus laid his hands on his eyes again; and he looked intently and his sight was restored, and he saw everything clearly."
— *Mark 8:25*

QUOTATION

"Although the world is very full of suffering, it is also full of the overcoming of it."
— *Helen Keller,* Sunbeams, *page 102*

THE MAYO CLINIC, founded by the Mayo brothers, retains its fame, but seldom is heard the name of Dr. William J. Mayo's first surgical nurse. She was Sister Mary Joseph Dempsey.

Julia Dempsey, born on May 14, 1856, in Salamanca, New York, spent her youth in Salamanca and in Rochester, Minnesota. In August 1878, she became Sister Mary Joseph of the Congregation of Our Lady of Lourdes, a Franciscan Third Order Regular. She was assigned to various teaching positions.

In 1889, she was asked to return to Rochester, Minnesota, where her congregation was building a hospital in the wake of a terrible tornado. She studied nursing and in 1890 became a surgical nurse. The hospital medical staff was made up of Dr. William Mayo and his two sons, Charles and William. Sister Mary Joseph served as surgical nurse until 1915. She also served as superintendent of the hospital from 1892 until 1939.

She oversaw the expansion of the hospital from forty-five to six hundred beds, the updating of facilities and the opening of a school of nursing for the training of sisters and laywomen. She helped organize the Catholic Hospital Association. Her medical and administrative skills contributed much to the success of the Mayo Clinic. She died March 29, 1939, at Rochester, Minnesota.

REFLECTIONS

- What is your experience of nuns and other religious in the medical profession? Have you ever been in their care?
- When have you had to act as nurse to a child or family member? How did that experience broaden your understanding of those who do it every day?

PRAYER

When we are ill and in need of medical care,
May we find your presence, God,
In the hands and hearts
And healing skills of medical professionals.
Amen.

 *May 15*

EMILY DICKINSON

Poet · U.S. · 1839–1886

SCRIPTURE THEME

Passing

"And the peace of God, which surpasses all understanding, will guard your hearts and your minds in Christ Jesus."

— *Philippians 4:7*

QUOTATION

*"Who built this little alban house
And shut the windows down
So close my spirit cannot see?"*

> — *Emily Dickinson, "Bring me the sunset in a cup," Selected Poems and Letters of Emily Dickinson, page 44.*

IN THE HOME OF EMILY DICKINSON at Amherst College in Massachusetts, visitors can see the re-created room where Emily's imaginative life and work took place. The two front windows have thin curtains that let in the light of day and offer a full view of life passing by.

Her poetry speaks of "the world passing by"—the world she came to know through these two windows. And the perceptions of the outer world and the inner world that Emily made sitting at her writing table between these two windows resulted in nearly two thousand poems.

These poems were arranged in neatly tied packages and placed in her desk, only to be discovered after Emily's death by her sister, Lavinia.

Among other photos in her room, Emily kept ones of Charlotte Brontë and Elizabeth Barrett Browning, for she greatly admired the spirit of these writers.

REFLECTIONS

- Read a volume of Dickinson's poems. Does their brevity strike you as a strength or a weakness?
- When have you felt the need to hide a talent or hobby? When have you simply wanted to keep your work to yourself?

PRAYER

In the certain slants of light
That shine through the windows of our lives,
May we see your divine presence and give you thanks.
Amen.

 *May 16*

MARGARET OF CORTONA

Franciscan tertiary, penitent • Italy • 1247–1297

SCRIPTURE THEME

Forgiveness

"Therefore, I tell you her sins, which were many, have been forgiven; hence she has shown great love. But the one to whom little is forgiven, loves little."

  — Luke 7:47

QUOTATION

"The time is fulfilled, and the kingdom of God has come near; repent, and believe in the good news."

  — Mark 1:15

MARGARET WAS BORN AT LAVIANO, TUSCANY, IN 1247. There are several saints named Margaret, but this one was the daughter of a Tuscan peasant family. She lost her mother in childhood and was not loved by her stepmother. From the ages of eighteen to twenty-seven, Margaret lived openly as the mistress of a nobleman near Montepulciano. She bore him a son.

After her lover met a violent death, Margaret and the baby were given a home by a family in Cortona. Her father refused to allow her to come back home.

A gradual conversion led Margaret from self-indulgence to self-denial. She became a Franciscan tertiary and both worked for a living and performed charitable acts while she raised her son. When her son went to a Franciscan novitiate, Margaret established a community dedicated to nursing the sick, especially the poor.

Her life grew increasingly austere and reclusive. A revelation inspired her to call others to repentance, and so she assisted many from far and near in reforming their lives. She spent her last years as a contemplative and mystic.

She died in 1297 at age fifty at Cortona. Her feast on February 22 was approved for the Diocese of Cortona in 1515. She was canonized a saint for the Universal Church in 1728 with her feast on May 16. Her body, said to be uncorrupt, lies at rest in a church in Cortona. Margaret is called "the Magdalene of the Franciscans."

REFLECTIONS

- Are there stories in your own family about unmarried mothers who found kindness among family or friends?
- What can you do for unmarried mothers in need?
- What role does penance and penitence play in your spiritual life?

PRAYER

Have mercy, O God of Love,
Have mercy on me,
And forgive my sins.
Turn my heart from wrongdoing,
Turn my heart toward you
In lasting repentance and love.
Amen.

May 17

CONSTANCE BAKER MOTLEY

Lawyer • U.S. • 1921—

SCRIPTURE THEME

Cries of the poor

"You should rather open your hand, willingly lending enough to meet the need, whatever it may be…. Give liberally and be ungrudging when you do so, for on this account the LORD *your God will bless you in all your work and in all that you undertake."*

— *Deuteronomy 15:8, 10*

QUOTATION

"You win by preparation and experience—that's all. Preparation and experience."

— *Constance Baker Motley,* Famous American Women, *page 320*

BORN ON SEPTEMBER 14, 1921, Constance was the sixth of nine children born to parents who came to Connecticut from the British West Indies. They did not understand American ways of segregation, and from childhood on up, Constance observed certain differences in treatment of Blacks and Whites. Her interest in history and current events increased her awareness of the inequality accorded Blacks.

The Lloyd Gaines school case in Missouri caught Constance's attention and firmed up her resolve to become a lawyer. She studied at Fisk and at New York University. At Columbia University, she came to know Thurgood Marshall. In 1946, Constance married Joel Motley and they had a son.

Constance specialized in school and college segregation cases. She prepared arguments for the landmark Supreme Court decision of May 17, 1954, which desegregated schools. She devoted herself to the *James Meredith* v. *Mississippi University* case for over two and a half years and was thrilled when he received his diploma.

In the 1960's, Constance focused her attention on inadequate schooling for Black children. She served in the New York State Senate, as president of the Borough of Manhattan and as U.S. district judge for New York City. She worked tirelessly for true and just constitutional interpretation with equality of protection under the law.

REFLECTIONS

- Has desegregation of schools affected your life? How?
- Do you still find evidence of lesser education or opportunities because of race or other reasons?
- Have you ever been denied an opportunity of education or employment because of your ethnic background? Have you ever denied an opportunity to someone else for the same reason?

PRAYER

We pray for those
    Victimized by racial tensions
    And for those who work
    Toward harmony and peace.
    Amen.

For those who tirelessly work
    For equality of protection
    By law and by practices,
    For those hurt by sexism and racism,
    We pray for God's blessing
    On their work and their success.
    Amen.

 *May 18*

MARY McLEOD BETHUNE

Educator • U.S. • 1875–1955

SCRIPTURE THEME

Neither slave nor free

"There is no longer Jew or Greek, there is no longer slave or free, there is no longer male and female; for all of you are one in Christ Jesus."
   — Galatians 3:28

QUOTATION

"The true worth of a race must be measured by the character of its womanhood."
   —Mary McLeod Bethune, The Quotable Woman, 1800–On, *page 157*

EARLY IN LIFE, MARY MCLEOD NOTICED AND QUESTIONED WHY IT WAS that White folks could read and Black folks were not allowed to learn. Born in South Carolina on July 10, 1875, Mary was the first child in her family born free rather than slave. She grew up proud of her African heritage because of the stories told to her by her grandmother, Sophia.

The McLeod family held family prayers every morning and evening. And while they couldn't read the prayer books at church, they loved to hear the words of the preacher and the singing of the choir.

Mary's mind was quick and her thoughts deep, and though she was a champion cotton picker, she yearned to read. When schooling was available, she was sent, and it changed her life overnight. Later, a Quaker woman paid Mary's fees for a girls' seminary and a year's study at the Chicago Mission Training School.

When Mary graduated at nineteen from the Mission Training School, she was refused an assignment because there were no openings for Black missionaries in Africa. Disappointed, Mary was able to find a teaching position in Georgia. In the church choir, she met Albertus Bethune and married him in 1898.

Seeing a crying need, Mary started a school at Daytona Beach, Florida. She taught, wrote letters, baked, gave talks, sang and did anything she could think of to promote the school. Soon, there were 250 students and the Bethune-Cookman College campus was started. She relied on interracial cooperation and fought for women's rights as well as Black freedom. She added a hospital, a library and community conferences, and the college grew.

The poet Langston Hughes felt Mary's influence. She advised him to tour and give poetry readings, which gave him some income. Mary began to travel in national and international circles. On a trip to Europe, she had an audience with Pope Pius XI. Mary got to know Eleanor Roosevelt and their friendship helped Eleanor overcome her prejudices.

In her sixties, Mary served as adviser to the National Youth Association, and then was put in charge of Black Affairs for the NYA. She formed the Federal Council on Negro Affairs, called the "Black Cabinet," a group who met in her home to work against discrimination in government.

In May 1949, Mary returned to her cottage at Bethune College, and she died there in 1955. A noted journalist of the time called her one of the ten most important women in America.

Mary McLeod Bethune's home is preserved as she left it on the Bethune-Cookman College campus in Daytona Beach, Florida. The Bethune Museum and Archives in Washington, D.C., contains memorabilia of Mary as well as changing exhibits on Black women.

A statue of Mary McLeod Bethune, unveiled in 1974, stands in Lincoln Park in Washington, D.C. This memorial was the first monument of a Black person on public land in the U.S. capital.

REFLECTIONS

- What family prayers are in use in your home—meal prayers, bedtime, special days? Which prayer traditions from your youth have you abandoned?
- Make a list of ten women you consider most important in your own life, in the U.S., in history, in the Church, in the world.
- Read some of Langston Hughes's poetry, keeping in mind that he always remembered Mary's affirmation and advice.

PRAYER

Forgive our sins of racism and sexism,
O God of unity,
And strengthen our resolve
To be inclusive of all peoples.
Amen.

May 19

LORRAINE HANSBURY

Playwright • U.S. • 1930–1965

SCRIPTURE THEME

Gifts

"Now there are varieties of gifts, but the same Spirit; and there are varieties of services, but the same Lord."

— 1 Corinthians 12:4

QUOTATION

"There is always something left to love. And if you ain't learned that, you ain't learned nothing."

— *Lorraine Hansbury*, The Quotable Woman: 1800–On, *page 51*

IN HER LANDMARK DRAMA, *A RAISIN IN THE SUN*, Lorraine examines the question "What happens to a dream deferred?" asked by Langston Hughes in one of his poems. In the film version, one geranium plant on the kitchen windowsill images the hopes and conflicts of the dream of leaving the Chicago ghetto in which the family lives.

Lorraine, born May 19, 1930, in Chicago, to a prosperous Republican family, studied African history and began writing early in her career. She won the Best Play of the Year award in 1959 for *A Raisin in the Sun*.

The Sign in Sidney Brustein's Window was Lorraine's second commercially produced play. Her subsequent plays dealt with black concerns in Africa as well as in America. In fact, her philosophy and presentation rendered a deep and lasting influence in the theater of Black performers and Black audiences. Lorraine died January 12, 1965.

REFLECTIONS

- Try to see the film or musical version of *A Raisin in the Sun*.
- What image matches your hopes and aspirations?

PRAYER

Grant us the vision, O God,
To see in windowsill treasures
The hopes and dreams
Of those who dwell within.
Amen.

 *May 20*

ANTOINETTE BLACKWELL

Clergywoman • U.S. • 1825–1921

SCRIPTURE THEME

Pastor

*"He will feed his flock like a shepherd;
he will gather the lambs in his arms,
and carry them in his bosom,
and gently lead the mother sheep."*

— Isaiah 40:11

QUOTATION

"The sexes in each species of beings...are always true equivalents—equals but not identicals."

— Antoinette Blackwell, The Quotable Woman, 1800–On, *page 49*

IN 1853, ANTOINETTE WAS GIVEN A PERMANENT APPOINTMENT as a Congregational pastor, thus becoming the first formally appointed female pastor in the United States. She had previously completed a theological course though the authorities refused to degree or license her. She worked as a lecturer and itinerant preacher.

Born on May 20, 1825, in Henrietta, New York, Antoinette was a precocious child and spoke up at Congregational Church meetings. She attended Oberlin College where she obtained a literary degree before pursuing her theology interest.

After her 1853 appointment as pastor, she pursued her interest in reform movements, especially those involving women's rights, temperance and abolition. Her religious convictions changed, and in 1854, she became a Unitarian. In 1856, she married Samuel Blackwell, a brother of Drs. Elizabeth and Emily Blackwell. Another Blackwell brother married Lucy Stone, and this whole family became involved in women's rights.

After her marriage, Antoinette retired from public life. She pursued studies in social and physical sciences and wrote several books. Later in life, she resumed some lecturing. Her husband died in 1901. She died November 5, 1921.

REFLECTIONS

- Do you find it amazing that women in the mid–nineteenth century were seeking equality in church ministry?
- What values of your larger family have been handed on to you?
- In what roles of pastoral ministry are women of your church involved?

PRAYER

In many ways, you call us as women, O God,
To be of service as pastoral and caring ministers.
Strengthen us to follow your plans for leadership
And service in our church communities.
Amen.

May 21

MARY ROBINSON

President, politician, lawyer, professor • Ireland • 1944—

SCRIPTURE THEME

Conscience of a leader

"For I also am a man set under authority, with soldiers under me; and I say to one, 'Go,' and he goes, and to another, 'Come,' and he comes, and to my slave, 'Do this,' and the slave does it."

— *Luke 7:8*

QUOTATION

"You have a voice, I will make it heard."

— *Mary Robinson's 1990 campaign slogan,* Current Biography, *April 1991, page 50*

BORN AS MARY BOURK IN COUNTY MAYO ON MAY 21, 1944, Mary grew up with four brothers in a Roman Catholic home. Both of her parents were physicians. Mary received an excellent education in Ireland, in Paris and later in the United States.

Mary greatly admired her grandfather and dreamed of being a lawyer like him. She studied law at Trinity College, a Protestant institution. When she married a law classmate, Nicholas Robinson, outside the faith, her parents refused to attend the wedding. In 1967–1968, Mary attended Harvard Law School and found excitement in the U.S. civil rights movement.

Back in Ireland, Mary joined the law faculty of Trinity and gained a seat in the Senate (Seenad), the upper chamber of Parliament, where she championed liberal causes and women's rights. She made a name for herself as a lawyer in both Irish and English courts. She also worked for the reconciliation of Northern Ireland with the Republic of Ireland.

Mary was elected president of Ireland and was sworn in on December 3, 1990. Though the office is largely ceremonial, Mary's hope was to effect changes. In 1997, she became the U.N. High Commissioner for Human Rights. Mary and her husband are the parents of three children and live in Dublin.

REFLECTIONS

• Mary Robinson remains personally opposed to abortion while insisting on the right to information about abortion for those who wish it. How do you feel about this?

- Are there mixed marriages in your family? What tensions does this create? What opportunities for growth and blessings?

PRAYER

When we raise our voices
To be heard by others,
Let us pray for discernment
To speak messages and values
Born of sincere prayer.
Amen.

May 22

RITA OF CASCIA

Wife, mother, Augustinian nun • Spain • 1377–1437

SCRIPTURE THEME

Nothing is impossible

"For truly I tell you, if you have faith the size of a mustard seed, you will say to this mountain, 'Move from here to there,' and it will move; and nothing will be impossible for you."

— *Matthew 17:20*

QUOTATION

"Faith is the first factor in a life devoted to service. Without faith, nothing is possible. With it, nothing is impossible."

— *Mary McLeod Bethune,* Women of Faith and Spirit, *page 33*

RITA (MARGARITA) WAS BORN IN 1377 IN THE UMBRIAN HILLS OF ITALY, in the same general area as Saint Francis of Assisi. She wished to become a nun but married because her parents wished it. Her husband became unfaithful and violent. After eighteen years of marriage, he was brought home to her, murdered. Her sons wanted to avenge his death, but she prayed they would not. Both of them died before they were able to get involved in murder.

Rita went to the Augustinian convent for admission but was told that widows were not accepted. She went back a second and third time, and the rule was changed in her favor. She became a prayerful nun with a special devotion to the Passion.

Disease afflicted her the last years of her life. She died May 22, 1437.

Her body never corrupted and in 1900, she was canonized. She has been invoked as the saint of desperate and impossible cases. A new basilica was built at Cascia in 1946. Her body lies enshrined there, and the tomb attracts countless pilgrims.

REFLECTIONS

- What do you do when things seem desperate or impossible?
- Rita prayed that her sons not become guilty of revenge and murder. Her prayer was answered in that they became ill and at Rita's urging forgave her father's killer. What do you think of this example of prayer and forgiveness?

PRAYER

Forgive us, O God of pardon and peace,
For any moments of revengeful thoughts,
And lead us through prayer
Toward windows of reconciliation.
Amen.

May 23

MARGARET FULLER OSSOLI

Transcendentalist writer, feminist • U.S., Italy • 1810–1850

SCRIPTURE THEME

Courage

"Finally, be strong in the Lord and in the strength of his power."

— *Ephesians 6:10*

QUOTATION

"I am 'too fiery'…yet I wish to be seen as I am, and would lose all rather than soften away anything."

— *Margaret Fuller,* Remember the Ladies, *page 98*

MARGARET WAS BORN IN 1810, ON MAY 23. By the age of four, she had learned her numbers, and by six was reading Latin classics and translating them into English, all this by instruction of her father. He also taught her to carry on excellent conversations, formulating her thoughts before she spoke.

While Margaret advanced well with book knowledge, she was lacking in social skills until an understanding teacher assisted her with this. She prepared her young brothers for college by tutoring them and did much of the sewing and housework because her mother was frequently ill.

In 1835, she met Ralph Waldo Emerson and hoped to advance the relationship. But her father's sudden death put her, at age twenty-five, in charge of the household. In time, she became a teacher at Bronson Alcott's school and made further acquaintance with the Emersons. She took other teaching positions, completed a translation of some of Goethe's works and became interested in women's rights. She observed that women were handicapped by lack of formal schooling and lack of opportunities to use what knowledge they did acquire.

In 1839, Margaret called together twenty-five distinguished New England women for the first of several "conversations" on various topics. The women came together for intellectual stimulation, and the group was the forerunner of women's study clubs, feminist conferences and colleges for women. One of the participants in the 1839 group was Elizabeth Cady Stanton.

Margaret worked with Emerson on *The Dial*, the transcendentalist magazine, and her work as editor kept the magazine at its high level. Her work also brought her into touch with the circle of great minds in New England and stimulated her writing. In 1843, her article promoting the idea that a woman must fulfill herself as an individual caused a sensation and led Horace Greeley to invite her to become editor at the *New York Tribune*. Margaret accepted and became the first woman to be editor on any major newspaper.

Her 1845 book, *Woman in the Nineteenth Century,* became the "bible of feminists" and the most talked-about book of the day. Both her newspaper reporting and her book shocked many with truth as she saw it. In 1846, she became a foreign correspondent for the *Tribune* and sent back interesting observations from Europe.

She secretly married Giovanni d'Ossoli and had a son during the Italian Revolution. Their marriage remained secret because of involvement in efforts to establish a revolutionary Roman republic. She died with her husband and baby in a shipwreck in 1850 as they neared the New Jersey coast on their way home. She was forty years old.

REFLECTIONS

- Are you satisfied with the intellectual stimulation you experience in your life now? That you experienced in your younger years?
- Do you belong to any women's study or discussion groups?
- Do you seek an intellectual basis for your faith life and spiritual practices?

PRAYER

In our communications,
O Word Incarnate,
May we have
The courage of our convictions
And the clarity of our commitments.
Amen.

 *May 24*

QUEEN VICTORIA

Queen · England · 1819–1901

SCRIPTURE THEME

Ruler

"Happy are your people! Happy are these your servants, who continually attend you and hear your wisdom!"

— *2 Chronicles 9:7*

QUOTATION

"Now let me entreat you seriously not to do this; not to let your feelings (very natural and usual ones) of momentary irritation and discomfort be seen by others; don't (as you so often do) let every little feeling be read in your face and seen in your manner, pray don't give way to irritability before your ladies. All this I say with the love and affection I bear you—as I know you have to contend with and struggle against."

— *Queen Victoria, in a letter to Princess Royal,* The Quotable Woman, 1800-On, *page 40*

A WHOLE ERA OF HISTORY IS NAMED FOR HER—THE VICTORIAN AGE. She was born May 24, 1819, and named Alexandrina Victoria. An only child, she was raised by her mother. Her father died before her first birthday.

When George IV died, Victoria was recognized as heir to the throne. She was only eleven, so her uncle reigned as regent. At eighteen, Victoria took over and asserted her independence. In 1840, she married Prince Albert. They had nine children.

Victoria gave Florence Nightingale wholehearted support and instituted the Victoria Cross for bravery. After Albert's death in 1861, Victoria became a recluse. Coaxed back into public life by 1864, she was named Empress of India in 1876 because of her great interest in that colony.

From the age of thirteen, Victoria kept a journal with vivid details and did many drawings in sketchbooks. She was also a prolific letter writer. As she aged, her popularity increased. In 1887 and 1897, the fiftieth and sixtieth years of her reign, national jubilees were celebrated. She died January 22, 1901.

REFLECTIONS

- For all her dour appearance, Victoria loved her husband and children. What values, attitudes, accomplishments do you associate with the Victorian era?

- In what areas of your life do you have complete control? Do you rule with wisdom?

PRAYER

Strengthen us, God of love,
To show kindness, gentleness
To those we dislike.
Amen.

 *May 25*

DOROTHEA LANGE

Photographer • U.S. • 1895–1965

SCRIPTURE THEME

Watching, seeing

"The eye is not satisfied with seeing."

— *Ecclesiastes 1:8*

QUOTATION

"It came to me that what I had to do was to take pictures and concentrate upon people, only people, all kinds of people."

— *Dorothea Lange*, Dorothea Lange: Life Through the Camera, *page 20*

DOROTHEA LANGE SPENT MANY OF HER CHILDHOOD AFTERNOONS waiting in the New York City library for her mother's workday there to end. And while she waited, she looked out the windows and watched.

"I looked into all those lives so strange to me," she said. "I watched." She liked to watch people through the windows, and with an intense look, she focused on details.

Dorothea was born May 25, 1895. Her mother spent what money she could on books and records. Her father's Shakespeare books provided her with stories that she loved. Dorothea loved to be free to walk all over the crowded streets of New York City. Walking and watching, reading and plays and art shows—these were Dorothea's main education. Her formal schooling did not hold her interest quite as well.

At seventeen, she took a beginner's job with Arnold Genthe, the photographer famous for his photos of the 1906 San Francisco earthquake. From him, she got a look into the world of celebrity. She also learned how he focused the camera on the plainest of women and photographed the inner light he saw in each one. Eventually, she set up her own photo lab in the chicken coop.

In a moment of revelation during a vacation in the Sierra Mountains, Dorothea had a great spiritual experience. She determined that people, and only people, should be the subjects of her work.

Another turning point came to Dorothea as she stood one day at her studio window. Gazing at the street below, she noticed an unemployed young man, and it came to her that real life was on the streets more than in the celebrities who came to the studio.

She began focusing her camera on the homeless, the hungry—people she found in the everyday world. One of her best-known photographs, "White Angel Bread Line," is from the early 1930's.

Dorothea was invited to exhibit her work as documentary photographs; they had the power to inform the mind and to move the heart. Dorothea remained committed to people, to the truth of reality about them, to respect for each person. She photographed the migrant workers in California. Her famous photo "Migrant Mother" comes from this series and has been called one of the greatest American photographs.

At the end of the 1930's, a Guggenheim Fellowship enabled Dorothea to photograph Western religious communities such as the Mormons. In the early 1940's, Dorothea was asked to do a photo record of the internment of Japanese Americans on the West Coast. This she did with a deep sense of respect and concern for the dignity of the people. She did further series about ethnic groups on the West Coast.

Later in her life she did a series on relationship, the warm and intimate moments of everyday life. She did a special project about the Mormons with Ansel Adams for *Life* magazine; he did the landscapes while she did the people. *Life* sent her abroad to do a photo story on the people of rural Ireland.

In 1964, she learned that she had cancer and only a year to live. She worked on a photo essay about the life of rural women in America, and she prepared a one-woman show of her life's work for the Museum of Modern Art in New York City. She died October 11, 1965. She was seventy.

REFLECTIONS

- Have you experienced a moment of special insight or revelation, a spiritual intuition that set the course of your life or part of it?

- How do photographs preserve your memories of the past? Do you regret not having taken pictures of certain occasions? What special moments can you capture for your memory today?

PRAYER

As we look through
The lens of our experiences,
May we remain ever focused on you,
O God, for you are
The still point of our turning world.
Amen.

May 26

SALLY RIDE

Astronaut · U.S. · 1951—

SCRIPTURE THEME

Majesty of the heavens

"I am the root and the descendant of David, the bright morning star."

— *Revelation 22:16*

QUOTATION

"Our exploration of the planets represents a triumph of imagination and will for the human race. The events of the last twenty years are perhaps too recent for us to adequately appreciate their proper historical significance. We can, however, appraise the scientific significance of these voyages of exploration: They have been nothing less than revolutionary both in providing a new picture of the nature of the solar system, its likely origin and evolution, and in giving us a new perspective on our own planet Earth."

—*NASA Advisory Committee,* The New York Public Library Book of Twentieth Century American Quotations, *page 380*

"A WOMAN'S PLACE IS NOW IN SPACE." This was told to Sally Ride as she became the first U.S. woman to travel in space. Two Soviet women were the first women in space, one in 1962 and one in 1982, a few months before Sally's six-day space flight.

Born May 26, 1951, Sally was always a self-motivated intellectual with a love for math, science and sports. Sally studied to be an astrophysicist, that is, one who studies the physical and chemical traits of celestial matter. In 1977, NASA was looking for mission specialists and encouraged women to apply. Sally did, along with eight thousand others. In 1978, she learned of her acceptance as an astronaut and began her intensive and rigorous training. In July 1982, Sally married Dr. Steven Hawley, a fellow astronaut. She was selected as one in a crew of five for the space shuttle *Challenger* that same year.

The *Challenger* lifted off on June 18, 1983. Sally could see through the spacecraft windows a whole new view of the Earth, where the oceans looked like tiny water droplets, and a whole new sense of space, with endless pinpoints of light in the stars, planets and galaxies. She returned to Earth famous. While she responded to her public obligations, she prepared for her second space flight in October 1984. On that mission, Sally helped deploy the Earth Radiation Budget Satellite.

After the Challenger explosion in 1986, Sally was appointed to the presidential commission that investigated the situation. In 1987, she resigned from the space program to accept a science fellowship for international security at Stanford University Center for International Security and Arms Control. She worked there as a physicist. In 1989, she became director of the California Space Institute and a professor at the University of California.

REFLECTIONS

- Do you ever dream of traveling in space? What kind of adventures would you like to have?

- How do you feel when you look at the stars? Humbled? Awestruck? Indifferent?

PRAYER

Peering through the spaceship windows
Of our imagination,
We are in awe, O Creator,
At your majesty and splendor and glory.
Amen.

 *May 27*

RACHEL CARSON

Marine biologist · U.S. · 1907–1964

SCRIPTURE THEME

Ocean

"Thus far shall you come, and no farther,
and here shall your proud waves be stopped."
— *Job 38:11*

QUOTATION

"Entire species of animals have been exterminated, or reduced to so small a remnant that their survival is doubtful. Forests have been despoiled by uncontrolled and excessive cutting of lumber; grasslands have been destroyed by overgrazing.... We have much to accomplish before we can feel assured of passing on to future generations a land as richly endowed in natural wealth as the one we live in."
—Rachel Carson, Wit and Wisdom of Famous American Women, *page 48*

WHEN RACHEL CARSON worked for the U.S. Fish and Wildlife Service, she took an underwater diving trip to learn more about the ocean. What she saw through the windows of her diving helmet became one of the greatest experiences of her life and contributed to her book *The Sea Around Us.* From early childhood, Rachel had dreamed of seeing the ocean.

Born inland on May 27, 1907, near Pittsburgh, Pennsylvania, Rachel learned about nature and science from her parents. Rachel loved to read, and one of her favorite authors was Beatrix Potter, with her stories about rabbits and other animals. And Rachel wanted to be a writer.

When Rachel went to Pennsylvania College for Women, she studied English but later switched to biology. After graduation, she got a job at the U.S. Bureau of Fisheries and did some pamphlet writing for them. Eventually, she began writing magazine articles and books, all the while learning more about the environment. Her books *The Sea Around Us* and *Under the Sea Wind* became best-sellers.

When she worked for the Fisheries, Rachel complained about having only one small window, saying that it was "like working at the bottom of a well." Later, when Rachel was able to build her own house by the sea, she had windows near her desk in her workroom through which she could see both the woods and the water.

During the 1950's, Rachel came to realize that chemicals were poisoning the environment, and she went to work on researching the facts. When *Silent Spring* was published in 1962 and translated into dozens of other languages in 1963, an impact was made and laws limiting chemical pollution began to be made.

Rachel knew she had cancer, and some chapters of *Silent Spring* showed how poisons in the environment cause cancer. She died April 14, 1964. Her book about children and nature, *A Sense of Wonder*, was published posthumously.

REFLECTIONS

- Have you read any articles or books on ecofeminism, which holds that the best interests of the planet need the nurturing, caring decisions of women? How do you feel about this idea?

- A long quote from a biography about Rachel was used at her funeral. What words will you leave behind?

- Rachel Carson shared her mother's love of books and nature. What loves have you and your mother shared?

PRAYER

We see and hear your powers and presence
In the ebb and flow of tides on the seashore.
Be for us, the Lord of the sea and sky.
Amen.

May 28

MARGARET POLE

Wife, mother, countess, martyr • England • d. 1541

SCRIPTURE THEME

Honesty

"Finally, beloved, whatever is true, whatever is honorable, whatever is just, whatever is pure, whatever is pleasing, whatever is commendable, if there is any excellence and if there is anything worthy of praise, think about these things."

— *Philippians 4:8*

QUOTATION

"Remember that nothing is small in the eyes of God. Do all that you do with love."

—*Saint Thérèse of Lisieux*, Quotable Saints, *page 117*

MARGARET POLE WAS HIRED by King Henry VIII of England as governess for Princess Mary and called by King Henry "the saintliest woman in England."

After Henry announced his divorce of his wife Catherine and intended marriage to Anne Boleyn, Margaret left the royal court.

In 1536, Margaret's son, Reginald Pole (soon to be made a cardinal), wrote a treatise against Henry's divorce and claim to be head of the Church of England. Reginald was in Rome, but the rest of the Pole family was still in England. Henry determined to get rid of every last one of the Pole family.

Margaret was among those who supported Queen Catherine in her claim as Henry VIII's wife and queen. For opposing Henry VIII in his divorce of Catherine and marriage to Anne Boleyn, Margaret was imprisoned without a trial.

Once arrested, Margaret was never brought to trial because no jury would have ever convicted her. Margaret and her family were deprived of their rights.

After two years, Margaret was led out of the tower and beheaded on May 28, 1541. She was beatified in 1886.

REFLECTIONS

• Ponder how the activities of Henry and Reginald affected Margaret's life and how she remained good and honest through it all.

- How have their activities affected your life and those of modern-day people?
- Reflect on how far-reaching certain actions can become.

PRAYER

For all who suffer unjustly
At the hands of ruthless rulers,
We pray that they may have strength
To bear their afflictions
And faith to unite all with God.
Amen.

 *May 29*

CHRISTINE DE PISAN

Feminist, intellectual · Italy · 1364–1430

SCRIPTURE THEME

Wisdom

"For the LORD gives wisdom;
from his mouth come knowledge and understanding."
— *Proverbs 2:6*

QUOTATION

"We are all pilgrims and wayfarers in this life....
Arise then, pilgrim, shake off sleep for this is not the hour for sleeping."
—*Christine de Pisan,* The Quotable Woman: From Eve to 1799, *page 67*

CHRISTINE WAS THE DAUGHTER of an Italian astrologer and physician, and she received an excellent education from him. Christine and her mother joined him in Paris when he was employed by the French court.

Christine married a French official when she was fifteen. When he died two years later, she supported herself and her children by writing for noble patrons. She wrote history, philosophy, biography and poetry. She also wrote songs and ballads that reflected her sadness and loneliness.

Christine insisted on the right of women to be educated and defended the rights of women in general. Her words record the famous deeds of women, and her views were often quoted in the fifteenth century.

In 1414, Christine retired to a convent and wrote her last work, a song in honor of Joan of Arc. She is recognized as an important poet in French literary history.

REFLECTIONS

- One wonders how and why Christine's feminist views were hidden from view for five centuries. How many windows of women's insight had shutters closed and nailed tight in the course of history?

- Do you ever wonder why the writings and wisdom of women seem to have been downplayed?

PRAYER

We praise you, God, for all the women
 Over all the centuries who have shared
 Their wisdom and knowledge of you
 With each other and with succeeding generations.
 Amen.

For women who make their living by writing,
 We pray for inspiration,
 Satisfaction in creativity,
 And devotion to truth.
 Amen.

May 30

JOAN OF ARC

Visionary, saint, national hero • France • c. 1412–1431

SCRIPTURE THEME

Voice of the Lord

"A voice says, 'Cry out!'
 And I said, 'What shall I cry?'"
  — Isaiah 40:6

QUOTATION

"In God's name! Let us go on bravely!"

—*Joan of Arc,* The Last Word, *page 15*

THE LAND OF JOAN'S BIRTH (MODERN FRANCE) was dominated by the English. Joan was born into a peasant family and helped to care for the sheep. When she was thirteen, she began to hear the voices of Saint Margaret, Saint Catherine and Saint Michael. These voices bade her seek out the King of France (the Dauphin) and help him recapture France from the English. This she did by rallying an army and freeing Orleans and other French cities from English power. When the French king was crowned on July 17, 1429, Joan was present.

Joan was betrayed by the Duke of Burgundy and sold for ten thousand gold francs to a French bishop who served the English cause. This bishop had Joan tried for treason and heresy, and his court had her burned at the stake. The written documents of the trial stand as important historical testimony. In due time, the trial of Joan of Arc was revived and the decision reversed.

Church approval came in the form of beatification and then canonization in 1920, but for five centuries, popular acclaim and devotion had celebrated her innocence, courage and martyrdom.

Mark Twain considered her the greatest woman who ever lived, and he spent many years researching her life. He wrote a book from the point of view of Joan's fictional secretary and captured the spirit of Joan's heroism as soldier and as woman on trial. The book *Saint Joan* has been recently republished.

Other literary treatments of Joan of Arc include works by Bernard Shaw and G. K. Chesterton.

REFLECTIONS

- Women serving in the military offer varying points of view concerning peacekeeping activities, combat duty and the like. Did you serve in the military or have friends who did? How do you feel about it?
- If you are currently serving in the military, what does Joan of Arc have to say to you?
- Artists over the centuries have found inspiration in the life and death of Joan of Arc. See if your local art museum has any pieces related to Joan.
- Titles abound in the case of Joan of Arc—Maid of Orleans, Savior of

France, to name a few. If you read Mark Twain's book *Saint Joan*, take note of all the titles he gives to her.

PRAYER

May our eyes
Be like clear-shining windows
Revealing the purity and sincerity
And fidelity of our souls.
Amen.

 *May 31*

ELIZABETH OF THE VISITATION

Cousin of the Virgin Mary, mother of John the Baptist • Israel • 1st century

SCRIPTURE THEME

Prophecy

"Blessed are you among women, and blessed is the fruit of your womb."
— Luke 1:42

QUOTATION

"The moment your greeting sounded in my ears, the baby leapt in my womb for joy."
—Elizabeth, Luke 1:44

THERE IS A CHURCH IN TIMAU (a remote village 120 miles north of Nairobi, Kenya, in East Africa) dedicated to Saint Elizabeth of the Visitation. A lovely mural depicts the village of Timau, with an African Elizabeth greeting an African Mary. The tabernacle rests in the wall between the two women, and rightly so, for Christ met John while both were in the wombs of their pregnant mothers.

The Gospel of Luke tells us Elizabeth lived with her husband, Zechariah, outside Jerusalem. Elizabeth offered hospitality to Mary and received from Mary the womanly concern and help women give to pregnant mothers.

At the birth of John, it was really Elizabeth who named him John. After the birth of John, the Gospels never again mention Zechariah or Elizabeth, but it is likely that the couple lived out their years at Ain

Karim watching John grow and leave home.

REFLECTIONS

- Prayerfully consider Elizabeth as she awaits the birth of her baby, and the joy she experiences when Mary arrives.
- Reflect on the husband-wife relationship of Zechariah and Elizabeth, and on their faithful observance of Jewish religion in awaiting the Savior.

PRAYER

In our visits,
May we always bring
The joy of Christ's presence
To each other.
Amen.

 *June 1*

SOJOURNER TRUTH

Abolitionist, reformer • U.S. • d. 1883

SCRIPTURE THEME

Truth

"Truthful lips endure forever,
  but a lying tongue lasts only a moment."

  — Proverbs 12:19

QUOTATION

"Where did your Christ come from? From God and a woman. Man had nothing to do with him. If the first woman God ever made was strong enough to turn the world upside down all alone, these women together ought to be able to turn it back and get it right-side up again. And now that they are asking to do it, the men better let 'em."

  — Sojourner Truth, Women of Faith and Spirit, *page 23*

ON JUNE 1, 1843, GUIDED BY VISIONARY VOICES, Isabella Van Wagener quit her job, took the name of Sojourner Truth and began preaching at revival meetings.

In the late 1790's, she was born a slave named Isabella and mothered at least eight children by a fellow slave, Thomas. In 1827, she fled to the Van Wagener farm. When she gained her freedom, she moved to New York with the surname of Van Wagener. From her childhood, she conversed easily with God.

After 1843 she talked and preached widely on abolition of slavery, suffrage for women, and Union causes. She worked to reform prostitutes. Her "Ain't I a Woman" speech made at a women's rights convention is worth quoting and remembering. In 1864, she was received by Abraham Lincoln and stood nearly as tall as he.

She retired in 1875 but still received visitors from all over the country. She died at about age eighty-five at Battle Creek, Michigan, on November 26, 1883.

REFLECTIONS

- Have you ever had to change your name? What did it mean to you? To others?

- Do you listen to your inner voice? Do you act on its suggestions?

PRAYER

Lord, you have many names
That reveal truths about you.
May the names by which we call each other
Reveal truth and beauty and goodness
As reflections of your presence in our midst.
Amen.

 *June 2*

MARTHA WASHINGTON

Original First Lady • U.S. • 1731–1802

SCRIPTURE THEME

Hospitality

"Contribute to the needs of the saints; extend hospitality to strangers."

— Romans 12:13

QUOTATION

"The greater part of our happiness or misery depends on our dispositions, and not on our circumstances. We carry the seeds of the one or the other with us in our minds wherever we go."

— *Martha Washington,* The Quotable Woman: From Eve to 1799, *page 251*

BORN ON JUNE 2, 1731, MARTHA WASHINGTON was the very first to become First Lady of the United States. Martha Washington was an aging grandmother when George Washington was inaugurated as first president of the new nation. Nearly sixty with snow-white hair, Martha may have preferred a quieter home life at Mount Vernon to sharing her husband with the whole country.

But share she did, and she was able to find some joy in it. She became friends with Abigail Adams, wife of the vice president. (Abigail wrote the now-famous "Remember the Ladies" letter.)

In the early days of her married life with George, Martha excelled at sewing, spinning, cooking and the supervision of her elegant household. As the plight of the American colonies worsened, Martha was one of the first to forsake tea and fancy English goods for coffee and homespun goods. She supported the patriot cause.

Eventually, Martha joined George in the war effort, helping to sew soldiers' clothing and caring for wounded in camp hospitals. She spent that bitter cold winter at Valley Forge when she likely longed for the blazing hearth of Mount Vernon. And Martha went with George to Philadelphia when the capital was moved there, and adapted to the social customs there.

After President Washington's farewell address, Martha rejoiced to return to old-fashioned housekeeping. George died in 1799. Before her death in 1802, Martha burned all the letters she had from George. She did not leave these to be shared with the country.

REFLECTIONS

- What qualities do you feel a First Lady must bring to her role? What do you do to make visitors (perhaps friends of your husband) feel comfortable in your home?
- When have you forsaken your personal comfort in support of a larger cause? Would you be willing to do it again?

PRAYER

To welcome guests with a heart of hospitality
Was the gift of Martha Washington
And Martha of Bethany.
Let us pray for the grace of hospitality
In our lives.
Amen.

June 3

GLADYS AYLWARD

Missionary · England and China · 1903–1970

SCRIPTURE THEME

Release from bondage

"He has sent me to proclaim release to the captives."

— *Luke 4:18*

QUOTATION

"Oh, God! Here's me, here's my Bible, here's my money, use us, God, use us."
— *Gladys Aylward*, Saints of the Twentieth Century, *page 7*

GLADYS WAS BORN IN LONDON ON JUNE 3, 1903. She left school at fourteen to work as a parlor maid, all the while longing to be a missionary. In 1930, with money she had saved, Gladys bought a train ticket to China. Once there, she joined an elderly Scottish missionary named Miss Dawson. Together they set up The Inn of the Sixth Happiness as a place for travelers. By learning the local dialect, Gladys won the respect of the local Chinese. The two missionary women taught the gospel to those who would listen.

Gladys was appointed official foot inspector of the area to help enforce the new law against foot binding. She became a Chinese citizen in 1931.

During World War II, Japanese soldiers invaded the province. Gladys was able to lead a hundred children on a long mountain march to safety. For months into years, Gladys lived as a fugitive, bringing medical help to one village after another.

She preached and lectured back in England in the late 1940's and early 1950's and then returned to Taiwan to assist refugees and orphans. Only five feet tall, Gladys was known as "The Small Woman" (*Ai Weh Teh*). Using this title, Alan Burgess wrote a book about her in 1957. Ingrid Bergman starred in the film *The Inn of the Sixth Happiness*, which helped make Gladys famous. Gladys died January 1, 1970.

REFLECTIONS

- In early June 1989, at Tiananmen Square, Chinese students seeking greater freedom were massacred. Do you have any memories of that event? Would you have had the courage to stand up to the soldiers as the students did?

- What do you know about the ancient custom of foot binding? What forms of disfigurement are acceptable in our culture? What is the difference?

PRAYER

May the religious fervor and missionary dedication
Shown us in the life of Gladys
Inspire our willingness to create inns of happiness
Wherever we live the gospel.
Amen.

June 4

SOONG CHING-LING

Chinese women's movement leader, political leader • China and U.S. • 1893–1981

SCRIPTURE THEME

Power

"For the kingdom of God depends not on talk but on power."
— 1 *Corinthians* 4:20

QUOTATION

"Let us exert every ounce of man's energy and everything produced by him to ensure that everywhere the common people of the world get their due from life. This is to say that our task does not end until every hovel has been rebuilt into a decent house, until the products of the earth are within easy reach of all, until the profits from the factories are returned in equal amount to the effort exerted, until the family can have complete medical care from the cradle to the grave."
— *Soong Ching-ling,* The Quotable Woman: 1800-1981, *page 247*

BORN MAY 29, 1893, IN SHANGHAI, Ching-ling was educated in China and at Wesleyan College for Women in the United States. She returned to China in 1913 and two years later married Sun Yat-sen, who, in 1921, became president of the Republic of China. He was ousted in 1922 by a Chinese warlord. When he died in 1925, Ching-ling chose to devote her life to the ideals they shared about creating a new China. In 1927, her sister Mei-ling married Chiang Kai-shek, leader of the Nationalist Party. Ching-ling, in opposition to these politics, moved to the U.S.S.R. for two years.

She kept her links with the Chinese Communist Party. During World War II, she set up the Chinese Defense League for aiding children and those in need of medical care. She was prominent in the Chinese women's movement and in international relations. In 1950, she was awarded the Stalin Peace Prize. Ching-ling was made honorary president of the Women's Federation of China in 1957. Her later years were lived in Shanghai. She was admitted to the Communist Party in 1981. She died that same year.

REFLECTIONS

- What are your political beliefs? How do you contribute to your local government?

- When have you disagreed with a friend or relative over political issues? How did you resolve your differences?

PRAYER

Sisters often differ from one another,
As did Ching-ling and Mei-ling,
As did Martha and Mary.
May we grow in our respect for
And dialogue with all of our sisters,
In families and faith communities,
In neighborhoods and in the global village.
Teach us wisdom, teach us love, O God,
In our public lives and in our private affairs.
Amen.

 *June 5*

SOONG MEI-LING

Activist for New Life Movement and Cultural Revolution · China · 1897—

SCRIPTURE THEME

Values

*"So teach us to count our days
   that we may gain a wise heart."*
— *Psalm 90:12*

QUOTATION

"When you pray, don't insult God's intelligence by asking Him to do something which would be unworthy of even you, a mortal."

—*Soong Mei-ling,* A Book of Days, *page 325*

MEI-LING, THE YOUNGEST SISTER OF CHING-LING, received her education from ages seven to sixteen in the United States. She married Chiang Kai-shek in 1927 and worked closely with him as his secretary and English interpreter as he became leader of the Nationalist Party. The two sisters differed as to political views. Ching-ling abandoned the Nationalist Party and left the country while Mei-ling became active in the New Life Movement of the 1930's, which advocated a return to Confucian values.

Mei-ling held some government positions and served as adviser to her husband as head of state. During World War II, she was a successful propagandist for the Nationalist cause. She toured the United States for this purpose in 1942–1943. When the Nationalists fled to Taiwan, she removed herself from public life. She took up residence in the United States after her husband's death in 1975. In 2001, she reached the age of 104.

REFLECTIONS

- What do you know about the political struggles in China? Do your feelings lean more toward empathy? Suspicion?
- What are you doing to promote peace and stability around the world? What can you do?

PRAYER

Differing windows of opportunity open
Even to sisters in the same family.
May we be graced with the ability
To transcend our differences
And the strength to be our sisters' keepers.
Amen.

June 6

MADELEINE ALBRIGHT

Secretary of State • Czechoslovakia and U.S. • 1936—

SCRIPTURE THEME

Ambassador of peace

"You have increased the nation, O LORD,
*   you have increased the nation; you are glorified."*

    — *Isaiah 26:15*

QUOTATION

"Force alone can be a blunt instrument, and there are many problems it cannot solve."

    — *Madeleine Albright,* The Quotable Woman, *page 611*

IN JANUARY 23, 1997, Madeleine Korbel Albright was sworn in as Secretary of State for the United States. She is the first woman to hold this high-ranking position.

Born in Prague, Czechoslovakia (now Czech Republic), in 1936, Madeleine grew up in the Catholic faith. Her father served as a diplomat in the homeland.

During World War II, her family fled from the Communist takeover and lived in western Europe. Madeleine learned four languages while living in five different countries. Later, the Korbel family came to the United States.

Madeleine graduated from Wellesley College and studied for her master's at Columbia University. She worked in government jobs and as a professor of international relations.

At the time of her marriage in 1959, she joined the Episcopal Church. She had three daughters, two of them twins.

From 1993 to 1997, she served as ambassador from the United States to the United Nations.

Madeleine places high priority on the values of democracy, respect for human rights and dignity. She goes about her diplomatic roles with charm, grace, confidence, humor and a certain toughness. When she made a round-the-world courtesy tour shortly after her swearing in, she also took time in the evenings to chat on the Internet with some elementary school students back in the United States.

She visited her homeland and came to know that she had Jewish roots and that her father's parents had died at the concentration camp at Auschwitz. In December 1997, Madeleine made an African tour in which she pleaded for concern for war-torn refugees.

Always, Madeleine gives first place to people, and her attention to women's issues across the globe has endeared her to many.

REFLECTIONS

- Have you learned later in life of some dark family secret? How did it affect you? What helped you integrate this new piece of information and the related emotions into your total life story?

- Have you learned the language of another country? Do you encourage children to do so? How about the customs, folklore and holidays of other cultures and countries?

PRAYER

For those who have endured great tragedy
And still had the courage to reach out

To others in need,
We pray that they may inspire us
To find our way out of the darkness
And embrace the light.
Amen.

June 7

ANNE OF ST. BARTHOLOMEW

Secretary to Saint Teresa • Spain • d. 1626

SCRIPTURE THEME

Companion, friend

*"Some friends play at friendship
  but a true friend sticks closer than one's nearest kin."*

— Proverbs 18:24

QUOTATION

"It is with straw that I light my fires."

— *the answer Anne received from the Lord when she pleaded her incompetence to lead others,*
Lives of the Saints, *page 205*

MANY GREAT WOMEN have had a beloved and trusted companion and assistant. Anne was such a person for Teresa of Avila. Anne was blessed with common sense and practicality and accompanied Teresa on several of her journeys. Anne wrote a vivid description of Teresa's last journey and her last days on earth. She was at Teresa's bedside when she died.

As a young child near Avila, Anne tended sheep. At age twenty, she entered the Carmelite convent at Avila and professed her vows as a lay sister rather than a choir sister. Lay sisters generally attended to practical things, such as food and guests. Choir sisters spent hours in spiritual reading, writing and singing of the Divine Office. Sometimes, lay sisters were uneducated and could neither read nor write, but this wasn't true of Anne. She simply preferred to remain a lay sister.

After Teresa's death, Anne was part of the company of Carmelites who founded a new convent in France. Anne was coerced into becoming a choir sister and served as prioress at Pontoise and then at Tours. A Carmel foundation in the Netherlands saw Anne on the move again. She served as prioress at the house in Antwerp.

While at Antwerp, Anne wrote instructions for her Carmelite sisters and also her own autobiography. When Antwerp was threatened by outside conquerors, it was Anne's prayers that saved the city. She was called the Liberator of Antwerp, and to this day, her memory is honored in that city.

Anne died on June 7, 1626. An estimated twenty thousand people came to file past her casket and pray. She was beatified in 1917.

REFLECTIONS

· Whom would you hope to have at your side when you die?

· Pray for those who are your best friends and closest companions.

PRAYER

As Anne and Teresa were companions and friends;
As Ruth and Naomi were companions and friends;
May we find in our friends the companionship we need;
May we give to our companions the friendship they need.
And, may we rejoice in companionships and friendships
Which nurture our minds and our spirits.
Amen.

June 8

BARBARA BUSH

First Lady • U.S. • 1925—

SCRIPTURE THEME

Charity

"She was devoted to good works and acts of charity."
— Acts 9:36

QUOTATION

"You have to love your children unselfishly. That's hard. But it's the only way."
— *Barbara Bush,* The Quotable Woman, *page 71*

WHEN BARBARA BECAME FIRST LADY, she changed the beauty salon room of the White House into a delivery room and nursery for Millie, her springer spaniel. Six puppies were born with Barbara serving as midwife. This serves as an image of the First Lady who wished to be down-to-earth rather than sophisticated, and who furthered the administration's appeal to family life with her aura as grandmother.

Barbara was born June 8, 1925, and married George Bush in 1945. She is mother of six children, one of whom died young. Two of her sons became governors, one eventually becoming president of the United States in 2001.

In her younger years, Barbara made a career of community service. As First Lady, she sought to better society as an advocate for improved literacy. She also encouraged others to assist at shelters for the homeless, at Head Start programs and at AIDS hospitals.

REFLECTIONS

- What do you expect first ladies to contribute to the nation's cultural and spiritual life?
- Have you helped someone learn to read? How would your life change if you could not read?

PRAYER

May we make windows of opportunity
For compassion and services in your name,
O God of mercy and caring love,
As we view the needs of our society
For literacy, homes, health care,
Education, and family values.
Amen.

June 9

GABRIELLE BOSSIS

Actress, playwright • *France* • *1874–1950*

SCRIPTURE THEME

Joy
"Make a joyful noise to the LORD, all the earth;
break forth into joyous song and sing praises."
— *Psalm 98:4*

QUOTATION

"In your soul there is a door that leads to the contemplation of God—but you must open it."

— *Gabrielle Bossis*, Revelations of Women Mystics, *page 159*

BORN IN FRANCE IN 1874, Gabrielle grew from a shy and fearful child to a joyous and sociable young woman into a well-known and successful actress and playwright. And all the while she maintained her professional career, she carried on a marvelous inner dialogue with her "darling God" as she called him.

Though her spiritual director urged her to join a convent, she was led by an interior guide to decide against this. She never married. With an amazing harmony, she continued in her theatrical vocation while thriving on a deep spiritual life.

While traveling to Canada in 1936, at age sixty-two, Gabrielle experienced a greater intensity of dialogue with her inner voice. What her "darling God" communicated to her, she wrote in a diary, *Lui et Moi (He and I)*. The first French edition sold out rapidly. A second edition with a preface by Daniel Rops expanded into seven volumes, including a biography of Gabrielle. An English version of two volumes was published in 1969.

Gabrielle lived a long, healthy life. In 1950, she suffered heart difficulties and died June 9, at age seventy-six.

REFLECTIONS

- Gabrielle lived with a joyful spontaneity and ease, enjoying many temporal goods. Her only renunciation seems to be that of marriage and motherhood. She was totally in love with her "darling God." What does this say to you about human pleasures?
- For Gabrielle, God was always near—behind a veil, a curtain; just beyond the door, the window. When do you feel close to God?

PRAYER

Teach us, please,
O God of Light,
To look for you
In the various windows
Of our busy lives.
Amen.

June 10

JUDY GARLAND
Actress • U.S. • 1922–1969

SCRIPTURE THEME

"O sing to the LORD a new song
for he has done marvelous things."
   — *Psalm 98:1*

QUOTATION

"We cast away priceless time in dreams,
Born of imagination, fed upon illusion,
and put to death by reality."
   — *Judy Garland,* The Quotable Woman: 1900–Present, *page 263*

BORN ON JUNE 10, 1922, in Wisconsin, Frances Gumm appeared in vaudeville and on the variety stage at an early age, touring with her two older sisters as the Gumm sisters.

She adopted the stage name of Judy Garland, and by age thirteen, she was appearing in MGM films. She partnered with Mickey Rooney in several films. Judy described her acting career in Anne Edwards's *Judy Garland* as one who felt exploited by the studio, kept awake with "pep-up pills" to perform for many hours, then given sleeping pills for a few short hours of sleep. As her career progressed, Judy became more involved with drugs and alcohol, all the while performing to large and appreciative audiences.

In 1939 she starred in *The Wizard of Oz*, for which she won an Academy Award, and from which she became forever associated with the song "Somewhere Over the Rainbow."

Judy performed as a star in films that included *Easter Parade* and *Meet Me in St. Louis*. Health problems, precipitated by her personal habits, led to the termination of her MGM contract in 1950. She then toured Europe and the United States as a popular singer. In the later 1950's and into the 1960's, she resumed some film work and a bit of television.

Her daughter, Liza Minnelli, was born in 1946 and has become a big star in her own right. Judy died on June 22, 1969.

REFLECTIONS

• Judy was born into a performing family, and the tradition is carried on with her daughter. Have careers been handed down in your family?

- If you are a mother, what do you most treasure about your daughter? Or, as a daughter, what do you most value about your mother?

- Listen to the lyrics of "Somewhere Over the Rainbow." What is its message for you? Do you have a favorite song that expresses your values?

PRAYER

Thank you, God, for rainbow dreams.
May you be the rainbow
Beyond the storms of life.
Amen.

June 11

JEANNETTE PICKERING RANKIN

Politician, pacifist · U.S. · 1880–1973

SCRIPTURE THEME

Peace
"And the land had rest from war."
  — *Joshua 11:23*

QUOTATION

"I want to stand by my country, but I cannot vote for war."
  — *Jeannette Rankin,* Notable American Women, *page 566*

JEANNETTE IS REMEMBERED as being the only member of Congress to vote against U.S. entry into both world wars. When she voted against entry in World War I in 1917, her career was marked by her choice. She believed in a global society of peace and became one of the finest representatives of a generation of female pacifists.

Jeannette was born June 11, 1880, in the Montana Territory. Her mother was a New England schoolteacher who had gone west. Her father was a rancher and lumber merchant. Frontier society offered women career opportunities, and all six Rankin sisters pursued professional ambitions. Montana granted the vote to women before the Nineteenth Amendment. This aided Jeannette in her political career. After college, Jeannette tried teaching, sewing and social work, but only when she became involved in the suffrage movement and its linkage to peace did she find some sense of fulfillment.

She campaigned as a Republican and won a seat in Congress as representative from Montana. Jeannette worked on legislation for women and children; she worked toward a federal suffrage amendment.

In 1919, Jeannette accompanied Jane Addams and Florence Kelley to the International Congress of Women in Zurich. This organization became the Women's International League for Peace and Freedom. In 1928, Jeannette founded the Georgia Peace Society, and in 1929, she became involved with the National Council for the Prevention of War. She ran again for Congress and won. On December 8, 1941, hers was the single vote cast against U.S. entry into the war. After her term as representative, Jeannette returned to Montana, where she took up ranching and caring for her elderly mother. She traveled abroad to study pacifist methods, especially those of Gandhi in India.

During the 1950's, she opposed the Cold War, including U.S. involvement in Korea. In the late 1960's, the Jeannette Rankin Brigade demonstrated against the Vietnam War. At the age of eighty-eight, she considered running again for Congress, but her health kept her from doing so. She died May 18, 1973.

REFLECTIONS

- Who were the pacifist voices you heard during the Persian Gulf War? During Vietnam? Was your own among the voices for peace?

- How do you promote the cause of peace? How do you promote peace in your own home and workplace?

PRAYER

People in every age have sought peace,
O God—in you,
And among the people who dwell on earth.
Grant us windows of peace in our times
And strengthen us to work for peace
By acting justly, loving tenderly and working humbly
With you and all your creatures.
Amen.

 *June 12*

ANNE FRANK

Diarist • Germany and Holland • 1929–1945

SCRIPTURE THEME

Optimism

"Now faith is the assurance of things hoped for, the conviction of things not seen."

— *Hebrews 11:1*

QUOTATION

"I don't think of all the misery, but of all the beauty that still remains."

— *Anne Frank,* The Quotable Woman, *page 144*

FOR ANNE FRANK, THERE WAS A WINDOW, a very small window, in the attic space above the warehouse where she lived in hiding for two years. And it was to that window that she took her diary to ponder and pray and write about the meaning of life.

Born June 12, 1929, in Germany, Anne and her family escaped to Amsterdam in 1933. When the Nazis occupied the Netherlands in 1941, the Jewish Frank family was at first persecuted, and then forced into hiding. They were found in 1944 because of an informer and sent to prison camps. Anne died of typhus at the Belsen camp in early March 1945, perhaps on March 2. The rest of the family also died, except for her father, who was in a hospital at the time Auschwitz was liberated. A family friend gave him all of Anne's writings. In 1947, an edited version of Anne's diary was published in German and translated in 1953 as the *Diary of a Young Girl.* The book became a symbol of what happened to Jews under the Nazi regime and was translated into thirty languages as well as adapted for stage and screen.

The Amsterdam house is preserved as a museum in memory of Anne and all young Jews who died. A statue of Anne stands near the house. Some observe March 2, the probable date of her death, as Anne Frank Day. Others, in the spirit of Anne's affirmation of life, celebrate her birthday.

REFLECTIONS

- Anne found reason to hope as she sat near her attic window. What windows offer you hope?

- When have you provided shelter to someone during a time of persecution? When have you been betrayed?

PRAYER

May the glimpses we have into the hearts of others
Inspire us, O God, to renewed faith
In the goodness of humanity
As your image and likeness.
Amen.

 *June 13*

DOROTHY SAYERS

Mystery novelist • England • 1893–1957

SCRIPTURE THEME

Mystery

"What is your life? For you are a mist that appears for a little while and then vanishes."

— *James 4:14*

QUOTATION

"Perhaps it is no wonder that the women were first at the Cradle and last at the Cross. They had never known a man like this Man—there never has been such another. A prophet and teacher who never nagged at them, never flattered or coaxed or patronized; who never made arch jokes about them, never treated them either as 'The women, God help us!' or 'The ladies, God bless them!'; who rebuked without querulousness and praised without condescension; who took their questions and arguments seriously; who never mapped out their sphere for them, never urged them to be feminine or jeered at them for being female; who had no axe to grind and no uneasy male dignity to defend; who took them as he found them and was completely unselfconscious. There is no act, no sermon, no parable in the whole Gospel that borrows its pungency from female perversity; nobody could guess from the words and deeds of Jesus that there was anything 'funny' about woman's nature."

— *Dorothy Sayers,* A Matter of Eternity, *pages 95–96*

DOROTHY WAS BORN JUNE 13, 1893, at Oxford, England, and became one of the first women to graduate from Oxford University. She worked at teaching and advertising before she turned to writing detective stories. These were very successful, especially because of the characters Lord Peter Wimsey and Harriet Vane.

Dorothy was mother to an illegitimate son, John Anthony, born January 3, 1924. The care of the child was delegated to a relative. In 1934, Dorothy "adopted" the child as her own.

She married Mac Fleming, an ex-army officer, in 1926, after his divorce was finalized. While he lived an alcoholic lifestyle with Dorothy's royalties, she remained loyal to him though unhappy. He died in 1950.

In the 1930's, Dorothy turned to specifically religious subjects. Her verse play and radio drama, *The Man Born to Be King*, was the *Godspell* of her day.

As part of the Oxford intellectuals, Dorothy was a leading voice of Christianity in the twentieth century. She recognized parallels in the roles of artist and theologian and promoted the communication of the gospel to ordinary readers as well as intellectuals.

Dorothy devoted time to the translation of Dante's *Inferno* and *Purgatorio* with commentaries, and also became involved in social work. She died in 1957.

REFLECTIONS

- How does your work communicate your religious beliefs? How are you persuaded by the writings of others to change something in your spiritual life?

- Read some of Dorothy's detective stories, such as *Whose Body?* and *Busman's Honeymoon*. How does her approach differ from that of other mystery writers?

PRAYER

Jesus, we are called to be your disciples,
And so we pray for a singleness of heart
And a hospitality of service
As we listen to your voice
And speak with our voices
In the rounds of our daily lives.
Amen.

 *June 14*

HARRIET BEECHER STOWE

Novelist, abolitionist • U.S. • 1811–1896

SCRIPTURE THEME

Inner life

"I pray that, according to the riches of his glory, he may grant that you may be strengthened in your inner being with power through his Spirit."
— *Ephesians 3:16*

QUOTATION

"If women want any rights they had better take them, and say nothing about it."
— *Harriet Beecher Stowe,* Words of Women, *page 18*

BORN ON JUNE 14, 1811, in Connecticut, Harriet was the daughter of a Calvinist minister. All five of her brothers became ministers. Harriet received a good education, and when she moved with her family to Ohio, she learned firsthand about the Underground Railroad.

She married Calvin Stowe in 1836 and moved to Maine with their seven children when he took a teaching position. Harriet wrote thirty books and many poems, short stories and magazine articles.

Inspired by a vision, *Uncle Tom's Cabin* became an international best-seller and greatly added to the growing national resistance to slavery. The book also had international impact, as it was translated into every European language. The book is said to have inspired Siamese and Russian slaveholders to free their slaves. Published in 1873, Harriet's book *Women in Sacred History* offers "a history of Womanhood under Divine Culture" in the thirty or so biblical biographies.

Harriet died in 1896.

REFLECTIONS

• Have you read *Uncle Tom's Cabin*? What effect did it have on you? How did it expand your understanding of slavery?

• What is the best way to influence public opinion about an issue? When have you tried to persuade people to see an issue your way?

PRAYER

Spirit of God,

We ask for the wisdom
To find goodness
In each and every person
And for the courage
To use our talents
To affirm that goodness.
Amen.

 *June 15*

GERMAINE OF PIBRAC

Devout shepherd · France · 16th century

SCRIPTURE THEME

Good Shepherd

"I am the good shepherd. I know my own and my own know me."
— John 10:14

QUOTATION

"Every individual is representative of the whole...and should be intimately understood, and this would give a far greater understanding of mass movements and sociology."
— *Anaïs Nin,* Sunbeams, *page 126*

A SHEPHERD IN LATE SIXTEENTH-CENTURY FRANCE, Germaine suffered many afflictions. She was born with a paralyzed right hand and suffered from scrofula, which is tuberculosis of the lymph glands. She was young when her mother died and mistreated by her stepmother. Her father never showed her any affection. Indeed, she was practically banished from the family home and ordered to tend sheep in the areas surrounding Toulouse.

Despite all this, or maybe because of it, she nurtured a wonderful inner life. She left her pastures to attend daily Mass, and the rosary was her constant companion. She gathered the local children for lessons on the basics of faith. She shared with the poor any stale bread doled out to her.

Her stepmother once accused her of stealing bread from home. When Germaine was ordered to show what lay hidden in her apron, a beautiful array of summer flowers appeared there.

Dead at twenty-two, Germaine's body was still not decayed fifty years later. During the year of exposition of her body, many miracles were reported.

REFLECTIONS

- Making the best of circumstances emerges as a theme in reflecting on Germaine's life. "When life gives you lemons, make lemonade" is one way to put it. When have you made the best of a difficult situation? How important is it to maintain a cheerful attitude in challenging circumstances?
- Bring to prayer an area of hardship in your life. How can you bring it to a beautiful and spiritual resolution?
- Think about the adage "Bloom where you are planted." How can you make a dark situation brighter?

PRAYER

We pray in the spirit of Germaine,
In the daisy, let us see,
That you, O God, are mystery.
Amen.

 *June 16*

JOYCE CAROL OATES

Writer, critic, teacher • U.S. • 1938—

SCRIPTURE THEME

Hometown

"I have inscribed you on the palms of my hands;
your walls are continually before me."

— *Isaiah 49:16*

QUOTATION

"I begin with the proposition that the impulse to create, like the impulse to destroy, is utterly mysterious. That it is, in fact, one of the primary mysteries of human existence. We can't hope to explain it but we can't, evidently, resist speculating about it."

— Joyce Carol Oates, in (Woman) Writer: Occasions and Opportunities, *page 3*

Born on June 16, 1938, Joyce Carol Oates grew up in an Irish-Catholic, working-class family in Lockport, north of Buffalo, New York. Joyce earned her bachelor's degree at Syracuse University and her master's degree in English from the University of Wisconsin.

Joyce began her writing career as a child, and during her college years, she wrote a novel each semester. After some time in doctoral studies at Rice University, she left the school to pursue writing as a full-time career. She made a name for herself with short stories and novels and continued with poetry and critical essays and, eventually, drama.

In 1960, she married Ray Smith, and together they founded the Ontario Review Press. Joyce taught English courses at the University of Detroit from 1961 to 1967, and after that at Windsor, Ontario.

Joyce continues to write as a prolific novelist and short story writer, with over sixty books to her credit. Using Gothic horror, realism and other creative forms of fiction, Joyce focuses her attention on how much of experience is beyond human control. Using violence, Joyce focuses on the struggle of her characters in the midst of circumstances beyond their control. Critics compare her gothic tales of dismal lives to those written by romantic and naturalist authors. Feminist consciousness runs through her fictional creations.

REFLECTIONS

- Have you read anything by Joyce Carol Oates? What was your reaction?

- Is there an outstanding female author in your area? Does she use local settings and customs in her works? How do local details make a story come alive for you? How do they change your experience of familiar places?

PRAYER

With grateful hearts, we praise you,
O God of our mother and father,
For our families and our hometowns—
The people with their gifts and values,
The settings, the folklore, the customs,
The special situations we treasure.
Amen.

June 17

BARBARA MCCLINTOCK

Geneticist, winner of Nobel Prize in Medicine • U.S. • 1902–1992

SCRIPTURE THEME

Solitary reaper, gleaner

"Let her glean even among the standing sheaves, and do not reproach her."
— *Ruth 2:15*

QUOTATION

"[She] invited me in, stating that it was time that I learned to do the things that girls should be doing. I stood there and looked at her. I didn't say anything, but I turned around and went directly home, and told my mother what had happened. My mother went directly to the telephone and told that woman, 'Don't ever do that again!'"
— *a childhood memory of Barbara McClintock,* The Triumph of Discovery, *page 71*

FOR BARBARA, THERE WAS A CERTAIN ONENESS IN ALL THINGS, and she lived by her mystical and intuitive sense of unity. She pursued Tibetan Buddhism and practiced a kind of global, nonlogical thinking that sometimes made communication with others confusing. Barbara also had a strong sense of solitude and deep dedication, single-mindedness and joy, which she brought to her scientific research. Born on June 17, 1902, Barbara, even as a child, was solitary and sensitive. She studied at Cornell University, where she got interested in genetics studies with corn. At the beginning of her postgraduate career, she discovered and identified maize chromosomes under the microscope, a major breakthrough. With Harriet Creighton, Barbara published their research findings in August 1941. Their work and paper became the cornerstone of experimental genetics. Cornell and the cornfields became Barbara's home.

She gave some time to the University of Missouri and to the Cold Spring Harbor genetics department. In 1944, Barbara was named to the National Academy of Science. The Genetics Society elected her as its first female president.

At Cold Spring Harbor, Barbara studied mutations in corn plants and developed a theory of "jumping genes," an idea ahead of its time. In the 1970's, the scientific community began to understand how right Barbara had been. In 1981, she was recognized with several awards and a fellowship. In 1983, she was awarded the Nobel Prize for Medicine.

In her late eighties, Barbara was still working, mostly alone, in her laboratory or her cornfield. She died in 1992.

REFLECTIONS

- Do you work better alone or with others? What sort of activities occupy your solitary time?

- Have you ever experienced conflict between intuitive thinking and logical thinking? To which are you more inclined?

- Barbara was once locked out of her laboratory and had forgotten her key. She managed to find an open window and in "unladylike" fashion climb in. A passing photographer captured her in the act. When have you had to circumvent doors that were locked to you?

PRAYER

In our moments of solitude, O God,
May we glean insights of wisdom
And reap fruits of prayerful presence.
Amen.

June 18

JEANNE MANCE

Nurse, cofounder of Montreal • France and Canada • 1606–1673

SCRIPTURE THEME

Medicine

"...[C]ure every disease and every sickness."
— *Matthew 10:1*

QUOTATION

"'Why,' a seventy-six-year-old woman was asked, 'are you seeking therapy at your age?' Reflecting on both her losses and her hopes, she answered, 'Doctor, all I've got left is my future.'"
— Judith Viorst, Sunbeams, *page 147*

IN MONTREAL, CANADA, there stands a bas-relief monument of Jeanne Mance dressing an American Indian boy. It was in 1643 that Jeanne made friends with Algonquin families and gave nursing care to their children.

Jeanne was born in France on November 12, 1606, to a family of the lower nobility. There were twelve children. Jeanne was always deeply religious but did not feel called to become a nun. She may well have heard tales about New France (Canada) as she grew up.

In her twenties and still not married, Jeanne felt that she had a mission in New France. A wealthy widow asked Jeanne to nurse the sick in a hospital in the new colony of Montreal. The ships sailed in June 1641. The group spent the first winter near Quebec.

Jeanne made friends with the hospital and school nuns already in New France and learned nursing skills from them. Also, one by one, she became godmother to forty godchildren, some French, some American Indian.

In May 1642, Jeanne was with the founding members of Montreal. She served as judge when disputes arose.

By October 1645, the hospital known as Hotel-Dieu of Montreal was built. In 1649, Jeanne visited France to solicit help for the hospital and the young colony. Back at Hotel-Dieu, Native American raids and massacres threatened the colonists' peace and safety.

In the winter of 1657–1658, Jeanne returned to France to secure hospital nuns. Typhus on the return trip nearly killed Jeanne.

Jeanne's part in the growth of Montreal is integral to the history of French Canadians. Jeanne's first biography was written by Marie Morin, who, as a young girl, came to Jeanne's home to do housework. Jeanne died June 18, 1673.

REFLECTIONS

- What role did women play in settling the frontier? What frontiers call to you?
- Are you a godmother? Who are your spiritual children?

PRAYER

Let us lift up in prayer
Those persons for whom
We are godmother
Or spiritual mother,
And those persons
Who are godmothers
Or spiritual mothers
For each of us.
Amen.

 *June 19*

ETHEL ROSENBERG

First American civilian executed for espionage • U.S. • 1915–1953

SCRIPTURE THEME

Liberty, freedom

"But those who look into the perfect law, the law of liberty, and persevere, being not hearers who forget but doers who act—they will be blessed in their doing."

— *James 1:25*

QUOTATION

"Always remember that we were innocent."

— *Ethel Rosenberg, in her last letter to her children before her execution,* Remember the Ladies, *page 113*

ON JUNE 19, 1953, ETHEL AND JULIUS ROSENBERG were executed as convicted spies at Sing Sing Prison at Ossining, New York. They were the first U.S. civilians to suffer execution for espionage, and the first to be so punished in peacetime.

The "death house letters" exchanged between the two before their execution and published for the public to read aroused much emotion and public protest. Nonetheless, the execution was carried out.

Ethel was sentenced for having typed some reports, outlining U.S. atomic research, sent to an alleged Soviet spy.

REFLECTIONS

- Does your state have the death penalty? How do you feel about this?
- What do you want your children or survivors to know about you before you die?

PRAYER

For all those sentenced to death, we pray,
That they may repent their crimes
And for those pronouncing death sentences,
That they are careful in their judgments
And find just ways
To deter crime.
Amen.

 *June 20*

LILLIAN HELLMAN

Dramatist • U.S. • 1905–1984

SCRIPTURE THEME

Conscience

"I have lived my life with a clear conscience before God."
— *Acts 23:1*

QUOTATION

"I cannot and will not cut my conscience to fit this year's fashions."
— *Lillian Hellman, in "Letter to the House Un-American Activities Committee," May 19, 1952, The Great Thoughts, page 179*

LILLIAN HELLMAN WAS BORN JUNE 20, 1905, in New Orleans and attended New York and Columbia Universities. She worked in a publishing house, reviewed books and served as a play reader. She is best remembered as a playwright.

By 1930, she was devoting much of her time to her own writing. *The Children's Hour,* which opened on Broadway in 1934 and ran for 691 performances, was her first great success. In 1939, *The Little Foxes* became her second. Both have been made into movies, as well as her later play, *Watch on the Rhine.* From 1935 on, she wrote directly for movies, both original pieces and adaptations. Some of her scripts included Anouilh's *The Lark.*

Later in life, she worked as an editor. She published in 1969 an autobiographical memoir called *An Unfinished Woman* and in 1976 a memoir of persons and politics called *Scoundrel Time.* In 1973, she published *Pentimento: A Book of Portraits,* also autobiographical. Lillian died June 3, 1984.

REFLECTIONS

- Consider the evolving career of Lillian. Has your own career changed over the years? By one thing leading to another? By conscious decision? Have you noticed the presence of God's Spirit in this?

- Do you think of yourself as a work in progress, an "unfinished woman"? What remains to be done?

PRAYER

We experience your presence, O God of the ages,
In all the stages of our lives and of our life's work.
We thank you for your guiding Spirit
And pray to follow where you lead us.
Amen.

 *June 21*

BENAZIR BHUTTO

Political leader, prime minister · Pakistan · 1953—

SCRIPTURE THEME

Daughter's rights

"...[Y]ou shall pass his inheritance on to his daughter."
— *Numbers 27:8*

QUOTATION

"People think I am weak because I am a woman. Do they know I am a Muslim woman and that Muslim women have a heritage to be proud of?"
— *Benazir Bhutto,* Benazir Bhutto, *page 62*

BENAZIR WAS BORN JUNE 21, 1953, in Pakistan to the wealthy Bhutto family. Before attending Radcliffe College in the United States and Oxford University in England, Benazir was educated at a private school in Pakistan run by Irish nuns. She was the first Bhutto woman to go to college.

In 1971, Zulfikar Al Bhutto, Benazir's father, became the new president of Pakistan. By 1977, when Benazir finished at Oxford, her father was prime minister in Pakistan. Benazir returned home hoping to enter foreign service. But her father was deposed in a military coup. Benazir and her mother were under house arrest and prison arrest several times. During his imprisonment Benazir's father both taught and inspired her with democratic ideals. The military regime executed him in 1979. Benazir movingly describes this ordeal in her autobiography, *Daughter of Destiny.* After her father's death, Benazir went to England for medical treatment.

After the end of martial law, Benazir returned to Pakistan and with her mother began to lead the Pakistan People's Party (PPP) founded by her father.

Benazir married Asif Zadari in December 1987 with an understanding that her devotion to political leadership would affect their marriage. Their first child, Bilawal, was born September 21, 1988.

When a free election was held in November 1988, Benazir was elected prime minister of Pakistan. At thirty-five, Benazir became the first female to lead a Muslim country in modern times and one of the youngest heads of state.

Benazir visited the United States in 1989 hoping to secure continued financial aid for Pakistan. Back home she was losing power and gaining critics. In January 1990, Benazir gave birth to her second child, Bakhtwaw, thus becoming the first modern leader to have a baby while in office.

In August 1990, Benazir was dismissed as prime minister of Pakistan with accusations of corruption. When the national elections were held in October 1990, Benazir was defeated. With the same vision of democracy that sustained her in her fight against the military dictatorship following her father's death, Benazir continued her efforts toward greater democracy for Pakistan.

REFLECTIONS

- As a young woman, Benazir observed the ancient Pakistani custom of wearing the burqa cloth, which hid all but her eyes. Her father permitted her to remove it. Who encouraged you to resist conformity?

- Benazir idolized her father, and he involved her in politics from an early age. What did you learn of politics from your parents?

PRAYER

For those who lead their countries
Through difficult political situations,
We beg your graces and blessings,
O God of justice and reconciliation.
Amen.

June 22

ANNE MORROW LINDBERGH
Writer • U.S. • 1906–2001

SCRIPTURE THEME

Seashore

"The voice of the LORD is over the waters."
— *Psalm 29:3*

QUOTATION

"It is not physical solitude that actually separates one from other men, not phys-ical isolation, but spiritual isolation. It is not the desert island nor the stony wilderness that cuts you off from the people you love. It is the wilderness of the mind, the desert wastes in the heart through which one wanders lost and a stranger. When one is a stranger to oneself then one is estranged from others, too."
— Anne Morrow Lindbergh, Sunbeams, *page 89*

IN *GIFT FROM THE SEA*, ANNE MORROW LINDBERGH reflects on women's struggles for identity. With seashore similes, Anne advises women to find times of solitude devoted to creativity, especially as a counterbal-ance to the many demands of marriage.

Anne was born June 22, 1906, into a family devoted to scholarship and books. She traveled in Europe with her parents and graduated from Smith College in 1928.

With her marriage to Charles A. Lindbergh in 1929, her private life changed into a very public one. Because of her husband's interests, she learned to fly planes and operate a radio.

The kidnapping and murder of their twenty-month-old son in 1932 brought a frenzy of public attention. In 1935, the Lindberghs moved to Europe. They returned to the U.S. in 1939.

Although a celebrity and a mother of a large family, Anne always devoted some time to her writing career. Her book of poems, *The Unicorn and Other Poems*, tells of the spiritual growth of a freedom-seeking person.

Volumes of Anne's letters and diaries reveal her determined spiritual independence. In all of her writing, Anne matches form to theme and uses several favorite images—seashells, birds, trees, mountains and sky.

REFLECTIONS

• Do you find places and spaces in your life for solitude and creativity?

- What thoughts does the ocean inspire in you?

PRAYER

Let us place in the windows of our minds
Some of our favorite images—
Seashells, trees, skies, mountains—
And see in each reminders of your presence,
O God and Source of all being.
Amen.

 *June 23*

SAINT AUDREY

Abbess • England • d. 679

SCRIPTURE THEME

Women's adornments

*"Can a girl forget her ornaments,
or a bride her attire?"*

— Jeremiah 2:32

QUOTATION

"It is difficult to see why lace should be so expensive; it is mostly holes."

— Mary Wilson Little, Beyond Bartlett, page 95

SAINT AUDREY (AETHYLRYTH, ETHELDREDA) was the Northumbrian queen and patron saint of Ely. Tradition has it that she died of a throat tumor, which she considered just punishment for her youthful liking for neck lace.

The word *tawdry* is short for Saint Audrey lace—neck lace bought at Saint Audrey's Fair in Ely, England. Tawdry has come to describe cheap and showy apparel.

Audrey was the most popular woman among the Anglo-Saxon saints for a very long time. She was the daughter of King Anna of East Anglia and sister to Saints Sexburga, Ethelburga and Withburga. Though she married twice, she remained a virgin.

After she entered the convent, she moved to Ely, where she was selected to serve as abbess of the double monastery. She lived a life of great holiness and simplicity.

Audrey died in 679. Her body remained incorrupt, and one of her hands is preserved in the church at Ely.

REFLECTIONS

- What sort of small vanities do you allow yourself? Why do they appeal to you?
- What is most delicate and fragile in your personality?

PRAYER

May we find joy
As the echo of your presence, O God,
In the simple pleasures of life—
Summer fairs and picnics,
Pretty things, and other good gifts.
Amen.

 *June 24*

SARAH ORNE JEWETT

Writer, mentor • U.S. • 1849–1909

SCRIPTURE THEME

Natural world

"They heard the sound of the LORD God walking in the garden at the time of the evening breeze."

— *Genesis 3:8*

QUOTATION

"A harbor, even if it is a little harbor, is a good thing, since adventures come into it as well as go out, and the life in it grows strong, because it takes something from the world and has something to give in return."

— *Sarah Orne Jewett*, Familiar Quotations, *page 816*

THE DAUGHTER OF A COUNTRY DOCTOR, Sarah received her education in literature and nature from her father as she accompanied him on his rounds. South Bewick, Maine, was Sarah's birthplace on September 3, 1849, her living place and her place of death on June 24, 1909. Sarah came to know intimately the people of southern Maine, which provided her with the details of her local-color writing.

Sarah's first novel, *A Country Doctor*, narrates a girl's early life, and is largely based on Sarah's own life. It is considered the most feminist of her works. Over the years, Sarah sustained several close female friendships; she never married.

A popular late-nineteeth-century card game called Authors carried Sarah's face as one of the very few women in the game. And this is how Willa Cather came to know of, and then to know, Sarah. Sarah offered Willa letters of advice; and Sarah's advice was sought by other young authors as well.

Willa highly praised Sarah's narrative of *The Country of the Pointed Firs*. The character sketches it contains hinge on the relationship and conversations of two New England women. One is the town herbalist, able to heal spiritual as well as physical ailments. This Mrs. Todd is also the focal point of communication and community in the little town on the seacoast of Maine.

Sarah wrote in the style of New England realism with an attention to personal point of view, celebrating the human effort to forestall spiritual destruction. The relationships of women to nature, to the community and to each other prevail throughout Sarah's writing. The realism of her time offered a way to express the existence of a matriarchal, marginal culture, which nourished strong, independent women. The short stories written by Sarah offer valuable themes in well-crafted prose.

REFLECTIONS

- How have you been shaped by the environment in which you were raised? In what ways do you rebel against it?
- Willa Cather and other young writers saw Sarah as a mentor. Who have been your mentors in your chosen field of interest?

PRAYER

We praise you, storytelling God,
For dear old houses,
And dear old women,
And dear old stories.
Amen.

June 25

MIRIAM AMANDA "MA" FERGUSON

Governor • U.S. • 1875–1961

SCRIPTURE THEME

Political leader

"He made him overseer of his house and put him in charge of all that he had."

— Genesis 39:4

QUOTATION

"The land is a mother that never dies."

— Maori saying, Sunbeams, *page 32*

MIRIAM AMANDA WALLACE WAS BORN IN TEXAS IN 1875 to a wealthy family. She attended a prep school away from home and a woman's college.

She met James E. Ferguson, a lawyer with real estate and banking interests, and married him in 1899. For the first fifteen years of their marriage, she tended the home and the children while he took care of business. When James ran for governor and won, Miriam became the First Lady of Texas. Governor Ferguson was reelected in 1916. In 1917, he was accused of illegal campaign funding and other financial abuses, impeached and permanently banned from holding public office in Texas.

After several political fights, James announced in 1924 that his wife would run for governor. Reporters shorted Miriam Amanda to "Ma," a nickname she hated, but it stuck. Ma was elected, and during her first term, she fought the Ku Klux Klan. She also removed the ban on her husband and made him streets commissioner. (The Texas Supreme Court later overturned Ma Ferguson's removal of the ban.)

Ma ran for reelection in 1926 and 1930 but was defeated. In 1932, she was reelected governor of Texas. She focused her attention on reduction of government spending during the early days of the Depression. She did not run in 1934 but ran successfully in 1940. Ma lived out her days as the "grand old lady" of Texas politics until her death at age eighty-six, on June 25, 1961.

REFLECTIONS

- The year 1992 was called "the year of women politicians" because many women came into their own. Do you have a favorite female politician? Which of her qualities do you most admire?

- What are your own political concerns, goals and dreams? How do you pursue them?

PRAYER

Forgive us, God,
When we attach nicknames
That are offensive or hateful to others.
Teach us, God, to listen and hear
What names others wish to hear.
Amen.

June 26

PEARL BUCK
Novelist • U.S. and China • 1892–1973

SCRIPTURE THEME

Solid foundation

"Everyone then who hears these words of mine and acts on them will be like a wise man who built his house on rock."

— *Matthew 7:24*

QUOTATION

"You cannot make yourself feel something you do not feel, but you can make yourself do right in spite of your feelings."

— *Pearl Buck,* A Book of Days, *page 102*

IN HER BOOK *THE BIG WAVE*, Pearl tells the story of two boys living in Japan, one in the highlands as a farmer and one near the sea as a fisherman. When the big wave destroys the fishing village and Jiva's family, he finds a home with Kino and his farm family. In due time, Jiva returns to the seashore and builds a new home. In the old home, there were no windows facing the sea. In the new home, Jiva builds a window facing the sea so he can see it. He shows his courage by being willing to see the risks of danger.

Pearl, born June 28, 1892, was the daughter of American missionaries who took her to live in China when she was an infant. She lived in China and absorbed its culture until turmoil there forced her to return to the United States in 1932. She raised nine Asian children as well as her own daughter.

Most of Pearl's writings attempt to explain China and other Asian countries to the Western world. *The Good Earth,* considered by many to be her best work, tells of Chinese peasants. It became a worldwide bestseller and won the 1931 Pulitzer Prize.

Pearl wrote biographies of her mother, *The Exile;* of her father, *Fighting Angel;* and of her mentally retarded daughter, *The Child Who Never Grew.* Pearl's writing was popular for its simple style, traditional values and universal themes. By 1972, she had published more than eighty-five books. When she died on March 6, 1973, she had twenty-five more ready for publication.

Pearl genuinely liked ordinary people and devoted her writings to their interests. She was awarded the Nobel Prize in 1938 for her portrayals of Chinese life and for great biographies.

REFLECTIONS

- What risks frighten you? Which do you tackle head-on?
- What experiences have opened new cultures to you?

PRAYER

May we walk gently
With our God
And one another
On this good earth.
Amen.

 *June 27*

HELEN KELLER

Deaf and blind campaigner • U.S. • 1880–1968

SCRIPTURE THEME

Vision

"Then the eyes of the blind shall be opened,
And the ears of the deaf unstopped."

— Isaiah 35:5

QUOTATION

"When indeed shall we learn that we are all related one to the other, that we are all members of one body? Until the spirit of love for our fellow men, regardless of race, color or creed, shall fill the world, making real in our lives and our deeds the actuality of human brotherhood—until the great mass of the people shall be filled with the sense of responsibility for each other's welfare, social justice can never be attained."

— *Helen Keller,* Wit and Wisdom of Famous American Women, *page 49*

BORN IN ALABAMA IN 1880, Helen became both blind and deaf from a disease, probably scarlet fever, before her second birthday. Until she was seven, she survived and behaved as an "untamed creature." When Anne Sullivan, who had been blind as a child, came to teach Helen, there was quite a struggle between teacher and student until Helen's mind grasped connections between life and language. With Anne's perseverance, Helen learned a manual alphabet and then Braille. She learned to read, write and speak, as well as ride and swim. Anne saw Helen through her college years at Radcliffe, where Helen became quite a scholar, and graduated *cum laude* in 1904. Helen published her first book, *The Story of My Life*, when she was twenty-three. But this was just the beginning.

Helen, with Anne, toured the country giving lectures in order to raise money for the American Foundation for the Blind. Helen developed a great consciousness for the value of each human spirit. She became a symbol of hope for persons with disabilities and differences as she championed various causes.

In 1936, Anne's death precipitated a crisis for Helen, which is described in her *Journal*, published in 1938. Helen wrote *Teacher: A Biography of Anne Sullivan Macy*, which was published in 1954. Polly Thompson served as Helen's secretary from 1914 to 1960, and as a close friend over those many years.

In 1955, Helen received an award from President Eisenhower's Commission on Employment of the Handicapped. In 1964, the Presidential Medal of Freedom was given to Helen along with four other women.

During Helen's lifetime, *The Miracle Worker* was performed on stage and in film. It is still viewed by television and video audiences. Memorable is the scene of water running over the child Helen's hands while her mind grasps the idea that "everything has a name."

After World War II, Helen toured Africa, Asia and Europe with her message of courage and hope for persons with disabilities. She died June 1, 1968, at age eighty-eight.

REFLECTIONS

- When did you first learn to read—to know that things had names? What lasting effect did this have on you?

- When have you helped another to read and learn new things?

PRAYER

May we look the world
Straight in the eye,
Straight in the face,
And see the face of God
And see God there,
Eye to eye.
Amen.

June 28

MOLLY PITCHER

Battlefield hero • U.S. • 1754–1832

SCRIPTURE THEME

Water

"Everyone who thirsts,
come to the waters."

— *Isaiah 55:1*

QUOTATION

"Your job is to help somebody."

— *Family motto of Sadie Delany,* The Quotable Woman, *page 330.*

MARY LUDWIG HAYS, WITH MANY OTHER SOLDIERS' WIVES, was with the American troops on June 28, 1778, at the Revolutionary War Battle of Monmouth. It was a very hot June day, and Mary kept up a supply of drinking water from her pitcher to the men. The soldiers called her "Molly Pitcher."

When her husband collapsed from the heat, Molly took his place at the gun and remained there until the battle was finished. For this heroism, she received a government pension in her later years.

Molly was born October 13, 1754, and grew up on a dairy farm in New Jersey. At fifteen, she was employed as a house servant to a doctor. She married John Hays who served in the Seventh Pennsylvania Regiment of the Revolutionary War. John died in 1789. Molly later married John McCauley.

Molly died January 22, 1832. In 1876, her grave was given a special marker. In 1916, a statue was erected in her memory.

REFLECTIONS

- How do you feel about the role of women in war? As soldier? As auxiliary service? As healer?

- Another Revolutionary heroine, Margaret Corbin, also took over the gun when her husband was killed. She was injured and disabled and received a lifetime solder's half-pay pension. When have you or someone you know taken on an unconventional role because of a husband? To whom have you given "a cup of cold water" in the name of Jesus?

PRAYER

Jesus, Living Water,
We pray to you,
May we respond with "Yes"
To each one who asks
For a drink.
May we give water, refreshment and rest
In your name.
Amen.

June 29

SAMANTHA SMITH

Ambassador of peace to U.S.S.R. • U.S. • 1972–1985

SCRIPTURE THEME

Peacemaker

"A harvest of righteousness is sown in peace for those who make peace."

— James 3:18

QUOTATION

"Why do you want to conquer the world, or at least our country?"
— *letter to Soviet leader,* Contemporary Newsmakers, *1985, page 99*

SAMANTHA, AT AGE ELEVEN, became internationally known as an ambassador of peace between the United States and the Soviet Union. When she was ten, Samantha wrote a letter to Soviet leader Yuri Andropov. In the letter, she expressed her fears of nuclear war, which she had heard discussed on television news. She also asked him why he would want to conquer any other country.

The following year, the Soviet newspaper *Pravda* ran part of Samantha's letter, and she then wrote a second letter requesting a reply. A 500-word telegram from the Soviet leader invited Samantha and her parents to visit the Soviet Union as his guests. The visit focused on Soviet schoolchildren—Samantha never got to see Andropov, who claimed a busy schedule. International news highlighted the visit, and Samantha became an instant celebrity with appearances on news telecasts and talk shows.

Born on June 29, 1972, Samantha's ordinary childhood and school years changed after her Soviet visit. She liked being in the public eye and at age twelve began to do television work with her father as her manager.

While returning home to Maine from England, where she had completed the filming for four episodes of the television series *Lime Street*, her airplane crashed. Samantha and her father, as well as some other passengers, were killed. That was August 25, 1985. Samantha had just turned thirteen.

REFLECTIONS

· Travel increases understanding of and respect for other cultures. In what ways have your travel experiences opened windows for you?

· How can children learn to be advocates and ambassadors for peace? What about adults?

PRAYER

As ambassadors for peace,
Let us turn to the Prince of Peace
For inspiration and courage.
Amen.

June 30

MOTHER MARY FRANCIS BACHMANN

Wife, mother, widow, religious founder • Bavaria and U.S. • 1824–1863

SCRIPTURE THEME

Widows

"The woman was left without her two sons and her husband."

— *Ruth 1:5*

QUOTATION

"She who stands in need of no one has many friends."

— *from the* Advice of Mother M. Francis *to her spiritual daughter (translated from the German)*

THE FOUNDERS OF MANY RELIGIOUS CONGREGATIONS, especially in the United States, were women who had married and raised a family, who became widowed, who felt called by God to give certain services to the poor or the sick, to children or the elderly.

This was just the case with Maria Anna Bachmann, born on November 14, 1824, immigrant wife of Anthony Bachmann from Bavaria, mother of four children and widowed at age twenty-seven by the sudden death of her husband. When her sister, Barbara Boll, moved in to help with the children, the two women were amazed to discover that they both felt drawn to religious life.

The two women attended daily Mass while sharing their little house on Apple Street in Philadelphia. They cared for the children and took in young working girls as boarders. In 1854, Anna Dorn, a young Franciscan tertiary, found her way to the Bachmann home and took up residence in her home. Anna became the third founding member of the community.

Meanwhile Bishop John Neumann had visited with Pope Pius IX during a trip to Rome. The pope, also a Third Order Franciscan, encouraged Bishop Neumann to found a community of Franciscan sisters in his Philadelphia Diocese.

The three women were clothed in the religious habit at a ceremony with Bishop Neumann presiding on April 9, 1855, as the founding sisters of the Congregation of the Sisters of Saint Francis of the Third Order Regular. Anna Bachmann became known as Mother Mary Francis and served as superior of the new community.

She also raised her four children. John served as a soldier in the Civil War and died at age seventeen. Aloysius became a priest for the Diocese of Buffalo. The two girls became sisters of Saint Francis—Cunigunda was known as Sister Mary Francis, and Johanna as Sister Mary Robertine, both in the Buffalo branch of the congregation.

The sisters began to care for the sick poor in their own homes and took on the task of teaching in the parish school. As more women joined the community, some were sent to establish missions in Syracuse, Utica and Buffalo.

In late 1862, Mother Francis visited the Buffalo foundation and remained until February 1863. Upon her return to Philadelphia, she faced the reality of tuberculosis. In June, she died and was buried in a plain pine coffin in her religious habit.

REFLECTIONS

- What contributions do widows make in your local faith community?
- Have you thought about a second career? What changes in your family circumstances contribute to this?

PRAYER

For all those women who were mothers
Of families and of religious communities,
We praise and thank you, Mother-God.
Amen.

July 1

PAULI MURRAY
Lawyer, Episcopal priest · U.S. · 1910–1985

SCRIPTURE THEME
Proud shoes, feet

"How graceful are your feet in sandals,
O queenly maiden!"
— Song of Solomon 7:1

QUOTATION
"Now I was empowered to minister the sacrament of One in whom there is no north or south, no black or white, no male or female—only the spirit of love and reconciliation drawing us all toward the goal of human wholeness."
— Pauli Murray, The Last Word, page 57

THE CONTRIBUTIONS TO SOCIETY MADE BY PAULI MURRAY are primarily service contributions. She served as lawyer and as Episcopal priest. And as a Black woman, she faced many challenges and sufferings.

Born November 20, 1910, Pauli was orphaned at age three and raised by an aunt in the home of her maternal grandparents. She graduated from Hunter College in New York but was denied admittance to the University of North Carolina because of her race. Under the guidance of Stephen Vincent Benét, Pauli wrote poetry and prose. He urged her on in the writing of an epic poem about Blacks in America and published it as "Dark Testament" in 1943.

Pauli graduated with honors from Howard University Law School in Washington, D.C., but was kept out of Harvard Law School because she was a woman. She obtained her master of arts from the University of California Law School and her doctorate from Yale. She took jobs as lecturer and lawyer, including some time at the Ghana School of Law in West Africa.

Involvement in social activism brought Pauli into contact with Eleanor Roosevelt. Pauli's activism in the course of rights for Blacks also got her jail sentences. Pauli felt called to and pursued church ministry. She studied and was ordained on January 8, 1977. Her first time to celebrate the Holy Eucharist as an Episcopal priest came on February 13, 1977, at the little chapel in North Carolina where her grandmother had been baptized.

In her autobiography, *Song in a Weary Throat*, Pauli tells of her growth in social and spiritual service. She described that Eucharist in the chapel of her grandmother's Baptism as having come full circle. Her earlier book, *Proud Shoes: The Story of an American Family*, tells the story of her ancestors. She speaks of their dignity as well as their degradation.

After her ordination, Pauli served in a parish in Baltimore with extended ministry to churches in Pittsburgh and Washington, D.C. She continued writing in areas of theology and social concern. She especially liked to challenge politicians and newspapers by letters on issues that mattered to her.

Pauli died July 1, 1985.

REFLECTIONS

- Pauli was Black, woman, lawyer, Episcopal priest—and each of these gave her joy and gave her pain. What key words describe you? What are your joys, your pains?

- Pauli preferred Black to Negro, and she liked the word Black to be capitalized. What are terms applied to your own ethnic background? What do you like or dislike about the words? How sensitive are you to terms preferred by others?

- Pauli saw the differences of culture, race, nationality, appearance and religion as windows of enrichment. Have you reduced any barriers to full acceptance of other human beings?

PRAYER

O Christ Jesus,
In you there is no north or south,
No east or west.
May we all be one in you
And united with each other.
Amen.

July 2

JEAN CRAIGHEAD GEORGE

Artist, writer, naturalist • U.S. • 1919—

SCRIPTURE THEME

Wilderness

"A voice cries out:
'In the wilderness prepare the way of the LORD,
make straight in the desert a highway for our God.'"

— *Isaiah 40:3*

QUOTATION

"Animals are such agreeable friends—they ask no questions, they pass no criticisms."

— *George Eliot*, The New Book of Christian Quotations, *page 11*

JEAN'S BOOK *JULIE OF THE WOLVES* WAS VOTED in 1973 as one of the ten best children's books of the last two hundred years. This story of an adolescent Eskimo girl tells the conflict of traditional ways and contemporary "civilization." The book won the 1973 Newbery Medal.

Jean was born July 2, 1919, in Washington, D.C., and worked as an artist, writer and naturalist. She usually lives with the wild animals she writes about and reports that over the years she has kept at least 170 wild animals.

Her characters are typically adolescents, sometimes girls and sometimes boys. Some of her popular books are *My Side of the Mountain, The Summer of the Falcon, Hook a Fish, Catch a Mountain, Who Really Killed Cock Robin?* and, of course, *Julie of the Wolves.* The young characters in these books, who want to be accepted as individuals, learn to achieve this by becoming capable outdoors people. They learn independence and self-reliance from the natural environment.

Jean's writing harmonizes the natural world with fiction, and the beautiful with grim natural realities. Animal lore and human growth are told with such detail that adults as well as young people enjoy reading Jean's books.

REFLECTIONS

• Is your prayer life sometimes nurtured by the mysteries of the natural world?

- What have been your experiences with animals? Tame animals? Wild ones?

- What do you do when you are terrified by the enormity of natural disasters?

PRAYER

May we see you, Creator God,
Through the windows of the natural world,
Your tranquillity, your beauty, your harmony.
And in the grim natural realities,
May your presence still offer us
A window of hope.
Amen.

July 3

FLORENCE ALLSHORN

Missionary · England and Uganda · 1887–1950

SCRIPTURE THEME

Christ in others

"On that day you will know that I am in my Father, and you in me, and I in you."

— *John 14:20*

QUOTATION

"I can't dislike people, I take Jesus Christ too seriously."

— *Florence Allshorn*, Saints of the Twentieth Century, *page 103*

FLORENCE WAS BORN IN 1887 AND GREW UP IN ENGLAND. She was active in her church and was appointed to the Sheffield Cathedral staff in 1918. In 1920, she was on a boat to Uganda headed for the mission at Inganga, fifty miles north of Lake Victoria. The woman in charge of the girls' boarding school had been through seven helpers already. No one could live with the matron for long. Florence was about to be the eighth to leave when she learned the key lesson of her life.

An old African woman spoke to Florence about Jesus as Savior, even of this difficult situation at the school. Florence made up her mind to love this cantankerous mission woman, and there was a great improvement.

Tuberculosis forced Florence to return to Europe for surgery and rest. In 1928, she began work at a college for women training as missionaries. Realizing the disillusionment many suffered after a few years in mission work, Florence set about establishing a place of refuge for returning missionaries.

In the mid-1940's, St. Julian's became a house of hospitality for missionaries and others. Florence served as head of the expanding group as they moved from house to farm to estate. And always, Florence nurtured the best in others by accepting them as they were and loving them into their better selves.

Florence died July 3, 1950.

REFLECTIONS

- Which people bring out the best in you? Which bring out the worst in you? How can you resolve to always be your best?

- Have you ever dreamed of being a missionary? What do you think would be most difficult about life and work in the mission fields? Most rewarding?

- Visit with a missionary to learn how home visits help to renew their strength and spirits.

PRAYER

May we take you, Jesus,
Seriously enough
To accept all persons
Even when they disappoint
Or displease us,
And love them as you do.
Amen.

July 4

INDEPENDENCE DAY

U.S. • 1776

SCRIPTURE THEME

Freedom

"For the yoke of their burden,
and the bar across their shoulders,
the rod of their oppressor,
you have broken as on the day of Midian."
— Isaiah 9:4

QUOTATION

"Give me your tired, your poor,
Your huddled masses yearning to breathe free,
The wretched refuse of your teeming shore,
Send these, the homeless, tempest-tossed to me;
I lift my lamp beside the golden door!"
— Emma Lazarus's words at the base of the Statue of Liberty

THE STATUE OF LIBERTY, sculpted by Frederic Auguste Bertholdi and presented to the people of the United States by the people of France, continues to welcome citizen, visitor and immigrant to the land of the free.

A bronze version of the Statue of Liberty was erected in 1876, on the hundredth anniversary of Independence Day, in New York City's Union Square, and still stands there. Cities and towns across the country have their own statues, large and small, in parks and on high buildings, all commemorating that July 4, 1776, Declaration of Independence.

In 1976, the bicentennial anniversary of U.S. independence was celebrated with gala events in the harbor waters around Miss Liberty. And as the years pass, this statue continues to represent for Americans and the world the spirit of liberty and freedom and justice.

REFLECTIONS

· Does your town or city have a Statue of Liberty?

· What does the Statue of Liberty mean to you? Does our nation still strive to uphold her promises?

• Watch for the use of the statue in art, advertising, replicas and entertainment. How is it used or misused? When do you find it trivialized?

PRAYER

We pray to you, Author of Liberty,
For peace as we work for justice,
For justice as we work for peace,
So that there may be
Liberty for all.
Amen.

 *July 5*

CATHERINE MUMFORD BOOTH

"Mother" of the Salvation Army • U.S. • 1829–1890

SCRIPTURE THEME

Women's care for those in need
"She opens her hand to the poor,
and reaches out her hands to the needy."
— *Proverbs 31:20*

QUOTATION

"When I became ninety I had been passed over as a speaker at a Salvation Army gathering, and this depressed me. So, to comfort myself, I said, 'Lord, help me to be reconciled to old age.' Well, the next day, the telephone rang and it was the BBC asking if they could interview me."
— *Catherine Booth,* Harper Religious and Inspirational Quotation Companion, *page 305*

BORN IN ENGLAND IN 1829 to an itinerant Methodist preacher and his wife, Catherine Mumford was a sickly child drawn to things religious. She read the Bible through several times before she turned thirteen. At sixteen, she had a religious experience of great happiness, which sustained a lasting courage.

At twenty-six, she married William Booth, a minister, and the two worked happily together preaching and praying among the poor. Catherine believed in women's active participation in the church, and she preached with great fervor.

In 1861, William Booth became an independent revivalist. This meant an itinerant life among the poor people of London's East End for both of them. Catherine, as team worker with her husband, nurtured this seed of the mission that became the Salvation Army. She designed the Salvation Army woman's uniform—a plain tunic and blouse plus a Quaker bonnet. Additionally, Catherine brought up her eight children with a sense of service to the church. Her seventh child, Evangeline, born December 25, 1865, the same year as the founding of the Salvation Army, later became the first and only woman to serve as general of the international Salvation Army (1924–1939). Daughters-in-law and other members of the extended Booth family joined in serving the poor, outcasts and prisoners. The Booth family spread its ministry worldwide. In 1888, Catherine learned that she had cancer. She preached her last message to fifty thousand people on the occasion of the Salvation Army's twenty-fifth anniversary.

Catherine died October 4, 1890, and fifty thousand people filed past her coffin. Some of Catherine's writings and books, especially *Female Ministry, Life and Death, Popular Christianity* and *Practical Religion*, are still being read, especially by Salvation Army women.

REFLECTIONS

- Catherine helped to define the role of women in the Salvation Army and to promote the use of women's gifts and talents. How is your local church doing in this regard?
- How do you (can you) affirm and encourage the contemporary service to the poor of your local Salvation Army?
- Pray for women you know whose human goodness and practical compassion bring hope to the poor.

PRAYER

May we see you, God,
Through the eyes of the poor
And in the eyes of the poor.
Amen.

 *July 6*

MARIA GORETTI

Child martyr · Italy · d. 1902

SCRIPTURE THEME

Forgiveness

"Love your enemies and pray for those who persecute you, so that you may be children of your Father in heaven."

— *Matthew 5:44*

QUOTATION

"Yes, for the love of Jesus I forgive him. May he be with me in Paradise, and may God forgive him because I have already done so."

— *Maria on her deathbed*, Mothers of the Saints, *page 215*

THE STORY OF MARIA'S LIFE is also the story of the teaching and example of her mother, Assunta. Assunta was born in Italy about 1866. She never learned to read or write. She married Luigi Goretti in 1886. Maria was the third of seven children. Always very poor, the family shared land and living space with the Serenelli family. Assunta taught her children to live for God, while the boys of the Serenelli family were allowed pornographic magazines. Maria was young when her father died of malaria. While Assunta and the other children did the field work, Maria often tended the baby and did the housework.

Alessandro Serenelli, eighteen, began to bother Maria when she was alone, trying to seduce her and threatening her if she ever told her mother. On July 5, 1902, while others were harvesting beans, Alessandro tried to rape twelve-year-old Maria. When she fought back, he stabbed her fourteen times. Maria was taken to the local hospital.

Before she died on July 6, she forgave her murderer. Alessandro's trial resulted in thirty years of hard labor, and for eight years he showed no sign of repentance. Gradually, he changed and repented for his sins. Some eighteen years after Maria's death, Alessandro came to Assunta and begged her forgiveness, which she granted.

Assunta lived to see her daughter canonized in 1950 and is the only mother ever to be present at her child's canonization.

REFLECTIONS

- The greatness of Assunta and Maria lies more in their compassion and their graced ability to offer forgiveness than in purity or anything else. Is there someone you need to forgive?

- How do you think young people best learn the values and virtues of purity and chastity?

- What sense of God and goodness do you attribute to your parents' way of bringing you up?

PRAYER

Strengthen us, O God of love,
To choose fidelity to you
In our moral and ethical choices,
And bless with your healing love
All victims of rape and pornography.
Amen.

July 7

MARGARET WALKER

Author · U.S. · 1915–1998

SCRIPTURE THEME

Jubilee

"They shall be released in the jubilee."
— *Leviticus 25:31*

QUOTATION

"Everything I have ever written or hoped to write is dedicated...to our hope of peace and dignity and freedom in the world, not just as black people, or as Negroes, but as free human beings in a world community."
— *Margaret Walker, The Quotable Woman: 1800–On, page 342*

IN 1966, MARGARET PUBLISHED *JUBILEE*, an epic novel that tells the story of Vyre in her passage to womanhood and her freedom from slavery. Biblical overtones in prose that is poetic and rhythmic convey deep spiritual convictions.

Margaret was born July 7, 1915, to middle-class parents, both of whom were university graduates. Margaret earned a bachelor's degree, a master's degree and a doctorate. She worked as a writer, editor and teacher. She married in 1943 and became the mother of four children.

As director of the Institute for the Study of History, Life, and Culture, Margaret organized Black culture writers' conferences. As young as twelve, Margaret was writing poetry. She received awards for *For My People*, which uses jazz rhythms and blues metrics, with clearly Black poetic substance and structure. In *How I Wrote Jubilee,* Margaret writes of the research into and inspiration of the life of her maternal great-grandmother, Vyre, the hero of *Jubilee*. Margaret died November 30, 1998.

REFLECTIONS

- What do you know of your grandparents and great-grandparents? How does your sense of heritage affect your day-to-day living?

- How have your favorite writers been influential in effecting freedom for others? Does this help you to appreciate their work more deeply?

PRAYER

In learning about
Our foremothers and forefathers,
May we come to a gratitude
For the values of faith and freedom
They have given us.
Amen.

July 8

KATHE KOLLWITZ

Artist • Germany • 1867–1945

SCRIPTURE THEME

Mother

*"He gives the barren woman a home,
    making her the joyous mother of children."*

— *Psalm 113:9*

QUOTATION

"Strength is: to take life as it is and, unbroken by life—without complaining,

and overmuch weeping—to do one's work powerfully."
— *Kathe Kollwitz*, The Diary and Letters of Kathe Kollwitz, *page 78*

THE VISUAL IMAGES MADE BY KATHE present women in one of three stances: protecting of life with her arms, embracing or reaching out, or strengthening herself by placing her hands on her head or over her eyes.

Further, Kathe's central concern is with the maternal woman. Women's arms and bodies are used to protect, surround and shelter children, and in distilling the essence, Kathe affirms the relationship and values of life given, nurtured, defended and mourned when lost.

Kathe, born July 8, 1867, lived as mother and as artist in Germany during World War I. The destruction of her artworks and the death of her son on the Belgian front caused her enormous suffering.

Her strong love resulted in the powerful cultural image of maternal figures who evidence vulnerability and confidence in an active choice to care for children. The contemporary crisis over the abortion issue calls for cultural expressions in visual, theater and literary arts of life affirmed, protected and fortified. Kathe did this in her lithographs, sculptures and woodcuts. As a creative woman, she invites others to see and value the human capacity for enduring life's sorrows and to resist the obliteration of life.

Kathe's life and art asserts and affirms faith in mothers protecting, embracing and fortifying the young life. Kathe managed to be mother and artist.

REFLECTIONS

- Try to see Kathe's visual art in art books—especially *Seed Corn Must Not Be Ground, Mother Group, Woman Thinking, Tower of Mothers,* her *Pieta,* and *Mary and Elizabeth.*

- How do you protect, embrace and fortify life in the creative or domestic arts you engage in?

- Do you try to balance a creative art with another job, as well as family or community responsibilities? How does it go for you?

PRAYER

Direct our hearts and hands,
O Source of all life,
To the affirmation, protection, and fortification of life,
Especially the lives of children.
Amen.

 *July 9*

ROSE HAWTHORNE LATHROP

Caregiver for cancer patients • U.S. • 1851–1926

SCRIPTURE THEME

Lepers

"I do choose. Be made clean!"

— *Mark 1:40*

QUOTATION

"I will see all things only through the presence of God, thus freeing myself of personality and forgetting my existence. I will regard creatures in the spirit of Jesus Christ."

— *Rose Lathrop*, Modern Saints: Their Lives and Faces, *page 285*

ROSE HAWTHORNE WAS BORN ON MAY 3, 1851. She was the third child of Sophia and Nathaniel Hawthorne, the famous writer. From her parents, Rose learned kindness and compassion. Brought up as a Unitarian, Rose had a close encounter with Catholicism while still quite young. One day, while walking in the Vatican gardens with her family on a trip to Rome, she literally bumped into Pope Pius IX. He patted her head and blessed her. Rose always treasured that moment.

Rose's father died when she was thirteen, and her mother died before Rose was twenty. Rose married George Lathrop in 1871. Their only child died at four of diphtheria.

George and Rose studied the Catholic religion and were baptized in 1891, twenty years into their marriage. George had a long-term drinking problem, and by 1893, the couple separated. George died in 1898. Rose felt called to care for destitute cancer patients, and she chose to live in the tenements of the lower East Side of New York City. Here, Rose wrote numerous newspaper articles telling of the needs of the cancerous poor. When Alice Huber came to join her in direct care of the poor with cancer, the two women decided to choose some form of religious life. They became Dominican tertiaries and wore the Dominican habit.

Rose became Sister Mary Alphonsa, and Alice became Sister Mary Rose. After much prayer, they were able to buy a building for their cancer patients. Mother Alphonsa believed in keeping patients happy and sometimes bought even luxury items for them—like a parrot, or a dog, or a radio. One of her dreams, a new fireproof building, was begun before her death in July of 1926.

Bishop Walsh of Maryknoll preached at her funeral. The Dominican Servants of Relief, founded by Rose Hawthorne Lathrop, continue to work among poor cancer patients in several dioceses in the United States.

REFLECTIONS

- Call to mind what literature you may have read by Rose's father, Nathaniel Hawthorne. How would exposure to such an imagination empower her in her empathy for the suffering? When have you felt especially close to someone in need?

- How do small kindnesses and little luxuries ease the pain of illness or loss? Is there someone for whom you can provide this relief?

PRAYER

Through the intercession of Rose,
We pray that we may be generous
In service to those
Who suffer from cancer
And other terminal illnesses,
And we pray that
When we are afflicted ourselves,
We may accept the suffering
With hope in Jesus.
Amen.

 *July 10*

EVA LAVALLIERE

Actress, mission nurse • France • 1866–1929

SCRIPTURE THEME

Orphan

"In you the orphan finds mercy."

— Hosea 14:1

QUOTATIONS

"I thank you, O my God, that You have given me shelter beneath Your roof. Abandonment, love, trust—such is my motto."

— Sister Eva Lavalliere, Modern Saints: Their Lives and Faces, *page 391*

EUGENIE WAS BORN ON THE MEDITERRANEAN COAST of France in 1866. Her brother was the favored child, and Eugenie felt unloved. She spent some years at a Catholic boarding school. She always remembered her First Communion as a day of rare peace.

At eighteen, Eugenie witnessed the murder of her mother by her father and his suicide. Eventually, she met and joined a theatrical troupe, and her stage life as Eva Lavalliere began. She became internationally famous for her comedy and wit, her vitality and enigmatic manner. She had several lovers and bore one daughter, Jeanne. None of this made Eva happy, and she contemplated suicide several times.

While vacationing with her companion, Leona, Eva had conversations with the parish priest. A book he gave her, *The Life of Mary Magdalene*, changed Eva's life forever. In June 1917, Eva returned to the sacraments. She wanted to join a Carmelite convent, but none would take her. She called herself "Earth's eternal orphan." Eva settled in a small house with Leona. She joined the Third Order Secular of Saint Francis and took the name Sister Eva Marie of the Sacred Heart of Jesus. The sisters had a daily schedule of prayer, good works, almsgiving, spiritual reading and meditation. Though her health was frail, Eva spent several months each year as a mission nurse in North Africa, nursing Arab children in French Tunisia.

As a sign of her new life, Eva decided to give up all cosmetics and hair coloring. She kept notebooks of her spiritual reflections. In 1928, Eva became seriously ill. Leona took care of her. Eva's daughter, Jeanne, showed up "to help," but actually had in mind to make her mother addicted to cocaine so she could then make money from selling it to her mother. The doctor caught on and ordered Jeanne out. Eva, however, was addicted by then and needed the drug until her death.

Eva's last days were very painful, but she had a certain peace in all her sufferings. She died in 1929, on July 10, of peritonitis.

REFLECTIONS

- When has reading a book dramatically changed your life? Do you revisit the book to reaffirm those changes?
- Do you write your spiritual reflections in a journal or notebook? How do you measure your spiritual growth?

PRAYER

> May those who are orphans
> Or feel orphaned by life's circumstances
> Find in God a loving parent—
> A mother and father,
> And may they find in human companions
> Friendship and love and care,
> And a sense of family.
> Amen.

 *July 11*

SAINT OLGA

Wife, mother, grandmother, ruler · Russia · 10th century

SCRIPTURE THEME

Generations

> *"For the Lord is good;*
> *his steadfast love endures forever,*
> *and his faithfulness to all generations."*
> — *Psalm 100:5*

QUOTATION

"Every day is a messenger of God."
> — *Russian proverb,* The New Book of Christian Quotations, *page 56*

THE RUSSIAN NATION WAS CONVERTED TO CHRISTIANITY during the reign of Vladimir, king and saint, but this was foreshadowed by the Baptism of Saint Olga, King Vladimir's grandmother. In 913, Prince Igor married Olga, a woman of lowly birth. She became regent when he was assassinated in 945. Olga ruled until 955 when her son Svyastoslav took over.

In her seventies, Olga went to Constantinople and was baptized as Helen. Returning to Russia, she tried to spread the Christian faith. Missionaries came from Trier (Germany) under the leadership of Saint Adalbert. Vladimir gained the throne in 987 and was baptized. His faith became by rule the official faith of the Russian people.

REFLECTIONS

- Do you have memories of some aspect of your faith learned from or shared with a grandparent?
- Find out the stories of your grandparents or great-grandparents—their religion and church. What religious customs and traditions have remained in the family?
- Russian nesting dolls are a symbol of eternal life, showing how life goes on from generation to generation. In your experience, how is faith handed down from generation to generation?

PRAYER

May we rest and nest in you, O God,
As a child on its mother's lap,
As a bird in its nest.
And may we be blessed
From generation to generation
With generous mother love.
Amen.

July 12

GERTRUDE BELL

Traveler, negotiator · England · 1868–1926

SCRIPTURE THEME

Travel to new places

"Go from your country and your kindred and your father's house to the land that I will show you."

— *Genesis 12:1*

QUOTATION

"The world of adventure and of enterprise, dark with hurrying storms, glittering in raw sunlight, an unanswered question and unanswerable doubt hidden in the fold of every hill. Into it you must go alone...roofless, defenseless, without possessions. The voice of the wind shall be heard instead of the persuasive voices of counselors, the touch of the rain and the prick of the frost shall be spurs sharper than praise or blame."

— *Gertrude Bell*, Gertrude Bell, *page 31*

GERTRUDE WAS BORN TO A PROSPEROUS MIDDLE-CLASS FAMILY on July 14, 1868. Two years later, when her mother died in childbirth, Gertrude took special interest in the baby, Maurice. Later, with a stepmother and more children, Gertrude was torn between conformity and liberal behavior. Gertrude attended Queen's College and Lady Margaret Hall, Oxford, with history as her specialty. In 1892, Gertrude visited the Middle East, where her uncle was ambassador to Tehran. She also took desert journeys, engaged in Alpine mountain climbing and round-the-world Cook's tours. By 1907, her interest and travel centered on Asia Minor.

She worked in Asia Minor with archaeologist Sir William Ramsay and wrote her findings for archaeology journals. She also translated Persian poetry into English.

In 1913, she became involved in military intelligence and worked as such in Cairo during World War I. In 1916, she took up work as secretary to Sir Percy Cox in Basra. In 1917, Gertrude made her home in Baghdad and helped negotiate the dismantling of the British mandate in Iraq. She supported Faisal in his claim to the throne.

Gertrude was conservative on women's issues and was a founding member of the Anti-Suffrage League.

On rare occasions, she visited England, but Baghdad remained her home. On July 12, 1926, she died of a drug overdose, just two days short of her fifty-eighth birthday. She is buried in Iraq.

REFLECTIONS

- What traveling have you been able to do? How did your experiences change your understanding of other people and yourself?
- Have you sometimes loved the distant, the unknown, the foreign, the mysterious? What, for you, is the attraction?

PRAYER

In all our travels, O God,
May we notice your presence—
In the adventure and culture,
In the places and peoples—
And praise you always.
Amen.

July 13

BARBARA JORDAN

Politician, lawyer • *U.S.* • *1936–1996*

SCRIPTURE THEME

Hard work

"We must work the works of him who sent me while it is day."

— John 9:4

QUOTATION

"I never intended to become a run-of-the-mill person."

— *Barbara Jordan*, Newsweek, *November 4, 1974*

ON JULY 13, 1992, BARBARA JORDAN GAVE THE KEYNOTE SPEECH at the Democratic National Convention. Here's how she got that far.

Born in Houston on February 21, 1936, Barbara grew up in a Baptist minister's family. She studied hard and received a good education. She also loved music and learned to play the guitar. When she was in tenth grade, Barbara heard Edith Spurlock Sampson, a lawyer from Chicago, give a speech. Barbara decided to become a lawyer and went to Texas Southern University where debating became her favorite activity. She liked to hear other viewpoints and learned to speak her own views clearly.

Barbara went to study law at the University of Boston and enjoyed more freedom than in segregated Houston. She returned to Texas to start up her law practice and work for desegregation and civil rights in her home state.

In 1960, the Democratic vice presidential candidate was Lyndon Baines Johnson. He and Barbara became friends by working together on political activities. In 1962 and 1964, Barbara ran for the Texas state senate but lost. In 1966 she won, and, in 1967 she was sworn in. She gained respect and admiration as the first Black state senator since 1883. In 1972, Barbara was elected president pro tempore of the senate. On June 10, 1972, she was governor for one day.

In 1972, Barbara was elected to the U.S. House of Representatives, the first Black woman from a southern state to serve in Congress. She became a member of the Congressional Black Caucus, and she served on the House Judiciary Committee. Barbara gained national recognition and received several awards and special assignments. In 1978, she retired from public life and took up teaching as a public service profession. She gave lectures and wrote a book about her life.

REFLECTIONS

- Some have considered Barbara Jordan as an excellent candidate for a Cabinet member, an ambassador, a Supreme Court justice or even president of the United States. How do you feel about a woman in these positions?
- Barbara was brought up to believe that she could accomplish nearly everything by hard work and brain power. How do you feel about hard work in achieving your goals?
- What does "women's work" mean to you? To society? Do these definitions fit what women's work actually is?

PRAYER

O God,
Grant success to the work
Of our hearts
And heads
And hands.
Amen.

July 14

KATERI TEKAKWITHA

Mohawk convert to Christianity · U.S. and Canada · d. 1680

SCRIPTURE THEME

Path

"Happy is everyone who fears the LORD
who walks in his ways."

— *Psalm 128:1*

QUOTATION

"The Navajo and Pueblo Indian tribes who danced the rituals...as partners in the cosmic process, attuned me to the universally primal—rather than to either the 'primitive' or the 'civilized.'"

— *Barbara Morgan,* The Quotable Woman: 1800–On, *page 274*

KATERI IS THE FIRST NATIVE AMERICAN TO BE CALLED BLESSED by the Catholic Church. She was born near Auriesville in what is now New York State, of a Mohawk father and a Christianized Algonquin mother.

When Kateri was four, a smallpox epidemic killed her parents and her brothers. Her uncle, an anti-Christian Mohawk chief, became responsible for Kateri. Jesuit missionaries from France, and perhaps contact with Christianized American Indians, influenced Kateri, and she was baptized on Easter Sunday, April 18, 1676, with the name Katherine (Kateri in Mohawk).

Hostility and persecution from her own tribe members followed, and she fled to a mission near Montreal where she received her First Communion on Christmas Day of 1677.

Her spirituality and asceticism impressed all who knew her. She took a private vow of virginity in 1679, very unusual for a Mohawk woman who would depend completely on a husband for support. She died April 17, 1680, at the Montreal mission.

Native American and French alike treasured her memory. In 1932, the formal cause for her beatification was presented. In 1943, she was recognized as one with heroic virtue, and in 1980, three hundred years after her death, she was beatified by Pope John Paul II.

REFLECTIONS

- What are your feelings about women who must depend upon the support of a husband? What effect, if any, does this factor have upon the marital relationship?

- Do you practice any form of asceticism? Are there some ascetic practices that appeal to you?

PRAYER

May each of us radiate
The beauty of the inner goodness
And enable others to find
The secret of true beauty
In the Trinity-God
Who dwells in our hearts.
Amen.

 *July 15*

MARY WHITE OVINGTON
Civil rights activist • U.S. • 1865–1951

SCRIPTURE THEME
Rights

"I am about to die; of what use is a birthright to me?"
— Genesis 25:32

QUOTATION

"A right which goes unrecognized by anybody is not worth very much."
— *Simone Weil,* The Beacon Book of Quotations by Women, *page 276*

MARY WAS ONE OF THE VERY FEW WHITE PERSONS belonging to the National Association for the Advancement of Colored People (NAACP). Indeed, she was one of the founding members of 1909, when the goals of the NAACP were considered far-fetched by both Blacks and Whites.

Born April 11, 1865, in New York City, to an upper-middle-class family, Mary studied at Lacker Collegiate Institute and Radcliffe College. Forced to leave school when family finances suffered reverses, Mary put her reform interests to work as a social worker at Greenpoint Settlement. Inspired by a speech of Booker T. Washington on racial discrimination, Mary took a job at Greenwich Settlement House, and began a study of how Blacks lived in New York City. Looking for ways to effect positive changes in society, Mary joined the Socialist party. In 1911, her book *Half a Man: The Status of the Negro in New York* was published. Mary worked as an officer and a major policy maker in NAACP. She remained active in the organization for more than forty years. She served as mediator of disputes. She promoted suffrage for Black women and pressed for school desegregation.

During the 1920's, Mary wrote book reviews affirming the artists of the Harlem Renaissance. She wrote books on the NAACP and on Black leaders. She also wrote novels. In 1947, Mary retired from the NAACP. After several years of ill health, she died July 15, 1951, at the age of eighty-six.

REFLECTIONS

• What cross-cultural, cross-racial experiences have you had? How have these shaped your views on social issues?

- How have you and your family been affected by desegregation? Does more desegregation need to happen in your local schools, workplace or community?

PRAYER

Bless all those, O God,
Who think and work
For justice and peace
Across the lines of race.
Amen.

July 16

MARIE MADELEINE POSTEL

Educator • France • d. 1846

SCRIPTURE THEME

Courage
"Take heart, son; your sins are forgiven."
— *Matthew 9:2*

QUOTATION

"I want to teach the young and inspire them with the love of God and a liking for work. I want to help the poor and relieve some of their misery."
— *Marie Madeleine Postel*, Lives of the Saints, *page 255*

BORN IN FRANCE, JULIE POSTEL GREW UP a bright and determined woman. When she was eighteen, she set up a school for poor children. After the French Revolution, she saw great need for sacramental preparation for children and for works of mercy.

The idea of forming a congregation grew in her mind, and in 1807, she and three companions made the vows of religion. Julie became known as Marie Madeleine. The four women instructed two hundred girls.

The community began to grow and so did the educational program. Sister Marie Madeleine was considered an educational pioneer in her ideas, methods and curriculum. She died in 1846, at the age of ninety, with her community at 150 members. In 1908, Pope Pius X beatified her and in 1925, Pope Pius XI canonized her.

REFLECTIONS

- Call to mind any women religious you may have had in school or met at a parish or hospital or wherever. What energy, courage and originality did they possess?

- How does your view of work improve when you think of it as God's work?

PRAYER

Grant us courage, O God,
To meet the challenges of our times,
To perform the works of mercy
For those in need.
Amen.

July 17

OPENING OF WOMEN'S RIGHTS NATIONAL HISTORIC PARK AND NATIONAL WOMEN'S HALL OF FAME

Seneca Falls, New York • 1968

SCRIPTURE THEME

Remembering

"My child, do not forget my teaching,
but let your heart keep my commandments."

— *Proverbs 3:1*

QUOTATION

"The history of mankind is a history of repeated injuries and usurpation on the part of man toward woman, having in direct object the establishment of absolute tyranny over her. He has created a false public sentiment by giving to the world a different code of morals for men and women, by which moral delinquencies which exclude women from society, are not only tolerated, but deemed of little account in men. He has endeavored, in every way that he could, to destroy her

*confidence in her powers, to lessen her self-respect, and to make her willing to
lead a dependent and abject life."*

— *from the* Declaration of Sentiments, The Great Thoughts, *page 457*

TUCKED AWAY IN A ROW OF STORES in the Historic District of Seneca Falls,
New York, the National (U.S.) Women's Hall of Fame is housed in the
building formerly used as the Seneca Falls Savings Bank, which was constructed in 1916.

Area residents of Seneca Falls founded the Hall of Fame in 1968 with
no physical home. The first twenty members were inducted in 1973 and
included Susan B. Anthony, Marian Anderson, Margaret Chase Smith
and Elizabeth Cady Stanton. A major fund-raising event secured the
building, and new members were added to the permanent exhibit.

Large panels with photographs and biographical information celebrate
and honor the accomplishments of women by areas of achievement—art,
science, humanitarianism, education, athletics and government. There
are both historic and contemporary honorees, and a national committee
selects new members. Also in Seneca Falls, the Women's Rights National
Historic Park includes Elizabeth Cady Stanton's home, and the former
Wesleyan Chapel. And in nearby Waterloo, the park includes the homes
of Jane Hunt and Mary Ann McClintock. The Ladies of Seneca Falls met
in each other's homes to discuss and formulate ideas that led to their
Declaration of Sentiments.

REFLECTIONS

- Who are your heroines? Which women do you place in your own personal hall of fame?

- How have men's attitudes toward women changed during your lifetime? How much change is yet needed?

PRAYER

We want to honor in perpetuity
All those women
Whose contributions are of value
To our lives and our countries.
May God bless our efforts.
Amen.

July 18

JANE AUSTEN
Novelist · England · 1775–1817

SCRIPTURE THEME

Books

*"Have I not written for you thirty sayings
of admonition and knowledge,
to show you what is right and true."*

— *Proverbs 22:20-21*

QUOTATION

"What did she say? Just what she ought, of course. A lady always does."

—*Jane Austen,* The Quotable Woman: From Eve to 1799, *page 362*

SOME RANK JANE RIGHT UP THERE WITH SHAKESPEARE as one of England's two greatest writers. But since Jane never signed her name to her own works, no one had any sense of her greatness during her lifetime. Jane was born December 16, 1775; she was the seventh of eight children in a family in which the father was a church rector. Her education included languages and literature, as well as needlework and music. She began to write in her early years.

Pride and Prejudice was completed by the time she was twenty-one, though not published for another fifteen years. During her twenties and thirties and very early forties, she wrote all her novels. They were published anonymously, and, though good reviews appeared in the *Quarterly*, Jane received no praise and very little money for her published novels.

Jane never married, and to some extent remained on the margin of society for lack of money. Yet she was a keen observer of life in her limited situation. Her portrayal of the joys and sorrows of manners and morals in rural England offers a sense of female values and imposed limits. This was both her art and her life.

Jane became seriously ill early in 1817 and died July 18. She was not quite forty-two years old.

REFLECTIONS

- If you have a great love of reading and learning, to whose example and encouragement do you attribute it?

- As you read Jane's novels, notice how she accommodates women's dreams and hopes to the existing social structures. Do you find that contemporary women think or write this way?
- Jane gives her characters intellect, feeling and moral sense. How well do women fare in these respects in other novels you read?

PRAYER

When we find ourselves
In isolation on the fringes,
May we remember your presence,
Dear God,
And turn to you in prayer.
Amen.

July 19

ROSALYN YALOW

Medical researcher, Nobel Prize winner • U.S. • 1921—

SCRIPTURE THEME

Healing

"He laid his hands on a few sick people and cured them."
— *Mark 6:5*

QUOTATION

"We cannot expect in the immediate future that all women who seek it will achieve full equality of opportunity. But if women are to start moving towards that goal, we must believe ourselves or no one else will believe in us; we must match our aspirations with the competence, courage and determination to succeed."
— *Rosalyn Yalow,* And Then She Said..., *page 9*

ROSALYN SUSSMAN WAS BORN JULY 19, 1921, in the South Bronx. Her mother, Clara, was from a German immigrant family; her father of Ukrainian immigrant parents. Ros, as she was called, taught herself to read before she entered kindergarten. She used the public library and enjoyed movies, roller skating and baseball games at Yankee Stadium. During her school years, Ros helped her mother with the sewing she took in. An excellent student, Ros especially liked math, and eventually chemistry and logic. She entered Hunter College at age fifteen. Reading a biography of Marie Curie further inspired Ros to concentrate in physics. Finding a graduate school was difficult, but the University of Illinois at Urbana accepted her. She met Aaron Yalow on the first day of school. They married in June 1943 and set up a kosher home.

In 1946, Ros returned to Hunter College to teach physics but had her heart set on physics research. When she accepted a job in hospital radiotherapy service, she became immersed in biomedical investigation. She learned medicine from Solomon Berson, a new resident at the hospital, and they became research partners for twenty-two years.

The Yalows had two children; both parents helped with the children, and both parents kept their careers. The research of Ros and Sol led to the discovery of RIA (radio-immuno-assay) in 1956. RIA uses immunologic methods and radioactive tools to measure substances. One of the applications related to insulin.

In 1972, Sol Berson died of a heart attack. With a new work partner, Ros published more than sixty papers and received several medical awards, including the 1976 Albert Lasker Prize. In 1977, Ros received half the Nobel Prize in Medicine.

In 1978, Ros declined the *Ladies' Home Journal* Woman of the Year Award because she wanted to see women and men on equal footing. She had struggled and searched in her college years, her marriage and her professional career for that equality and did not wish her achievement to be called remarkable for a woman.

By the 1990's, Aaron had retired from teaching and Ros was becoming involved in public affairs.

REFLECTIONS

- Reflect on the joys and hardships of a husband and wife, each with their own careers. How are the challenges of a dual-career couple different from those of others?

- Ros was scolded by some for working while her children were young. What is your view of mothers who must work outside the home? How does society view them?

- How do you feel about programs and awards geared specifically toward women? Do they hamper the cause of equality or promote it?

PRAYER

> With gratitude, we pray,
> For those who work in research
> For medical techniques
> That benefit humankind.
> Amen.

 *July 20*

JUDY COHEN CHICAGO

Artist • U.S. • 1939—

SCRIPTURE THEME

Song of Songs

*"You have ravished my heart, my sister, my bride.
You have ravished my heart with a glance of your eyes."*

— *Song of Solomon 3:9*

QUOTATIONS

"Then we began to make choices based on three criteria: (1) Did the woman make a significant contribution to society? (2) Did she attempt to improve conditions for women? (3) Did her life illuminate an aspect of women's experience or provide a model for the future?"

— *Judy Cohen Chicago,* The Dinner Party, *page 98*

BORN IN CHICAGO, JUDY COHEN did her college work at the University of California at Los Angeles from 1960 to 1964. In 1961, she married Jerry Gerowitz. He died two years later. Judy devoted her time to teaching art until 1969. Judy married Lloyd Hamrol in 1969 and continued teaching in California and Wyoming.

The feminist art movement interested her, and she helped found the Feminist Studio Workshop in Los Angeles. In the late 1970's, Judy devoted herself to overseeing the creation and display of *The Dinner Party*. Though some of Judy's artwork shocks in its boldness, *The Dinner Party* contributes to understanding woman's history. It consists of a large triangular table, set with thirty-nine ceramic dinner plates and embroidered place mats, each of which symbolizes someone important in the history of women. The floor under the table is inscribed with 999 names of women of achievement.

Two books describe this joint project: *The Dinner Party: A Symbol of Our Heritage* focuses on the 999 and more women, each by name with a short write-up, and on the 39, by illustrations of the dinner plates; *The Dinner Party: Embroidering Our Heritage* concentrates on the place mats or runners. The compendium of women's lives reads as a history of women from goddesses to contemporary artists and authors.

REFLECTIONS

- How do you deal with people whose opinions are radically different from your own? Do you block them out entirely, or do you try to find something of value in their perspectives?
- Judy considers Georgia O'Keefe, Louise Nevelson, Emily Carr and Barbara Hepworth among the greatest influences on her art career. Who has influenced your career or personal life? How does it help to know that other women have shared your struggles and succeeded?

PRAYER

By seeing the strength of other women,
May we come to know ourselves
And our capabilities.
May all women come to your table,
O nourisher and provider,
And know that there they are remembered.
Amen.

 *July 21*

FRANCES PARKINSON KEYES

Novelist · U.S. · 1885–1970

SCRIPTURE THEME

Religion

"For every house is built by someone, but the builder of all things is God."
— *Hebrews 3:4*

QUOTATION

"Well, it's a good thing to trust in Providence. But I believe the Almighty likes

a little cooperation now and again."
— Frances Parkinson Keyes, The Last Word, *page 57*

FRANCES WAS BORN JULY 21, 1885. Her formal education was in Boston, Switzerland and Berlin. She read a great deal. Married in 1904, she had three children. Frances began writing and publishing after her marriage because of critical financial need. She became the author of several saints' lives, including *Bernadette of Lourdes* and *Mother Cabrini*. She also has a long list of novels to her credit.

In her fiction, Frances creates heroines who are young and naive, beautiful and in love with older men. Some have personal careers, but most choose marriage. Her fictional women accept hardship well and are loyal and competent persons, and generally find fulfillment in motherhood.

Frances found religion important and often describes religious practices in her novels. In 1940, she completed *Along a Little Way*, which tells of her gradual conversion to Catholicism.

Her husband, Henry Wilder Keyes, served three terms in the U.S. Senate, and Frances shared her thoughts in a monthly column, "Letters From a Senator's Wife," for fourteen years. She also did some travel writing.

This rather prolific if somewhat sentimental author challenges her readers to transcend provincialism and to take a wide-angle look at the world. She is listed in *Catholic Authors: 1930–1947*.

REFLECTIONS

- Many authors are autobiographical in their writing, even if subconsciously. Is this a case of life informing art or the reverse?
- Think of someone with whom you generally disagree. What is that person's reading taste? How might this contribute to the differences in your views?

PRAYER

We are grateful for religion—
Its truths and its heroes—
For giving us picture-window views
Of life at its best.
Amen.

 *July 22*

MARY MAGDALENE

Follower of Jesus • Israel • 1st century

SCRIPTURE THEME

Mary Magdalene

"Mary stood weeping outside the tomb."

— *John 20:11*

QUOTATION

"I have seen the Lord."

— *Mary Magdalene, John 20:18*

SCRIPTURE SCHOLARS GENERALLY AGREE that Mary Magdalene is a person in her own right and not to be confused or identified with Mary of Bethany or the unnamed sinful woman in Luke 7:36-50.

Mary Magdalene, or Mary of Magdala, was healed by Jesus in the "casting out of seven devils," which may be a first-century Palestinian expression for serious illness. Mary was one of the women who followed Jesus about and helped to provide for him and the twelve apostles.

Mary stood at the foot of the cross, assisted in the burial, arrived at the empty tomb and first beheld the risen Christ, carrying news of his resurrection to the apostles.

REFLECTIONS

- Prayerfully read John 20:1-2, 11-18.
- What do you do when people disbelieve your faith and your witness to the goodness of God and resurrection of Jesus?

PRAYER

May we see you,
Lord Jesus,
In the resurrection
Of each new day.
Amen.

July 23

SUSANNAH WESLEY

"Mother of Methodism" • *England* • *c. 1669–1742*

SCRIPTURE THEME

Faithfulness

"Him alone you shall worship; to him you shall hold fast, and by his name you shall swear."

— *Deuteronomy 10:20*

QUOTATION

"Get as deep an impression on your mind as is possible of the constant presence of the Great and Holy God. He is about our beds and about our paths and spies out all our ways."

— *Susannah Wesley,* People Whose Faith Got Them Into Trouble, *page 84*

BORN IN ENGLAND IN 1669 OR 1670, Susannah was the twenty-fifth child of a nonconformist clergyman at odds with the officially established Anglican religion. The question of whether to conform or not affected all of Susannah's life. At thirteen, she chose to join the established church, believing that God's will required obedience to the law of the land.

At nineteen, she married Samuel Wesley and influenced him to worship with the established church. Samuel became an Anglican clergyman. Susannah and Samuel had nineteen children in twenty-one years, but ten of them died as babies.

Samuel was imprisoned over religious dissent to the 1662 Act of Uniformity, which required complete assent to everything in the Anglican *Book of Common Prayer*, and Susannah was left to provide for the children. The same enemies who imprisoned her husband also slashed her cows and burned her garden, but Susannah was steadfast in prayer and she survived.

Susannah kept her appointed times for prayer. Her children knew they needed to be quiet whenever she flung her long white apron over her head for a few moments of prayer, and at certain hours, Susannah went to the quiet of her room for prayer. Considering her home and children as her place of ministry, Susannah taught her children in a household school six hours a day.

She made a practice of giving each child one full hour alone with her individual attention each week. In her adult faith development, Susannah began to lean more toward the nonconformity of her childhood and struggled with questions about the authority of God and personal conscience. She and Samuel had strong differences of opinion about religious matters, but a very faithful love.

In 1709, their home caught fire and all escaped except six-year-old John. He stood in the frame of a window afraid to jump. A neighbor, standing on Samuel's shoulders, was able to reach John just as the roof collapsed. John lived to become the founder of Methodism. Another of Susannah's sons, Charles, wrote over a thousand hymns, including "Christ the Lord Is Risen Today" and "Hark the Herald Angels Sing."

John and Charles went as missionaries to the American Indians in the colony of Georgia but returned to England when the mission failed. When Samuel died, Susannah stayed in touch with her several children. When John and Charles began preaching in nonconformist ways, Susannah supported them and sometimes, literally, stood right beside them.

Her last days were spent at the old factory building that John used as Methodist headquarters. She died there on July 23, 1742.

REFLECTIONS

- Susannah may be remembered as the mother of John Wesley and wife of Samuel Wesley, but she is a woman of faith in her own right. Reflect on the importance she gave to prayer, to education of children, to an honest search for truth. How important are these ideas in your life?

- One of Susannah's house rules was that no girl was taught to sew until she could read. Reflect on this approach to the gift of intelligence in girls.

PRAYER

O great and holy God,
Become impressed so deeply
Upon our minds and hearts
That we are mindful of your presence
In our waking and in our sleeping.
Amen.

 *July 24*

AMELIA EARHART

Aviator • U.S. • 1898–1937

SCRIPTURE THEME

Wings

"He came swiftly upon the wings of the wind."

— *Psalm 18:10*

QUOTATION

"Courage is the price that life exacts for granting peace.
The soul that knows it not, knows no release
From little things,
Knows not the livid loneliness of fear
Nor mountain heights where bitter joy can hear
The sound of wings."

— The Harper Religious and Inspirational Quotation Companion, *page 115*

BORN JULY 24, 1898, IN KANSAS, Amelia Mary was named after her two grandmothers. Amelia's mother had been adventurous; she had ridden circus horses, and she had climbed to the top of Pike's Peak, the first woman to do so. Amelia's father was a lawyer and judge.

Amelia worked as a nurse during World War I and trained further at Columbia University medical school. During these years, she also trained as a pilot.

In 1928, Amelia became famous as the first woman to fly across the Atlantic; she was passenger and log keeper. On May 20–21, 1932, she flew a solo flight across the Atlantic. Amelia, married to George Putnam, the publisher, lectured on the promotion of economic opportunities for women, including the aircraft industry.

Amelia continued to fly, setting many records and becoming active in many aviation organizations. In 1937, she set out with Fred Noonan on a round-the-world flight. Their plane disappeared mysteriously near Howland Island in the Pacific. Her death is given as July 2, 1937. Though many speculations have been made, the mysterious disappearance has never been explained. Letters from Amelia to her mother and sister were found years later in an attic. Their publication reveals the more private life of the famous and adventurous aviator.

REFLECTIONS

- As children, Amelia and her sister Muriel experimented with motion and speed—in a homemade roller coaster, for example. What childhood interests led to your career or serious hobbies?

- How have you been emboldened by the courage of women who are your friends or family members?

PRAYER

Gather us under your great wings,
O God of the skies,
So that our journeys and homecomings
May receive your protection.
Amen.

July 25

MADALEVA WOLFF

Poet, nun, educator • U.S. • 1887–1964

SCRIPTURE THEME

Education

*"Keep hold of instruction; do not let go;
guard her, for she is your life."*
— *Proverbs 4:13*

QUOTATION

"I like to go to Marshall Field's in Chicago just to see how many things there are in the world that I do not want."

— *Mother Mary Madaleva*, Simpson's Contemporary Quotations, *page 191*

IN THE 1940'S, SISTER MADALEVA'S INTEREST in the education of women in the religious life and the religious education of all women led to the first Catholic graduate program in theology for women at St. Mary's College, Notre Dame, Indiana. In the 1950's, Madaleva's leadership and vision led to the Sister Formation Conference and better education and training of young women for religious ministry.

Born May 24, 1887, Mary Evaline, nicknamed Eva, had a happy childhood in a small Wisconsin lumber town. Her family valued education, and it was always assumed that the children would go to college. Eva attended the University of Wisconsin at Madison and then transferred to St. Mary's College at Notre Dame. A friendship made there with Sister Rita Hefferman, as Eva studied literature with this teacher, led Eva to the novitiate of the Holy Cross sisters. She made permanent vows in the community and was assigned to teach at St. Mary's College.

With the religious name of Sister Madaleva, Eva completed a master's degree in English, and later a doctorate. She became a noteworthy poet and did some other writing. She served as a college president for over thirty years.

Madaleva's writing tended toward love, serenity, beauty and tranquillity, not horror, terror or despair. All of her poetry reflects this. Madaleva also wrote her autobiography called *My First Seventy Years*.

In 1961, Sister Madaleva retired. She died on July 23, 1964.

REFLECTIONS

- Reflect on your own experience of higher education. Was it essential to the goals you have achieved? Would further education be a wise choice for you?

- How have you encouraged other women to expand their potential through higher education?

PRAYER

May we find in the wonder windows
Of our everyday lives
Moments of tranquillity and beauty
That speak of the very presence of God.
Amen.

July 26

SAINT ANNE

Mother of Mary, grandmother of Jesus • *Israel* • *1st century*

SCRIPTURE THEME

Providence

"I do not want what is yours but you; for children ought not to lay up for their

parents, but parents for their children."

— 2 Corinthians 12:14

QUOTATION

"This is adoration: not a difficult religious exercise, but an attitude of the soul."

> — *Evelyn Underhill,* The Harper Religious and Inspirational Quotation Companion, *page 20.*

SAINT ANNE, NOT MENTIONED IN SCRIPTURE, comes to us via tradition. One source says that she, like her husband, Joachim, was of the tribe of Judah; they both lived saintly lives and had great herds. The Church of St. Anne in Jerusalem was built on the space where it is believed that Anne and Joachim made their home.

Saint Anne was very popular in the East with at least three feasts among the Greeks. The crusades brought devotion to her back to Europe. Saint Anne is greatly honored in Brittany, France, where people claim she appeared from 1623 to 1625. There is a major shrine there dedicated to Saint Anne d'Auray.

In the Americas, Saint Anne is honored by a great shrine church called Saint Anne de Beaupre on the St. Lawrence River above Quebec City. In 1658, a small shrine was planned for the site. When Louise Guimont, unable to walk, was miraculously cured, devotion to Saint Anne grew. Later a large basilica was built there. Among the main attractions are an eight-foot statue of Saint Anne, made of oak, and a major relic of Saint Anne—her forearm.

In Brittany, a pilgrimage is held each year on July 25 to the place where it is believed Saint Anne appeared to a poor man named Yvon. The women of Brittany wear special embroidered costumes as they walk in the candlelight and torchlight procession toward the church built at the site of the appearances. The pilgrims stay for two days remembering and celebrating the appearance of Saint Anne on French soil in the seventeenth century.

There is an old French saying: "Dead or alive, every Breton must go to Saint Anne's church at Auray." The devotion to Saint Anne d'Auray spread throughout Europe and to the New World, especially to Saint Anne de Beaupre in Quebec, Canada.

REFLECTIONS

- How important are grandparents in the life of a child? What role, if any, did yours play? How would your grandmother have lived had she been born in your generation? Do your choices differ? Why?

- If you are, or might become, a grandmother, how do you see your role?

PRAYER

Show us, O God of vision,
How to find in our grandmothers
Special windows onto all our ancestors—
Their lives and values and visions.
Amen.

 *July 27*

GERTRUDE STEIN

Writer • U.S. and Europe • 1874–1946

SCRIPTURE THEME

Fame, identity

"You are the light of the world…. Let your light shine before others."
— *Matthew 5:14, 16*

QUOTATION

"Considering how dangerous everything is nothing is really very frightening."
— *Gertrude Stein,* And Then She Said, *page 21*

BY THE TIME SHE WAS SIX, Gertrude had lived in Pennsylvania, Vienna, Paris, Maryland and California. She was one of five children. By the time Gertrude was seventeen, both of her parents had died.

Gertrude loved to read and pursued college, where she was guided into philosophy and psychology by William James. She experimented with automatic writing, a use of associative and generally abstract patterning of narrative, akin to stream-of-consciousness writing.

After a trip to Europe, she pursued medical studies at Johns Hopkins for two years. Then she abandoned it and moved to Paris where she lived for thirty-four years. There, she became a connoisseur of art and developed her literary style in a "stream of consciousness writing using the free association of ideas and words." She became world famous for her recognition of emerging talent.

Saturday evenings at the Stein apartment attracted artists and writers from all over the world. Gertrude had a genius for interpersonal relationships and human interchange. During World War I, she learned to drive and helped deliver supplies to hospitals. *The Autobiography of Alice B. Toklas*, which Gertrude collaborated in writing with Alice, was published in 1933 and became a best-seller. It also brought Gertrude invitations to lecture in the United States, and she enjoyed being a celebrity. Gertrude returned to Paris, where she was a leader in the expatriate world. In 1946, she became ill with cancer and died on July 27.

REFLECTIONS

- Have you tried to read stream-of-consciousness writing? What sort of insights can it provide?
- How do art and literature nurture your soul, your spiritual well-being?
- Do you have a special friend/confidant? How has this friend opened windows onto the world to you?

PRAYER

May we find in art and literature,
O Eternal Word and Wisdom,
Images which strengthen our faith in you.
Amen.

July 28

BEATRIX POTTER

Children's book author, illustrator · *England* · *1866–1943*

SCRIPTURE THEME

Children

"Whoever welcomes one such child in my name welcomes me."
— *Matthew 18:5*

QUOTATION

"Once upon a time there were four little Rabbits, and their names were—Flopsy, Mopsy, Cottontail, and Peter."
— Beatrix Potter, The Quotable Woman: 1800–1981, *page 124*

BEATRIX WAS BORN JULY 6, 1866, in London and lived a rather isolated childhood in a large mansion. She loved small animals and had some as pets. Beatrix developed a keen sense of observation, which she put to good use in her watercolor drawings.

She began telling animal tales to amuse sick children, and this is how Peter Rabbit, Jemima Puddleduck, Jeremy Fisher, Tom Kitten and other lovable characters came to be.

At forty, Beatrix purchased and moved to Hill Top Farm and in the next eight years created thirteen new books for children with her writing and illustrations. When Beatrix married William Heelis in 1913, she set aside her books and devoted herself to her husband. She became a good farmer and sheep breeder. It was in the rural beauty of England's Lake District and in married life that Beatrix found the greatest contentment.

She died July 28, 1943.

REFLECTIONS

- What in your life appeals to the child in you and nourishes childlike qualities?
- How do you cherish and nurture the innocence of the children in your life?

PRAYER

Creator God,
Maker of all living creatures,
We humbly pray
For a truthful respect
Toward the animals of your creation.
May we delight in their antics,
Rejoice in their services to humanity,
Protect their right to live,
And respect your purpose
In giving them life.
Amen.

July 29

SAINT MARTHA

Friend of Jesus • Israel • 1st century

SCRIPTURE THEME

Hospitality

"Martha, Martha, you are worried and distracted by many things; there is need of only one thing."

— *Luke 10:41*

QUOTATION

"I think I have never heard a sermon preached on the story of Martha and Mary that did not attempt, somehow, somewhere, to explain away its text. Mary's of course was the better part—the Lord said so, and we must not precisely contradict Him. But we will be careful not to despise Martha. No doubt, He approved of her too. We could not get on without her, and indeed (having paid lip-service to God's opinion) we must admit that we greatly prefer her. For Martha was doing a really feminine job, whereas Mary was just behaving like any other disciple, male or female; and that is a hard pill to swallow."

— *Dorothy Sayers,* A Matter of Eternity, *page 95*

MARTHA'S NAME COMES FROM THE ARAMAIC *MARTA,* meaning "lady of the house." She was just such in the household at Bethany. Many tales are told about the last years of Martha and her family. Saint Gregory the Great popularized a legend about an oarless boat that drifted from Palestine to Marseilles, carrying Martha, Mary Magdalene and Lazarus to France. Some legends say that Mary is buried in France. Another tradition has Martha and Mary living out their last years with Mary, Mother of Jesus.

The home of Martha, Mary and Lazarus at Bethany always had an open door for Jesus, for his apostles and certainly for the mother of Jesus whenever she came to the area.

Martha was probably the eldest of the three. The Gospel passage clearly says that it was her (Martha's) house. She is remembered as a busy, practical, efficient housewife.

REFLECTIONS

• What is your form of hospitality toward those who visit your home?

- How do you welcome people of other cultures to your workplace or community?

PRAYER

As we busy ourselves
By washing the windows
For the sake of hospitality
And household stewardship,
Let us also still ourselves
To find your real presence, God,
In the midst of our busyness.
Amen.

 *July 30*

EMILY BRONTË

Novelist · England · 1818–1848

SCRIPTURE THEME

Strength

"Whoever serves must do so with the strength that God supplies."
  — *1 Peter 4:11*

QUOTATION

"No coward soul is mine,
No trembler in the world's storm-troubled sphere:
I see Heaven's glories shine,
And faith shines equal, arming me from fear."
  — Emily Brontë, The Great Thoughts, *pages 50–51*

THE BRONTË FAMILY HAS AN INTERESTING STORY, sad in its many deaths and uplifting in its strength of spirit, sometimes spoken and sometimes not.

Emily wrote one novel, *Wuthering Heights,* and penned many lines of poetry. She was a good housekeeper and caretaker of her brother in his bouts with alcoholism and drugs. The cold she caught the day of his funeral led to her untimely death at age thirty. For Emily, the inner world of God and the outer world of spirit united in true mystical fashion. The voices in her poems echo the visionary quality of her novel. To appreciate the elements of her poetry is to grasp the meaning of her fiction, which typifies and yet transcends Gothic romance.

Infinity and eternity mattered to her, and what she experienced in the natural and domestic world provided glimpses into that world beyond.

REFLECTIONS

- How has care for an ill family member weakened you? How has it made you stronger?
- Do you ever transcend the everyday by focusing your thoughts on the eternal? How does this kind of thinking change your perception of daily challenges?

PRAYER

Heaven's glory shines through
The windows of faith and courage.
May we find these windows
To strengthen our spirits,
Especially in moments of darkness.
Amen.

July 31

MARY NOAILLES MURFREE
Author · U.S. · 1850–1922

SCRIPTURE THEME

History, memory

"Jerusalem remembers...
All the precious things
That were hers in days of old."

— *Lamentations 1:7*

QUOTATION

"Remember me when I am gone away
Gone far away into the silent land."

— *Christina Rossetti*, The Beacon Book of Quotations by Women, *page 272*

MURFREESBORO IN TENNESSEE, the birthplace of Mary Murfree on January

24, 1850, was named for Mary's grandfather in the early 1800's. Mary also died in Murfreesboro, on July 31, 1922.

Mary's formal education began in Nashville, and after the Civil War continued in Philadelphia, where the family lived for a time. In 1869, the family moved back to Murfreesboro and Mary began to write short stories, some of which were published in Lippincott's *Magazine* and in *The Atlantic Monthly*. She used the pen names of R. Emmett Dembry and Charles Egbert Craddock. In 1884, her first book, *In the Tennessee Mountains*, collected several of her stories.

Several books of stories, serialized novels and novels followed in the 1880's and early 1900's. When the real identity of Charles Egbert Craddock was revealed in 1885, Mary became quite a celebrity. Her local-color themes and mountain dialect add to the realism of American fiction.

REFLECTIONS

- Have you ever needed to use (or wished you had used) a pseudonym or pen name? Why do so many women choose this course?

- Has anything—a town, street or building, perhaps—been named for your foremothers or forefathers? What sense of heritage do you carry?

PRAYER

Strengthen in us, O God,
A sense of family history
So we may appreciate
The lives of family members
And affirm the heritage
Of special gifts of nature and grace.
Amen.

August 1

MOTHER MARIANNE OF MOLOKAI

Franciscan missionary to lepers • U.S. • 1838–1918

SCRIPTURE THEME

Leprosy

"Go, wash in the Jordan seven times, and your flesh shall be restored and you shall be clean."

— 2 Kings 5:11-14, 27

QUOTATION

"I am not afraid of any disease, hence it would be my greatest delight even to minister to the abandoned 'lepers.'"

— in *"Letter of Mother Marianne,"* A Song of Pilgrimage and Exile, *frontispiece*

BARBARA KOOB WAS BORN JANUARY 23, 1838, in Germany. Her family moved to the United States and settled in Utica, New York, in 1840. The family came to a German settlement and Catholic parish named St. Joseph's. By 1855, Barbara had finished school and was working in a factory job.

After her father's death, Barbara applied for admission to the Franciscan Sisters, whom she had come to know in Utica. She was sent to Syracuse for her novitiate and was given the name Sister Mary Anna, which was spoken as Marianna and became Marianne.

Sister Marianne taught school and served as administrator and superior in Utica, Syracuse and Oswego. She served as secretary to Mother Bernardine; she also became her confidant and adviser.

During her second term as provincial superior, Mother Marianne received a letter of invitation from a priest in Hawaii. After tedious discussion and arrangements, Mother Marianne and six others set off in October 1883 by train to San Francisco and by boat to the Sandwich Islands. They were welcomed in Honolulu in early November.

There were difficulties with language, buildings and the health board, but eventually the sisters ministered to the Hawaiian people. In 1888, Mother Marianne and her helpers were established at the leper settlement on the island of Molokai. Father Damien, the saintly priest of Molokai, visited them up until his death in 1889.

Mother Marianne died in the summer of 1918. The cause for her beatification and canonization were introduced into Rome in 1983. Today, the Syracuse Franciscans still carry on ministry in Hawaii.

REFLECTIONS

- For a long time Mother Marianne felt called to Hawaii's lepers but went through several other experiences with patience and hope until her dream materialized. How have you waited for your dreams?
- Read *A Song of Pilgrimage and Exile: The Life and Spirit of Mother Marianne of Molokai*, by Sister Mary Laurence Hanley, O.S.F., and O. A. Bushnell.

PRAYER

Jesus, you reached out to heal lepers.
Grant us the courage
Through our kindness
And prayers,
To heal those we encounter.
Amen.

 August 2

OUR LADY OF THE ANGELS

Costa Rica • 1636

SCRIPTURE THEME

Angels

"But the angel of the LORD called to him from heaven."
— *Genesis 22:11*

QUOTATION

"Take shelter under the Lady's mantle, and do not fear. She will give you all you need. She is very rich, and besides is very generous with her children. She loves giving."
— *Blessed Raphaela Maria*, Quotable Saints, *page 101*

SOME THREE HUNDRED YEARS AGO IN COSTA RICA, a native girl, while looking for firewood, found a black stone image of the Virgin Mary holding the Child Jesus. As the story goes, every time she took the stone home or tried to move it, the stone returned to its original place near Cartago. The priest in the girl's parish felt that the Virgin wanted a church built on that spot. When the church was completed, they named it Nuestra Señora de los Angeles. It was on August 2, 1636, that the Black Madonna was found, and Franciscans have observed August 2 as the feast of Our Lady of the Angels.

When Costa Rica gained independence, it took the Black Madonna as the country's patron. This was affirmed in a decree from Rome in 1914.

REFLECTIONS

- What are your favorite titles of Mary? Why?
- Many countries, cities, schools and organizations have their own special devotion to Mary or claim her as a patron under a specific title. Have you ever belonged to such an organization?

PRAYER

Dear Lady of the Angels,
And dear Mary greeted by an angel,
Teach us to recognize the messengers sent to us by God,
Teach us to receive the messages sent to us by God,
Teach us to become messengers of God to the people around us.
Amen.

August 3

FLANNERY O'CONNOR

Novelist, short story writer • U.S. • 1925–1964

SCRIPTURE THEME

Sin, grace

"They are now justified by his grace as a gift, through the redemption that is in Christ Jesus."

— *Romans 3:24*

QUOTATION

"Does one's integrity ever lie in what he is not able to do? I think that usually

it does, for free will does not mean one will, but many wills conflicting in one man. Freedom cannot be conceived simply."

— Flannery O'Connor, Sunbeams, *page 71*

MARY FLANNERY O'CONNOR WAS BORN MARCH 25, 1925, in Atlanta, Georgia. Brought up Roman Catholic in the midst of Southern fundamentalist Protestants, she graduated from the Women's College of Georgia at Milledgeville (now Georgia College) and received her master's degree from the University of Iowa.

Her short stories depicted poor Georgian people seeking in desperation for spiritual meaning. Using grotesque characters, Flannery's fiction reveals the import of grace as supernatural goodness in battle with evil and horror.

Flannery's physical health was limited by lupus, which made her weak and crippled. Awards and grants enabled her to continue writing. She continued her hobby of raising peacocks and writing when she was able, until her death on August 3, 1964, a few months before her fortieth birthday.

REFLECTIONS

· Read one of Flannery O'Connor's short stories. What insight can you gain from the characters' spiritual struggles?

· Have you ever been limited in your goals or life's work by chronic illness? How have you overcome such illness?

PRAYER

Illumine our souls, O God,
With the light of your grace.
Amen.

 *August 4*

JUSTINE MERRITT
Peacemaker · U.S. · 1924—

SCRIPTURE THEME
Cloth
"Their clothing is blue and purple;

They are all the product of skilled workers."
— Jeremiah 10:9

QUOTATION

"Every stitch is a prayer."
— Justine Merritt, Western New York Catholic, *January, 1990*

JUSTINE MERRITT, BORN IN THE EARLY 1920's, lived an ordinary life as student, wife, mother. Then she had a spiritual awakening and became a peace activist. She was the energy and inspiration behind the ribbon that encircled the Pentagon and Capitol building in Washington, D.C., on August 4, 1985.

"I ask you to place on fabric what you cannot bear to think of as lost forever...in apartheid, in religious war, in environment, in whatever fear or pain you have." With these words, Justine Merritt, writer and storyteller, invited the world to create the ribbon around the earth.

A Ribbon Event in August 1985 in Washington, D.C., was composed of 27,000 pieces of fabric on which people had placed symbols of what they could not bear to think of as lost forever in nuclear war. The ribbon and the persons holding it stretched around the Pentagon, the White House and the Capitol, symbols of military, personal and political power. The timing focused on the fortieth anniversary of the bombings of Hiroshima and Nagasaki.

While some challenged the Peace Ribbon Project by asking, "How many votes did it change?" Justine simply asks, "How many lives did it change?" Justine explains that every piece of that ribbon was "a work of the heart," a work of peace. "Every stitch is a prayer." And in the new ribbon—the ribbon around the earth—every stitch is a prayer, a loving thought, a good energy. Justine suggests that individuals pray for others like themselves while doing the needlework. She says: "If you're a nurse, a tired nurse, pray for the nurse in the AIDS wing, the nurse on the Gaza Strip, the nurse in a motherhouse infirmary. If you're a grandmother, pray for the grandmothers in Bangladesh, in South Africa, in your own city. If you're an oppressed person, homeless and hungry, pray for those like yourself in South Africa, in New York City."

"This new ribbon," says Justine, "is building a community of prayer, of prayer-ers, a community of intercessory prayer." And she explains that it is the prayer for one another that will circle the earth more truly than even the cloth ribbon.

REFLECTIONS

- For additional information about The Ribbon Around the Earth (or The Pentagon Ribbon), write to The Ribbon Around the Earth, 855 N. Jefferson St., Arlington, VA 22205.

- When have you adopted the cause of peace? What can you do to be a peacemaker in your own home and community?

PRAYER

O Creator, who made a rainbow
To circle the earth,
May we wrap our earth
In a ribbon of prayer
For each other and for peace.
Amen.

 *August 5*

CLEMENTINE ANUARITE

Virgin, martyr • Zaire • 1941–1964

SCRIPTURE THEME

Virginity

"Do not be afraid...for you have found favor with God."
— *Luke 1:30*

QUOTATION

"Pray for me. I prefer to die instead."
— Blessed Clementine, The Seed, *December 1989, page 12*

IN EASTERN ZAIRE IN AFRICA, in the town of Wamba, Nengapeta Anuarite was born in 1941. Her father had a chance to visit Palestine where he learned about Christ. He and his family became Christians, and Nengapeta was baptized as Alphonsine.

She attended primary school and then lived at the convent of the Holy Family Sisters at Bafwabakka. On August 5, 1959, at age eighteen, she took her first vows of chastity, poverty and obedience as Sister Marie Clementine. She developed special devotions to the Holy Eucharist and the Virgin Mary.

She taught at a girls' boarding school and was remembered by both students and staff for her kindness.

In 1964, civil war broke out in Zaire. The rebel movement, called *Simbas* (Swahili for "lion"), attacked the country from the East. Many people, including missionaries, were killed. A band of these rebels entered the convent, rounded up the sisters and put them on a truck to take them to the rebels' headquarters. The group leader ordered all medals and rosaries to be thrown away.

One of the officers tried to entice Sister Marie Clementine, but she resisted. Angered, he hit her on the head and ordered her killed. Two soldiers stabbed her with knives. And so, she died as virgin and martyr on December 1, 1964, at age twenty-three.

The Church in Zaire made an official investigation into Sister Marie Clementine's life in 1978. When Pope John Paul II visited Zaire in 1980, he approved the cause for her canonization. In his 1985 visit, the pope proclaimed her blessed at a solemn Mass in Kinshasha, the capital of Zaire. Her full name is Sister Marie Clementine Nengapeta Anuarite; she is fondly called Blessed Clementine, and the Church in Zaire has developed a liturgy in her honor.

REFLECTIONS

- Are you involved in efforts to raise awareness of political instability around the globe? Are you able to see how it affects individual lives and how individuals can work to stop it?
- Rape is a cause for concern for every woman. How do you cope with your own fears of rape and crime?

PRAYER

For women who have been raped,
We pray that they may experience
The healing presence of God
And the healing presence
Of their families and friends.
Amen.

August 6

LUCILLE BALL

Comedian, actress • U.S. • 1911–1989

SCRIPTURE THEME

Laughter

*"Blessed are you who weep now,
 for you will laugh."*

— Luke 6:21

QUOTATION

"Luck? I don't know anything about luck. I've never banked on it, and I'm afraid of people who do. Luck to me is something else: hard work—and realizing what is opportunity and what isn't."

— Lucille Ball, The Quotable Woman: 1900–Present, *page 152*

LUCILLE WAS BORN IN CELERON, a suburb of Jamestown, just south of Buffalo, New York, on August 6, 1911. She always wanted to be an actress, and at fifteen she left high school to go to New York City for drama school. She worked for a time as a model.

At age seventeen, Lucy became ill with rheumatoid arthritis, which caused her two years of paralysis. It was the years of the Great Depression when Lucy recovered, and she got by with money earned from modeling and acting as an extra in films.

She played in several movies during the 1930's. In 1940, she played in the film *Too Many Girls* with Desi Arnaz, whom she married the same year. They maintained their separate careers, he as a bandleader and she as an actress.

During the 1940's, Lucy continued to play major roles in comedies. In 1950, she and Desi launched a radio program, and in October 1951, they began the *I Love Lucy* show on TV. It became a favorite TV show and in 1956 won an Emmy award. Reruns of Lucy's shows have been playing all over the world ever since.

Lucy and Desi divorced in 1960. Two years later Lucy became president of Desilu Productions and returned to TV with *The Lucy Show*. When she sold the company in 1967, Lucy formed her own company, Lucille Ball Productions. She produced a third television series, *Here's Lucy*, from 1968 to 1974.

Lucy was among the first female TV stars, and she insisted on Desi Arnaz as her TV husband when studio executives feared that viewers would not relate to a Hispanic. In the early days of her show, Lucy appeared pregnant, one of the first women to do so on TV. In 1985, Lucy returned to television in *Stone Pillow,* a movie about a bag lady. She was the funny lady of TV, but she also lent her acting to serious issues.

Lucy died in 1989, and many of her best shows reappeared on TV in her memory. In 1993, Lucie Arnaz put together a home movie film of the lives of her parents. The film was shown on national TV.

REFLECTIONS

- What are your favorite comedy shows and comedians? What can you learn from your own taste in comedy?

- Do you, or someone you know, have a disabling illness? How does laughter help in coping with difficult times?

PRAYER

Give us joy and laughter,
O God,
And delight
To balance our afflictions.
Amen.

 *August 7*

MOTHER MAGDALEN DAEMEN

Religious founder • Netherlands • 1787–1858

SCRIPTURE THEME

Poor giving to poor
"She out of her poverty has put in all she had to live on."
　— *Luke 21:4*

QUOTATION

"The feeding of those that are hungry is a form of contemplation."
　— *Simone Weil,* The Beacon Book of Quotations by Women, *page 159*

CATHERINE DAEMEN WAS BORN NOVEMBER 19, 1787, in the southern part of the Netherlands to a simple country family. As a teenager, she worked as a domestic servant in a nearby village. Just before her twentieth birthday, she made profession in the Third Order Secular of Saint Francis. She often referred to that day, October 12, 1817, as the greatest day of her life.

Catherine and others in the Third Order spent time with the children as well as the poor and the sick. In 1825, Catherine went to Heythurpsen to care for neglected children. Other women joined her in this service project. They built themselves a house and lived a simple life of prayer and service.

On May 10, 1835, the women moved to a larger house and began living as a religious community with the name of the Sisters of Saint Francis of Penance and Christian Charity. Catherine became known as Sister Magdalen. The community followed the rule of Third Order Franciscans.

In 1840, Mother Magdalen resigned her office and lived a life of service and prayer until her death on August 7, 1858.

REFLECTIONS

- What do you consider the greatest day of your life? Why?
- What cooperative efforts of women to provide healing and care for children, the sick, those in need and the environment are present in your community? What can you do to support their efforts?

PRAYER

Wherever women gather
In your name, O God,
To live simple lives
Of prayer and service,
May you be in their midst.
Amen.

August 8

MARJORIE KINNAN RAWLINGS

Novelist • U.S. • 1896–1953

SCRIPTURE THEME

Animals

"Let the earth bring forth living creatures of every kind."

— *Genesis 1:24*

QUOTATION

"He found himself denying this so-called force of gravity. It could not be what tied men to earth. It was a heavy weight, an unendurable pressure from the outer-land, and if a man could once break through it, soar high like a bird, he would be free, would meet, would join, something greater than he, and be complete at last."

— *Marjorie Kinnan Rawlings,* The Quotable Woman: 1800-1981, *page 254*

HER PULITZER PRIZE–WINNING STORY OF 1938, *THE YEARLING*, remains a favorite. Born of her experiences in the hamlet of Cross Creek in northern Florida, this story reveals Marjorie's kinship with nature. More of the same is contained in *Cross Creek*, a poetic prose collection of her memories of life among the Crocker people of north Florida. Both books have been made into movies.

Marjorie, born August 8, 1896, married Charles Rawlings in 1918 and worked as a reporter and feature writer while trying her hand at fiction. In 1928, she bought a forty-acre orange grove at Cross Creek and settled there. She managed the grove, became acquainted with the local people and wrote stories that sold. She was a keen observer and rendered the Crocker dialect and humor in a convincing manner. While working on a biography of Ellen Glasgow, Marjorie died December 14, 1953, at age fifty-seven.

REFLECTIONS

- What can we learn about people by learning their local dialect?
- How do you react to a colorful dialect? With interest? Amusement? Scorn? What do your attitudes reveal about you?

PRAYER

May the animals of our earth
Inspire us, O Creator of all,
To make peace and to live gently.
Amen.

 *August 9*

EDITH STEIN

Jewish convert to Catholicism, Carmelite nun who died at Auschwitz · *Poland and Germany* · *1891–1942*

SCRIPTURE THEME

Holocaust

"'The songs of the temple shall become wailings in that day,' says the Lord GOD;
'the dead bodies shall be many,
   cast out in every place. Be silent!'"
   — *Amos 8:3*

QUOTATIONS

"And there is no profession which cannot be practiced by a woman."
   — *Edith Stein,* Essays on Woman, *page 47*

EDITH WAS BORN TO JEWISH PARENTS ON OCTOBER 12, 1891, in Wroclaw, which has belonged to both Poland and Germany. In her autobiography, Edith explains the importance to her mother of October 12 being Yom Kippur that year.

At seven, Edith was aware of an inner life that she could not express. Although she attended Jewish services with her family, by thirteen she claimed to be an atheist. She was a bright student and at twenty-five had her doctorate in philosophy. She enjoyed hiking, the visual arts and good conversations and had a strong social conscience.

The strength of spirit she saw in a Christian friend and the autobiography of Saint Teresa of Avila, which she read in a single night, led to her conversion to Catholicism. She taught school and translated Catholic philosophical works while she pondered becoming a Carmelite. She wrote, gave lectures, deepened her interior prayer and waited. In 1933, she was accepted at the Cologne Carmel in Germany, where she was known as Sister Teresa Benedicta of the Cross. She was allowed to continue her writing as well as attend to domestic chores.

By 1938, the persecution of Jews in Germany was in earnest. Kristallnacht, the night of November 9, 1938, when all the windows of synagogues, Jewish homes and businesses were broken and up to forty thousand Jews were sent to concentration camps, meant fear for the Carmelite nuns because of Edith. In December 1938, Edith fled to the Carmel at Echt in Holland, where she offered her sufferings as sacrifice for peace.

In 1942, Jewish members of Dutch religious orders were arrested. Edith and her sister Rosa were among those picked up in early August and sent by train to Auschwitz.

Edith died there August 9, 1942.

REFLECTIONS

- Although Edith was an intellectual, she was persecuted because of her heritage rather than her ideas. When have you suffered because of your ethnicity or family background? Does it matter why someone suffers?

- Read Edith's *Essays on Woman (Die Frau)*.

PRAYER

Strengthen us, O God, in our trials
With the calmness and composure
That enable us still
To reach out to others in need
In the name of Jesus.
Amen.

August 10

MARIA DROESTE

Devotee to the Sacred Heart • *Germany and Portugal* • *d. 1899*

SCRIPTURE THEME

Heart

"Trust in the LORD with all your heart."
  — *Proverbs 3:5*

QUOTATION

"The heart outstrips the clumsy senses, and sees—perhaps for an instant, per-haps for long periods of bliss—an undistorted and more veritable world."
  — *Evelyn Underhill,* Beacon Book of Quotations by Women, *page 148*

MARY WAS THE DAUGHTER of two eminent German Catholic families. Poor health kept her from entering the convent, but she made a vow of chastity and lived a life of prayer and works of mercy while remaining at home.

Mary felt called to aid neglected girls. By her mid-twenties, with improved health, she entered the Good Shepherd Nuns with the name Sister Mary of the Divine Heart. She made religious vows in the convent at Muenster, her native city, and had charge of the girls there. She moved to Portugal and was appointed superior of the convent in Oporto. A spinal condition made an invalid of her.

Because of her private revelations, Pope Leo XIII agreed to write the encyclical *Annum Sacrum*, which urges devotion to the Sacred Heart, in May 1899, and to consecrate the human race to the Sacred Heart in June 1899.

Mary died June 7, 1899, just three days before the universal consecration to the Sacred Heart.

REFLECTIONS

- When have you been reluctant to follow your heart? What are your private revelations?

- What devotions renew your spirit? When do you most need them?

PRAYER

Sacred Heart of Jesus,

Bless our homes,
Our hearts, our lives.
Amen.

 *August 11*

CLARE OF ASSISI

Founder of Poor Clares • Italy • 1193–1253

SCRIPTURE THEME

Poverty

*"Those who try to make their life secure will lose it, but those who lose their life
will keep it."*

— *Luke 17:33*

QUOTATION

*"Sisters, beware of all pride, vain ambition, envy, greed, and of taking part in
the cares and busy ways of the world..."*

— *Clare of Assisi,* The Quotable Woman: From Eve to 1799, *page 58*

IN ASSISI, THE BASILICA DI SANTA CHIARA holds the Cimabue paintings that
depict the highlights of Clare's life. One shows Bishop Guido handing
Clare an olive branch on Palm Sunday. The story behind the art recalls
the Palm Sunday of Clare's decision to secretly flee her family to follow
the way of Francis. The bishop's gesture affirmed and assured Clare of
her vocation.

The eighteen-year-old Clare was inspired by a Lenten sermon preached
by Francis in thirteenth-century Assisi. The opposition Clare met with
from her family did not deter her from following the poverty of Christ as
Francis was living and teaching it.

Clare lived at the convent of San Damiano for nearly forty years. San
Damiano was the church that Francis rebuilt in the early days of his conversion. In establishing the Second Order of Franciscans, to be known
worldwide as the Poor Clares, Francis gave this church and convent to
Clare, her sister Agnes and the other women of Assisi who chose the
cloister over their worldly castles.

In the refectory at San Damiano, the tables used by Clare and her sisters still remain. And these are the tables where the pope dined with

Clare and her sisters and insisted that Clare rather than himself bless the bread of the meal.

The window at the top of the wall is where Clare met the Saracens in 1241 after they had used ladders to scale the wall. Clare literally stared down the enemy until they fled. She and her sisters then turned to prayer, and a violent storm kept the Saracens from attacking Assisi itself.

The final days of Clare's life were spent on a small terrace on the sunny, south side of the convent overlooking the valley. Here she tended flowers and prayed. Once when illness confined her to bed, she had a vision of the Mass in her room. This is why she has been named the patron of television.

REFLECTIONS

- Clare stared down her enemy with a steadfast gaze and prayer. How do you deal with your enemies?

- Television offers us windows on the whole world, on the global village. Do you allow what you learn from TV to affect your sense of prayer and service? Are there some TV shows that you would be better to ignore?

PRAYER

Through the intercession of Clare,
Patron of television,
May we use TV programs
As windows onto our world
And onto eternity.
Amen.

 *August 12*

KATHERINE LEE BATES
Author, educator • U.S. • 1859–1929

SCRIPTURE THEME

Natural beauty

"Let the sea roar, and all that fills it;
let the field exult, and everything in it."

— *Psalm 96:11*

QUOTATION

"It was then and there, as I was looking out over the sea-like expanse of fertile country spreading away so far under those ample skies, that the opening lines of the hymn floated into my mind. That the hymn has gained, in these twenty-odd years, such a hold as it has upon our people, is clearly due to the fact that Americans are at heart idealists, with a fundamental faith in human brother-hood."

— *Katherine Bates,* Give Her This Day, *page 231*

REMEMBERED FOR HER POEM "AMERICA THE BEAUTIFUL," Katherine had a long career as a college teacher and author. She was born August 12, 1859, in a Massachusetts town named Wellesley, where she grew up and graduated from Wellesley College. Forty years of her life were devoted to the college as instructor in English, professor and department head. She retired in 1925 as professor emeritus.

Over these same years, Katherine wrote several books—scholarly works, poetry and travel books. It was in 1893 while she was on a tour of the western states and in awe of the view of Pike's Peak that Katherine was inspired to write her famous poem. Revised over the years from 1895 to 1911, the poem was set to the music of Samuel A. Ward's "Materna" and became something of an unofficial national hymn.

In Wellesley, Katherine died on March 28, 1929.

REFLECTIONS

- From time to time, there arise discussions on which patriotic hymn should be the official national anthem of the United States. What are your thoughts?
- Have you seen Pike's Peak or another snow-capped mountain? What is your experience of natural beauty? What feelings does it summon?

PRAYER

May God shed grace on America
And bless its peoples
With true freedom and peace.
Amen.

August 13

LUCY STONE
Feminist • U.S. • 1818–1893

SCRIPTURE THEME

Violence toward women

"But he would not listen to her; and being stronger than she, he forced her."
— *2 Samuel 13:14*

QUOTATION

"The widening of woman's sphere is to improve her lot. Let us do it, and if the world scoff, let it scoff—if it sneer, let it sneer."
— *Lucy Stone, The Quotable Woman: 1800–On, page 37*

IN THE 1820'S WHEN LUCY WAS A SCHOOLGIRL, the stagecoach passengers passing through town would throw out tracts and pamphlets for the students to read. Eager to get these, Lucy climbed out an open window of the schoolhouse and got to the reading material before others grabbed it all. This angered her teacher who made her reenter the schoolroom via the same window.

Born August 13, 1818, Lucy learned early in life that a girl's world was limited. She felt angry when her brothers were allowed to read. Her anger turned to despair when the Bible was quoted to reinforce men's dominion over women. She determined to learn Greek and Latin to see if the Bible had been translated correctly. Despite her father's strong opposition, she made plans for college. After working and saving for nine years, she went off to Oberlin College in Ohio, the only one at the time to admit women on an equal basis with men. Her goal was to become an educated and independent woman.

Lucy insisted that women had a right to speak in public, and she pursued a lecturing career, working for a time as an abolitionist lecturer for William Lloyd Garrison's Anti-Slavery Society. Her interest in women's rights grew, and she began listening to the wrongs done to women.

When she got in trouble with church authorities for removing her bonnet in the Congregational church because its heaviness gave her a headache, she stood her ground and convinced them it was right for her to do so, though they required her to remain in the rear of church.

Though she had resolved never to marry, for the sake of keeping her freedom, in 1855 she did marry Henry Blackwell, brother of Elizabeth Blackwell. Lucy kept her maiden name, and the couple protested the marriage laws that deprived women of their rights to property and children.

Lucy retired from public life to care for her daughter, Alice, who was born in 1857.

By 1867, the women's suffrage movement caught Lucy's attention and involvement. Lucy advocated a city-by-city, state-by-state approach, while Elizabeth Cady Stanton and Susan B. Anthony went national. In 1870, Lucy started the *Woman's Journal*, and she and her husband were editors. Lucy's daughter, Alice, who never married, carried on the work of the magazine.

Lucy died October 18, 1893. The bust of Lucy Stone that was on display at the Chicago's World Fair in 1893 was later placed at the Boston Public Library.

REFLECTIONS

- Lucy Stone has been called "the morning star of the women's rights movement." What would life be like without some of the rights we now take for granted—suffrage, property ownership, wages, education? What rights are yet to be won?

- Responsible feminism sorts out basic human rights and freedoms from license to do anything one wants. How do you apply the pro-choice notion of abortion to responsible feminism?

PRAYER

May we be willing
To climb in and out of windows
In our search for you, O Eternal Truth.
Amen.

August 14

CATHERINE FITZGIBBON

Social worker • England and U.S. • 1823–1896

SCRIPTURE THEME

Orphans

"As a mother comforts her child,
  so will I comfort you."
— Isaiah 66:13

QUOTATION

"A Child of Happiness always seems like an old soul living in a new body, and her face is very serious until she smiles, and then the sun lights up the world."
— *Anne Camero*, Beacon Book of Quotations by Women, *page 48*

CATHERINE WAS BORN MAY 11, 1823. At age nine, she moved from England with her family and settled in Brooklyn, New York. There, she attended St. James parish school.

In 1950, Catherine entered the Sisters of Charity, where she was known as Sister Mary Irene. She taught school, and when infants were left on the convent steps, she was appointed to take care of them. Soon, other sisters were appointed to help, and they established the Foundling Hospital on October 11, 1869. Sister Mary Irene also organized a laywomen's auxiliary to assist the hospital.

Sister Mary Irene also provided for other aspects of foundling care. She organized a foster care and adoption program and established a shelter for unwed mothers. Her special work became the rehabilitation of unwed mothers.

Associated with the Foundling Hospital, Sister Mary Irene established a maternity hospital, a children's hospital, and a hospital for convalescent children. She also opened a day nursery for preschool children. For twenty-seven years, she served as superior of the Foundling Hospital. The techniques she introduced for reducing the spread of disease were adopted by hospitals all over the United States.

Sister Mary Irene died in New York City on August 14, 1896, at age seventy-three.

REFLECTIONS

• What do you know about services in your area for women with unplanned pregnancies? How can you help?

· How do you contribute to the welfare of the children in your community?

PRAYER

As we reach out our hearts and hands
To the foundlings and orphans
And refugee children of our world,
To the children in our midst
Who are sick, or poor, or have special needs,
We remember, Jesus,
That you once were a child,
And ask the blessing
Of your smile upon all children.
Amen.

 *August 15*

CATHERINE DE HUECK DOHERTY

Prophetic laywoman, spiritual guide • *Russia and Canada* • *1897–1985*

SCRIPTURE THEME

Solitude

"Turn to me and be gracious to me,
  for I am lonely and afflicted."

— *Psalm 25:16*

QUOTATION

"Acquire inner peace and a multitude will find their salvation near you."

— *Catherine Doherty*, A Book of Days, *page 312*

IN AN ERA WHEN THE RUSSIAN *PERISTROIKA* AND *GLASNOST* have become household words, so, too, many have learned of *poustinia*. And this they learned from the Russian-born Catherine de Hueck.

"I was born in a Pullman car," Catherine often told her listeners, and so she was. Her father, Colonel Theodore Kolychkine, and his wife, Emma Thompson, had traveled to an industrial fair at Gorki and made camp in the Pullman car because the hotels were full. Catherine was born a few weeks earlier than expected and immediately baptized in the local Russian Orthodox Church.

As Catherine grew up, she and her mother brought food, medicine and clothing to needy neighbors, and this they did twice weekly. Catherine attended a Roman Catholic school, and also experienced the Russian Orthodox religion. She lived in several countries and learned at least a half dozen languages. Catherine was especially drawn to Saint Francis of Assisi.

In 1912, at age fifteen, Catherine married a cousin, Boris de Hueck. During World War I, Catherine served as a Red Cross nurse in the Russian army. In the late 1920's, the de Huecks moved to Canada and settled near Toronto.

Catherine worked as a salesperson and also traveled about giving lectures on the events in Russia. When her marriage broke up, Catherine moved in the direction of becoming a lay apostle, devoted to the gospel and social justice. She took up residence in the slums and began a friendship house for the poor. The Friendship House movement grew from Toronto to Hamilton and Ottawa.

In the mid-1930's, Catherine visited Dorothy Day, founder of the Catholic Worker movement, and the two became fast friends. In 1938, Catherine founded a Friendship House in the Harlem section of New York City. There she met Eddie Doherty, the journalist, already twice widowed. In 1943, they married, and in 1947, they purchased land and a small cottage in Combermere, Canada. There they devoted themselves to farming and literary work. In time, they built little huts—*poustinias*—where individuals could withdraw for solitude and prayer. This became the setting for the community of Madonna House.

In 1955, Catherine and Eddie pledged mutual chastity, and in 1969, Eddie was ordained a priest in the Melkite Oriental Rite, which allows married clergy. Eddie died in 1975 at age eighty-four.

Catherine died December 14, 1985. Madonna House continues to flourish.

REFLECTIONS

- Read one of Catherine's many books: *Dear Sister, Poustinia, Sobornost, Strannik, I Live on an Island, The Gospel Without Compromise, Not Without Parables, Poems.*

- *Staretz* means "a person of spiritual wisdom." Do you have a *staretz*, someone who counsels you in difficult times?

In our moments of darkness,
May we learn from the staretz,
The wise woman in our lives,
To turn to the God of light.
Amen.

 *August 16*

JOAN DELANOUE

Religious founder • France • 17th century

SCRIPTURE THEME

Avoiding selfishness

"Each of us must please our neighbor for the good purpose of building up the neighbor."

— *Romans 15:2*

QUOTATION

"In the different voice of women lies the truth of an ethic of care, the tie between relationship and responsibility, and the origins of aggression in the failure of connection."

— Carol Gilligan, The Quotable Woman: From Eve to 1799, *page 106*

IN THE VILLAGE OF SAMUR, FRANCE, a woman named Joan and her family made their living selling religious bric-a-brac and trinkets to pilgrims at the shrine of Our Lady of Ardilliers. After her parents died, Joan inherited the shop. She made the most of it, even keeping the shop open on holy days and Sundays.

One day a pilgrim woman, an elderly visionary, spoke to Joan about her true vocation. Joan went to see a priest who advised her to keep her shop closed on Sundays. Gradually, Joan saw that her vocation was to serve the poor. She began to give away her possessions and went to care for poor children who lived in a stable.

Eventually, Joan set up a hospice called Providence House. She took in beggars and the poor. She gave up her store in order to offer hospitality to the needy. She is the patron of those caught in selfishness.

She founded a congregation to carry on her work, the Sisters of Saint

Anne. She took the name of Sister Jane of the Cross. The houses she established and the congregation she founded were especially devoted to the care of elderly women.

REFLECTIONS

- How do you keep holy the Sabbath? Could certain changes bring more holiness to your life?
- Are there shelters in your area for the homeless, the poor, the disabled? How can you be of service to them and the residents there?
- Do you have one or more elderly women to whom you go for advice?

PRAYER

May we set aside the bric-a-brac
Of our cluttered lives
And find joy in simple hospitality,
In woman-to-woman talk over a cup of tea.
And may we bring a cup of tea
And talk with you, God, woman to woman.
Amen.

 *August 17*

BARBARA RUCKLE HECK

Religious leader · Ireland and U.S. · 1734–1804

SCRIPTURE THEME

Preaching

"And how are they to hear without someone to proclaim him?"

— *Romans 10:14*

QUOTATION

"Philip, you must preach to us, or we shall all go to hell, and God will require our blood at your hands."

— *Barbara Ruckle Heck,* Women and Religion in America, *Vol. 2, page 328*

BORN IN 1734 IN COUNTY LIMERICK, IRELAND, Barbara was a member of a group of religious refugees who migrated to America in 1760. Her husband, Paul, was also part of the group. Both their families had been converted to Methodism by disciples of John Wesley. Barbara and Paul were married in 1760, the same year they set sail for America. They settled in New York City.

In 1766, Barbara urged her cousin Philip Embury to resume lay preaching and teaching of the beliefs of Wesley. She organized the Methodist Society and was responsible for the opening of Wesley Chapel, the first Methodist chapel in the United States, in 1768. In 1769, Methodist missionaries from England arrived to assist them. Around 1770, the Hecks resettled in what is now Washington County in New York State. Again, Barbara led the organization of a Methodist Society and then a church. In 1774, they moved with others to Canada to escape Whig persecution. They settled near Montreal, where Barbara continued to be a leading voice in organizing Methodist services.

Barbara, known as "the Mother of American Methodism," died in Canada on August 17, 1804.

REFLECTIONS

- What role did women play in establishing the church you attend? What role do they play in its continuing ministry?
- Do you practice the same religion as your parents? How did your family come to this faith?

PRAYER

We hear you, Spirit of God,
We hear your voice,
As you call women
To be of service to your Church.
Amen.

 *August 18*

HELENA OF CONSTANTINOPLE

Empress, builder of basilica, finder of true cross · *Asia Minor* · *3rd century*

SCRIPTURE THEME

Cross

"For the message about the cross is foolishness to those who are perishing, but

to us who are being saved it is the power of God."

— 1 Corinthians 1:18

QUOTATION

"Nearer, my God, to Thee, Nearer to Thee; E'en though it be a cross That raiseth me."

— *Sarah Adams,* Harper Religious and Inspirational Quotation Companion, *page 123*

HELEN WAS BORN IN ASIA MINOR ABOUT 270, possibly an innkeeper's daughter. She married Constantius Chlorus, a Roman general, but he divorced her when he became emperor in 292. Her son, later the Emperor Constantine, respected and honored her.

Helen was converted to Christianity late in life by her son. She was devout and generous and made a long pilgrimage to the Holy Land. She had basilicas built at Bethlehem and the Mount of Olives. She was buried at Rome, but her body was later moved to Constantinople. Roman coins were minted to honor her.

Both Trier (now in Germany) and England claimed her as their own and honored her as the mother of the first Christian emperor. She was also honored for her miracles surrounding the discovery of the true cross of Jesus.

The story is told that on one of her pilgrimages, she had excavations made near Calvary and among the rubble she discovered some crosses. Miracles seem to have identified the cross on which Jesus died.

The British poet Cynewulf celebrated this in his finest poem, "Elene," written in the ninth century. Several other British poems celebrate the cross, notably "The Dream of the Rood" by an Anglo-Saxon poet.

The feast of the Finding of the True Cross (formerly on May 3) was suppressed in the 1969 revision of the Roman calendar. More than 135 dedications of monasteries and churches to Saint Helen are noted in England. The island of Saint Helena was named for her by Spanish sailors, who discovered it on her feast day.

Helen is responsible for the building of the basilica at Trier, where Constantine resided. Current excavations at that site are disclosing history about the fourth century. Trier considers her one of its patron saints.

REFLECTIONS

- Do you wear a cross or have one on display in your home or place of work? How often do you meaningfully reflect upon what this symbol means to you?

- What is your opinion of the legends surrounding the one true cross? Are they an aid to faith, or a distraction?

PRAYER

> May the crosses
> That we wear around our necks
> And that we hang on our walls
> Serve as reminders of the one true cross
> Of our salvation.
> Amen.

 *August 19*

SISTER ALPHONSA

Visionary • India • 1910–1946

SCRIPTURE THEME

The East

"As far as the east is from the west,
so far he removes our transgressions from us."

— *Psalm 103:12*

QUOTATION

"I assure you that as far as human judgment can be relied on, this young nun was almost as saintly as the Little Flower of Lisieux."

— said by Alphonsa's spiritual director at her funeral, Modern Saints: Their Lives and Faces, *page 393*

CALLED ANNAKUTTI, THIS CHILD WAS BORN to a doctor in India and his wife, who died a few weeks after giving birth. The child's full name was Anna Muttathupundatu. The family was Syrian Catholic. Annakutti's aunt became a second mother to her while Anna attended the state primary school and high school.

By age thirteen, Annakutti wished to enter a convent but was promised for marriage by her aunt. She deliberately burned and disfigured herself and so escaped marriage. Her aunt persisted with marriage plans, but Anna's uncle came to her rescue.

Anna was permitted to join the Clarist Sisters of Malabar, a community of Third Order Franciscans. She received the name of Sister Alphonsa.

Both before and after her entry into religious life, Alphonsa had dreams and visions of saints. She did some teaching but frequently suffered from ill health. Serenity, good advice and effective prayer were noted during her lifetime.

She died July 28, 1946, not quite thirty-six years old.

After her death, people who asked Sister Alphonsa's intercession with God were amazed at having their prayers answered with healing and favors and they talked about it a great deal. An unauthorized devotion sprang up and Sister Alphonsa's fame spread. People from all over India came to visit her tomb.

The Cardinal Secretary of the Sacred Oriental Congregation began preliminary investigations for her beatification and canonization. In 1970, Sister Alphonsa's writings were approved.

REFLECTIONS

- Do you know someone whom you believe to be saintly or especially holy? How do such people influence the lives of those around them? How do you influence the lives of those you know?

- Have you ever had a vision of a special mentor? What would your favorite saint say to you?

PRAYER

Through the intercession of your saints,
O God of our dreams and visions, may we experience grace
As a sign of your saving presence.
Amen.

 August 20

ANNE HUTCHINSON

Religious liberal • England and U.S. • 1591–1643

SCRIPTURE THEME

Exile

*"In you, O LORD, I seek refuge;
do not let me ever be put to shame."*

— *Psalm 31:1*

QUOTATION

"Give me Christ, I seeke not for graces, but for Christ, I seeke not for promises, but for Christ, I seeke not for sanctification, but for Christ, tell not me of meditation and duties, but tell me of Christ."

— *Anne Hutchinson,* The Quotable Woman: From Eve to 1799, *page 138*

ANNE MARBURY WAS BORN IN ENGLAND, probably in the spring of 1591. Her father was a silenced clergyman who insisted his daughter be brought up in an atmosphere of learning.

At twenty-one, she married William Hutchinson, a merchant, in August 1612. A Puritan minister named John Cotton inspired Anne. A year after John Cotton sailed to the Massachusetts Bay Colony in the New World, Anne with her husband and children followed.

And so, at age forty-three, Anne began a new life with a position of influence in the Puritan community. She held regular religious meetings in her home, which attracted merchants and ministers alike. She began to offer her own views on theology, which she attributed to the influences of Cotton Mather. In time, her adherence to the "covenant of grace" and rejection of the "covenant of works" led to factions and the "Antimonian Controversy."

In 1637, with a change of governor, Anne was banished from the Massachusetts Bay Colony and excommunicated from the Puritan Church. She moved with her family to Aquidneck, now called Rhode Island.

Anne's husband died in 1642. Anne then resettled on Long Island. On August 20, 1643, she was killed by American Indians.

REFLECTIONS

- Anne took excommunication and banishment with a sense of equanimity. How do you respond to setbacks and ostracism?
- Anne's view of salvation centered on grace alone, teaching that good works are irrelevant. What is your view on this?

PRAYER

When we meet opposition
For our religious views,
May we turn anew
To our God for strength
To love tenderly,
To act justly,

And to walk humbly
With our God.
Amen.

August 21

VICTORIA RASOAMANARIVO
Witness to faith • Madagascar • 1848–1894

SCRIPTURE THEME

Love

"It bears all things, believes all things, hopes all things, endures all things."
— *1 Corinthians 13:7*

QUOTATION

"You can put me to death, but you have no right to shut the church."
— *Victoria Rasoamanarivo,* Saints in the Making, *page 69*

BORN IN 1848 IN MADAGASCAR, Victoria grew up with customs and beliefs that focused on ancestors. The reigning queen outlawed Christianity and punished any who believed in it with persecution and death.

Later, French Jesuits and other missionaries came and Victoria was enrolled in a mission school. Though her family opposed it, Victoria was baptized on November 1, 1863.

Many people of Madagascar struggled to keep their native religion and to get rid of European colonialism. When Victoria chose to remain Catholic, she forsook her right to be buried in the family ancestral tomb, a heroic choice at age fifteen or sixteen.

She lived an extraordinary life of prayer, both publicly and privately. She felt drawn to religious life but was advised to give Christian witness as a layperson. This advice proved providential, for in 1883, all priests and religious were banished from the island of Madagascar. Victoria was able to remain, and the island's Catholics considered her the pillar of their faith.

In 1864, Victoria married the eldest son of the prime minister, a husband picked for her by her family. She lived in the humiliation of his shameful dissoluteness for twenty years. Victoria baptized her husband just before his death in 1887. After his death, she simply continued her devotions and her charity.

After a very short illness of internal bleeding, Victoria died on August 21, 1894. She was buried in the family tomb, all threats of exclusion now forgotten. In 1961, as her cause for canonization progressed, her remains were moved to a Catholic cemetery, as was her wish.

REFLECTIONS

- The age-old conflict between family and national traditions and what colonial powers impose affected Victoria profoundly. How do these conflicts affect you? Have you ever been torn between family tradition and the views of your religion or larger culture?
- Many people have negative views about those born to wealth and position. What are your views? What would you do differently if your birth circumstances had been different?

PRAYER

May we be prayerful and holy
In the ways we lead others
To justice and freedom.
Amen.

 *August 22*

SATAKO KITAHARA

Pharmacist, social worker, junk collector • Japan • 1929–1958

SCRIPTURE THEME

Service to the poor

"For the LORD hears the needy,
  and does not despise his own that are in bonds."
  — *Psalm 69:33*

QUOTATION

"Spiritual truth is truth in whatever age, but the tasks of its service change as society changes."
  — *Dorothy Thompson,* The New York Public Library Book of Twentieth Century American Quotations, *page 357*

BORN IN AN AFFLUENT FAMILY ON AUGUST 22, 1929, Satako grew up in a Tokyo suburb. She learned what was required of proper Japanese young women.

During World War II, Satako worked at an aircraft factory. Near the end of the war, she fell ill with tuberculosis. When her health improved, Satako studied at the Pharmaceutical College. In a chance encounter with two Catholic nuns, Satako came to learn about the Church and the faith of Christians. Satako was baptized with the name Elizabeth on October 30, 1949. In that same year, she graduated as a pharmacist.

A Franciscan named Brother Zeno labored in Japan on behalf of the poor, especially Tokyo's outcasts who were known as Ant People. Satako came to know of his efforts and decided to help him. She came to their slum area and organized a Christmas program. She obtained a ragpicker's large wicker basket and scavenged for reusable junk along with the residents.

Many thought Satako had gone mad from the stress of the war. They failed to see the mystical values of her spirituality. Satako received a license to collect junk in Tokyo. This was her chosen vocation. Additionally, she instructed the children in grammar and singing, and supervised their afternoon baths. Satako became known as "The Mary of Ant Town."

In time, Satako no longer returned to her affluent home at night. She took up residence in Ant Town. The effects of tuberculosis made Satako very ill by 1957. She died January 23, 1958, at age twenty-eight. Her grave on the outskirts of Tokyo remains a shrine where people come to pray.

REFLECTIONS

- Have you ever had firsthand contact with homeless or slum people? What difference can you make in the life of someone desperate?

- Is poverty a reasonable choice? Is wealth always a good thing? Does our society agree with you?

PRAYER

Through the intercession
Of this patron saint
Of homeless garbage pickers,
We pray to God
For better conditions
For those who are homeless
Or in need of food and clothing,

And we resolve to reflect on our role
In bettering conditions
For the homeless and hungry.
Amen.

 *August 23*

ROSE OF LIMA

Mystic, lay Dominican • Peru • 1586–1617

SCRIPTURE THEME

Path to God

*"Fools think their own way is right,
but the wise listen to advice."*

— *Proverbs 12:15*

QUOTATION

"Rose of my heart, you are my little chosen Bride."

— *words of the child Jesus to Rose,* The Book of Saints, *page 290*

THIS NEW WORLD SAINT WAS THE DAUGHTER of a conquistador from Puerto Rico. She was born in Lima, Peru, in 1586 and baptized Isabella. Her nickname Rose became her given name, and rightly so, for when convent life was denied her, she helped to support her family by selling flowers.

She became a member of the Third Order of Saint Dominic and wore the habit at the small hermitage she had on her family's property. She lived a life of austerity, sometimes placing a crown of thorns on her head. In many ways her life paralleled that of Saint Catherine of Siena, especially in her remaining at home, living an ascetic life and receiving mystical graces.

A group of people living in Peru were associated with the Dominicans during the time Saint Turibius of Mongrovejo was archbishop. These included Saint Martin de Porres and Blessed Juan Massias as well as Rose.

Rose practiced many penances and austerities, sometimes to the great dismay of her mother. She also took pity on sick people, especially the poor. Rose even nursed some of them in rooms of the home left empty by the marriages of her sisters.

At thirty-one years of age, Rose died. Thousands of people flocked to the funeral to see her, to touch her. Many miracles happened. Hundreds of Native Americans of Lima asked for Baptism. And the mother who objected to Rose's penitential ways became a nun herself.

Rose is the first American-born person to be canonized a saint of the Church. Her canonization took place in 1691.

REFLECTIONS

- Rose, like Catherine of Siena, chose to live the life of a religious at home when denied life in a convent, and grew in holiness by doing so. How do you find God's plan when the path seems blocked?

- Many are drawn to religious life but are unable to shoulder its responsibilities. How can you begin to live a more holy life in your present circumstances?

PRAYER

May Rose of the Americas inspire us
To prayer and service
As we make our journey toward God.
Amen.

 *August 24*

SIMONE WEIL

Philosopher, mystic · France · 1909–1943

SCRIPTURE THEME

Concern for poor

"In your goodness, O God, you provided for the needy."

— *Psalm 68:10*

QUOTATION

"When an apprentice gets hurt, or complains of being tired, the workmen and peasants have this fine expression: 'It is the trade entering his body.' Each time that we have some pain to go through, we can say to ourselves quite truly that it is the universe, the order and beauty of the world, and the obedience of God that are entering our body."

— *Simone Weil,* Sunbeams, *page 75*

CONSIDERED ONE OF THE MOST IMPORTANT religious philosophers of the twentieth century, Simone was born February 3, 1909, in Paris, to a wealthy Jewish family. She loved sunsets and flowers even as a child. Her intelligence led her to excellence in studies and much independent thinking.

She studied philosophy, taught school and wrote articles. She took a job as a car machinist in order to experience the sufferings of manual laborers.

From the age of twelve, Simone suffered greatly from migraine headaches. In the midst of these violent headaches, she recited over and over George Herbert's poem "Love," and she experienced the mystical presence of Christ's love in her affliction.

With a serious migraine headache, Simone once visited a Portuguese village, and upon hearing the fishermen's wives singing a poignant song, she called to her mind the Volga boatman song. And in the midst of her migraine, Simone experienced a moral empathy for all who have experienced deep sadness and related it to the faith of Jesus' first followers.

Several spiritual experiences—hearing the Gregorian chant at Solesmes Abbey, sensing the presence of Saint Francis at Assisi, reading George Herbert's poem "Love"—deepened her desire and search for truth.

Simone was a thinking woman who applied her intellect to the service of others in compassion. At age five, she deprived herself of sugar so soldiers might have it. She was not an intellectual snob but an intelligent minister, testing truth in living like peasants and factory workers. Though she looked at Christianity and felt at home in Catholic churches, she chose to remain unbaptized because she was unhappy with the Catholic exclusion of other religions. Her spiritual director, Father Penn, claimed her to be Christian and saint.

By 1943, Simone suffered seriously from ill health. She was eating too little and working too hard. She died August 24, 1943, at age thirty-four.

REFLECTIONS

- When Simone suffered intense headaches, she would repeat from memory the poem "Love" by George Herbert, and this helped her transcend the pain. How do you deal with pain?
- Sometimes ill health and physical suffering are the occasion of special graces and insights. Has this ever been your experience?

PRAYER

You are present to us, O God,

In every sunset and every flower.
We thank you.
Amen.

 *August 25*

ALTHEA GIBSON

Tennis player • U.S. • 1927—

SCRIPTURE THEME

Fight the good fight

"Do you not know that in a race the runners all compete, but only one receives the prize?"

— *1 Corinthians 9:24*

QUOTATION

"I always wanted to be somebody."

— *Althea Gibson,* The Quotable Woman: 1900–Present, *page 312*

ALTHEA WAS BORN AUGUST 25, 1927, on a cotton sharecropper's farm in South Carolina. The Depression forced her family north in search of work, to where Althea sometimes lived with aunts or uncles. Alcohol, truancy and other problems affected Althea's school years. She learned boxing as self-defense on the streets of Harlem in New York City and enjoyed nearly every sport.

At age fourteen, she discovered tennis. Benefactors helped her perfect her game. She won championships and broke the racial barrier in tennis. In 1955–1956, Althea did a goodwill tennis tour throughout Southeast Asia. In 1959, she released a record album, *Althea Gibson Sings*, and appeared in a film, *The Horse Soldiers*.

In 1964, in her late thirties, she began a professional golf career and met with moderate success. Her outstanding success lies in the inspiration she provides to all athletes.

REFLECTIONS

• Althea titled her autobiography *I Always Wanted to Be Somebody* (1958). Another of Althea's books is *So Much to Live For* (1968). What do these titles mean to you?

- What sports do you enjoy? How does physical activity fit into your sense of well-being?

PRAYER

We run to you, God,
As the prize of our lives.
Amen.

 *August 26*

ELIZABETH BICHIER DES AGES

Founder of religious congregation • France • 1773–1832

SCRIPTURE THEME

Faith

"If you have faith the size of a mustard seed, you will say to this mountain, 'Move from here to there,' and it will move; and nothing will be impossible for you."

— *Matthew 17:20*

QUOTATION

"A religious awakening which does not awaken the sleeper to love has roused him in vain."

— *Jessamyn West,* The New York Public Library Book of Twentieth Century American Quotations, *page 357*

ELIZABETH WAS ONE OF THOSE CATHOLICS who supported the underground ministry of priests during the difficult days of the French Revolution.

Born in 1773 in Poitiers, Elizabeth was the daughter of a public official and the niece of a priest who greatly influenced her spiritual life. She felt drawn to the contemplative religious life but was advised by Father Andre Fournet (Saint Andre) that she had a genius for active work in the world.

She received preparation in a Carmelite novitiate. Then, with five companions, she began a congregation that taught children and sheltered the sick and aged. With approval of their rule, the community was named Daughters of the Cross. By 1830, sixty convents were established.

Elizabeth suffered from poor health and died peacefully on August 26,

1832. She was canonized by Pope Pius XII in 1947.

REFLECTIONS

- Elizabeth helped rebuild the faith in France after the destruction of the Revolution. What are the differences between active and contemplative ministry? To which do you feel called?

- Have you ever followed a different path in life because of advice you were given? Are you grateful? Resentful?

PRAYER

Thank you, God, our counselor,
For the advice and wisdom sent our way
By people of faith and compassion.
Amen.

August 27

MOTHER TERESA OF CALCUTTA

Missionary to poor, religious founder · *Yugoslavia and India* · *1910–1997*

SCRIPTURE THEME

The poor, destitute

"Why did I come forth from the womb
to see toil and sorrow,
and spend my days in shame?"

— *Jeremiah 20:18*

QUOTATION

"I try to give the poor people for love what the rich could get for money. No, I wouldn't touch a leper for a thousand pounds, yet I willingly cure him for the love of God."

— *Mother Teresa of Calcutta*, Sunbeams, *page 130*

AGNES GONXHA BOJAXHIU WAS BORN AUGUST 17, 1910, in Skopje, Yugoslavia, near the border of Albania. She was a happy child and had a happy childhood. When she was twelve, she joined the Sodality of Our Lady. When she heard about missions in India, she knew she wanted to become a missionary there.

At eighteen, she went to the Irish Sisters of Loreto in Dublin. She learned English and took the name of Teresa. She was sent to Darjeeling and later to Calcutta to teach school. Here she learned the languages of Bengali and Hindi and began making trips to the Calcutta slums.

On September 10, 1946, while riding a crowded train, Sister Teresa experienced a call from God to go and work among the very poorest in the slums. Mother Teresa received permission from the pope to found a new congregation. She chose the traditional Indian sari with a blue border as the habit for her nuns, who were called the Missionaries of Charity. The sisters began bringing the sick and dying to a building where there was no door in the open archway. Anyone was welcome at any time. Mother Teresa befriended the governor and Prime Minister Indira Gandhi.

Volunteers came from all parts of the world to work with Mother Teresa and her sisters. The volunteers and sisters kept an austere schedule of prayer, work, simple meals and lots of love. They especially reached out to abandoned babies and to those with leprosy. They set up mobile clinics and established other homes for the neglected.

Mother Teresa was awarded the Nobel Prize for Peace in 1979. In 1990, Mother Teresa was named "person of the decade" by a Bombay magazine. She opened a home for children in Romania, where an epidemic of AIDS affected hundreds, and continued her works of mercy well into the new decade.

Mother Teresa died in 1997. Her funeral was attended by tens of thousands and internationally broadcast.

REFLECTIONS

- What have been your personal experiences with the destitute poor?
- Have you experienced a "call within a call" as Mother Teresa did?
- Why do you think Mother Teresa had such universal appeal?

PRAYER

May we make of our lives
And our service to others
Something loving and beautiful
For you, O God.
Amen.

August 28

SAINT MONICA

Mother of Augustine • North Africa • b. 332

SCRIPTURE THEME

Persistence in prayer

"We, for our part, will devote ourselves to prayer and to serving the word."
— Acts 6:4

QUOTATION

"Yes, provided he wants what is good."

> — Monica's response when asked whether a person who has what he wants is happy, Lives of the Saints, *page 308*

MONICA WAS BORN IN 332 AT NAGOSTE, NORTH AFRICA. Her marriage to Patricius brought his mother to the new household; both husband and mother-in-law gave Monica some difficult times. Monica had three children: Augustine, Navigius and Perpetus.

Most of what is known about Monica comes from Augustine's *Confessions.* Her patience over many years along with her prayers for him eventually brought about a moral conversion. With the guidance of Saint Ambrose in Milan, Augustine was baptized with Monica present. Monica took part in the conversations of Augustine and his friends and showed herself well versed in Scripture.

Monica fell ill at Ostia and died there.

REFLECTIONS

- Augustine considered Monica his spiritual as well as physical mother. Do you consider someone a mother or father in the spirit?
- What role did your mother or father play in your faith development?

PRAYER

As Monica and her son Augustine,
While overlooking the sea of Ostia,
Shared a mystical presence of God;
May we experience God
In the company of a loved one.
Amen.

August 29

ELIZA ANN STARR

Artist, writer • U.S. • 1824–1901

SCRIPTURE THEME

Art, color

"He made its posts of silver,
*   its back of gold, its seat of purple;*
its interior was inlaid with love."

— *Song of Solomon 3:10*

QUOTATION

"We need love and creative imagination to do constructive work."

— *Paula Ollendorf,* And Then She Said..., *page 55*

A CONVERT TO CATHOLICISM, Eliza was born August 29, 1824, as the second of four children in a family that held Unitarian beliefs. Eliza's parents believed in education and urged their children to pursue it. Eliza studied painting and art in Boston.

At age twenty-one, Eliza began a religious search and in 1854 converted to Catholicism. Her art and her religion found expression in tutoring, teaching and lecturing. She settled in Chicago and contributed to the cultural life there.

Her art studio was destroyed in the great Chicago fire in 1871, and she relocated to St. Mary's at South Bend, Indiana. Her reputation grew, especially in Catholic circles, with her essays on art and poems appearing in both Catholic and secular periodicals. Eliza established an art department at St. Mary's in South Bend and continued to combine teaching with artistic expression.

In 1881, Eliza published two volumes called *Pilgrims* and *Shrines* based on her travels in Europe. She authored several devotional books that she also illustrated, among them *Isabella of Castile* (1889) and *Christian Art in Our Own Age* (1891).

The University of Notre Dame awarded her the Laetare Medal in 1885. She also was honored with a medallion from Pope Leo XIII and a gold medal at the Chicago Columbia Exposition in 1893.

Eliza died on September 7, 1901, at the home of her brother.

REFLECTIONS

- Visit an art gallery or studio to see paintings done by women. What special insight do these works possess?

- What are your creative outlets? How do you nurture your imagination?

PRAYER

May the works of artists and poets
Serve as windows
Onto your truth and beauty,
O Divine Artist.
May we each nurture
In our individual lives
A sense of the artistic,
A taste of the creative, a feel for the imaginative,
And recognize in each other
The artist at work
And the artist as work.
Amen.

August 30

MARY SHELLEY

Novelist • England • 1797–1851

SCRIPTURE THEME

Imagination, dreams

"Let the prophet who has a dream tell the dream, but let the one who has my word speak my word faithfully."

— *Jeremiah 23:28*

QUOTATION

"It is hardly surprising that women concentrate on the way they look instead of what was in their minds since not much has been put in their minds to begin with."

— *Mary Shelley,* The Quotable Woman, *page 144*

THE FIRST SCIENCE FICTION NOVEL, *FRANKENSTEIN*, written by Mary Shelley in 1815, remains one of the most famous horror stories. And many do not realize that the book was written by a woman or by one so young. Mary was eighteen when she wrote it, and twenty-one when it was published.

Born on August 30, 1797, in England, Mary Godwin was the daughter of Mary Wollstonecraft, the first of British feminist pioneers, and William Godwin, a philosopher. Mary, but a few days old when her mother died, was raised in an atmosphere of liberal thought by her father and step-mother. At age sixteen, she eloped with the poet Percy Bysshe Shelley and moved to Switzerland with him.

In a group of literary friends who decided each would write a tale of the supernatural, Mary wrote the story of a tormented scientist who created a living and alarming being.

Much of Mary's short married life was given over to bearing and caring for children. Only one lived beyond infancy. After her husband died in 1822, Mary wrote novels and travel accounts to support herself and her son. She also started a biography of her husband but did not complete the work before she died in 1851.

REFLECTIONS

- How were you shaped by the circumstances of your birth and upbringing? How might your mother have felt had you eloped to Switzerland with a poet at sixteen? How would you feel if your daughter did it?
- Read (or reread) *Frankenstein*. How is it different from the story you remember?

PRAYER

We share in your creativity, O Creator,
In what we think and feel and imagine,
In what we build and shape and fashion.
Amen.

August 31

MARIA MONTESSORI

Educator • Italy • 1870–1952

SCRIPTURE THEME

Creativity, children

"They laughed at him. But when the crowd had been put outside, he went in and took her by the hand, and the girl got up."

— *Matthew 9:24*

QUOTATION

"The first idea that the child must acquire in order to be actively disciplined is that of the difference between good and evil; and the task of educators lies in seeing that the child does not confound good with immobility, and evil with activity."

— *Maria Montessori,* And Then She Said..., *page 12*

CASA DEI BAMBINI (THE CHILDREN'S HOUSE) was Maria's dream come true for the children of the San Lorenzo slum district on the outskirts of Rome. On January 6, 1907, the three- to six-year-old "urchins," as they were called, were welcomed by Maria as she set about guiding their learning through sensory experiences.

Though she was lecturer, doctor and campaigner for women's rights, Maria is best remembered for revolutionizing the early education of children. What she did gained worldwide acceptance; preschool and kindergarten programs bear her name everywhere.

Born August 31, 1870, in eastern Italy, Maria was an only child. When she was five, the family moved to Rome and Maria went to school there. Interested in mathematics, Maria and a few other girls were allowed to attend a boys' secondary school. When Maria chose to study medicine, her father strongly disapproved while her mother encouraged her. In 1896, Maria became the first Italian woman to become a doctor. She worked with people who were institutionalized for their disabilities, ran a clinic for women and children and traveled to give lectures on feminist issues.

Kept secret at the time, Maria had a son named Mario. The father was Dr. Guiseppe Montesano, who never married Maria. The boy was sent to live with a family in the country, and at fifteen finally learned who his mother was. His crisis propelled Maria into new directions. She began to explore new ways of teaching young children. After the 1907 Casa dei Bambini, others were opened in Rome and Milan. In 1910, Maria published her ideas in a book called *The Montessori Method*. She stressed that children like freedom of choice about learning materials, that they enjoy silence and peace so they can come to organization and cleanliness by themselves.

The Montessori method caught on and Maria traveled all over the world to train teachers. She also faced criticism from those who disagreed with her methods.

In 1922, under Benito Mussolini, Maria was made chief inspector of schools for all of Italy. In 1934, when Mussolini wanted schoolchildren to join his Fascist youth organization, Maria broke with him, closed all her schools and moved to Spain.

Mario, whom she called a nephew, came to be Maria's assistant. From 1937 to 1939, they lived in Amsterdam near the International Montessori Association. In 1939, Maria and Mario moved to India, where the environment suited her contemplative, mystic nature and the wisdom of her years was respected. Her last years, 1945 through 1952, saw travel to Pakistan and various parts of Europe. A planned lecture tour of Africa never took place because of her death of a stroke on May 6, 1952. She was eighty-one.

Maria's presence remains in every classroom, toy store or playroom where her vision of childhood is nurtured. In 1990, there were 130 approved Montessori schools in the United States and at least 4,000 "nonapproved" schools that use some of her methods in their programs.

REFLECTIONS

· How, in your experience, do children learn? How do you learn?

· What emphases were most evident in your education? Were you ever considered "uneducable" by one of your instructors? How do such labels affect children?

PRAYER

May we see you, Jesus,
In the face of every child,
And love you dearly
In securing the rights of every child.
Amen.

September 1

ANNA COMSTOCK

Naturalist, illustrator • U.S. • 1854–1930

SCRIPTURE THEME

Growth of corn, grain

"The earth produces of itself."

— *Mark 4:28*

QUOTATION

"Each person has his own safe place—running, painting, swimming, fishing, weaving, gardening. The activity itself is less important than the act of drawing on your own resources."

—*Barbara Gordon,* The Quotable Woman, *page 20*

ANNA WAS BORN SEPTEMBER 1, 1854, in western New York and educated in local schools at Otto and Randolph. She taught school briefly and then went to Cornell University for further education. In 1878, she married John Comstock, an entomologist on the Cornell faculty. Anna shared his interest in insects, and she became adept at making insect illustrations.

When John was appointed by the U.S. Department of Agriculture as its chief entomologist, Anna was appointed his assistant. In 1885, she completed her degree in natural history at Cornell. She made engravings for the plates in her husband's books as well as books of her own.

In 1888, Anna was among the first four women admitted to the National Honor Society for the Sciences. In 1895, her appointment to a New York State committee on agriculture offered her the opportunity to organize nature study for the public schools. Anna prepared classroom materials and trained teachers via the Cornell extension services. At the turn of the century (1899), Anna became the first woman to teach as an assistant professor at Cornell. She was promoted to professor in 1920. Anna also served as editor on nature magazines. After 1922, she taught only in the summer sessions.

The League of Women Voters chose Anna as one of the twelve greatest living American women in 1923. She died August 24, 1930.

REFLECTIONS

• Go for a nature hike on your own or with an organized group.

- What is your "safe place"? When are you forced to draw on your own resources?

PRAYER

In praising your every creature,
O Creator-God, we praise you
And your marvelous works.
Amen.

September 2

QUEEN LILIUOKALANI OF HAWAII

Queen · Hawaii · 1838–1917

SCRIPTURE THEME

Stand firm in faith

"Fight the good fight of the faith; take hold of the eternal life, to which you were called."

— *1 Timothy 6:12*

QUOTATION

"The Hawaiian people have been from time immemorial lovers of poetry and music, and have been apt in improvising historic poems, songs of love, and chants of worship, so that praises of the living or wails over the dead were with them but the natural expression of their feelings."

—*Queen Liliuokalani*, The Quotable Woman: 1800–On, *page 72*

ORIGINALLY NAMED LYDIA KAMEKEHA PAKI, Liliuokalani was born in Honolulu, Hawaii, on September 2, 1838, and received her education at a royal school run by American missionaries. She was part of the royal court of Kamehameha III. She married in 1862. Her husband was a Boston sea captain and a Hawaiian government official.

After her older brothers died, Liliuokalani was established as ruler, serving as regent for another brother. In 1891, she ascended to the throne, the first woman ever to do so. As queen, she tried to restore traditional autocracy to the throne in a domineering manner, which clashed with economic and military agreements of Hawaii with the United States.

She was forced aside by a Committee of Public Safety. In order to prevent bloodshed, she agreed to a provisional government. Her followers attempted an unsuccessful revolt while Liliuokalani was held under house arrest. In 1895, she abdicated the throne but continued to fight against the U.S. annexation of the islands. She served as head of the *Onipa'a* ("Stand Firm") movement with the motto of "Hawaii for Hawaiians."

Hawaii was annexed to the United States in 1898, the same year that Liliuokalani published *Hawaii's Story by Hawaii's Queen* and composed the song "Aloha Oe." Liliuokalani lived quietly on a government pension in Honolulu until her death on November 11, 1917. She was generally revered by islanders and visitors alike.

REFLECTIONS

- When have you been forced to give up control over something? What was the result?
- How does music ease your suffering after a traumatic event? To what songs do you often resort in times of pain?

PRAYER

May an aloha spirit
Grow in our welcoming others
And bidding them good-bye.
Amen.

 *September 3*

PRUDENCE CRANDALL

Teacher • U.S. • 1803–1890

SCRIPTURE THEME

Time for every purpose

"For everything there is a season, and a time for very matter under heaven."
— *Ecclesiastes 3:1*

QUOTATION

"What do we live for, if it is not to make life less difficult for each other?"
—*George Eliot*, The Quotable Woman, *page 41*

During the night Prudence heard eggs breaking against the windows of her home and school in Canterbury, Connecticut. With her typical courage and determination, Prudence went out before daybreak and scrubbed those windows clean. She did not want her newly arrived students who were Black and female to see such signs of hatred.

It was 1843, and the New England town was fiercely opposed to the education of Blacks. Prudence, on the other hand, had experienced a spiritual clarity in realizing that education should be for all.

Born September 3, 1803, Prudence was raised in a Quaker home and educated at a boarding school. She became a teacher and in 1831 opened a private academy for girls in Canterbury. It was soon recognized as the best of its kind.

The trouble began when Prudence allowed her Black servant to sit in on classes. The ideas of William Lloyd Garrison about abolition of slavery deepened the conviction of Prudence and she closed her "white" school and reopened it for "young ladies and misses of color."

The town fathers arrested and imprisoned Prudence for violation of the "Black Law," which forbade education of Blacks from other states. The trial was nasty, and Prudence was convicted. Later, a court of appeals reversed the conviction, but local opposition turned into mob violence.

Prudence was forced to give up her school. She married and moved to Illinois where she and her husband opened another school. She lived out her last years with her brother in Kansas.

In 1886, the legislature of Connecticut offered Prudence an apology and a small pension. She died in 1890, on January 28.

REFLECTIONS

- Watch the Walt Disney television movie *She Stood Alone*, which portrays the courage of Prudence Crandall in opening the first school for Blacks.

- William Lloyd Garrison inspired Prudence in her choices. Who inspires you in difficult decisions and sustains you with strength during suffering?

PRAYER

When persecution and hatred
Smear eggs on the windows of our lives,
Strengthen us, O God,
To wash them clean
And go on with our dreams.
Amen.

September 4

ROSE OF VITERBO

Preacher • Italy • d. 1252

SCRIPTURE THEME

Youth

"I am young in years,
and you are aged;
therefore I was timid and afraid
to declare my opinion to you."

— *Job 32:6*

QUOTATION

"Prayer reveals to souls the vanity of earthly goods and pleasures. It fills them with light, strength and consolation, and gives them a foretaste of the calm bliss of our heavenly home."

—*Saint Rose of Viterbo*, Quotable Saints, *page 188*

ROSE WAS BORN IN THIRTEENTH-CENTURY ITALY, into the midst of division between emperor and pope, of division between Guelfs and Ghibellines.

Something of a child prodigy, she began at age twelve to speak out for loyalty to the pope. She spent the next four years speaking the cause on the streets of Viterbo despite threats from her father. Eventually, the city mayor banished her and her family from the city.

Rose went on to other towns where she continued her preaching. She foretold the death of the emperor and returned to Viterbo. She sought admittance to a convent but was refused, so she returned to her father's house until her death at age seventeen, in 1252.

She was buried at the church, but her relics were later moved to the very convent that refused her.

She was canonized in 1457. Each year, her relics are carried in procession through the streets of Viterbo, the same streets where she did her preaching.

REFLECTIONS

- Rose's life work was essentially accomplished during her early teen years. What young teens do you know? What do they contribute to the life of the church?

- How can you foster courage in a young person you know?

PRAYER

May we listen, Lord,
To the voices of teens
And to their unspoken concerns
And find inspiration
In their faith and service.
Amen.

 *September 5*

MARIA ASSUNTA PALLOTA

Missionary • Italy and China • 1878–1905

SCRIPTURE THEME

Single-minded devotion

"Set your minds on things that are above, not on things that are on earth."
— Colossians 3:2

QUOTATION

"The one great aim of her life is the glory of God. The one great example of her life is the incarnate God. The one great devotion of her life is the will of God. The one great longing of her life is union with God. The one great reward of her life is the vision of God."
—Mother Harriet Monsell, Simpson's Contemporary Quotations, *page 192*

BORN IN PICENA, ITALY, of devout and hard-working parents, Maria developed a habit of prayer. She helped to teach catechism in her village. At twenty, when her parents were able to spare her, she entered the Franciscan Missionaries of Mary in Rome.

Maria spent the next five years in various convents in Rome doing domestic, infirmary and catechetical work. Then she spent a year in Shansi province of northern China as a cook. On April 7, 1905, she died in a typhus epidemic.

The Franciscan Missionaries of Mary were founded in India. They are called the White Franciscans because of the color of their habit. They have had eight of their sisters beatified.

REFLECTIONS

- Have you ever had to postpone career decisions because of family responsibilities? How do you feel about it now?
- What is your opinion of domestic work? Do you find spiritual enrichment in daily chores, or merely drudgery?

PRAYER

God, we ask your blessings on all those
Who live and labor
In unfamiliar cultures,
And we pray that we may all grow
In multicultural understanding.
Amen.

September 6

JANE ADDAMS

Social reformer • U.S. • 1869–1935

SCRIPTURE THEME

Beneficence

*"Happy are those who consider the poor;
the* LORD *delivers them in the day of trouble."*

— *Psalm 41:1*

QUOTATION

"In his own way each [one] must struggle, lest the moral law become a far-off abstraction utterly separated from his active life."

—*Jane Addams, in* The Quotable Woman: 1800–1981, *page 108*

JANE WAS BORN SEPTEMBER 6, 1860, IN ILLINOIS. Her mother died when she was an infant, so she was raised by her widowed father and stepmother. Jane's father died when she was twenty-one.

Jane studied at the Women's Medical College in Philadelphia, but illness forced her to withdraw. During a European tour with her stepmother, she became conscious of urban poverty. When she decided to found a settlement house, she bought Hull House in Chicago's immigrant section.

The publication in 1895 of the *Hull House Maps and Papers* brought the influence of Jane's ideas to national attention. Protective legislation, union recognition and treatment of urban juvenile crime were among her successes in social justice and human rights activities.

Leadership and writing continued to occupy Jane's attention right up to World War I. While most know of her connection with Hull House, too few remember her peace activities during World War I. She continued her campaign for the disadvantaged, lending her energies to women's suffrage, civil rights, women's education and women's employment.

The Daughters of the American Revolution considered her "the most dangerous woman" in the 1920's because she took the side of Blacks, immigrants and disadvantaged groups, all considered "foreigners" by the DAR. Jane gradually received recognition and acclaim. She shared the Nobel Peace Prize in 1931 and donated her share of the prize money to the Women's International League.

REFLECTIONS

- If Jane had succeeded at medical school, she may have never brought hope to the varied immigrant population of Chicago. When have you been discouraged in one endeavor only to find success in another?
- How do less fortunate persons benefit from your beneficence?

PRAYER

Teach us, God,
To face life's disappointments
By looking to other windows of opportunity
To find your plan and design for life.
Amen.

 *September 7*

GRANDMA MOSES

Folk painter • U.S. • 1860–1961

SCRIPTURE THEME

Beauty, art

"I have filled him with divine spirit, with ability, intelligence, and knowledge in

every kind of craft."

— *Exodus 31:3*

QUOTATION

"I think real hard till I think of something real pretty, and then I paint it."

—*Grandma Moses,* Women of Achievement, *page 209*

ANNA MARY ROBERTSON, born on September 7, 1860, in rural New York State, was one of ten children. As a child, Anna sometimes painted on old windowpanes from discarded windows. Once she even salvaged the window from an old caboose and painted on this, covering it with scenes.

At twelve she was hired out for domestic work, and then she married Thomas Moses in 1887. He was one of the hired farmhands. They lived in Virginia for many years before returning to New York State. They had ten children, five of whom died in infancy.

After Thomas's death in 1927, Grandma Moses took up painting as a hobby. She was sixty-seven. She had painted some as a child and had done embroidery over the years. Now she turned to oils. She developed a technique of seeing a scene through a window and painting what she saw. By changing her angle of vision to the left or to the right, she could frame the scene in a number of ways. This approach had a lasting influence on her style.

In 1938, a collector discovered her genius for painting, bought everything she had painted and put her work into exhibition. Her exact and lively depictions of country life gained her international fame.

All told, she painted some two thousand pictures in the last thirty years of her life. She died December 13, 1961, at Hossick Falls, New York.

REFLECTIONS

- Spend some time looking at one of Grandma Moses' paintings.
- What new things might you begin in the second half of your life?

PRAYER

We rejoice, O God,
In the simplicity of rural life
And in the beauty
Of artists who portray
The simple scenes of country life.
Amen.

September 8

QUEEN ELIZABETH I

Queen • England • 1533–1603

SCRIPTURE THEME

Queen

"When the queen of Sheba heard of the fame of Solomon, she came to Jerusalem to test him with hard questions."

— 2 Chronicles 9:1

QUOTATION

"All my possessions for a moment of time."

—Queen Elizabeth, *last words,* The Beacon Book of Quotations by Women, *page 321*

HER RULE AS QUEEN LASTED FOR FORTY-FIVE YEARS and gave her name to a whole era of flourishing culture and nationalism in British history.

Elizabeth, daughter of Henry VIII and Anne Boleyn (whom Henry married secretly after his "divorce" of Catherine of Aragon), was born September 7, 1533. After the execution of Anne in 1536, Elizabeth was declared illegitimate. Her status was restored by Parliament in 1544.

Elizabeth was not the boy her father wanted, and Henry VIII went on to his third wife who did give him a son, Edward. Elizabeth and Edward grew up together and were fast friends. Both received a good education.

When Henry died, Edward, at age nine, took the throne. At fifteen, he died of tuberculosis. Mary, Henry's first daughter, became queen. During the reign of Mary I, a Catholic, Elizabeth was imprisoned for her Protestant views. When Mary died in 1558, Elizabeth succeeded to the throne. There was an elaborate coronation ceremony on January 15, 1559.

Efforts were made to make England Catholic once again. Mary Stuart, Queen of Scots and grandchild of Henry VII, and also Catholic, was seen by some to be the rightful heir to the throne, rather than the "illegitimate" Elizabeth. After much intrigue, Mary was accused of treason and Elizabeth signed the death warrant.

Yet another effort to make England Catholic came from the Spanish Armada, but they were defeated by Elizabeth's army. England remained non-Catholic.

By 1570, Elizabeth was excommunicated from the Roman Catholic Church. The reign of Elizabeth was a time of more balanced politics and greater tolerance of religious differences. During the Elizabethan era, there was a kind of peace and prosperity for forty years in which art and culture could thrive. William Shakespeare's plays were written and performed, not only for the royalty but also for the common folk. Explorers went out to new parts of the world. Scientists and other thinkers advanced the ideas of Renaissance and Reformation.

Elizabeth never married, though she had suitors. Some say that Elizabeth liked to have her power and authority without any interference from a man. By 1600, plagues, bad weather, heavy taxes, repression of Catholics and Puritans, and a number of other things caused Elizabeth to lose her popularity as queen. In her late sixties, Elizabeth grew sad and ill. She died March 24, 1603, at age sixty-nine.

REFLECTIONS

- Learn more about the art and music, poetry, drama, literature, explorations and discoveries during the Elizabethan era.
- If you had been Queen Elizabeth, what might you have done about Catholics? Puritans? Protestants? How far do you think the practice of tolerance of other religions should go? When does a religion become a cult?

PRAYER

To do our part
In family, in society, in Church
To create an environment
In which the arts flourish
And in which artists are nourished.
Amen.

September 9

PHYLLIS WHITNEY

Author · U.S. · 1903—

SCRIPTURE THEME

Cross-cultural experience

"After this I looked, and there was a great multitude that no one could count, from every nation, from all tribes and peoples and languages."

— *Revelation 7:9*

QUOTATION

"Picking up the pad, Christy carried it to window light and studied it carefully."
—Phyllis A. Whitney, Rainbow in the Mist, *page 203*

PHYLLIS WHITNEY IS A POPULAR AND PROLIFIC WRITER with dozens of novels and juvenile fiction books to her credit. She has also taught courses in writing and written books for would-be authors. Early in her career, she worked in a bookstore and served as the editor of the children's book page at two different newspapers.

Born September 9, 1903, of American parents in Japan, Phyllis spent her childhood living in Japan, China and the Philippines. Her father was an American businessman in the Orient. When her father died, Phyllis was fifteen. She and her mother moved to California and later to Texas. She graduated from high school in Chicago. At forty-seven, she married a businessman, and they had one daughter.

The novels written by Phyllis total more than fifty and are of three types: novels for young people, mysteries for young people and adult novels—mostly Gothic romances. Most of her young adult novels appeal to girls rather than boys.

In her adult novels, Phyllis creates women concerned about their identities in a sophisticated and psychological manner, with special attention to relationships between mother and daughter.

REFLECTIONS

- Is Phyllis Whitney one of your favorite popular authors? Which other popular authors do you read and like?
- What part does light reading play in your recreation?
- What added dimension can a person of cross-cultural experiences bring to the writing of a book?

PRAYER

For the children of the world, we pray
That we may give them roots,
That we may give them wings,
That we may give them windows.
Amen.

JAPANESE MARTYRS

Japan • *d. 1622*

SCRIPTURE THEME

Martyrdom

"When Herod saw that he had been tricked by the wise men, he was infuriated, and he sent and killed all the children in and around Bethlehem who were two years old or under."

— *Matthew 2:16-17*

QUOTATION

"Jesus, receive our souls."

—*Japanese martyrs*, Lives of the Saints, *page 326*

WHEN JAPANESE CHRISTIANS WERE TIED TO STAKES AND BURNED on September 10, 1622, at Nagasaki, entire families were among those killed and later beatified.

An English skipper reported seeing children and women martyred. "Among them little children five or six years old burned in their mother's arms, crying out, 'Jesus, receive our souls.'"

REFLECTIONS

- Have you reflected upon the reality of your own death? How do you envision it?
- When have you faced difficulty with bravery? When have you found bravery lacking?

PRAYER

For the sake of Christ,
May we stand brave
Even in the face of death
Rather than deny
Our faith in Christian truths.
Amen.

September 11

MARY WHITNEY

Astronomer • U.S. • 1847–1921

SCRIPTURE THEME

Stars

"The heavens are telling the glory of God;
and the firmament proclaims his handiwork."

— Psalm 19:1

QUOTATION

"Light tomorrow with today."

—Elizabeth Barrett Browning, Quotable Women, *page 421*

BORN SEPTEMBER 11, 1847, Mary was a good student and entered college with advanced standing. Her entire career was devoted to good education, especially of women in the sciences.

It was the influence of Maria Mitchell at Vassar College that got Mary Whitney interested in astronomy. With her own Alvan Clark telescope, Mary observed the solar eclipse in August 1869. After her master's degree at Vassar in 1872, Mary went to Zurich to study celestial mechanics. In 1881, she returned to Vassar as an assistant to Maria Mitchell and in 1888 succeeded Maria as director of the observatory at the college and as professor of astronomy.

Mary developed an ambitious research program in astronomy at Vassar, and her students secured professional positions in observatories. In 1899, she became a founding member of the American Astronomical Society. She retired from Vassar in 1910.

Mary died January 20, 1921.

REFLECTIONS

- Go out on a starry night and look up. Which constellations can you name?
- What do you know about prominent women in science?

PRAYER

May we find God's presence
As we dream of stars

And as we ponder the heavens
And as we search the skies,
For the heavens are telling
The glory of God
And the firmament proclaims
The presence of God.
Amen.

 *September 12*

PENINA MOISE

Poet, writer of Jewish hymns • U.S. • 1797–1880

SCRIPTURE THEME

Song

"I will sing to the LORD because he has dealt bountifully with me."

— Psalm 13:6

QUOTATION

"Lay no flowers on my grave. They are for those who live in the sun, and I have lived in the shadow."

—Penina Moise's last words, Notable American Women, *Vol. 2*

BORN ON APRIL 23, 1797, Penina was the sixth of seven children in the family of Sarah and Abraham Moise in Charleston, South Carolina. Penina's formal schooling ended at age twelve when her father died, but she continued to study and write at night after her workdays of making lace. By 1830, Penina had published poems in newspapers and journals. *Fancy's Sketch Book*, a small volume of her poems, was published in 1833.

As a member of the Beth Elohim Congregation, Penina practiced her religion devoutly and served for many years as superintendent of Sunday school. Over the years, she wrote verses and hymns on Jewish themes, many of which were published in 1856 in *Hymns Written for the Use of Hebrew Congregations,* and some of which are still used in the standard hymnal of congregations of American Reform Jews.

The Moise family was active in support of the Confederacy and forced to leave Charleston during the war. After the war, though blind by then, Penina and her widowed sister Rachel Levy conducted a school for girls.

Penina continued to write verse, which her niece Jacqueline Levy wrote down. Penina never married. She died on September 13, 1880, at age eighty-three. She is buried in Beth Elohim's old cemetery in Charleston.

REFLECTIONS

- Try to learn more about other Jewish women as artists, leaders and humanitarians, for example, Rabbi Sally Priesand and Henrietta Szold.
- Consider that Mary of Nazareth was a Jewish woman. Prayerfully read her hymn—the Magnificat—in Luke's Gospel.

PRAYER

For those who are blind, we pray, O God,
That they may find windows
In their hearts and minds.
For those who live in shade and shadow,
We pray that they may find sunshine
In their faith in you.
Amen.

September 13

CLARA SCHUMANN

Pianist, composer, teacher · Germany · 1819–1896

SCRIPTURE THEME

Music

"I will proclaim your name to my brothers and sisters,
in the midst of the congregation I will praise you."

— *Hebrews 2:12*

QUOTATION

"And when she will have left us, will our faces not light with joy in thinking of her, of this magnificent woman..."

—*Johannes Brahms of Clara,* Women: Around the World and Through the Ages, *page 167*

BORN SEPTEMBER 12, 1819, in Germany, Clara Wieck was the daughter of a composer and received a thorough musical education. She gave her first piano recital at age nine and her first concert tour at age eleven. All of Europe called her a prodigy by the time she was sixteen.

Clara fell in love with one of her father's pupils, Robert Schumann. Against her father's wishes, Clara and Robert were married. She sacrificed her career for the sake of his; soon, they had eight children to care for.

Clara did take some concert tours, taught piano and composed a little, but mostly she devoted her energies to promoting her husband's career and, after his death, his works and reputation. She also promoted the music of her close friend Johannes Brahms.

REFLECTIONS

- When caught in the tension between others' needs and your own, how do you resolve the conflict?
- Do you believe that there are creative ways for a contemporary woman to pursue an artistic talent or other career while being a wife and mother? Why or why not?
- Do you feel that a woman should sacrifice her hopes of a career in order to nurture someone else's talents?

PRAYER

May we find harmony
In our relationships
And in our musical experiences,
O God of harmony,
And peace in you.
Amen.

September 14

EDEL QUINN

Catholic action • Ireland and Kenya • 1907–1944

SCRIPTURE THEME

Wisdom, humor

"Wisdom is vindicated by her deeds."

— *Matthew 11:19*

QUOTATION

"The spiritual journey is the soul's life commingling with ordinary life."

—*Christina Baldwin,* Beacon Book of Quotations by Women, *page 305*

BORN IN IRELAND ON SEPTEMBER 14, 1907, Edel Quinn was supposed to be named Adele. The parish priest thought she was being named after the edelweiss mountain flower and spelled it Edel.

Edel was a cheerful child, a daily communicant and unselfishly considerate of others. She longed to become a cloistered nun, but family needs prompted her to get a job as a secretary-typist. When she was free to consider entering the Poor Clares, she was found to have tuberculosis and went for rest and treatment.

She became interested in and joined the Legion of Mary, and, among other things, she did rescue work among the street girls in Dublin. When the legion wanted someone for East Africa, Edel was willing. In 1936, she went to Mombasa, Kenya, and then inland to Nairobi, Kenya. There she set up two branches of the legion, one for Africans, the other for Europeans and Indians. When she held the annual membership ceremony, it was the first time in East Africa when the different races came together for a religious purpose.

Edel traveled throughout Kenya, Uganda, Nyasaland and Tanganyika, establishing the Legion of Mary. The bishops there found this form of Catholic action a special gift of life for the Church.

Malaria complicated Edel's health situation, and she returned to Nairobi in 1944. She died there on May 12.

Cardinal Suenens of Belgium wrote an account of her life and of her work in Africa. The cause of her beatification was introduced in 1957.

REFLECTIONS

• There may be Legion of Mary groups in your area. When have you found the society of other religious-minded women helpful?

- Have you been to an event that draws people from varied ethnic and racial groups? How did you feel about it?

PRAYER

Let us pray for a sense of wisdom
To know that there is a time for laughter,
To know that joy is the echo
Of God's life in us and among us.
Amen.

September 15

MARY OF SORROWS

Sorrowing mother · Israel · 1st century

SCRIPTURE THEME

Mary's sorrows

"...and a sword will pierce your own soul too."
   — *Luke 2:35*

QUOTATION

"I am a woman of a sorrowful spirit."
   —*Hannah, 1 Samuel 1:15*

JEANNE BRADY, A NURSE WHO SPENT TWO YEARS in a mission hospital in northern Kenya, tells the story of a fifteen-year-old Samburu boy dying of leukemia. His mother, tall and slender and straight, as is typical of Samburu people, came each day to feed him. And when he couldn't keep food down, she stood by him; she stayed by his bedside. After a time, she would leave the hospital and return to her village and the needs of the rest of her family.

One day, sensing the boy's weakness, the mother asked Jeanne to help her position the boy so he could face the east and see God when the Great Spirit came for him and so that God could see the boy's face. And then the mother left.

When the mother returned the next time, Jeanne met her at the mission gate and told her the boy's spirit had gone. The Samburu do not look upon their dead but continue to remember them as they knew them in life; they mentally converse with them as though still living. These African peoples maintain spiritual presence with their ancestors and family members as well as with their God.

Jeanne speaks of how this Samburu mother took the news of her son's death with great courage and strength—a *stabat mater* who stood by her son in life and in death.

The gospel scene of Mary standing at the foot of the cross reminds and affirms all the *stabat maters* throughout history who stand by those who are loved.

REFLECTIONS

- Read *Stabat Mater: Noble Icon of the Outcast and the Poor,* a book by Peter Daino, S.M., (New York: Alba House, 1988), which reflects on Mary as model in an East African context.

- Prayerfully read the several verses of the *Stabat Mother* hymn or listen to a sung version.

PRAYER

For every mother
Who stands
At the death of a child,
We pray for strength and courage.
Amen.

September 16

ANNE DUDLEY BRADSTREET

Poet · England and U.S. · 1612–1672

SCRIPTURE THEME

God in nature

"The pastures of the wilderness overflow,
the hills gird themselves with joy,
the meadows clothe themselves with flocks,
the valleys deck themselves with grain,
they shout and sing together for joy."

— *Psalm 65:13*

QUOTATION

"Authority without wisdom is like a heavy axe without an edg[e], fitter to bruise than polish."

—*Anne Dudley Bradstreet*, The Quotable Woman: From Eve to 1799, *page 151*

BORN IN 1612, ANNE SPENT HER YOUTH IN ENGLAND. Her father believed in educating his daughter, and Anne had access to the wonderful library of her father's friend the Earl of Lincoln.

In 1628, Anne married Simon Bradstreet, and in 1630, they came to Massachusetts Bay Colony, where Anne's father was governor. Though the Puritan woman's place was in the home, Anne continued her reading and writing. She wrote poems about biblical themes, and her brother-in-law liked them well enough to take them back to England and get them published. The title, *The Tenth Muse Lately Sprung Up in America*, astonished people as much as the fact that the book of poems was written by a woman.

Anne revised and rewrote, and when the American edition was completed in 1678 (six years after her death), her reputation as poet became firmly established.

Her poems include love poems, domestic poems, religious poems and death poems. "Contemplations" has become a highly regarded poem in its recognition of the presence of God in nature.

Anne also wrote spiritual commentaries on the Psalms, Proverbs and Ecclesiastes, short prose pieces and a brief autobiography. She died September 16, 1672, at age sixty.

REFLECTIONS

- Read a poem or two by Anne Bradstreet. How do her perceptions color your view of nature?
- What is your experience of poetry writing? Do you find the idea inviting? Daunting?

PRAYER

May the beauties of the natural world
Serve as windows onto your eternal beauty, O God,
As we grow in our contemplative awareness
And love of you.
Amen.

September 17

HILDEGARD OF BINGEN

Mystic, writer, healer · *Germany* · *1098–1179*

SCRIPTURE THEME

Spring

"He makes me lie down in green pastures;
he leads me beside still waters;
he restores my soul."

— *Psalm* 23:2-3

QUOTATION

"You most glorious greenness,
You take root in the sun,
And in the clear day-brightness
You shine forth in a wheel
Which no earthly excellence comprehends."

—Hildegard of Bingen, The Quotable Woman: From Eve to 1799, *page 47*

One of Hildegard's lasting works is her book *Scivias* (from *sciens vias Domini*, "one who knows the ways of God"), born of her experience of spiritual awakening. Hildegard integrates religion, science and art in her writing and illustrations.

Born in 1098 on the Nahe River in Germany, Hildegard was placed in a convent at age seven and educated in the Benedictine traditions of prayer and work, Scripture and spinning. By the time she was eighteen, Hildegard received the habit and took the vows of a Benedictine nun. When she was thirty-eight, Hildegard was appointed abbess.

At age forty-two, Hildegard had her spiritual awakening and spent the next ten years writing *Scivias* by dictating the text to a secretary and by putting her visions into paintings. During this period of her life, she established her community at Bingen, where the Nahe River flows into the Rhine. Later, she established a second monastery on the opposite side of the Nahe River, and in both places, the nuns were skilled in music, song and art.

Hildegard also traveled about preaching to nuns and monks, to clergy and church officials and to the laity. Many cathedrals and monasteries were accessible by boat along the Rhine River and its tributaries. In conjunction with Bernard of Clairvaux, Hildegard preached and popularized the Second Crusade to the Holy Land.

When she was in her eighties, Hildegard and her nuns were placed under interdict because they allowed in their cemetery the burial of a revolutionary youth who had been excommunicated. Hildegard lamented this silencing of music and prayer. Just before her death on September 17, 1179, the interdict was lifted.

Formal canonization never took place in Hildegard's case, though three attempts were made. Devotion to Hildegard was permitted by the Church from the fifteenth century on, with the title of saint.

Hildegard also wrote and practiced the medieval art of healing. Her learning in science and medicine was recognized even during her lifetime. Her understanding of the circulation of the blood and mental instability preceded and paved the way for later scientific studies and discoveries.

REFLECTIONS

- What have been the spiritual awakenings, small or large, in your life?
- Do women preach in your church? How do you feel about this?

PRAYER

May we behold you, God of light,
In the brightness of the morning sun
Coming through the windows;
In the brilliance of noonday sun
Shining through our windows;
In the radiance of setting suns
Seen from our western windows;
May we behold you
And dwell with you in light.
Amen.

September 18

MARGARET SLACHTA

Social worker • Hungary and U.S. • 1884–1974

SCRIPTURE THEME

Listening heart

"Speak, LORD, for your servant is listening."

— *1 Samuel 3:9*

QUOTATION

"We are to be pioneers for a better world, working for social reform not through decrees imposed by power but through renewal of the spirit from within. The society, crying out for liberation, challenges us to continue the redemptive mission of Christ."

—*Margaret Slachta,* The Spirit of Margaret Slachta Lives On, *page 4*

IN A NORTHERN CITY OF HUNGARY, Margaret was born September 18, 1884, as the second of six daughters, to an affluent and cultured middle-class family. She trained as a teacher with graduate studies in history, German and French. She took a teaching position and in 1907 was appointed prefect of the Budapest State Teachers' College. During those years, Margaret met two prominent women, Edith Farkas and Charlotte Koranyi, who were active in the promotion of women's rights and in the social mission of the Church. When the Social Mission Society was established by Edith Farkas, Margaret resigned her teaching position and became a member.

Margaret made a speech on women's rights in industry in 1909 and organized women for social service and political action. In 1920, Margaret was the first woman elected a member of the Hungarian Parliament. Her priorities were the social and political equality of women as well as housing, land reform and rights of workers.

Margaret's vision of the social implications of the gospel led her to found the Sisters of Social Service as a religious community devoted to direct service, legislation and political activity on behalf of the poor and oppressed. She became especially involved and outspoken against the persecution of the Jews by the Nazis. She took up the cause of the Slovakian Jews with Pope Pius XII. When Hitler moved into Hungary in 1944, Margaret opened the convents of the Sisters of Social Service and hid more than a thousand Jews.

Margaret was again elected to the Hungarian Parliament after World War II, but her Christian convictions were unpopular. In 1949, Margaret left Hungary for the United States. She lived with the Sisters of Social Service in Buffalo, New York. She died January 6, 1974, at St. Francis Hospital in Buffalo.

REFLECTIONS

- How does the gospel influence your concern for society as a whole? What have you done to continue "the redemptive mission of Christ"?
- What social ills in your community call for your involvement?

PRAYER

Guide us, Spirit of God,
To hear the cry of the oppressed
And turn toward them with the same compassion
That Christ showed for us.
Amen.

September 19

RACHEL LYMAN FIELD

Novelist • U.S. • 1894–1942

SCRIPTURE THEME

Quilts, patches

"Therefore every scribe who has been trained for the kingdom of heaven is like the master of a household who brings out of his treasure what is new and what is old."

— *Matthew 13:52*

QUOTATION

"You're just given so much to work with in a life and you have to do the best you can with what you got. That's what piecing is. The material is passed on to you or is all you can afford to buy... That's just what's given to you. Your fate. But the way you put them together is your business."

—*Anonymous,* And Then She Said..., *page 50*

WITH A SPECIAL FONDNESS FOR IMAGES OF QUILTS IN HER WRITING, Rachel achieved a creative integration of old and new in her novels. Her adult novels depict female characters in situations where endurance, strength and breadth of compassion are illustrated through the metaphor of trees. These novels are *All This and Heaven Too, And Now Tomorrow* and *Time Out of Mind.*

In her best work for young people, the history of a wooden doll is told by the doll herself. Rachel won a Newbery Medal for that book, *Hitty: Her First Hundred Years. Calico Bush* and *Hepatica Hawks* narrate the isolation of young girls.

Born September 19, 1894, in New York City, Rachel began her career as a writer of children's literature. She wrote plays and poems in a variety of types and forms. Rachel married Arthur S. Pederson in 1935 and did some writing with him.

She died March 15, 1942.

REFLECTIONS

- What literary images speak best to you of women—quilts, trees, windows, birds, others?
- In what area of your life do you find yourself piecing together the best of what's old and new?

PRAYER

May we find the truths of our lives
In keeping the best of what is old
And piecing with it what is new
So that we may weave and craft a story
That will keep others warm at night.
Amen.

September 20

WINNIE LETS

Joyful Christian • *England* • *1907–1972*

SCRIPTURE THEME

Joy

"I will rejoice in the LORD;
  I will exult in the God of my salvation."

— *Habakkuk 3:18*

QUOTATION

"People need joy quite as much as clothing. Some of them need it far more."

—*Margaret Collier Graham,* Beacon Book of Quotations by Women, *page 177*

WINNIE, CRIPPLED WITH ARTHRITIS AND IN CONSTANT PAIN, managed to come in her wheelchair to church every Sunday morning. It took her three hours to get dressed and ready, but every Sunday she would be there at the Northhampton church near a modern housing development.

Born in Northhampton in 1907, Winnie lost both her father and her stepfather by the time she was a teen. She got work in a box-making factory and at a shoe factory. While caring for an elderly aunt and uncle, she worked as linen mistress at a hospital. Eventually, her arthritis kept her at home, where she made boxes once more.

In the mid-1960's, Winnie married, but a stroke left her husband an invalid. She cared for him though she was nearly as disabled as he was. By Christmas of 1971, he was in the hospital and within the year, they both died.

Despite all this hardship, maybe because of it, Winnie was a joyful Christian. It is her joy that her congregation remembers. Her parish congregation remembers in particular a Palm Sunday procession in which Winnie was pushed around in a wheelchair with her palm branch on her lap and her voice raised in singing.

Winnie is one of those countless holy people who are saints in a real sense but generally unknown beyond their own parishes and families.

REFLECTIONS

- Who comes to mind when you think of unsung saints and heroes?

- What enables a person to keep a sense of joy in the midst of difficulties? Is this something you make an effort to do?

PRAYER

May we find in persons
With debilitating diseases and disabling conditions
A source of strength and courage
To face life's difficulties
With graced good humor and honest acceptance,
We pray to you, God.
Amen.

September 21

AGNES AND COLUMBA KIM

Martyrs · Korea · 19th century

SCRIPTURE THEME

Hymns at the cross

"Now when the centurion who stood facing him, saw that in this way he breathed his last, he said, 'Truly this man was God's Son!'"

— *Mark 15:39*

QUOTATION

"Over my spirit flash and float in divine radiancy the bright and glorious visions of the world to which I go."

—*Saint Teresa of Avila,* Quotable Saints, *page 49*

DURING THE 1592 JAPANESE INVASION OF KOREA, some Koreans were baptized as Christians. Because Korea generally refused contact with the outside world, evangelization was difficult. Only in 1777 did some Christian literature make its way into Korea from Jesuits in China. Home churches grew as educated Koreans studied Christianity. By 1790, there were four thousand Catholics. None of them had ever seen a priest. When a few Chinese priests and French missionaries came, the Catholics rapidly grew to ten thousand.

During the nineteenth century, the church flourished in Korea, mostly under lay leadership, but severe persecutions of the Church erupted in 1839, 1846 and 1867. All told, 103 Korean Catholics and some French missionaries were martyred. Among them were Saint Andrew Kim Taegon, a native priest, and men, women and children of all ages.

Among the women were Columba and Agnes Kim, sisters, who were imprisoned, tortured and eventually beheaded. Columba was twenty-six. Agnes, twenty-four at the time of her death, was tormented and crucified before being beheaded.

Religious freedom came for the Koreans in 1883. In the 1990's, there were about 1.7 million Catholics in Korea.

The Korean martyrs were canonized in 1984 by Pope John Paul II on his visit to Korea.

REFLECTIONS

- What is the role of the laity in the contemporary church? How do you feel about this?
- What are some of the current roadblocks to evangelization at home and abroad? What do you think can help?

PRAYER

May we be patient
In the small crosses of daily life
And ready for the big crosses
That may come our way.
Amen.

September 22

ALICE MEYNELL

Poet, essayist • England • 1847–1922

SCRIPTURE THEME

Patron of arts

"Like good stewards of the manifold grace of God, serve one another with whatever gift each of you has received."

— *1 Peter 4:10*

QUOTATION

"I shall not hold my little peace; for me there is no peace but one."

—*Alice Meynell*, The Quotable Woman: 1800–1981, *page 82*

BORN IN 1847, ALICE SPENT MUCH OF HER CHILDHOOD with her sister Elizabeth in Italy and Switzerland. They were educated by their father.

Raised in the Anglican religion, Alice converted to Catholicism in 1872. Five years later, she married Wilfred Meynell, a journalist, and they became the parents of eight children. One daughter, Viola, became a novelist and poet. In 1929, Viola wrote a memoir of her mother, and in 1952, of her father.

Alice's first book of poetry, *Prelude*, appeared in 1875 and heralded seven more volumes in the next twenty-five years. Her meditative poetry was praised and well received. In 1895, Alice was nominated for poet laureate. *The Rhythm of Life*, published in 1893, was one of several volumes of Alice's essays.

The Meynells befriended the poet Francis Thompson and counted other British writers among their friends. Their household became a cultural center.

REFLECTIONS

- Do you know a home where literature and the arts flourish? Were you raised in such a home?
- How has your experience of the arts informed your religious sensibilities?

PRAYER

Let us thank God
For those magnanimous women
Who have made it their practice
To be patrons of the arts
And who have nurtured the genius
Of many an artist.
Amen.

September 23

LOUISE NEVELSON

Sculptor, feminist • U.S.S.R. • 1900–1988

SCRIPTURE THEME

Maker of art

"She puts her hands to the distaff,
and her hands hold the spindle."

— *Proverbs 31:19*

QUOTATION

"The freer that women become, the freer will men be. Because when you enslave someone—you are enslaved."

—*Louise Nevelson*, The Quotable Woman: 1900–Present, *page 22*

LOUISE BERLIARVSKY WAS BORN in Kiva, Russia, on September 23, 1900, and moved to Maine with her parents in 1905. She graduated from high school in 1918, and married Charles Nevelson in 1920. The couple settled in New York City.

Louise studied voice, drama and painting. In the early 1930's, she intensified her study of painting, spending time in Europe. By 1940, she was doing sculpture in stone, plaster, terra cotta, metals and woods. She was praised for her originality. Some of her larger abstract pieces bear resemblance to Aztec and Mayan forms. In the 1950's, her works moved toward assemblage, that is, complex, many-layered and made with multiple materials. Her works were exhibited in the United States and Europe.

In the 1960's and 1970's, Louise accepted commissions for sculptures at the Albany South Mall, at the New York City Trade Center and for the Good Shepherd Chapel at St. Peter's Lutheran Church in New York City. Other celebrated pieces done by Louise include "Sky Cathedral," "Homage to the World" and "Tropical Rain Forest."

Louise is acknowledged as an innovator in the field of sculpture.

REFLECTIONS

- Check to see if your local art gallery has anything by Louise Nevelson. Look for her sculptures in art museums when you travel.

- Do you like assembling various materials to create a table centerpiece, a decorative piece, a window display?

PRAYER

> Creators of art
> Tell truth in new ways.
> Grant us, Creator-Spirit,
> New eyes to see truth
> In created art
> And new hearts to believe
> In uncreated truth.
> Amen.

September 24

EDITH ELMER WOOD

Housing economist • U.S. • 1871–1945

SCRIPTURE THEME

Housing

"Come, my people, enter your chambers,
and shut your doors behind you."
— Isaiah 26:20

QUOTATIONS

"Home is not where you live but where they understand you."
—*Christian Morgenstern*, Sunbeams, *page 51*

EDITH ELMER WAS BORN SEPTEMBER 24, 1871, to Horace and Adele Elmer. Edith was the oldest of two children. As children, Edith and her brother moved frequently in the United States and overseas because of their father's military assignments. Their formal education came from tutors and governesses.

Edith received her bachelor of letters degree from Smith College in 1890. In 1893, Edith married Albert N. Wood. They named their four children Horace Elmer (who died as a small child), Thurston Elmer, Horace Elmer II, and Albert Elmer.

In 1906, Edith turned her attention to public health because of the lack of facilities to care for tuberculosis patients. Once she realized the connection between inadequate and poor housing to the spread of tuberculosis, Edith, at age forty-four, enrolled in graduate school to learn the concepts and skills of housing and social economy. She completed her master's degree in 1917 and her doctorate degree in 1919. She served on committees concerned about housing, taught, lectured and wrote articles, urging government involvement for low- and middle-income families as a public necessity and responsibility.

Edith became a leading authority on housing. She spoke highly of housing practices in England, Germany, Belgium and Holland. In the 1930's, she worked as adviser to many housing programs and reforms. She promoted "constructive" rather than "restrictive" housing legislation and projects.

As a young woman, Edith had written romantic fiction. In her middle and later years, most of Edith's writing was precise and realistic and devoted to housing problems and their solutions.

Edith died April 29, 1945, at the family home in New Jersey.

REFLECTIONS

- How can women keep their family names alive? Is this important to you?
- If you were to return (or have returned) to college in midlife or later in life, what would you want to study? Why?
- What are the housing needs in your area?

PRAYER

Keep our minds and hearts open, O God,
To always seeing and learning more
About the needs of others
And creative ways to meet the needs.
Amen.

 *September 25*

BARBARA WALTERS

TV journalist • U.S. • 1931—

SCRIPTURE THEME

Journalism, truth

"And they went out and proclaimed the good news everywhere."
— *Mark 16:19*

QUOTATION

"If we could harness the destructive energy of disagreements in politics, we wouldn't need the bomb."

—Barbara Walters, The Quotable Woman: 1900–Present, *page 356*

REMEMBERED AS THE FIRST NEWSWOMAN TO SERVE AS AN ANCHOR, Barbara was born September 25, 1931, in Boston. As a child, Barbara met famous people at the nightclubs owned by her father. At sixteen, Barbara moved to New York City, where her father opened his largest nightclub.

Admiring Katherine Cornell, Barbara decided she also wanted to be a stage actress. But that and teaching gave way to writing, first as an advertising writer and then as a TV news writer. Barbara also learned to produce TV programs.

Barbara was hired as a writer for the *Today* show, and she soon was earning more than $100,000 a year. She began to write features. She interviewed many famous people and developed the knack for putting them and herself at ease and for treating serious subject matter.

In 1963, Barbara married Lee Guber, a theater owner and producer. In 1968, they adopted a child and named her Jacqueline. Balancing her early morning appearances on the *Today* show and her family, Barbara also traveled on assignments to England, Persia, China and other places.

When Barbara was offered the coanchor spot on the ABC evening news, it came with a $1-million-a-year, five-year contract.

Her first news program with Harry Reasoner on October 4, 1976, was a success. Barbara did special correspondent assignments, interviewing foreign heads of state and national leaders. She also hosted a Sunday program called *Issues and Answers*. And she does special ABC programs, usually four a year, in which she interviews big celebrities.

In the 1970's, Barbara was named one of the Women of the Decade. In 1978, she received a prize for fine reporting along with John Chancellor and Walter Cronkite. In 1988, she assembled portions of her best specials for *The 50th Barbara Walters Special*. Barbara continues hosting special programs.

REFLECTIONS

- What women do you admire in TV news reporting and special programs? What role does the news play in your daily life?
- What special challenges do women face when trying to balance family and career? Do you feel that this is fair?

PRAYER

For all the women
Who work in the public media,
We ask your blessings, Spirit of Truth,
And your guidance
So that they may always speak truth
Carefully with love
And so contribute
To the goodness and well-being
Of society and individuals.
Amen.

 *September 26*

WINNIE MANDELA

Medical worker, anti-apartheid activist · *South Africa* · *1936—*

SCRIPTURE THEME

Freedom

"He has sent me to proclaim release to the captives."

— Luke 4:18

QUOTATION

"I married the struggle, the liberation of my people."

—*Winnie Mandela*, Winnie Mandela, *page 24*

WINNIE MADIKIZELA WAS BORN IN PONDOLAND, SOUTH AFRICA, on September 26, 1936, the fifth of nine children. Her mother was very religious and taught her children to pray regularly. Her father gave her a sense of African history and a desire for freedom from apartheid.

At sixteen, Winnie went to Johannesburg to train as a medical worker. There she saw the great inequalities of the apartheid system. Her friendships led to her meeting Nelson Mandela, the lawyer and leader in the African National Congress. He invited her to lunch, took her for a walk, saw her whenever he could. And then one day he told her where to get her wedding dress made. They were married in June 1958.

They lived in the shantytown of Soweto, but Nelson was away much of the time for legal and political situations. Winnie worked in the Women's Federation, and this eventually cost her the job she held at the hospital.

Both Winnie and Nelson spent time in prison for their activities. Two daughters were born, Zenani and Zindziseva, and the place they knew best as home was a farm at Rivonia in the outskirts of Johannesburg. Nelson continued to be away most of the time and came home only secretly and disguised. In 1963, Nelson was sentenced to life imprisonment. Zindzi was four; Zeni was five.

Because of threats, Winnie sent the two girls to Swaziland where they would be safe for school. Nelson lived out his imprisonment on Robben Island doing hard labor.

When Winnie was arrested and imprisoned, she suffered from a deep sense of hopelessness. But she never gave in, not even after 491 days of questioning, beating and poor food in solitary confinement.

Winnie was walking with the schoolchildren of Soweto in June 1976 when twenty thousand students staged an uprising. She witnessed the killings that resulted and was imprisoned for her support of the children. Later, Winnie was confined to a black township outside Brandfort. There she turned her tiny home into a clinic and welfare station with a pot of hot soup always on her stove.

In the 1980's, protests worsened and the government declared a state of emergency. Winnie was banned from speaking in public, which she defied. When she spoke at the funeral of some Black children, the entire globe heard her words and cheered her cause.

By 1990, Nelson was released from prison, and he and Winnie made tours around the world for the cause of equality in South Africa. In 1991, Winnie was tried and convicted for the deaths of some youths—a result of a skirmish involving her bodyguards. She was found guilty of assault and kidnapping. She appealed the punishment.

In the 1990's, both Winnie and Nelson continued to work for and hope for an end to apartheid.

REFLECTIONS

- Read Winnie's book *Part of My Soul Went With Him* (New York: W. W. Norton and Company, 1984).

- For what ideals would you be willing to sacrifice your time? Your family's safety? Your life?

PRAYER

Keep us mindful, Lord,

Of the injustices that surround us.
Do not let our vision be dulled
By convention and public opinion,
But keep us faithful
To your vision.
Amen.

September 27

CATHERINE MARSHALL

Inspirational writer · U.S. · 1914–1983

SCRIPTURE THEME

Living water

"The water that I will give will become in them a spring of water gushing up to eternal life."

— John 4:14

QUOTATION

"God insists that we ask, not because He needs to know our situation, but because we need the spiritual discipline of asking."

—*Catherine Marshall*, The New Book of Christian Quotations, *page 191*

BORN SEPTEMBER 7, 1914, Catherine grew up in a Presbyterian household with a minister-father. After college, she married Peter Marshall in 1936. Peter was a pastor and served as chaplain of the U.S. Senate in the late 1940's. After his death, Catherine wrote to support herself and her son. The book Catherine wrote about her husband, *A Man Called Peter*, appeared in 1951 and remained a best-seller for many years. Writing about Peter in this biography-autobiography fashion, Catherine set forth the story of their marriage and devotion to God in prose that is sincere and clear. The book was made into a successful movie in 1955 with Catherine's assistance.

Catherine was named Woman of the Year in literature in 1953 by the Women's National Press Club. Catherine also wrote articles for *Guideposts*, an inspirational magazine, and in 1959 married its editor, Leonard Earle Le Sound.

In 1967, Catherine's novel *Christy* was published. The story, based on the life of Catherine's mother, tells of a young teacher whose fortitude comes from her faith. In 1978, Catherine published a series of forty devotionals about the Holy Spirit.

She died in March 1983.

REFLECTIONS

· Do you like inspirational writing? What do you find most inspiring?

· What is your favorite biography?

PRAYER

May fortitude born of faith
Sustain our spirits
All the days of our lives
As we move beyond ourselves
To find God in our midst.
Amen.

 *September 28*

FRANCES WILLARD

Social reformer • U.S. • 1839–1898

SCRIPTURE THEME

Shake the dust and move on

"Wherever you enter a house, stay there until you leave the place. If any place will not welcome you and they refuse to hear you, as you leave, shake off the dust that is on your feet as a testimony against them."

— Mark 6:10-11

QUOTATION

"I regard the women's temperance movement as without parallel and without peer because it does not expect to win through any sleight-of-hand, it does not expect to surprise the enemy by skirmishes of night attacks, but in the strong day-light of reason, conscience, faith—it does expect to put to rout the armies of the aliens—those aliens of appetite, ignorance and greed which form the only hope of whisky makers and beer politicians."

—Frances Willard, Give Her This Day, *page 277*

CHURCHVILLE, NEW YORK, WAS THE BIRTHPLACE on September 28, 1839, of Frances Willard, daughter of two schoolteacher parents who both encouraged a good education. At age seven, Frances moved with her family to Janesville, Wisconsin. Following the example of her brother, she pursued a college education and graduated as valedictorian of her class in 1859. During an 1860 illness, she experienced a religious conversion and became a serious member of the Methodist Episcopal Church.

Frances taught school during the 1860's and served as secretary and fund-raiser for a Methodist ladies group. After a broken engagement with Charles Fowler, Frances never married.

Upon becoming president of the Evanston College for Ladies in 1871, Frances became the first American woman to head a college. In 1973, Frances resigned because of financial and power struggles. She became involved in the Women's Christian Temperance Union and was elected the local president in 1874 and editor of its periodical in 1877. She became the national president of WCTU in 1879 and remained so for the rest of her life. During her tenure, the organization grew both in size and in influence for women's rights issues.

Another "first" came in 1888 when Frances was the first woman elected as a delegate to the general conference of the Methodist Episcopal Church. Though she was never seated because of opposition from certain men, the conference praised her temperance work.

After her death on February 18, 1898, her friends promoted memorials in her honor. Seven years after her death, her statue was placed in the rotunda of the Capitol in Washington, D.C., and five years after that, she was honored by inclusion in the Hall of Fame for Great Americans.

REFLECTIONS

- If you have a college education, consider the teachers and administrators who impressed you. Who among them were women? If you do not have a college education, ponder whether that is still a possible window of opportunity for you.

- What causes or activities have you been pushed out of because of opposition from men? From other women? From both?

PRAYER

Show us your path, Jesus,
When we meet up
With those who oppose us.
Show us your will,

In deciding whether to stay in patience
Or shake the dust from our feet
And move on.
Amen.

September 29

CATHERINE MCAULEY

Founder of Mercy Sisters • Ireland • 1778–1841

SCRIPTURE THEME

Mercy

"Because the Lord your God is a merciful God, he will neither abandon you nor destroy you; he will not forget the covenant with your ancestors that he swore to them."

— *Deuteronomy* 4:31

QUOTATION

"The sisters are tired; be sure they have a comfortable cup of tea when I am gone...if you give yourself entirely to God—all you have to serve him, every power of your mind and heart—you will have a consolation you will not know where it comes from..."

—*Catherine McAuley on her deathbed,* 150th Anniversary of the Death of Catherine McAuley, 1841-1991

BORN IN DUBLIN IN 1778, Catherine grew up during times of hardship for Catholics because of British oppression. Catherine learned from her father to be generous to the poor. Catherine's mother sought social status and rejected Catholicism when her husband died. The remembrance of her father's faith sustained Catherine during the general turmoil.

Catherine spent time helping others. When she was forty, she inherited a fortune from a childless couple whom she had befriended. With the money she bought property and built a residence for women who would do social service work. The archbishop of Dublin suggested to Catherine that she establish a religious congregation. On December 12, 1831, Catherine and two others professed religious vows, thus establishing the Sisters of Mercy.

The nuns went out from their convent to visit the poor and care for them. Other bishops asked for similar assistance, and Catherine established twelve houses in Ireland and two in England. Catherine died November 11, 1841.

Her congregation spread worldwide. In 1990, Pope John Paul II declared Catherine venerable, the first step toward canonization.

REFLECTIONS

- Every religious community loves to retell the story of its foundation. If you have a favorite group of religious, ask them to tell you their founding story.
- Invite someone to have a "comfortable cup of tea" with you.

PRAYER

God of Mercy,
Teach us to bring mercy to others,
Offering "a comfortable cup of tea"
And a listening heart
To those who come into our day.
Amen.

September 30

SAINT SOPHIA

Legendary mother of Faith, Hope and Charity • Rome • 2nd century

SCRIPTURE THEME

Wisdom

"Wisdom cries out in the street,
in the squares she raises her voice."
— *Proverbs 1:20*

QUOTATION

"It is Sophia who gifts us with inner freedom."
—*said of Saint Sophia,* The Star in My Heart, *page 64*

SAINT SOPHIA, ACCORDING TO LEGEND, was the mother of three daughters, whom she named Faith, Hope and Charity. They lived in second-century

Rome and were arrested during the persecutions of the Emperor Hadrian. When they refused to deny the faith, the daughters were put to death. Saint Sophia, it is said, died shortly afterward while praying at their tomb.

There are several other saints named Sophia, mostly in the Eastern church, but not much is known about them. There is also a church in Constantinople dedicated to Holy Wisdom *(Hagia Sophia)*, also called Sancta Sophia.

In the scriptural book of Wisdom, Sophia becomes a person, a "she"— the feminine personification of God. In her book *The Star in My Heart,* Joyce Rupp devotes a chapter to Sophia. In a story, Rupp tells about a blackbird in a stairwell who failed to find the open window and fly to freedom. She speaks of Sophia as that presence who leads "the true self to the open window."

It has been said that "darkness shows us where the windows are." Perhaps that should be rephrased to say that "in the darkness, Sophia shows us where the windows are."

REFLECTIONS

- What truths have you been led to by the inner voice of wisdom?
- When have you experienced what is commonly called "women's intuition"? Are you able to rely on it?

PRAYER

Move us, Sancta Sophia,
Toward the open window,
Where there is freedom,
Clarity, truth, insight, vision,
Wisdom and prayer.
Amen.

 *October 1*

THÉRÈSE OF LISIEUX

Carmelite nun • France • 1873–1897

SCRIPTURE THEME

Littleness

"But you, O Bethlehem of Ephrathah,
who are one of the little clans of Judah,
from you shall come forth for me
one who is to rule Israel."

— Micah 5:2

QUOTATION

"Each small task of everyday life is part of the total harmony of the universe."

— *Thérèse of Lisieux,* Sunbeams, *page 16*

MARIE FRANÇOISE THÉRÈSE MARTIN WAS BORN AT ALENÇON IN 1873. Her father was a watchmaker, and Thérèse, the youngest, was the delight of her father's heart. Five of the Martin daughters became nuns, three of them Carmelites.

In 1888, at age fifteen, Thérèse entered the Carmelite convent at Lisieux, where two of her sisters and several cousins already lived. She lived a very "ordinary" life with its rounds of prayer and work. She developed a spirituality that she named her "little way." It was based on childlike trust and love for God.

In her twenties, Thérèse developed tuberculosis, which caused her much suffering. In 1895, at the request of her religious superiors, she wrote the recollections of her childhood and her later life. After her death at age twenty-four, on September 30, 1897, the edited version of what she wrote was published as *Histoire D'une Ame: The Story of a Soul.* The autobiography was translated into many languages and held great appeal.

The obscure nun of Lisieux became tremendously popular. Favors through her intercession abounded, and in 1925, Thérèse was canonized. Pilgrims flocked to the new church and shrine built in Lisieux to honor Thérèse.

Thérèse may be one of the most popular saints of modern times because she showed that anyone can become a saint; any ordinary person can attain sanctity.

In 1958, the English version of her unedited manuscript was published as *Autobiography of a Saint*. Others, including Dorothy Day, have written biographical studies of Saint Thérèse.

REFLECTIONS

- Try to read the *Autobiography* if you have never done so.
- Some hold the pious belief that Saint Thérèse sends roses when she hears pleas directed to her attention. Do you know anyone who has experienced this?

PRAYER

May we turn, as did Thérèse,
To the Holy Scriptures,
In which a single luminous word
May open infinite windows
For our souls.
Amen.

 *October 2*

RUTH BRYAN OWEN ROHDE

Diplomat, public official • U.S., England and Denmark • 1885–1954

SCRIPTURE THEME

Diplomacy

"Go to Nabal, and greet him in my name."

— *1 Samuel 25:5*

QUOTATION

"The future is made of the same stuff as the present."

— *Simone Weil*, On Science, Necessity and the Love of God, The Beacon Book of Quotations by Women, *page 131*

UPON HER APPOINTMENT AS MINISTER OF DENMARK IN 1933 by President Franklin Roosevelt, Ruth became the first woman to represent the United States to a foreign country. Ruth was also the first woman from the Deep South ever elected to Congress when she won a seat in 1928 for Florida's Fourth District.

Born on October 2, 1885, in Illinois, Ruth grew up in Nebraska and Washington, D.C. She learned from her father, William Jennings Bryan, the art of public speaking as well as politics and campaigning. She attended the University of Nebraska for two years.

Her first marriage to William Leavitt in 1903 ended in 1909. In 1910, she married Major Reginald Owen, a British army officer. During World War I, Ruth aided the war effort by serving as secretary-treasurer in England and as volunteer nurse with the British in the Middle East.

After the war, Ruth and her husband moved to Florida. Ruth became involved in the Chautauqua and Lyceum lecture circuits. Continuing her interest in things political, Ruth ran unsuccessfully for a congressional seat in 1926. Her 1928 run put her in Congress. Her husband died in 1927.

Her appointment as minister to Denmark lasted until her 1936 marriage to Borge Rohde, a Danish army officer. Also in 1936, Ruth made a national campaign supporting President Roosevelt's reelection.

As an author, Ruth wrote many books, including books on Danish and Scandinavian fairy tales. Ruth also worked for several peace organizations.

King Frederick IX of Denmark honored Ruth in 1954 with the Distinguished Service Medal. She died soon after, at age sixty-eight, on July 26, 1954.

REFLECTIONS

- What interests and skills of your father's or mother's have become part of your life?
- When have you felt the desire to work with a peace organization?
- Follow in the news the work of women serving in the U.S. Congress.

PRAYER

May each of us
Learn the skills of diplomacy
So we may be
Ambassadors of gospel values
In our relations
With all people, near and far.
Amen.

October 3

JACOBA OF SETTESOLI

Noblewoman, Franciscan • *Italy* • *d. 1239*

SCRIPTURE THEME

Death

"You are dust,
and to dust you shall return."

　— Genesis 3:19

QUOTATION

"In prayer last evening I heard a voice which said: 'If you wish to see Brother Francis alive, go at once to Saint Mary of the Angels; take with you whatever will be necessary for his burial as well as the refreshments that you used to provide for him when he was ill at Rome.'"

　— Jacoba of Settesoli, The Franciscan Book of Saints, *pages 118-119*

A YOUNG NOBLEWOMAN NAMED JACOBA (GIACOMA) living in Rome heard of Francis of Assisi and desired to make his acquaintance. When Francis was in Rome (in the 1220's) to see the pope about approval for his rule, Jacoba got her wish. She was so moved by his sermons that she transferred her possessions to her two sons (her husband was already deceased) and devoted her life to prayer and service in the Franciscan tradition.

She became a member of the Third Order and arranged for a hospice near the Trans-Tiber section of Rome, where she cared for Franciscan friars on their journeys. She was especially devoted to those who were ill.

When Francis felt that he was dying, he sent for her, as he had promised, in a letter that has been preserved. But even before the letter was sent, Jacoba and her two sons arrived at the bedside of Francis. Jacoba attributed her insight to a voice from God, which told her to go to Francis immediately.

Jacoba remained with Francis the last four days of his life and provided him with assistance and comfort. She provided his burial cloth and helped the friars in making funeral arrangements. She attended the funeral of Francis.

Afterward, Jacoba put her affairs in Rome in order, renounced the world completely and returned to Assisi, where she spent her remaining days close to the tomb of Francis, her spiritual father.

On February 8, 1239, she died and was laid to rest in the same church where Francis had been buried. Francis had fondly called her Brother Jacoba, and so she is remembered in Franciscan history.

REFLECTIONS

- What does the corporal work of mercy "bury the dead" mean to you?
- Think about funerals you have attended and the spiritual comfort they offer.
- How do you assist the bereaved—with presence, time, practicalities?

PRAYER

O God, may your angels bring
Into paradise the souls
Of our departed relatives and friends.
Amen.

October 4

ANNE SEXTON
Poet • U.S. • 1928–1974

SCRIPTURE THEME

Poetry, death

"Then the earth reeled and rocked;
the foundations also of the mountains trembled
and quaked, because he was angry.
Smoke went up from his nostrils,
And devouring fire from his mouth;
glowing coals flamed forth from him."
— *Psalm 18:7-8*

QUOTATION

"God owns heaven
but He craves the earth."
— *Anne Sexton,* The Quotable Woman: 1900–Present, *page 323*

BORN NOVEMBER 2, 1928, Anne had a New England childhood that meant winters with a favorite great-aunt in Weston, Massachusetts, and seaside summers in Maine. She has been described as a rebellious and demanding child. She felt her upper-middle-class parents, Ralph and Mary Staples Harvey, rejected her.

At age twenty, Anne married Alfred Sexton. They had two daughters. Suicidal tendencies often hospitalized Anne and strained her relationships with her young daughters and her husband. The marriage ended in divorce in 1973.

At twenty-eight, Anne renewed her earlier interest in poetry and studied at Boston University with the poet Robert Lowell and others. Sylvia Plath was a classmate. All these poets wrote in the confessional style of using details of their personal lives as metaphors, sometimes in exaggeration, for larger, universal problems.

Some readers of Anne's poetry were repulsed by her forthright use of bodily parts and experiences in her poetry. When Anne wrote about adultery, abortion, menstruation, masturbation, incest and drug addiction, she broke taboos and proprieties.

Her problems in relationships, her guilt, loss and insanity all became the basis for what she explored and expressed in her poetry. Her 1966 volume, *Live or Die*, became a Pulitzer Prize-winner for its affirmation of life in the "mad" persona. Anne's other works reveal her concern for womanhood and the religious aspects of the self. Her best poetry, in images of hyperbole, connect personal conflict to the universal search for separated selves.

Anne taught at Boston University for many years. At the same time that she was winning fellowships and prizes, she was receiving psychiatric care. Her growing dependence on sedatives and alcohol in the 1970's and the urging inner voices that had always plagued her preceded her death. Her suicide, by gassing herself in the garage, on October 4, 1974, was similar in method to that of her friend Sylvia Plath.

REFLECTIONS

- Read some of Anne's poems, especially "The Awful Rowing Toward God." Reflect on her struggles and on your own struggles.

- Have you ever tried to write poetry as you lived through an intense experience of suffering or of happiness? What was the result?

- Reflect on some intense experience of your personal life, and write words and images to express your recollection. Work at making it into a poem.

- Do you know anyone who has attempted, or committed, suicide? How were you affected?

PRAYER

O God, we sing in celebration
Of the women we are.
Give us the insight to appreciate ourselves,
And to know our own importance,
Especially to those we leave behind.
Amen.

 *October 5*

MARIE-ROSE DUROCHER

Founder of international congregation · *Canada* · *1811–1849*

SCRIPTURE THEME

Obedience

"We take every thought captive to obey Christ."
— *2 Corinthians 10:5*

QUOTATION

"Give me the spirit you want [the children I teach] to have."
—*Marie-Rose Durocher*, Quotable Saints, *page 141*

MARIE-ROSE WAS BORN NEAR MONTREAL, CANADA, IN 1811, the tenth of eleven children. Her childhood was filled with school, horseback riding and other activities.

By age sixteen, she wanted to enter a convent, but her poor health prevented it. When Marie-Rose was eighteen, her mother died. Her brother, a priest at Belveil, Montreal, invited her to come live with him. She worked in the parish and rectory until she was thirty-one.

Bishop Ignace Bourget, bishop of Montreal at the time, urged Marie-Rose to establish a religious community of women. She hesitated because her health was still frail.

With two friends, Melodie Dufresne and Henriette Cere, Marie-Rose moved across the St. Lawrence to Longueriel and set up house with thirteen young girls in a boarding school. In this setting, an international congregation (in both the United States and Canada) was founded, and the community of sisters dedicated themselves to education. They are called the Sisters of the Holy Names of Jesus and Mary.

Marie-Rose died in 1849 and was beatified in 1982.

REFLECTIONS

- Marie-Rose practiced the penances and austerities typical of her time. What penances and austerities do your life and time require of you?
- Marie-Rose moved ahead with founding the community because the bishop wished her to do so. How does her sense of deference compare with your own? Her sense of obedience?

PRAYER

Let us pray for teachers
As Marie-Rose prayed:
"Give me the spirit
You want the children
To have."
Amen.

 *October 6*

JIHAN SADAT

Social activist • Egypt • 1934—

SCRIPTURE THEME

Women's strength

"Finally, be strong in the Lord and in the strength of his power."
— *Ephesians 6:10*

QUOTATION

"It is a fact that I have enemies. But I believe also that the majority of women are with me. The old ways will never return."
— *Jihan Sadat, 1986 Current Biography Yearbook, page 485*

JIHAN, WHOSE NAME IN PERSIAN MEANS "THE WORLD," was born on an island in the Nile River, Egypt. She was the third daughter of four children. Her mother was from England and her father a descendent from Egyptian pharaohs. Nicknamed Jean, she attended a Christian missionary school while she lived and practiced the religion of Islam at home.

As a child in a warm and loving home, Jihan learned to love her country and her family.

Jihan went to secondary school in Cairo and at fifteen met Anwar Sadat, a twenty-nine-year-old former army officer just released from prison. Jihan and Anwar married on May 29, 1949. It was Jihan's choice—not a more typical arranged marriage.

While Anwar became more involved in the Egyptian revolution, Jihan had four children, three daughters and a son. During the 1967 Egyptian-Israeli War, Jihan served as a Red Cross volunteer. She also established a self-help cooperative in a Nile village.

In 1970, Anwar became president of Egypt. As the presidential couple, Jihan and Anwar made it clear that Jihan would be very involved in government affairs.

She continued her education and received her master's degree in Arabic literature in 1980. She established Children's Villages for orphans, increased her humanitarian efforts and worked with her husband in securing more rights for women and encouraging him in the Egyptian-Israeli peace mission.

For Jihan Sadat, as for all of Egypt, October 6 remains a day of great significance. It was on this day in 1973 when Egypt reclaimed land taken by Israel. It was also on this day, in 1981, that Anwar Sadat was assassinated. Jihan always returns to Egypt to honor her husband on this date.

After a period of mourning for her husband's death, Jihan resumed doctoral studies and continued her lectures at Cairo University. She also lectured in the United States and elsewhere on the status of women. In 1986, she completed her doctorate. She continues to observe her Muslim religion, praying five times a day as required.

Her autobiography, *A Woman in Egypt*, was completed in 1987.

REFLECTIONS

- Jihan affirms the traditional roles of women in family and child rearing while she encourages professional and social equality for women. How do you feel about this "both/and" approach to balancing women's lives?
- Many in the Arab world consider Jihan too liberal, while many in the West criticize her for being less than revolutionary. What do you say about her?

PRAYER

For women around the world,
We pray to you, God,

That their rights and freedoms
May be secured and protected.
Amen.

 *October 7*

OUR LADY OF THE ROSARY

SCRIPTURE THEME

Hail Mary

"Look, the young woman is with child and shall bear a son, and shall name him Immanuel."

— *Isaiah 7:14*

QUOTATION

"Greetings, favored one! The Lord is with you."

— *Luke 1:28*

IN 1571, CHRISTIAN EUROPEAN AND TURKISH FORCES BATTLED EACH OTHER at the Bay of Lepanto, off the coast of Greece. Pope Pius V, aware of the crisis, prayed the rosary to Our Lady of Victory. Thousands joined the pope, using the rosary as their weapon to forestall the planned invasion of Europe by the Turks.

The battle was won by the Europeans, and the pope ordered an annual feast to honor Our Lady of Victory.

Pope Gregory XIII changed the name to Our Lady of the Rosary. Recently the date was fixed as October 7.

REFLECTIONS

· For the past 500 years, the rosary has been the principal Marian devotion in the Church. Read more about the rosary devotion of the Dominicans, of Lourdes, of Fatima.

· Pray the rosary while meditating on the mysteries of Jesus and Mary.

PRAYER

Hail Mary, full of grace,
The Lord is with you.
Blessed are you among women,

And blessed is the fruit of your womb, Jesus.
Holy Mary, mother of God,
Pray for us sinners,
Now and at the hour of our death.
Amen.

 *October 8*

EMILY BLACKWELL

Surgeon, administrator • U.S. • 1826–1910

SCRIPTURE THEME

Healing

"Those who are well have no need of a physician, but those who are sick."
— Matthew 9:12

QUOTATION

"As teachers, then, to diffuse among women the physiological and sanitary knowledge which they need, we found the first work of women physicians."
— Elizabeth Blackwell, The Quotable Woman, 1800–On, *page 45*

WHEN EMILY CAME TO HELP HER SISTER Dr. Elizabeth Blackwell in the New York City Infirmary, the responsibility of management and fund-raising fell to Emily. The rapid growth of the services and the opening of a medical school were largely due to Emily's efforts. And when Elizabeth moved back to England in 1869, Emily took full responsibility for the operation of the hospital and school of nursing.

Emily, born on October 8, 1826, was five-and-a-half years younger than her sister Elizabeth. Emily was not quite six when the family moved to New York City. Both girls were well educated. Emily's interest in medical school led her to Rush Medical College in Chicago and later to the medical college of Western Reserve University in Cleveland. She received her degree in 1854 and then pursued further medical studies in Europe.

As dean of the nursing school founded by her sister, Emily saw the college develop a four-year program that graduated 364 women in thirty years. In 1899, Emily transferred her students to Cornell University Medical College, which had started accepting female students on a par with male students.

Emily continued her work with the infirmary until her death on September 7, 1910.

REFLECTIONS

- See the entry for Elizabeth Blackwell on February 3. How are these two sisters alike? Different?
- Have you ever experienced overshadowing by one of your sisters or brothers? How did it affect you?

PRAYER

Guide us, Jesus, Divine Physician,
In the spirit of your healing miracles,
As we are of service to others
In the areas of health and healing
And holistic living.
Amen.

 *October 9*

AIMEE SEMPLE MCPHERSON

Founder of International Church of the Foursquare Gospel • Canada and U.S. • 1890–1944

SCRIPTURE THEME

Ezekiel's vision

"As for the appearance of their faces: the four had the face of a human being, the face of a lion on the right side, the face of an ox on the left side, and the face of an eagle; such were their faces."

— *Ezekiel 1:10*

QUOTATION

"Don't ever tell me that a woman cannot be called to preach the Gospel. If any man ever went through one-hundredth the part of hell-on-earth that I lived in, they would never say that again."

— *Aimee Semple McPherson,* Remember the Ladies, *page 170*

AIMEE WAS BORN OCTOBER 9, 1890. Her early years saw her reared in the

Salvation Army and married to a Pentecostal evangelist, Robert James Semple. She was converted to her husband's religion and the couple went to China as missionaries.

Aimee's personal life has been described as "colorful" and "outrageous." She divorced her husband the same year she married him.

In 1910, Aimee returned to the United States and resumed work with her mother in the Salvation Army. Her second marriage in 1912 to Harold McPherson ended in divorce in 1921.

By 1915, she began a career as an itinerant preacher and healer. She also wrote and published a magazine. Her travels took her all over the United States and Canada, as well as to England, Australia and other countries.

Her revivals attracted thousands. She made her headquarters in Los Angeles and built her Angelus Temple there. In 1923, the temple was dedicated as the "Church of the Foursquare Gospel" based on Ezekiel's vision of a four-faced creature.

In the 1920's, Aimee had a romantic involvement with Kenneth Ormiston. In 1931 she entered into marriage with David L. Hutton. This marriage ended in divorce in 1934. Aimee was revered by many for her faith healings and her services to the poor, but others criticized her and called her "Jezebel."

Aimee's personal appeal and preaching along with her showmanship of robed choirs and costumed pageants and orchestral music attracted ever-larger crowds. Her services were broadcast on the radio.

In the 1930's, lawsuits and accusations of financial improprieties plagued Aimee, but none of this affected her loyal following. She founded a Bible college to train evangelists and missionaries. By the mid-1940's, Aimee's Foursquare Gospel movement had four hundred branches in the United States and Canada and two hundred missions overseas.

Death came for Aimee on September 27, 1944, from a sleeping pill overdose, which was declared accidental. Aimee's son, Rolf, carried on her work.

REFLECTIONS

- What do you think makes evangelism, especially fundamental evangelism, so appealing to people?
- Notice the use of communication media used by Aimee—preaching, radio, printed word, spectacle. What form of communication speaks most effectively to you? Why?

PRAYER

For the women who preach
By good example,
By writing and by speaking,
We ask your blessing, O God.
Amen.

 *October 10*

MOTHER ANGELA

Religious founder · Poland · 1825–1899

SCRIPTURE THEME

Humility

"For you have died, and your life is hidden with Christ in God."
— *Colossians 3:3*

QUOTATION

"My only duty is to pray for the sanctification of all the sisters and to place them in the hearts of Jesus and Mary, so that our congregation may conform to the designs of God."
— *Mother Angela,* Mother Angela and the Felician Sisters, *page 7*

BORN ON MAY 16, 1825, IN KALISZ, POLAND, Sophia Truskowska was the oldest of seven children. Her father was a lawyer. Both of her parents promoted religion, culture and education in their home. Sophia was educated by private tutors and at a girls' school. She also traveled with her father and was instructed by him.

In her early twenties, Sophia and her cousin Clothilde began to think more seriously about religious life. As a member of the Saint Vincent de Paul Society and of the Secular Third Order Franciscans, Sophia developed a sense of charity for those in need.

In 1854, Sophia founded the Institute of Miss Truszkowska for orphans and the aged. Most of her coworkers were Franciscan tertiaries and members of the society of Saint Vincent de Paul. The formal dedication of the several young women took place in Warsaw on November 21, 1855. Sophia became known as Mother Angela.

In 1860, Mother Angela founded the contemplative branch of the congregation and served as superior and spiritual mother to both branches. The group took the name of the congregation of the Sisters of Saint Felix of Cantalice, commonly called the Felician Sisters. Saint Felix was the patron saint of children. The suppression of the congregation in 1864 by the Russian government forced Mother Angela to relocate to Kraków where Austrian authority was in power.

In 1869, at age forty-four, because of ill health and total deafness, Mother Angela resigned from office and joined the ranks. For thirty years, she lived a simple, prayerful life. She died October 10, 1899, in Kraków, where she is buried.

In 1982, Pope John Paul II confirmed the decree of the heroic virtues of Mother Angela as Servant of God. On April 16, 1993, Pope John Paul II beatified Blessed Angela following a miracle obtained through her intercession. Lillian Halasinski of Dunkirk, near Buffalo, New York, received the miracle in the form of a cure of her diabetic neuropathy. Lillian and her daughter Geraldine attended the ceremonies in Rome and also visited the grave of Blessed Angela in Kraków.

REFLECTIONS

- If there are Felician Sisters in your area, learn more about their care of poor and deprived children and the aged and other forms of service. How can you assist in this type of ministry?
- Mother Angela tended flowers during her time of illness and spiritual trial. What activity brings you peace of mind?

PRAYER

Teach us, loving God,
To help all in need
Without distinction or discrimination;
To help all in need,
Friend and foe alike;
For everyone is our neighbor
And the globe is our neighborhood.
Amen.

 *October 11*

ELEANOR ROOSEVELT

First Lady, humanitarian, writer, diplomat • U.S. • 1884–1962

SCRIPTURE THEME

Political efforts, ambassador

"And how are they to proclaim him unless they are sent?"
— Romans 10:15

QUOTATION

"It isn't enough to talk about peace. One must believe in it. And it isn't enough
to believe in it. One must work at it."

— Eleanor Roosevelt, The New York Public Library Book of Twentieth Century
American Quotations, *page 471*

ELEANOR WAS BORN OCTOBER 11, 1884, and was educated at private schools
in the United States and England. Both of her parents died by the time
she was ten. She was raised by relatives.

At age seventeen, Eleanor worked as a volunteer in settlement schools.
In 1903, she married Franklin D. Roosevelt, her cousin. She was the niece
of Theodore Roosevelt. Franklin and Eleanor had six children; one died
in infancy.

After her husband's polio and paralysis, she became especially active
in his political career. In her own right, she became a great supporter of
women's and minorities' rights. She also devoted much time and energy
to the organization of volunteer services.

Eleanor, with two other women, founded a school and a craft factory.
In 1936, Eleanor began her newspaper column, "My Day," which made
her familiar in every American household.

She wrote books for children, her autobiography and other books.
After her husband's death in 1945, President Truman appointed her U.S.
delegate to the United Nations. Her role in establishing the Declaration
of Human Rights in 1948 was recognized with a standing ovation at the
United Nations.

She worked with several reform groups. Serving on the Commission
on the Status of Women in 1961–1962 was her last public position.
Eleanor died October 14, 1962.

REFLECTIONS

- What courage did Eleanor require to become politically active for the sake of her paralyzed husband? When have you had to develop strengths to compensate for the weaknesses of another?

- Many aspiring social reformers found a friend in Eleanor Roosevelt. What sort of social reform do you favor? How are you active in its support?

PRAYER

We pray that we may
Look to the future
With deep faith in God
And in the deep truth
Of our dreams.
Amen.

October 12

CARYLL HOUSELANDER

Mystic · England · 1901–1954

SCRIPTURE THEME

Psychological suffering

"Whenever you face trials of any kind, consider it nothing but joy, because you know that the testing of your faith produces endurance."

— James 1:2

QUOTATION

"Few mothers realize that their children are part of a whole and that the whole is the family of God, to whom every child born owes all the love and service of a brother or sister. Many mothers try to shield their children from the common life, to give them a sheltered upbringing, so to shield them from all risk or sickness or pain or poverty that they are shielded from vitality and the vast experience of living. They hate to see them grow or experience anything that will make them independent."

— *Caryll Houselander,* The Reed of God, *page 60*

BORN ON SEPTEMBER 19, 1901, Caryll became a member of the Catholic Church when she was about six and called herself a "rocking horse" Catholic rather than a "cradle" Catholic. In fact, Caryll titles her autobiography *A Rocking Horse Catholic*. She writes of memories—"isolated points that stand out" when she was between two and four years old.

The religious influence of Smoky, a family friend, and the example of the family physician are explained in Caryll's autobiography. Caryll describes long prayers at home and a great many Masses on Sundays—two Masses, plus catechism classes, plus benediction. She explains her first confession and Communion and the special inward change of her second Communion experience, which was given to her as Holy Viaticum during a strange illness.

Another focal point of Caryll's experience of Holy Viaticum centers on the real presence in the Blessed Sacrament and its connection to the Mystical Body.

Caryll's childhood experience of anxiety neurosis colored her attitude toward psychological suffering. She came to feel compassion for others with this kind of suffering and became convinced that "the only real cure for it is the touch of God."

The separation of her parents and her education at a French convent school gave Caryll the sufferings and joys of her later childhood years. In her mid-teens, Caryll returned to her mother in London. Further health problems forced her into the life of an invalid and morbid shyness. She continued her education at an English convent.

In July 1918, Caryll saw a vision of a Russian icon of Christ the King Crucified over London, and she began to associate the Passion of Christ with the sufferings of Russia. She wrote several books, including *The Way of the Cross, The Passion of the Infant Christ, The Reed of God* and *The Risen Christ*. She died on October 12, 1954.

REFLECTIONS

- What childhood memories offer focal points for your life?
- What psychological sufferings have helped shape your spirituality?

PRAYER

May we ponder icons
As windows
Into the spiritual world
And in them
Experience God's presence.
Amen.

October 13

MARGARET THATCHER

Prime minister • England • 1925—

SCRIPTURE THEME

Leadership

"Let your light shine before others, so that they may see your good works and give glory to your Father in heaven."

— *Matthew 5:14*

QUOTATION

"The only thing I'm going to do for you is make you feel freer to do things for yourselves."

— *Margaret Thatcher,* Margaret Thatcher: Britain's 'Iron Lady,' *page 55*

GRANTHAM, ABOUT A HUNDRED MILES FROM LONDON, is the childhood hometown of Margaret Thatcher. Margaret Hilda Roberts, born October 13, 1925, grew up in Grantham in the rooms above the grocery shop run by her father.

Her father was interested in religion and politics, and strong-minded Margaret received praise from him for her intelligence. She was determined to be a leader.

Margaret went to Oxford University, where she took up the study of chemistry. She was the first woman to be selected as the president of the Oxford University Conservation Association. It was during her Oxford days that Margaret decided she ought to be a member of Parliament.

She got involved with politics and met Denis Thatcher, whom she married.

Margaret rejoiced when Queen Elizabeth was crowned in 1953 and wrote an article which was headlined "Wake Up, Women!" Also in 1953, Margaret gave birth to twins and proceeded to combine career and family life quite successfully.

In 1959, Margaret took her seat as a member of Parliament. She was just thirty-four. In 1969, Margaret Thatcher was chosen to be the Shadow Secretary for Education, and in 1970, Secretary for Education.

In 1975, she was elected leader of her party, and in 1979, she became Great Britain's first female prime minister. She made her presence felt in England as well as in global politics.

In November 1990, Margaret left her role as prime minister and returned to private life. In June 1992, Margaret took the oath and was sworn in as a member of the House of Lords, an honorary position.

REFLECTIONS

- What qualities do you admire about Margaret Thatcher? What do you feel is the appropriate place for women with political skills?
- Watch for news stories on other women as world leaders.

PRAYER

We thank you, God,
Ruler of our universe,
For great women rulers of the past,
And pray that you gift
Those of the present
With wisdom and strength.
Amen.

 *October 14*

HANNAH ARENDT

Political scientist, philosopher · *Germany and U.S.* · *1906–1975*

SCRIPTURE THEME

Thinking

"Where is the one who is wise?"

— *1 Corinthians 1:20*

QUOTATION

"The sad truth is that most evil is done by people who never make up their minds to be either good or evil."

— *Hannah Arendt,* The Great Thoughts, *page 16*

BORN OCTOBER 14, 1906, in Germany, of German-Jewish parents, Hannah (Johanna) was educated in Germany, studied philosophy with Karl Jaspers as teacher and wrote her doctoral dissertation on Saint Augustine. Hannah fled to France when the Nazis came to power and then made her way to the United States. As a political theorist, she taught at various universities in the States.

In her best-known work, *The Origins of Totalitarianism*, Hannah describes how imperialism and anti-Semitism and "organized loneliness" contribute to the success of totalitarian movements. She also wrote *The Human Condition* and *On Revolution*.

The *New Yorker* magazine sent Hannah in 1961 to cover the trial of Adolf Eichmann. Hannah's observations and reflections led her to maintain a distinction between thinking and knowing. She said that Eichmann's monstrous crimes were related to his lack of thought.

Some considered Hannah elitist, but others saw that her sensitive writings held insight into the perplexities of modern times. Hannah forced her listeners and readers to think.

Hannah died December 4, 1975.

REFLECTIONS

- Someone has described the reluctance to do one's own thinking as "taking a moral vacation." How seriously do you do your own searching for truth, your own thinking and judging between good and evil?

- Some consider intellectuals elitist. Often, they are the thinkers who challenge others to satisfy the quest for meaning through honest thinking. What have you done lately, or what do you do regularly, to provide opportunities for intellectual growth?

PRAYER

Instruct us in your ways, O God,
And enable us to think
Deeply and clearly
About essential truths.
Bless the philosophers in our midst,
And help each of us
To philosophize a little
As we pray
About our daily lives.
Amen.

 *October 15*

TERESA OF AVILA

Carmelite reformer • Spain • 1515–1582

SCRIPTURE THEME

Water

"He leads me beside still waters;
he restores my soul."

— Psalm 23:2

QUOTATION

"Remember that you have only one soul; that you have only one death to die; that you have only one life, which is short and has to be lived by you alone; and there is only one glory, which is eternal. If you do this, there will be many things about which you care nothing."

—Teresa of Avila, The Quotable Woman: From Eve to 1799, *page 101*

HUMOR AND LIGHTHEARTEDNESS CHARACTERIZE THIS SAINT despite her trials and difficulties. Though she entered the Carmelite Convent of the Incarnation of Avila when she was twenty, she was forty when she seriously gave herself over to the service of God. She then devoted herself to the reform of her own life and that of the Carmelite convents.

Teresa was born in Avila in 1515. A lively and intelligent girl, she had a good upbringing.

On entering the Carmelite convent, Teresa enjoyed a life of relative ease and leisure. She entertained a wide circle of friends at the convent where the rules had been greatly relaxed. She was ill, probably with malignant malaria, and chose to ignore the practice of mental prayer.

When she was middle-aged, Teresa decided to reform her own life. She devoted herself to contemplative prayer. By 1562, she had established a new Carmelite convent under the strict and original form of the Carmelite rule. They were called the discalced because they went barefoot; the relaxed rule was called calced, meaning "shod."

Teresa spent twenty years traveling all around Spain. In all, she founded seventeen convents and insisted that they stay small, poor, enclosed and highly disciplined. She included daily mental prayer in their rule. With Teresa's help, Carmelite men also reformed their rule and way of life.

While maintaining a constant prayer life, Teresa attended to practical affairs. She also wrote spiritual and practical books, including her *Life of Teresa of Avila, The Way of Perfection, The Book of Foundations* and *The Interior Castle.* It is the spiritual truths about contemplative prayer in *The Interior Castle* that qualify Teresa as doctor of the Church, a title the Church gave to Teresa in 1970.

Teresa died in 1582 and was canonized in 1622. Several translations of her writings have been made. Also, three volumes of her letters have been published.

REFLECTIONS

- Read Teresa's *Pater Noster.*
- Read Teresa's words on the Samaritan woman and water in *The Interior Castle.*
- Pope John Paul II approved two forms of the Carmelite rule in 1991, which affirms a certain diversity of approach. Does your spiritual life tend to be highly disciplined or more relaxed?

PRAYER

"If, Lord, Thy love for me is strong
As this which binds me unto Thee,
What holds me from Thee, Lord, so long,
What holds Thee, Lord, so long from me?"
Amen.

 *October 16*

MARGUERITE D'YOUVILLE

Founder of Grey Nuns • Canada • 1701–1771

SCRIPTURE THEME

Hear the cry of the poor

*"Blessed are you who are poor,
for yours is the kingdom of God.
Blessed are you who are hungry now,
For you will be filled.
Blessed are you who weep now,
For you will laugh."*

— *Luke 6:20-21*

QUOTATION

"...[T]o live together...in perfect union and charity...to consecrate our lives...our work...for the poor."

— Commitment of Marguerite and all subsequent Grey Nuns, Lives of the Saints, *page 470*

MARGUERITE WAS BORN IN 1701 to a prominent family near Montreal in what was then called New France. Her father died when she was six. Relatives helped support her education at the boarding school of the Ursuline convent in Quebec City.

Marguerite married at twenty-one. Four of her six children died as infants, and her husband died when she was twenty-nine. Even before her husband's death, a spiritual conversion brought her to a greater piety and charity. She devoted herself to the care of her two sons as well as to prayer and charity for the poor.

In 1737, with three friends, Marguerite took noncanonical vows of chastity, poverty and obedience. The four women pledged themselves to service of the poor.

Marguerite and the others suffered misunderstanding from family and townsfolk. Marguerite's husband had trafficked in alcohol with the American Indians for fur pelts. By association, they were called *les grises,* which means "the grey ladies," an idiom for "drunken women." In 1755, eleven members of Marguerite's community took the habit of religious life and called themselves *"Les Soeurs Grises,"* "the Grey Nuns." They were also known as the Sisters of Charity of Montreal.

Marguerite died December 23, 1771. She was beatified on May 3, 1959, and canonized on December 9, 1990. This made her the first Canadian-born canonized saint.

REFLECTIONS

- Consider Marguerite as a wife, mother, widow, religious and servant to the poor. Which role most appeals to you?
- Marguerite's hands made lace and carried bricks, bathed frail bodies and buried the dead, drained swamps and built hospitals—all to serve the poor. How do your hands render service to the poor?

PRAYER

"Our Father,
Who art in heaven,
Hear the voice
Of Thy children on earth...
O Father,

Source of all love,
Multiply our works of charity
And render them fruitful
Into eternal life."
Amen.

 *October 17*

KAREN BLIXEN

Writer • Denmark and Kenya • 1885–1962

SCRIPTURE THEME

Parables

*"I will open my mouth in a parable,
I will utter dark sayings from of old."*

— Psalm 78:2

QUOTATION

"If only I could so live and so serve the world that after me there should never again be birds in cages..."

— Karen Blixen, And Then She Said, *page 14*

IN THE LATE 1980'S, THE FILM VERSION OF *BABETTE'S FEAST* made the rounds of movie theaters and entertained audiences with its story of devoted and extravagant love. Many were surprised to learn that the creator of the story also wrote *Out of Africa*, another popular film of the time.

Karen (Christence) Blixen, who wrote under the name of Isak Dinesen and other pseudonyms, was born on October 17, 1885, in Denmark. She studied in European cities and married her cousin, Baron Bron Blixen-Finecke, in 1914. She went with him to the highlands of Kenya in East Africa, where they tried to raise coffee. After their divorce, Karen continued to manage the coffee plantation by involving the local people. She also wrote stories during the rainy seasons.

In 1931, Karen left Kenya and devoted her time to professional writing, spinning charming and creative tales in both Danish and English. After a serious illness, Karen wrote her memoirs, *Out of Africa*, in which the Ngong Hills seen from her bungalow windows serve as a focal point.

Shadows on the Grass also tells of her days in Africa. Karen Blixen has a permanent place in modern European literature as a great storyteller.

She died September 7, 1962.

REFLECTIONS

- Watch *Out of Africa* or *Babette's Feast*.
- Karen's attitude toward native African people was considered colonial, sometimes arrogant. Still, she offered them opportunities for education and work. How do you view relationships between people of different races, especially unequal relationships?

PRAYER

We want to know you, O God,
And your story,
And we want to be
Part of your story.
Amen.

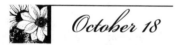 *October 18*

ANNIE SMITH PECK

Mountain climber • U.S. • 1850–1935

SCRIPTURE THEME

Mountains

"Come, let us go up to the mountain of the LORD,
to the house of the God of Jacob;
that he may teach us his ways
and that we may walk in his paths."

— Isaiah 2:3

QUOTATION

"While far below men crawl in clay and cold,
Sublimely I shall stand alone with God."

— *Mary Sinton Leitch,* The Quotable Woman 1800–On, *page 161*

ANNIE CLIMBED HER LAST MOUNTAIN, Mount Madison in New Hampshire, at age eighty-two. Her first was Mount Shasta in California, which she tackled at age thirty-eight. Her courage, endurance and physical strength were built as a child in competitive activities with her three brothers.

Annie was born October 19, 1850, in Rhode Island. She attended local schools and trained to be a teacher. She graduated with honors in 1873 from the University of Michigan. She taught in various schools, including Purdue University where she taught Latin. She took up advanced studies in German and became the first woman admitted to the American School of Classical Studies in Athens, Greece.

In 1885, Annie traveled in Greece and Germany. It was on this trip that the sight of the Matterhorn aroused her interest in mountain climbing.

In 1895, Annie became a celebrity when she climbed the Matterhorn. She pursued other mountains and supported herself by giving lectures, including some on the Chautauqua lecture circuit.

Annie climbed mountains in Mexico, Europe and South America, setting records of highest mountains climbed by women. At sixty-one, Annie climbed Mount Coropuna in Peru and planted a "Votes for Women" banner on its 21,250-foot peak. In 1927, the north peak of Mount Huascarin in Peru was named Cumbre Aña Peck.

Annie died in New York City on July 18, 1935.

REFLECTIONS

- What mountains—physical, spiritual, psychological—have you climbed?
- What would you like to (or are trying to) accomplish in your later years?

PRAYER

In facing mountains,
And in climbing mountains,
May we be strengthened
By a vision of our God
Who leads us up holy heights.
Amen.

October 19

AMANDA JONES

Developer of canning process • U.S. • 1835–1914

SCRIPTURE THEME

Inventions

"Whatever your hand finds to do, do it with your might."

— *Ecclesiastes 9:10*

QUOTATION

"My parents imagined that a child of three, exceptionally vigorous, who could name all the letters of the alphabet after a single telling, was old enough to go to school...."

— Amanda Jones, Give Her This Day, *page 299*

IN 1873, AMANDA INVENTED A CANNING PROCESS FOR FOOD using a vacuum and heated fluids. She obtained patents for her process, but a commercial venture using the process failed. In the 1880's, she invented and patented a liquid fuel burner, but the commercial venture using this also failed.

This enterprising woman was born October 19, 1835, in East Bloomfield, near Canandaigua, New York, and was educated in Black Rock and East Aurora, both near the city of Buffalo. Amanda also was tutored at home. For a time, she taught school and wrote poems, some of which were published. She moved to Chicago in 1869 and worked as editor and in other roles at various periodicals.

Her canning process and stove burner inventions led her to organize the Woman's Canning and Preserving Company in Chicago in 1890. The employees and stockholders of her company were women insofar as that was possible. Over the years, she continued to write and experiment. In the early 1900's, she received seven more patents, four in the canning processes and three connected to the fuel burner.

At an early age, Amanda converted to spiritualism and in 1910 published *A Psychic Autobiography*. She died March 31, 1914, in Kansas where she had lived since 1893.

REFLECTIONS

- What have you "invented"? How does your creativity bring joy to your life?

- Amanda combined scientific experimentation and invention with a love of writing poetry. What "opposites" are found in your activities?

PRAYER

We praise you, God,
For women with ideas
Who become "mothers of invention"
And improve the quality of life.
Amen.

 *October 20*

BERTILLA BOSCARDIN

Care of sick and of children · Italy · 1888–1922

SCRIPTURE THEME

Nursing
"He heals the brokenhearted,
and binds up their wounds."
— *Psalm 147:3*

QUOTATION

"To God all the glory, to my neighbor all the joy, to me the work."
—Bertilla Boscardin, Lives of the Saints, *page 382*

BORN IN 1888 NEAR VERONA, ITALY, Sister Bertilla was baptized Annetta. At sixteen, she entered the Sisters of Saint Dorothy at Vincenza. She trained as a nurse at Treviso.

When assigned to the children's ward, Sister Bertilla's devotion to the sick became well-known. During World War I, the Treviso hospital was taken over by the army and eventually was on the front line of attack. Sister Bertilla worked with courage and heroism among the patients, including the soldiers.

After the war, she was put in charge of the children's ward at Treviso hospital. In 1921, she had an operation, and never in good health, she died October 20, 1922, at age thirty-four.

The people of Treviso considered her an angel of mercy and had a plaque put in the hospital which describes her as "a soul of heroic greatness." Though an obscure nursing sister, her holiness touched the lives of patients. She was canonized in 1961, less than forty years after her death.

REFLECTIONS

- Who has been an "angel of mercy" to you in a hospital stay or serious illness?
- How have you remembered or honored those who have shown you kindness?

PRAYER

With gratitude, we pray
To you, God of mercy,
For all those who have been
"Angels of mercy"
In times of need.
Amen.

 *October 21*

MARGA RICHTER

Composer, pianist • U.S. • 1926—

SCRIPTURE THEME

Music

"Praise him with tambourine and dance;
praise him with strings and pipe!"

— *Psalm 150:4*

QUOTATION

"I just try to make my music as beautiful as I can, and hope others will find it beautiful too."

— *Marga Richter*, Women Composers, *page 204*

MARGA'S GRANDFATHER WAS RICHARD RICHTER, the German composer-conductor, and Marga's mother was Inez Chandler, a noted singer. And so, Marga was born into a musical family on October 21, 1926, one that always encouraged her musical talents and education. When Marga took up studies at the Juilliard School, the whole family moved from Wisconsin to New York to be with her. She completed her bachelor of music in 1949 and her master's degree in music in 1951.

In 1953, Marga married Alan Shelly, and their two children were born in 1956 and 1958. Marga enjoyed her years at home raising the children and composed some music in her spare time.

Marga has written music in a wide variety of genres. She has taught music and performed as well. She also supervises the recordings of her works. Her method of composing is slow. She never erases but rather throws what she has written on the floor, later to be retrieved if she decides she wants it back. She sometimes spends ten or twelve hours on a single measure.

Though her musical training was intense and comprehensive, she is a free spirit, composing in her own personal style and goal of beauty. One of her piano concertos, *Landscapes of the Mind,* is based on two paintings of Georgia O'Keefe—*Sky Clouds II* and *Pelvis I.* The music conveys the spaciousness and serenity of the paintings.

Marga devotes much of her time and thought to the concerns of women in music. She has said that it may well be that women express emotions in a way different than men.

Both of Marga's children have musical talent: Maureen studied sitar, an Indian lute, in India, and Michael became a professional pianist.

REFLECTIONS

- Is there some talent that has been handed down in your family for several generations—music, art, gardening? Do you enjoy the sharing of such a gift with someone else in your family?
- Are there women composing and performing in your area? Do you take advantage of opportunities to hear them?

PRAYER

For the gifts and talents
That are passed
From generation to generation,
For the enrichment and enjoyment
Of people near and far,
We praise you, God,
As giver of all good gifts.
Amen.

 *October 22*

DORIS LESSING

Writer • Iran, Rhodesia (Zimbabwe) and England • 1919—

SCRIPTURE THEME

Courage
"By his light I walked through darkness."
— *Job 29:3*

QUOTATION

"It seems to me like this. It's not a terrible thing—I mean it may be terrible, but it's not damaging, it's not poisoning to do without something one really wants.... What's terrible is to pretend that the second-rate is first-rate. To pretend that you don't need love when you do; or you like your work when you know quite well you're capable of better."
— *Doris Lessing,* The Quotable Woman: 1900–Present, *page 237*

DAUGHTER OF A BRITISH ARMY CAPTAIN AND HIS WIFE, Doris was born on October 22, 1919, in Iran. From 1924 to 1949, Doris lived with her family in Southern Rhodesia, now Zimbabwe.

From 1939 to 1943, Doris was married to Frank Wisdom. Her second marriage, to Gottfried Lessing in 1945, ended in 1949. She had three children. In 1949, Doris moved to England.

Much of her fiction deals with racial concerns and uses settings in South Africa. Her experience as a youth with Communist membership sensitized her to political and intellectual activists. Her disillusionment with Communism also appears in her writings.

In 1974, Doris completed *Memoirs of a Survivor*, a spiritual autobiography. A tendency toward moral mysticism colors the four books of the *Canopus in Argos Archives*.

REFLECTIONS

- Do you enjoy reading about other cultures? Why or why not?
- What kinds of truth do you find in fiction writing?

PRAYER

Instruct us, O God, in paths of truth
As we take seriously the fictional creations

Into the cultural and spiritual windows
Of people around the world.
Amen.

 *October 23*

HENRIETTA MEARS

Religious publisher, educator • *U.S.* • *1890–1963*

SCRIPTURE THEME

Enlightening
"Your word is a lamp to my feet
and a light to my path."
— *Psalm 119:106*

QUOTATION

"It made me gladsome to be getting some education, it being like a big window opening."
— *Mary Webb,* Beacon Book of Quotations by Women, *page 97*

HENRIETTA WAS BORN OCTOBER 23, 1890, in North Dakota and in her early years moved with her family to Minneapolis, Minnesota. The family joined the Baptist Church. By age twelve, Henrietta was teaching Sunday school.

After college, Henrietta became a schoolteacher. Invited by a Presbyterian pastor from Hollywood, Henrietta went to oversee and expand the Sunday school program there.

In her search for suitable church school materials, Henrietta saw the need for better publishing programs. In 1933, she founded Gospel Light Press and began printing Sunday school courses. She also founded the National Sunday School Association, revived the Sunday school concept and expanded it to include college-age students. Later in her life, she initiated Sunday school literature in foreign languages.

Henrietta died peacefully in her sleep on March 18, 1963, in Los Angeles.

REFLECTIONS

• Visit a religious bookstore and browse through the educational materials. What appeals to you? What were the strengths and weaknesses of your own religious education?

- Have you served as a Sunday school, Bible school, religious education or vacation Bible school teacher? Do you appreciate those who perform this valuable service?

PRAYER

Bless those who teach
Justice and peace and love,
For they shall shine as stars
For all eternity.
Amen.

October 24

BELVA LOCKWOOD

Lawyer • U.S. • 1830–1917

SCRIPTURE THEME

Lawyer

"If you obey my voice and keep my covenant, you shall be my treasured possession out of all the peoples."

— *Exodus 19:5*

QUOTATION

"I have been told that there is no precedent for admitting a woman to practice in the Supreme Court of the United States. The glory of each generation is to make its own precedents. As there was none for Eve in the Garden of Eden, so there need be none for her daughters on entering the colleges, the church, or the courts."

— *Belva Lockwood*, The Quotable Woman: 1800–On, *page 60*

BORN IN A LOG CABIN ON OCTOBER 24, 1830, near Lockport, New York, in a small town called Royalton, Belva Ann Bennett was the second of five children. She grew up doing farm chores and attending the local rural school. Belva liked school, and by age ten, she had read the entire Bible.

In order to earn some money to continue her education, Belva began teaching school at fourteen. She graduated from Girls' Academy in

Royalton in 1848. "Bell," as Uriah McNall called her, married him on November 8, 1848. Their daughter, Lura, was born in 1849. Uriah died in 1853 after injuries from a sawmill accident.

Though she needed the money, Belva turned down a teaching position because the trustees paid women less than men for the same work. She pursued further education at Gasport Academy, Genesee Wesleyan Seminary in Lima, and Genesee College at Syracuse, all in New York State. In 1857, Belva returned to her home area and became principal of the Lockport school district.

With Susan B. Anthony as a friend, Belva improved education for girls. Four years later, Belva moved to Gainesville, New York, as principal of the Female Seminary.

In 1866, Belva felt called to move beyond the classroom to pursue her interests in peace, women's rights, temperance and international relations. In 1868, Belva married Ezekial Lockwood, and their daughter was born in 1869—twenty years younger than Belva's first daughter. From 1869, Belva pursued a dream of becoming a lawyer and securing her right to practice law.

Belva was part of the July 4, 1876, women's demonstration in Philadelphia where the Declaration of Rights of Women was distributed. She continued to practice law and to work for women's suffrage. In 1884, the Equal Rights Party nominated Belva as a U.S. presidential candidate, and she became the first woman to actually run for president. (Victoria Woodhull was the first woman who announced her intention to run for president—in 1872—but then discovered she wasn't old enough to run.) Belva received some votes, both popular and electoral, and a great deal of criticism and mockery but never felt defeated. She was nominated again in 1888.

Belva prepared a bill for Congress in 1885 asking for an international court to preserve peace. The bill did not pass, but Belva was selected to attend international peace conferences for several years.

In a famous 1891 case, Belva defended the claims of the Cherokee Indian Nation for monies owed them by the U.S. government. In 1909, Belva was the first woman to receive the title of doctor of laws as Syracuse University bestowed the honorary degree on her.

Belva died on May 20, 1917.

In 1983, Belva was placed in the National Women's Hall of Fame at Seneca Falls, New York. In 1984, the Niagara County (New York State) Girl Scouts instituted a badge in her honor. In 1986, a U.S. postal stamp honored her. A portrait of Belva wearing legal robes hangs in the National Portrait Gallery in Washington, D.C.

REFLECTIONS

- When Belva wished to pursue her education and a career, finding proper care for her daughter became a problem. What is your attitude about child care for career and working mothers?
- How would you liked to be honored or remembered after your death—portrait, stamp, statue, memorial, scholarship?

PRAYER

Source and Giver of Law,
Lead us to make
Good laws for society
And to render interpretations
Of these laws
In justice and love.
Amen.

 *October 25*

JEANNE JUGAN

Founder of Little Sisters of the Poor · *France* · *1792–1879*

SCRIPTURE THEME

Care of aged

"So even to old age and gray hairs,
O God, do not forsake me,
Until I proclaim your might
To all the generations to come."

— *Psalm 71:18*

QUOTATIONS

"Little Sisters, take good care of the aged, for in them you are caring for Christ Himself."

—*Jeanne Jugan,* Modern Saints: Their Lives and Faces, *page 165*

BORN OCTOBER 25, 1792, in a small fishing village in Brittany, France, Jeanne Jugan lived in a one-room, earthen-floored cottage. Her father was lost at sea when she was three, and her mother struggled with poverty and the anticlericalism of the French Revolution. Jeanne learned her Catholic faith with a sense of service from her mother and other good women who ignored French laws forbidding religion. At sixteen, Jeanne began working as a domestic maid. When a sailor proposed marriage, she declined and dedicated her heart to God.

At twenty-five, Jeanne gave her clothes to her sisters and joined the Third Order of the Admirable Mother, founded by Saint John Eudes. She continued as a domestic maid. While employed by Mademoiselle Lecoq, the two spent time at Mass and prayer and also taught catechism to children.

When Jeanne was forty-five, she formed a community of prayer with seventy-two-year-old Françoise and seventeen-year-old Virginie. For service, they turned their attention to old women who had been abandoned. As a community, they took the name of Little Sisters of the Poor. By 1851, there were over a hundred sisters in the community and ten houses. When they received final papal approbation in 1859, there were thirty-six houses.

Jeanne lived her older years at the new motherhouse and was a delight to the postulants and novices with her good spirits and good advice. She never claimed the title of founder, and many of the younger members never knew she was. Jeanne died at age eighty-seven in 1879. She was beatified in 1982, on October 3.

REFLECTIONS

- What is your attitude about the elderly? Service to the elderly? The elderly poor?
- One story is told about how Jeanne put all the empty butter dishes in front of the statue of Saint Joseph. A few days later a donor showed up with a large donation of butter. How much do you rely on God's providence?

PRAYER

May we come to a deep resepct
O God ever ancient, ever new,
For the elderly among us,
For their lived experience,
For their wisdom,
And may we learn to listen to them
With appreciation and care.
Amen.

October 26

MARY ELLEN BEST

Painter • England and Europe • 1809–1891

SCRIPTURE THEME

Home

"By knowledge the rooms are filled
with all precious and pleasant riches."
 — *Proverbs 24:4*

QUOTATION

"Where they were liable to meet artists like Theodore Reiffenstein and Schmidt von der Launitz and her musical friends, who included Felix Mendelssohn, Clara Schumann, and Jenny Lind."
 — *Caroline Davidson,* The Art and Life of Mary Ellen Best 1809–1891, *page 42*

BORN IN YORK, ENGLAND, Mary Ellen grew up in an educated and cultured home. Mary Ellen was not quite nine when her father died. Mr. Best left his wife and two daughters well provided for financially; both Mary Ellen and her sister were sent to boarding schools.

Ellen loved painting, and she progressed in her skills under several drawing masters. Her education also made her well organized, family minded and happily independent. After school, she set herself up as a semiprofessional painter, specializing in watercolors. She continued to improve her technique as she went on sketching trips to art collections. In 1834, Ellen and her mother traveled through Holland and Germany. Ellen painted interiors of kitchens, bedrooms, sitting rooms and galleries as well as market and street scenes. Ellen also painted many watercolor portraits for family and for profit.

In 1838, Ellen and a female companion visited Holland, and in 1839, they traveled through East Germany. In January 1840, Ellen married Anthony Sarg, whom she had met in Frankfurt. They made their home in Nuremberg, Germany.

Ellen was the mother to Frank, born in 1840; to Caroline, born in 1842; and to Fred, born in 1843.

Ellen continued painting watercolors of the interiors of homes and did several portraits of her children, as infants, toddlers and growing children. She still considered herself an artist, though as mother and wife, she had less time to paint. After 1836, she ceased to exhibit her work, and after 1840, she ceased to sell her work.

What she painted in the 1840's, she did for herself. Whenever she painted, though, she drew admirers, for female painters in Germany, as well as in England, were a rarity at that time. Especially appealing among Ellen's paintings are those of church windows and the interiors of window-lit Dutch kitchens.

While Ellen's paintings abounded up until 1850, there is little evidence that she painted very much after that. A couple of portraits and an 1860 painting of "Roses in a Vase" done at Worms, where Ellen and her husband then resided, are all that have come to light from the 1850's through the 1870's.

Ellen's husband died in 1883, when she was seventy-four. She died of pneumonia on May 10, 1891, at the age of eighty-one.

REFLECTIONS

- In her youth, Mary Ellen loved travel and new experiences. She depicted the interior of buildings with great skill and sensitivity. What were the interests of your youth? How did you absorb and express what you experienced?

- It seems that in midlife, Ellen lost some of her energy and desire to paint. Her interests changed. What changes have you experienced as you have aged?

- As an artist, Ellen functioned in a "man's world," but she brought a "women's world" to her paintings. What do you bring of women to your activities?

PRAYER

May we find moments of prayer
As we gaze on church windows
And gaze out of kitchen windows
In our daily and weekly rounds
Of service and worship.
Amen.

October 27

EMILY POST

Writer on etiquette • U.S. • 1872–1960

SCRIPTURE THEME

Courtesy

"Do not seek your own advantage, but that of the other."

— 1 Corinthians 10:24

QUOTATION

"Manners are a sensitive awareness of the feelings of others. If you have that awareness, you have good manners, no matter what fork you use."

— Emily Post, The Quotable Woman, *page 177*

HER COLUMN, SYNDICATED BY OVER TWO HUNDRED PAPERS, helped to make Emily Post's name a household word. Her ideas on etiquette became household rules and rules for business and social life.

Emily was born October 27, 1872, and educated at private schools. She married in 1892 and divorced in 1906. To earn money, she began to write newspaper stories on interior decorating and architecture, and serials for magazines and light novels.

At her publisher's request, Emily put out a book called *Etiquette in Society, in Business, in Politics and at Home* in 1922. The charming way she wrote became popular, and her belief that good behavior was based on common sense and consideration for other people remained popular. Emily considered good manners to be built on simplicity and grace.

Emily kept abreast of changing times and adapted her material in subsequent reprintings to reflect telephone, television and airplane etiquette as these became part of daily life.

She spoke on radio programs in the 1930's, maintained a daily newspaper column and wrote several other books. In 1946, Emily founded the *Emily Post Institute for Gracious Living.*

Emily had two sons, Edwin and Bruce. Bruce died in 1927 at age thirty-two. Edwin became her adviser and manager for the Emily Post Institute.

Emily died on September 25, 1960.

REFLECTIONS

• What do you consider basic to etiquette and good manners?

- How do you feel about the way children are taught manners?

PRAYER

May we recognize in others
The dwelling place of God
And develop a sensitive awareness
Of the feelings of others
So that our manners may be
Considerate and sensible.
We make this and all our prayers
In the name of Jesus.
Amen.

 *October 28*

NAWAL EL SAADAWI

Author, physician · *Egypt* · *1930—*

SCRIPTURE THEME

Dignity of woman
"Strength and dignity are her clothing,
and she laughs at the time to come."
— *Proverbs 31:25*

QUOTATION

"The liberation of women is above all based on their capacity to think their own problems through and to link them to the total progress of the society and the world in which they live, to their capacity to develop a political and cultural consciousness."
— *Nawal El Saadawi*, And Then She Said…, *page 11*

NAWAL, THE DAUGHTER OF A CIVIL SERVANT, was born in Cairo, Egypt. Some time after graduating from Cairo University in 1955, Nawal studied at Columbia University in New York. Nawal worked as a physician of Cairo University Hospital and as a rural doctor. She also worked as a psychiatrist.

In 1972, Nawal's book *Women and Sex* stirred up a controversy because it discussed Arab taboos affecting women. Nawal lost her job as a director in the Ministry of Health.

In novels and short stories, Nawal expressed her feminist concerns about women's struggles for equality in Arab society.

In 1981, President Anwar Sadat of Egypt ordered Nawal and 1,535 other women arrested for publishing a feminist magazine. Only after the death of President Sadat on October 6 was Nawal released from prison by the succeeding President Hosni Mubarak. The ban on her books, however, remained in effect in Egypt and other Arab countries.

Nawal's book *The Hidden Face of Eve in the Arab World* was published in English in 1979. Nawal has especially opposed clitoridectomy (female circumcision), which is still practiced in many parts of the world. Much of Nawal's nonfiction writing deals with this topic. Her 1999 book, *Daughter of Isis,* is autobiographical.

REFLECTIONS

- Those who work with refugees tell horror stories of the ill effects of clitoridectomy on the health and psyche of women. How do you contribute to securing safety and dignity for those who are victimized?
- Pray for courage to write and speak what your spirit, mind and heart believe.

PRAYER

For the human rights
Of all peoples,
We pray to you, God.
Hear our prayer, O God,
And answer those who wait for you.
Amen.

 *October 29*

CATHERINE HAYES

Ballad singer, soprano • Ireland and England • 1825–1861

SCRIPTURE THEME

Ballad singer

"They and their kindred, who were trained in singing to the LORD, all of whom were skillful, numbered two hundred eighty-eight. And they cast lots for their duties, small and great, teacher and pupil alike."

— 1 Chronicles 25:7-8

QUOTATION

"The pleasure of listening to delightful notes, with delightful words, uttered with taste and feeling by an accomplished and intellectual singer, is one of the most perfect things that can fall to the lot of beings who are unable to hear the music of the spheres and the songs of Paradise."

— Eliza Leslie, The Quotable Woman: From Eve to 1799, *page 398*

CATHERINE WAS BORN TO A POOR FAMILY IN LIMERICK, IRELAND, on October 29, 1825. Bishop Knox of Limerick was influential in sending her to study music in Dublin. At fourteen she trained under Antonio Sapio. Her concert success brought her further study in Paris and Milan. At age twenty, she sang at La Scala and toured Europe to great applause.

In 1849, Catherine went to England, where she was employed at Covent Garden for a salary of £1,300. In 1851, she went on tour to the United States, where she made William Avery Bushnell her tour manager. She made a world tour of South America, Australia and India before returning to England in 1856. In 1857, Catherine and William were married. He died the following year after illness.

As a young widow, Catherine continued to sing. She became especially popular in London as a ballad singer. She died in England on August 11, 1861, shortly before her thirty-sixth birthday.

REFLECTIONS

- Catherine's voice was heard in many parts of the world. What is your dream for sharing your talents with the world?
- Catherine's education and career were launched by the kindly help of a bishop. How has your Church affirmed and encouraged your special gifts?

PRAYER

Through the open windows of our hearts, O God,
We hear the beauty of song as gift of hope.
May we live with hope and beauty
And find ways to share these.
Amen.

 *October 30*

ROSE WILDER LANE

Reporter, real estate agent • U.S. • 1886–1968

SCRIPTURE THEME

Women's strength

"I can do all things through him who strengthens me."
— Philippians 4:13

QUOTATION

"In that instant she knew the infinite smallness, weakness, of life in the lifeless universe. She felt the vast, insensate forces against which life itself is a rebellion. Infinitely small and weak was the spark of warmth in a living heart. Yet, valiantly the tiny heart continued to beat."
— Rose Wilder Lane, Young Pioneers, *page 99*

PERHAPS NOT QUITE AS WELL REMEMBERED AS HER MOTHER, Laura Ingalls Wilder of *Little House* fame, Rose Wilder was born on December 5, 1886, in De Smet, South Dakota, and traveled with her parents as a child of ten to Mansfield, Missouri.

When she left home, Rose became a telegraph operator and married a land speculator. After she and her husband divorced, Rose had to make her own way and worked as a reporter and became the first female real estate agent in the state of California. She began to write articles and short stories, and eventually novels.

Her pioneer novels tell of the strength and the sadness of the individuals who pioneered the settlements. *Let the Hurricane Roar* describes life on the Dakota frontier. It was Rose who encouraged Laura to put her memories on paper—which resulted in the *Little House* stories.

Laura and Rose had a close relationship. Evidence of this can be read in *On the Way Home*, Laura's diary of the trip from South Dakota to Missouri, and *West From Home*, Laura's letters to her husband, Manly, from her San Francisco visit to see Rose.

Rose pursued other interests and careers. Whatever she wrote praised the essential American spirit, especially as she saw it in American women.

In 1965, Rose was planning to serve as a war correspondent in Vietnam for Woman's Day when she suffered a heart attack. She died October 30, 1968.

REFLECTIONS

- What written records of your mother's life do you have? Letters, diaries, other?
- What have you written about yourself for your children, or nieces and nephews, to keep and cherish?

PRAYER

For those who nurture
And encourage others
In developing God-given gifts,
We praise you, God,
And thank you for the legacies
These affirmers give us.
Amen.

October 31

JULIETTE GORDON LOW

Founder of Girl Scouts • U.S. and England • 1860–1927

SCRIPTURE THEME

Love thy neighbor
"You shall love your neighbor as yourself."
— *Matthew 22:39*

QUOTATION

"It's better to be a real girl such as no boy can possibly be."
— *Juliette Gordon*, Juliette Gordon Low, *page 45*

JULIETTE MAGILL KENZIE GORDON, born October 31, 1860, was called "Daisy" right from her infancy. Her father was a Southerner and her mother a Yankee. When the Yankees captured her Savannah home during the Civil War, Daisy was still a small child. In fact, General Sherman paid a visit to her house, and she sat upon his knee.

Daisy learned early on to befriend the "enemy" both in the South and during her visits to Chicago. She loved art and drawing, and she grew fond of animals. She wrote poetry and little plays and started clubs to help others.

At fourteen, Daisy went off to boarding school. Her greatest friend was a Bible with a red alligator skin cover sent as a gift from her mother. Daisy felt close to God and to her parents when she read from it.

Daisy grew up into a pretty and popular young woman. In 1886, she married William Low, who was quite wealthy. Daisy lived a life of leisure in Europe and America. She learned that she could never have children, so she turned her energies to helping others. Her husband suffered from alcoholism and died in 1905.

Daisy turned to traveling and made friends everywhere she went. She met Sir Robert Baden-Powell, founder of the Boy Scouts, and from him learned about Girl Guides, which had already been established in England. Daisy started a troop for girls at her Scotland home.

The first official Girl Guide meeting in the United States was held March 12, 1912; March 12 is observed each year as the Girl Scout birthday. Daisy involved the girls in decision making, and soon troops were organized in many places.

Daisy began a pen pal plan with girls around the world. Her "International Post Office" helped build friendships worldwide. By 1920, forty-six countries were involved in Girl Guides and Girl Scouting.

In 1925, it was decided that the next International Conference was to be held at the yet-to-be-built Camp Macy in eastern New York State. Daisy knew she had only a few months to live because of cancer. Every effort was made to complete the camp facilities on time, and Daisy was proud to lead Robert and Olave Baden-Powell down the path at the camp lined with flags from many countries.

Daisy died on January 27, 1927. She was buried, as she wished, in her Girl Scout uniform.

REFLECTIONS

- Were you a Girl Scout? What memories do you have of your experience?

- How do you support organizations that foster the camaraderie and growth of young girls?

PRAYER

For Girl Scouts everywhere,
We pray to you,
O God of the universe,
That the friendships built among the girls
May work toward world peace and unity.
Amen.

November 1

SISTER FRANCES OF THE REDEMPTION

World traveler, mystic • Germany • 1947–1979

SCRIPTURE THEME

Wandering, restless, traveler

"They wandered in deserts and mountains."

— *Hebrews 11:38*

QUOTATION

"We were with Him in the dark, now He switches on the light."

— *Sister Frances,* Fascinated by God, *page 20*

FRANCES WAS BORN NOVEMBER 1, 1947, in Germany during the French occupation and learned both languages. She received almost no religious education during her childhood. At age twelve, she became curious and interested in the catechism classes her school companions attended. When she first heard about God, she was filled with joy. She was baptized by a military chaplain.

When Frances followed the French army to Algeria, she learned firsthand the sufferings of war in an Arab land. Back in France, she completed her degree. An attraction for quiet and solitude competed with her independent life as a university student and later as a world traveler. She wanted to write a thesis on the customs of the Popuan tribes. She pursued this for a while, and she traveled randomly, to Australia, to the Far East.

On a desert island not far from Hong Kong, she had a spiritual experience in which the certainty of God's existence exploded within her. It was such a profound experience that it changed her life forever. Her random journeys now had the focus of finding a solitary place where she could live a contemplative life.

She was advised to consider entering a Carmelite convent. When she received a permanent visa for India, she went to New Delhi to enter the Carmel there. Mystical graces made her cloistered life that of a true contemplative.

Sister Frances died November 7, 1979, at age thirty-two and as a temporary professed nun of the Carmel of Sitagarba. She was buried in a thicket of bamboo, a secluded place where she liked to go for her solitary prayer.

REFLECTIONS

- Do you have a favorite place (or places) for your solitary prayer?
- How international is your experience? How can you expand your horizons?

PRAYER

> In you, O God,
> Our restless hearts
> Were made to rest;
> May we find rest
> In moments of contemplation
> And mystical union with you
> Wherever our restless hearts may roam.
> Amen.

November 2

LOUISE IMOGEN GUINEY

Poet, scholar · U.S. and England · 1861–1920

SCRIPTURE THEME

Poetry

"The words of the mouth are deep waters;
the fountain of wisdom is a gushing stream."

— *Proverbs 18:4*

QUOTATION

"Quotations (such as have a point and lack triteness) from the great old authors are an act of filial reverence on the part of the quoter, and a blessing to a public grown superficial and external."

— Louise Imogen Guiney, Familiar Quotations, *page 860*

BORN JANUARY 7, 1861, Louise became a poet of the literary circle of Sarah Orne Jewett and Annie Adams Fields. Louise suffered ill health and also persecution as a Catholic, Irish and female. She worked at the post office and the public library before moving to England, where she did scholarly research at Oxford. Her personality remained lively and free spirited.

This is perhaps best seen in her letters, some of which were published in 1926.

Louise wrote critical essays and poetry, with *Patrino: A Collection of Essays* and *A Roadside Harp* considered her best in these genres. She also wrote biographies, including *Katherine Philips—The Matchless Orinda*.

Her great work of scholarship, an anthology of Catholic poets from Thomas More to Alexander Pope, was published posthumously in 1938. It was called *Recusant Poets*.

Her religious lyrics remain among the best of American contributions to the genre of religious poetry. Her lyrics were published in 1909 as *Collected Lyrics*. Louise died November 2, 1920, in England.

REFLECTIONS

· Do you find religious poetry helpful to your prayer life?

· Try to express your religious experiences in poetry. Do you find that it helps you to come to a deeper understanding?

PRAYER

We thank you, O Poet-God,
For the lovely lines penned by poets
Attuned to your beauty.
Amen.

 *November 3*

ANNIE OAKLEY

Sharpshooter · U.S. · 1860–1926

SCRIPTURE THEME

Sharpshooting

"David put his hand in his bag, took out a stone, slung it, and struck the Philistine on his forehead."

— *1 Samuel 17:49*

QUOTATION

"The results of philanthropy are always beyond calculation."

— *Annie Oakley,* Beacon Book of Quotations by Women, *page 244*

WHEN SHE DIED ON NOVEMBER 3, 1926, Annie left a legacy of kindness and generosity. Along with a legend of straight and accurate shooting, Annie was remembered for her philanthropy.

Born August 13, 1860, in a log cabin in Ohio, Annie grew up with Quaker parents and several siblings. When she was ten, her father died. Annie took up shooting game to help her family survive. Legend says that Annie shot and sold enough game to pay off the mortgage on the family farm and keep meals on the table.

At age fifteen, Annie won a shooting match against famous sharp-shooter Frank E. Butler. He admired her competence. The two married a year later and together toured the country presenting their demonstration of sharpshooting. Among their favorites were the shooting of a moving glass and the thin edge of a playing card. The act appeared at circuses and on vaudeville circuits. Annie took her stage name from a suburb of Cincinnati, Ohio. Frank dropped out of the show and became Annie's manager. They worked a short time for a circus. In 1875, they joined the Buffalo Bill Wild West Show. With Buffalo Bill, they toured the United States and Canada, England and Europe. In 1877, Annie Oakley met Queen Victoria in England. In Germany, she did her cigarette-shooting trick with the crown prince.

In 1901, Annie suffered temporary paralysis from injuries she received in a train crash. She left Buffalo Bill and did some drama and touring on her own. She taught trapshooting and demonstrated marksmanship to U.S. soldiers. She rejoined Buffalo Bill for his last season in 1917.

Upon retirement in 1922, Annie settled in Florida. She returned to her home state just before her death.

REFLECTIONS

- Did you ever dream of joining a circus or other special touring show? Would you still like to?

- What activities do you think of as being masculine? Which do you think of as feminine? Why?

PRAYER

For women who dare to be different,
Who have the courage
To be true to themselves, we pray,
And ask our God who creates us each
As unique and special
That we may affirm our own gifts
And those in each other.
Amen.

November 4

RAISSA MARITAIN

Scholar, writer · *Russia and France* · *1883–1960*

SCRIPTURE THEME

Assistance

"Do not forsake your friend or the friend of your parent."
 — *Proverbs 27:10*

QUOTATION

"In the modern social order, the person *is sacrificed to the* individual. *The individual is given universal suffrage, equality of rights, freedom of opinion; while the person, isolated, naked, with no social armor to sustain and protect him, is left to the mercy of all the devouring forces which threaten the life of the soul, exposed to relentless actions and reactions of conflicting interests and appetites.... It is a homicidal civilization."*
 — *Jacques Maritain*, Familiar Quotations, *page 969*

BORN NOVEMBER 4, 1883, IN RUSSIA OF JEWISH PARENTS, Raissa Oumansoff was raised in a strictly Orthodox fashion. The family moved to France in 1893 to escape persecution. Raissa, a brilliant student, studied at the Sorbonne, where she met Jacques Maritain. Together, they studied the writings of Saint Thomas Aquinas. And together, they collaborated on writing books and articles to explain Thomas Aquinas to twentieth-century readers.

Raissa and Jacques were in the forefront of the French Catholic revival movement of the early decades of the twentieth century. Raissa and her husband made their home near Paris and opened their home on Sunday afternoons to Catholic intellectuals. They also hosted a week's retreat each year.

In addition to collaborative works with her husband, Raissa wrote several volumes of poetry, a children's life of Aquinas and two books of memoirs, *We Have Been Friends Together* and *Adventures in Grace*. Raissa died September 12, 1960, in Paris.

REFLECTIONS

- What have you done in collaboration with another? How has it worked out for you?

- What can you do to foster the creativity of someone close to you?

PRAYER

May married couples be friends
In their lives together
And in their activities of collaboration.
Amen.

 *November 5*

BERTILLA OF CHELLES

Prioress in charge of queens • France • 7th century

SCRIPTURE THEME

Hospitality

"Be hospitable to one another without complaining."
— 1 Peter 4:9

QUOTATION

"Spiritual energy brings compassion into the real world. With compassion, we see benevolently our own human condition and the condition of our fellow beings."
— Christina Baldwin, The Beacon Book of Quotations by Women, *page 60*

BORN AROUND 635 IN FRANCE, Bertilla entered a Columban monastery and was trained in the Celtic tradition of prayer and hospitality. In the monastery hospice, she was in charge of providing for pilgrims, the poor and the sick.

When Bathildis, the queen of Clovis II, founded an abbey at Chelles, Bertilla was placed in charge. After the death of her husband, Queen Bathildis joined this monastery with Bertilla as her prioress. Queen Heresivith also joined the Chelles monastery with Bertilla as prioress.

Chelles became the model monastery of the seventh century and Bertilla the model prioress. Bertilla ruled the monastery for nearly fifty years and served as inspiration for other women to establish monasteries in their own countries. This included Saint Hilda who founded and governed a model monastery at Whitby in England.

Bertilla died about 705 at Chelles. Her relics are preserved at Chelles-Saint Andre.

REFLECTIONS

- Monasteries and abbeys were oases of humanity during the barbarous Dark Ages. What are some contemporary oases of humanity and Christian values?
- Bertilla ruled over queens, but she was chosen to rule because of her kind and considerate manner with others. How are you with people in your charge?

PRAYER

We pray for kindness and consideration
In our hospitality toward others,
In our manner of working with others.
Amen.

November 6

ANN ELIZA WORCHESTER ROBERTSON

Missionary to American Indians, Bible translator · *U.S.* · *1826–1905*

SCRIPTURE THEME

Missionary

"By God's will I may come to you with joy and be refreshed in your company."
— *Romans 15:32*

QUOTATION

"All American Indian poems are songs, and an Indian was once asked which came first, the words or the music. 'They come together,' he replied."
— *Marie Gilchrist,* The Quotable Woman: 1800–On, *page 241*

THIS MISSIONARY, DAUGHTER OF MISSIONARIES, was born November 7, 1826, in Tennessee. Ann Eliza Worchester, daughter of Samuel Austin Worchester and Ann Orr Worchester, moved as an infant from Tennessee to Georgia, then to Oklahoma. These moves kept the Worchester family as missionaries to the Cherokees as they were forced to move. Ann's father, a Congregationalist minister, had been imprisoned in Tennessee for refusal to recognize U.S. government authority over Cherokee land in Tennessee, and as devoted missionaries, he and his family went where the American Indians went.

In 1843, Ann was sent to an academy in Vermont and graduated in 1847. She returned to Oklahoma to help her parents with the mission. In 1849, she began work at a boarding school for labor training, which was cosponsored by the Creek Nation and the Presbyterian Church. In 1850, Ann married the school's principal, William Schenck Robertson, who was also a Presbyterian minister. At the time of her marriage, Ann converted from Congregationalist to Presbyterian.

Ann and William had four children. Ann oversaw housekeeping in her own home as well as the school, taught in the school and assisted her husband in translating Bible texts into Creek language.

Missionaries were expelled from some reservations during the Civil War because of new treaties with the Confederate government. The Robertsons worked in Kansas until they were recalled in 1866 by the Creeks. They reopened the school, produced a hymnal and continued Bible translations.

In 1880, the school burned and William died. Ann went to live with her daughter Alice in Muskogee, Oklahoma. She spent her remaining years translating Bible texts and completed the Creek New Testament in 1887. The University of Wooster granted her an honorary doctorate in 1892 for the Bible translation work. Ann died November 19, 1905, in Muskogee, a few days past her seventy-ninth birthday.

REFLECTIONS

- Have you ever dreamt of becoming a missionary to another people? What is attractive about this kind of life?

- Read more about Ann's daughter Alice Robertson, the second woman ever elected to the U.S. Congress.

- Read *Trail of Tears*, the story of Cherokees forced to move from Tennessee to Georgia to Oklahoma.

PRAYER

We praise you, God, for missionaries
Whose sympathies lie with indigenous peoples,
And whose services offer windows
Into the spirituality and cultures of others.
Amen.

November 7

MARIE CURIE

Chemist • Poland and France • 1867–1934

SCRIPTURE THEME

Research

"I...applied my mind to seek and to search out by wisdom all that is done under heaven."

— *Ecclesiastes 1:12-13*

QUOTATION

"You cannot hope to build a better world without improving the individuals. To that end each of us must work for his own improvement, and at the same time share a general responsibility for all humanity, our particular duty being to aid those to whom we think we can be most useful."

— *Marie Curie,* The Quotable Woman: 1800–On, *page 125*

MARYA (MARIE) SKLODOWSKA WAS BORN NOVEMBER 7, 1867, in Warsaw, Poland, at a boarding school where her mother was the principal. Her father taught physics and mathematics at a nearby high school. As a little child, Marie peered into the polished glass case of her father's collection of physics apparatus with great admiration, and this was a memory she treasured all her life.

When Marie was ten, her mother died of tuberculosis. Her oldest sister had died from typhus a bit before this.

Marie did very well in school, but higher education was not open to women in Poland at that time. Marie worked as a governess and as a teacher and studied all she could by herself. In 1891, she went to Paris to study at the Sorbonne, with a special interest in mathematics, physics and chemistry.

In 1894, Marie met Pierre Curie, and their relationship grew into friendship, love and partnership. Her marriage meant a choice for him and against returning to Poland. She became Madame Curie.

Marie gave birth to her first daughter, Irene, within a few months of publishing her first scientific work. She pursued her doctoral research in the area of uranium rays and named it radioactivity. With her insight about other radioactive elements, Pierre joined her research until they isolated polonium (named for Poland) and radium.

Along with other scientists, the Curies laid the groundwork for the discovery of atomic particles and the use of radium for treating cancer.

Marie was the first woman in Europe to receive a doctoral degree, and her examiner gave it to her "with great distinction." With Pierre, her husband, and Henri Becquerel, Marie received the Nobel Prize for Physics in 1903.

Both Marie and Pierre became ill from radiation sickness, and their lives were hectic with people interested in their work. In 1904, Marie had a second daughter, Eve. In 1906, Pierre was killed in a road accident. Marie took up his work as lecturer at the Sorbonne. In 1911, she received a second Nobel Prize.

During World War I, Marie and her daughter Irene devoted themselves to X-ray units for wounded soldiers. In the 1920's, Marie gave lecture tours to raise needed money.

Marie died July 4, 1934.

Her daughter Irene married the gifted scientist Frederick Joliot, and together they discovered artificial radiation, for which they won the 1935 Nobel Prize. Her daughter Eve wrote a biography titled *A Biography of Marie Sklodowska Curie*.

REFLECTIONS

- What is the role and value of science? What are its dangers?
- Marie's daughters carried on her heritage. As a daughter, what have you preserved of your mother's legacies to family, church, society?

PRAYER

As other daughters have carried on
Their mothers' legacy,
May we carry on the faith and love
Of our mothers and of our mother Church
In any manifestation to which we are called.
Amen.

November 8

DOROTHY DAY

Reformer • U.S. • 1897–1980

SCRIPTURE THEME

Work, workers

"Brothers and sisters, do not be weary in doing what is right."

— 2 Thessalonians 3:13

QUOTATION

"No one has the right to sit down and feel hopeless. There's too much work to do."

— Dorothy Day, Remember the Ladies, *page 260*

DOROTHY DAY WAS BORN NOVEMBER 8, 1897, and at age eight experienced a "sweetness of faith" at a Methodist Sunday school. She received her schooling in Chicago and at the Urbana campus of the University of Illinois. She began her journalism career at eighteen as a reporter.

As an activist for justice and peace, Dorothy had many stays in jail. She had a daughter, Tamar, by her common-law husband. In association with the theater for which she sometimes wrote, she had serious conversations with Eugene O'Neill about religion and death. She converted to Catholicism and tells that story in *From Union Square to Rome* and in *The Long Loneliness.*

Peter Maurin encouraged her to start a paper for the working population. She did so, selling the first edition on May 1, 1933. And she continued to publish *The Catholic Worker* for nearly fifty years.

Dorothy also established Catholic Worker houses and farms where the poor and homeless shared food and friendship. Both gentle and tough, Dorothy inspired a work and mission that continued to thrive after her death on November 29, 1980.

REFLECTIONS

- If there is a Catholic Worker house near you, pay a visit. What can you do to contribute to that work?
- Read *The Catholic Worker* newspaper.

PRAYER

> We pray for workers
> And unite our hearts and hopes
> In solidarity with them,
> Locally and globally.
> Amen.

 *November 9*

FLORENCE SABIN

Doctor, public health worker · U.S. · 1871–1953

SCRIPTURE THEME

Balance

"He changes times and seasons,
  deposes kings and sets up kings;
he gives wisdom to the wise
  and knowledge to those who have understanding."

  — Daniel 2:21

QUOTATION

"How came you to possess these many skills and virtues? It has been, I think, because of your great humanity. You have cared deeply for your kind. And men have come to recognize in you that rare total person—of wisdom and of senti- ment—heart and mind in just and balanced union."

  — said of Florence, Famous American Women, *page 371*

BORN ON NOVEMBER 9, 1871, to a father who had dreamed of being a doc- tor and to a mother who was health conscious, Florence took an early interest in things scientific. She thought she'd be a doctor, but in those days women didn't study medicine. Or did they?

Plans for Johns Hopkins University medical school included equal opportunity for women. The timing was fortunate, for Florence was encouraged by women who had donated sums of money for the medical school.

Dr. Franklin Page Mall, professor of anatomy, greatly influenced Florence in her learning and later in her style of teaching. His method, and later hers, was to stimulate and guide students toward independent learning and the joys of discovery on their own.

And Dr. Mall became more than a fine instructor to her. Florence was regarded as friend of the family. Dr. Mall encouraged her in her independent study of the brain. The model she made just before the turn of the century is still widely admired and used.

Florence studied the lymphatic system and blood vessels, publishing several papers in the early 1900's. She gave lectures in cities around the world and continued her teaching schedule while doing her research.

It is said that she was a thorough and demanding teacher. She must have been the same with her research, for students often mention catching a glimpse of her through the laboratory window late at night.

She was the first woman appointed full-time instructor at Johns Hopkins and the first woman to be elected president of the American Association of Anatomists.

In 1925, she was invited to join the Rockefeller Institute's scientific staff, the first woman to receive such an invitation as a full member. Again, her work was thorough and a source of inspiration. She studied tuberculosis intently.

When she retired at seventy-three and returned to her home state of Colorado, she served on a health committee where she led statewide reforms in legislation and special projects.

Several awards recognized her service to the betterment of health. She died in 1953.

REFLECTIONS

- Do you have any women among your personal physicians or other acquaintances who are doctors?
- Are there areas of health that women may handle even better than men? Vice versa?
- Some say women's health knowledge lags behind that of men's for lack of interested researchers. Would you encourage a friend to pursue the medical field?

PRAYER

We thank you, Incarnate God,
For the great wisdom,
For the great humanity
Of doctors and scientists
Devoted to the betterment of health.
Amen.

November 10

LUCRETIA MOTT

Reformer, feminist • U.S. • 1793–1880

SCRIPTURE THEME

Truth

*"I will walk with integrity of heart
   within my house.
I will not set before my eyes
   Anything that is base."*

— Psalm 101:2-3

QUOTATION

"The world has never yet seen a truly great and virtuous nation, because in the degradation of woman the very fountains of life are poisoned at their source."

> — Lucretia Mott, *speaking at the first Women's Rights Convention, 1848,* And Then She Said…, *page 52*

LUCRETIA SERVED AS WISE MOTHER AND ELDER STATESWOMAN to the women's rights movement. When the Seneca Falls convention happened in 1848, Lucretia was already fifty-five. Born on January 3, 1793, on Nantucket Island, Lucretia grew up among strong women often left alone while their menfolk were at sea. Building on her Quaker home life, she was educated at a Friends school. In 1821, she became a minister in the Quaker Society of Friends. And it was Lucretia who coauthored with Elizabeth Cady Stanton in 1848 the Declaration of Sentiments, which said: "We hold these truths to be self-evident: that all men and women are created equal…"

As a traveling Quaker minister, Lucretia relied on divine guidance. In her sermons, she nearly always spoke on women's rights and slaves' rights. She strongly believed that all human rights were connected, and thus she could never be of narrow mind or purpose.

Her husband and family were marvelously supportive of her; her Quaker friends sometimes less so. In one situation, Lucretia was the only voice raised against "civilizing" the Seneca people, allowing that the Seneca women might know better than Quaker women what was best for Seneca women.

In her 1849 *Discourse on Women*, Lucretia insisted on women's equality and right to be acknowledged as responsible and moral beings. In all her sermons and speeches, Lucretia advised women to enter the professions, to learn new skills and to get an education.

Lucretia promoted the idea of nonresistance—nonviolent resistance to civil authority. During the Civil War, which Lucretia opposed, she conducted religious services at the camps and brought food. Her notion of nonresistance led her to involvement with the Universal Peace Union and other peace societies.

Lucretia's motto and central concern always was "Truth for authority, rather than authority for truth," a motto she adopted from the preacher Nicholas Hallock during a controversy in the 1840's between conservative and liberal Quakers.

Lucretia's life was devoted to living truth in her personal life, in her family and church, and to sustaining truth in her fellow reformers and society's oppressed. She drew her strength from the spiritual depths of her own being, for she believed that the kingdom of God dwelt within each person.

Lucretia died on November 11, 1880.

REFLECTIONS

- Lucretia believed that critical thinking and sincere skepticism were religious duties. Do you think so?
- Do you see peace, equality, education, suffrage, human rights all of a piece, a seamless garment? Or do you focus your efforts on a single issue?
- How do you feel about the ideas of equality of men and women, of all races, of all nationalities, of all peoples?
- Were you taught critical thinking skills? How do you balance feelings with thinking?

PRAYER

May our contemplation
And our action
Open windows of tolerance
Toward equity for all.
Amen.

November 11

ABIGAIL ADAMS

First Lady, author of letters • U.S. • 1744–1818

SCRIPTURE THEME

Remembering

"The memory of the righteous is a blessing."
— Proverbs 10:7

QUOTATION

"In the new code of laws which I suppose it will be necessary for you to make, I desire you would remember the ladies and be more generous and favorable to them than your ancestors. Do not put such unlimited power into the hands of the husbands. Remember, all men would be tyrants if they could. If particular care and attention is not paid to the ladies, we are determined to foment a rebellion, and will not hold ourselves bound by any laws in which we have no voice or representation."

— Abigail Adams, in a letter to her husband, John, Wit and Wisdom of Famous
  American Women, *page 29*

ABIGAIL SMITH WAS BORN NOVEMBER 11, 1744, IN MASSACHUSETTS. She was a frail but intelligent child, and though she received no formal education, she read widely in both English and French. In 1764, her marriage to John Adams brought her happiness, and by 1774, they had five children. The next ten years saw John away from home much of the time for his political career.

Abigail's famous "Remember the Ladies" letter was written during that decade. Indeed, all of Abigail's letters are worth reading for their reports of how she managed the family farm and handled life in those difficult days, and for her lasting affection for John.

After the Continental Congress, Abigail and John resumed life together. She always supported his political career and moved with him to New York, Philadelphia and Washington, D.C., when his vice presidency and presidency took him to these cities.

During the last three months of her husband's presidency, Abigail became the first First Lady to live in the newly built White House. But she found it less than comfortable because it was not completely finished.

Abigail and John lived in retirement from 1801 to 1818. Abigail died on October 18, 1818. The first edition of her letters was published in 1840 by her grandson, Charles Francis Adams. Ever-expanding collections of her letters have been published since.

REFLECTIONS

- Read the published letters of Abigail Adams.
- Do you write or receive especially good letters of news and observations and concerns? Do you save well-written letters for family history and literary value?

PRAYER

Remember us, Lord;
Remember the women
And be generous and favorable to us.
Teach us to forgive history
Its shortcomings regarding women
And to live the present
And prepare for the future
With a greater sense
Of women's needs and concerns.
Amen.

November 12

ELIZABETH CADY STANTON

Reformer • U.S. • 1815–1902

SCRIPTURE THEME

Righteousness

"If you know that he is righteous, you may be sure that everyone who does right has been born of him."

— *1 John 2:29*

QUOTATION

"We still wonder at the stolid incapacity of all men to understand that woman feels the invidious distinctions of sex exactly as the black man does those of color, or the white man the transient distinctions of wealth, family, position, place, and power; that she feels as keenly as man the injustice of disenfranchisement."

— *Elizabeth Cady Stanton,* The Quotable Woman: 1800–1981, *page 26*

ELIZABETH WAS ELEVEN when her brother—the only boy in the family—died. And Elizabeth resolved to be all her brother was. She decided that meant education and courage, and she set about proving herself the equal of her brother. Indeed, she spent her whole life proving herself the equal of any man.

Born November 12, 1815, Elizabeth was one of five girls in the family. It was an era when girls were expected to grow up into wives and mothers and stay out of the man's world of business, politics and law, as well as the education that prepared men for these careers.

After her brother's death, Elizabeth persuaded her Presbyterian pastor to tutor her, and she learned well. The minister encouraged her to study Greek, Latin and mathematics. Even after Elizabeth rejected her strict religious upbringing, she kept her affection and admiration for the minister.

Elizabeth grew to hate the clothing and behavior considered suitable for a young lady. She came to fear organized religion and some of its teachings, though God and the Bible were important to her.

Elizabeth spent hours in her father's law library and early on developed sympathy for the women who were deprived by law of their children and their property.

Elizabeth was one of the best students at her school. No college at that time admitted women, so she went to Troy Female Seminary, run by Emma Willard. She married Henry Stanton in 1840 in a partnership of equals. Henry was active in antislavery lectures, and it angered Elizabeth that women were not allowed to take part.

Also in 1840, Elizabeth became acquainted with Lucretia Mott, and the two shared many of the same views. They talked about a women's convention, but other things kept them from doing it for some years.

Elizabeth started her family with the birth of her first child in 1842. She worked for a change in the laws concerning property for married women.

When the Stanton family moved to Seneca Falls, New York, Elizabeth missed the intellectual life of Boston. She found a new direction as she got involved with other reformers who organized the Women's Rights Convention in 1848. Elizabeth helped write a Declaration of Sentiments and a List of Resolutions, which included woman's right to vote. Though national and local reaction was largely negative, the women's efforts gained momentum.

Elizabeth also became friends with Susan B. Anthony of Rochester, New York, who was especially interested in temperance and the abolition of slavery. Elizabeth began to promote divorce as the solution to alcoholic husbands. She addressed the New York State Legislature on this and other issues of social and legal justice for women.

The Civil War and its aftermath divided energies as work for rights of Blacks increased. Elizabeth and Susan concentrated on women's voting rights. In her eightieth year, Elizabeth began to write her autobiography. She died in 1902.

REFLECTIONS

- Visit Seneca Falls and see Elizabeth Stanton's home, the Women's Rights National Historic Park, the National Women's Hall of Fame.
- What do you believe is the solution to marriages involving alcoholism and abuse?
- The Erie Canal provided the avenue of transportation for these women seeking to meet with others. What are today's avenues of communication for women seeking to meet with each other?

PRAYER

May we find strength, wisdom,
And inspiration
In the stories of the women
Of Holy Scriptures.
Amen.

 *November 13*

FRANCES XAVIER CABRINI

Missionary • Italy and U.S. • 1850–1917

SCRIPTURE THEME

Migrants, refugees, aliens, strangers
"I was a stranger and you welcomed me."
— *Matthew 25:35*

QUOTATION

"Renounce yourselves entirely if you wish to enjoy peace.... She who is not holy will make no one holy."
—*Frances Xavier Cabrini*, Lives of the Saints, *page 469*

BORN IN ITALY IN 1850, Francesca was the youngest of thirteen children of the Cabrini family. She grew up to be a teacher and was refused entry to two convents because of poor health.

While working at an orphanage, she founded the Missionary Sisters of the Sacred Heart. Mother Frances Xavier Cabrini had always hoped to work in China as her namesake had done, but when she became aware of the needs of Italian immigrants in America, she turned her attention to them.

She arrived in New York City in 1889 with six of her sisters and established a convent and orphanage. The sisters began adult classes for Italian immigrants and schools for the children.

Although Mother Cabrini found the English language difficult, she became an American citizen in 1909. She traveled all over the United States establishing convents, schools, hospitals and orphanages. She founded sixty-seven convents for her sisters throughout the world, including France, Spain, England, South America, the United States and Italy.

She died in Chicago on December 22, 1917, from malaria. Her congregation at that time numbered fifteen hundred.

She was canonized in 1946, the first American citizen to receive this honor. In 1950, Pope Pius XII named her patroness of all immigrants.

REFLECTIONS

- Mother Cabrini visited several large U.S. cities. For example, she visited St. Anthony's (Italian) Parish in downtown Buffalo, New York, around the turn of the last century and worshipped at the church located just behind City Hall. Does this sense of presence change the character of a place?

- What pressing contemporary need do you think Mother Cabrini would respond to? Is there something you feel inspired to do about a need you see?

PRAYER

Show us, dear God,
The place where you want us to be
That we may know your presence
In that place of your choice
And in the hearts of all persons
Who live in that place.
Amen.

November 14

FANNY MENDELSSOHN HENSEL

Piano virtuoso, composer • Germany and France • 1805–1847

SCRIPTURE THEME

Music

"Joy and gladness will be found in her,
thanksgiving and the voice of song."

— Isaiah 51:3

QUOTATION

"The lives of the musicians are imperfectly written for this obvious reason. The
soul of the great musician can only be expressed in music.... We must read them
in their works; this, true of artists in every department, is especially so of the
high priestesses of sound."

— *Margaret Fuller,* The Quotable Woman: 1800–On, *page 20*

FANNY WAS BORN IN HAMBURG, GERMANY, on November 14, 1805. She was
the oldest of four children; her famous brother, Felix, was four years
younger. Both Fanny and Felix received essentially the same musical
education and seem to have had equal talent. When Fanny was thirteen,
the family moved to Paris where both children continued their musical
education in piano and composition.

Fanny benefited from a heritage of musical tradition through the
female side of the family. Her aunt was an accomplished harpsichordist,
and her aunt's daughter was talented as well. Fanny's mother, Lea Solomon
Mendelssohn, was the Mendelssohn children's first musical teacher.

Bach's music became Fanny's favorite, along with music of Ludwig
van Beethoven and her brother. Fanny composed music—over four hundred works in the Baroque genres of cantata, oratorio, prelude and
fugue, and chorales for voice and piano. But Fanny's brother and father
discouraged publishing any of her compositions, while Felix's works
received great attention.

In 1822, the Mendelssohns began Sunday concerts at their home. In
1829, Fanny married Wilhelm Hensel, who continued the Sunday concerts after the death of Fanny's mother. Sebastian, Fanny's only child,
was born in 1830.

In the 1830's and 1840's, some of Fanny's compositions were published at her husband's persuasion. Fanny died of a stroke on May 14, 1847. She was forty-one years old.

Recent years have seen a new interest in Fanny's musical career and compositions. Her work is still being published and performed.

REFLECTIONS

- Have you ever put aside your plans and dreams for the sake of a brother or sister? By choice? By force? What did it mean for you?
- What role has music played in your life?

PRAYER

That girls may receive
The opportunities and education,
The encouragement and affirmation
Given to their brothers,
We earnestly beseech you, God.
Amen.

 *November 15*

GEORGIA O'KEEFE

Painter • U.S. • 1887–1986

SCRIPTURE THEME

Flowers

"Even Solomon in all his glory was not clothed like one of these."
— *Matthew 6:29*

QUOTATION

"I feel there is something unexplored about woman that only woman can explore...."
— *Georgia O'Keefe,* The Quotable Woman, *page 11*

GEORGIA WAS BORN NOVEMBER 15, 1887, in Sun Prairie, Wisconsin. Even as a small child, Georgia viewed the outer and inner realities—of seashell and prairie farm—with a freedom of expression. Later, flowers and the vast New Mexico landscapes provided her the same opportunity for abstraction of essence via paint on canvas.

Her adobe house in New Mexico was re-created at her direction to have large panes of glass so that she could look far out to the desert land-scape, and an inner patio so that she could see the center of her home.

She also looked through openings in sun-bleached bones, using them as small windows much like the viewfinder on a camera. What she saw were new dimensions on the world—light with greater intensity, colors with new relationships, scenes with new dimensions, objects with new perspectives.

Georgia's strong sense of solitude and her sense of her art as intimate visions made publicity and public viewing of her art difficult for her to accept.

Georgia died March 6, 1986. She was ninety-eight.

REFLECTIONS

- Do you need spaces of solitude for creativity?
- How comfortable are you in sharing your special gifts and talents with family and friends? With the general public?

PRAYER

O God, you are the focal point
On our horizon.
Give us the strength to follow the path
That leads to you.
Amen.

November 16

MARGARET OF SCOTLAND

Queen, reformer, benefactor · Scotland · 11th century

SCRIPTURE THEME

Justice

"Whatever is true, whatever is honorable, whatever is just, whatever is pure, whatever is pleasing, whatever is commendable, if there is any excellence and if there is anything worthy of praise, think about these things."

— *Philippians 4:8*

QUOTATION

"Be diligent in serving the poor. Love the poor. Honour them, as you would Christ himself."

—Louise de Marillac, Quotable Saints, *page 121*

MARGARET WAS PROBABLY BORN ABOUT 1045 in Hungary, of a German mother in exile. In 1057, she was brought to England but fled to Scotland during the Norman conquest of 1066. She married King Malcolm III (Canmore) in 1070 and became the queen of the land.

She had two daughters and six sons. One son became Saint David of Scotland. One daughter, Matilda, married Henry I of England.

Margaret was a strong-willed and influential woman both with her husband toward justice for the people of the kingdom and with Church authorities for reforms of religious and cultural life. She was also generous in providing for the poor and the sick, for pilgrims and travelers, for orphans and beggars.

Margaret died four days after her husband was killed, and she was buried with him at Dunfermline Abbey, which they had founded. She was canonized in 1250 and named the patron saint of Scotland in 1673.

REFLECTIONS

- Margaret organized guilds of women to make linens and vestments for church use. Some parishes still have such a group. Which of your skills would best serve your church?

- Margaret is the mother of a saint. How has the example of your own mother inspired you to goodness?

PRAYER

May every stitch
Made with loving hands
Be a prayer that mends our world
Torn by war and strife.
Amen.

November 17

ELIZABETH OF HUNGARY

Franciscan, caretaker of poor • *Hungary* • *1207–1231*

SCRIPTURE THEME

Bread for the poor

"The poor shall eat and be satisfied."

— *Psalm 22:26*

QUOTATION

"I heard a little bird singing and it sang so sweetly, I had to sing, too."

— Elizabeth on her deathbed, The One Year Book of Saints, *page 329*

ELIZABETH WAS BORN AS PRINCESS IN 1207, daughter of King Andrew II of Hungary. At age four, Elizabeth was brought to Thuringia to be brought up with Prince Louis, her future husband in an arranged marriage. They grew up fond of each other and were married when she was fourteen and he was twenty-one.

They had a wonderful marriage with three children. She carried on remarkable works of charity while he ruled the kingdom of Thuringia.

In 1227, when Elizabeth was only twenty, Louis died of malaria while on a crusade. Relatives of Louis tried to deprive Elizabeth of their home, but she received help from her aunt who was an abbess and her uncle who was a bishop.

She made provisions for her children, gave up all her possessions and joined the Third Order of Saint Francis. She built a hospital and took care of the sick, the poor, the destitute. Those she helped revered her as a saint.

She died at twenty-four on November 27, 1231. A great church was built at Marburg where she is buried.

She was canonized in 1235, only four years after her death. She is revered as a patroness of the Franciscan Third Order Secular.

REFLECTIONS

- Elizabeth is one of the most-loved saints of the German people, and her husband is honored as Saint Ludwig (German form of Louis). Do you know any married couples who embody holiness?

- How do you share your bread with the poor in your neighborhood? In the world?

PRAYER

May the marriage of Elizabeth and Louis
Offer us the witness of marital love
And inspire all married couples
To find love and beauty
In their marriage covenant.
Amen.

 November 18

ROSE PHILIPPINE DUCHESNE

Missionary to America • France and U.S. • 1769–1852

SCRIPTURE THEME

Frontier missions

"They were strangers and foreigners on the earth."
— *Hebrews 11:13*

QUOTATION

"Quah-kah-ka-num-ad" (*"Woman-who-prays-always"*).
— Rose's name among the Potawatomi people, The One Year Book of Saints, *page 330*

BORN IN FRANCE IN 1769, Rose entered the Visitation Order in 1788 during the middle of the French Revolution. The war disrupted convent life, and she was forced to return home. She aided fugitive priests, cared for the poor and the sick, taught schoolchildren and visited prisoners.

After the revolution, when the convent community of Visitation nuns could not be reassembled, she offered the convent to the Society of the Sacred Heart and joined that community.

When the bishop of New Orleans requested nuns for his huge Louisiana diocese, Rose went, arriving in 1818. She and her four nuns were sent to Saint Charles, Missouri.

During the next several decades, Rose established convents, orphanages, parish schools, schools for American Indians, boarding academies and a novitiate. She faced all the hardships and deprivations of pioneer life and came to be known as "the missionary of the American frontier."

Rose died November 18, 1852, at the age of eighty-three. She was canonized in 1988.

REFLECTIONS

- Do you have a nickname? What is its meaning? How did you get it?
- Consider the courage that frontier women needed. What is the frontier in your life?

PRAYER

May each generation of women
Face the new frontier of their times
With faith and fortitude and firm purpose.
Amen.

November 19

INDIRA GANDHI

Stateswoman · India · 1917–1984

SCRIPTURE THEME

Love of country

"My cities shall again overflow with prosperity; the LORD will again comfort Zion and again choose Jerusalem."

— *Zechariah 1:17*

QUOTATION

"You cannot shake hands with a clenched fist."

— *Indira Gandhi*, The Quotable Woman: 1900–Present, *page 210*

INDIRA WAS BORN IN INDIA, in the northern province of Kashmir, on November 19, 1917. Her father, Jawaharlal Nehru, was India's first prime minister. Nearly all of Indira's family was involved in politics, and nearly all of them spent time in jail because of their political beliefs. They lived in a time of transition from India as a British colony to India as an independent nation and followed the teachings of Mohandas Gandhi.

Mohandas Gandhi, known as Mahatma, led the Indian nationalist revolt against Britain and preached a doctrine of nonviolence in achieving political and social progress. He called for home industries and took on fasts to make his point. He was shot to death by a Hindu fanatic in January 1948.

At eleven, Indira organized a group of children called the Monkey Brigade to run errands for the Indian National Congress party. Indira received a good education, including time at a university called Visva-Bharati, as well as at Oxford University in England.

In 1942, Indira married Feroze Gandhi (not related to Mohandas). They both worked for India's freedom while they raised their family. In 1947, India gained its freedom with Indira's father as the first prime minister.

Indira devoted herself to assisting her father. She traveled the world with him. In 1955, she joined the committee for the Congress party, and in 1959, she became president of the party.

When her father had a stroke, Indira became his nurse until his death in 1964. The new prime minister gave Indira the job as minister of information and broadcasting. In 1966, Indira Nehru Gandhi became the new prime minister. She showed strong leadership and faced opposition with courage.

In 1984, Indira was shot while walking in her garden. Her death marked the outbreak of riots between opposing sects, particularly the Sikhs and Hindus. Indira's son Rajiv became the new prime minister.

REFLECTIONS

- You may wish to watch the video *Gandhi* for a sense of the India in which Indira lived.

- What are the responsibilities of empires toward their newly independent colonies?

PRAYER

May our hands be like open windows
As we work for the freedom
And human rights of all peoples.
Amen.

November 20

CORITA KENT

Artist, educator • U.S. • 1918–1986

SCRIPTURE THEME

The Word

"In the beginning was the Word, and the Word was with God, and the Word was God."

— John 1:1

QUOTATION

"One of the things Jesus did was to step aside from the organized religion of his time because it had become corrupt and bogged down with rules. Rules became more important than feeding the hungry."

— Corita Kent, The Quotable Woman: 1900–Present, *page 224*

FRANCES KENT, WHO USED CORITA AS HER PROFESSIONAL NAME, was born November 20, 1918. She was educated at Immaculate Heart College in Los Angeles and the University of Southern California.

In 1936, she joined the sisters of the Immaculate Heart of Mary with the name of Sister Mary Corita. She taught elementary school for a time and then became professor of art at Immaculate Heart College. She established herself as an artist and educator with an innovative and unique style. She used colorful and abstract shapes with messages from the Bible and contemporary culture. Her silkscreens reflected the issues of the 1960's and 1970's to which she gave her attention: women's rights and human rights, world peace and global nuclear disarmament.

In 1968, Corita left the sisterhood and set up an art studio in Boston. Her output of artwork gained popular attention in such things as a best-selling postage stamp, a 150-foot-high rainbow on a Boston gas storage tank and the 50-foot mural at the Vatican Pavilion of the 1964–1965 World's Fair. Corita's art is displayed in nearly fifty museums throughout the world.

In 1986, on September 18, Corita died in Boston of cancer. She was not quite sixty-eight.

REFLECTIONS

• Who is your favorite artist? What do you most admire about your favorite type of artwork?

- What is your opinion of public art and large installations?

PRAYER

We praise you and thank you, God,
For our individual and unique gifts
And pray to use these talents
In making our world
And our neighborhoods
Better places to live and play
And pray.
Amen.

November 21

PRESENTATION OF MARY

Israel · 1st century B.C.

SCRIPTURE THEME

In the temple

"When the time came for their purification according to the law of Moses, they brought him up to Jerusalem to present him to the Lord."

 — *Luke 2:22*

QUOTATION

"Home is the definition of God."

 — Emily Dickinson, Beacon Book of Quotations by Women, *page 137*

THIS FEAST, FOUND IN APOCRYPHAL RATHER THAN HISTORICAL LITERATURE, offers a basic theological truth about Mary. From her earliest years, she was dedicated and devoted to God.

In the *Protoevangelium of James,* an apocryphal gospel, the story is told of how Anne and Joachim presented Mary, at age three, in the temple at Jerusalem and offered her to God. Anne had made a promise to do so when she was still childless. The birth of Mary is also recorded in this apocryphal text.

By the sixth century, a church was built in Jerusalem honoring the

Presentation of Mary and the feast was widely celebrated in the Eastern Church. The feast was observed in the Western Church by the eleventh century. In the sixteenth century, the Presentation of Mary was made a feast for the universal Church.

REFLECTIONS

- In what ways did your parents dedicate your early life to God? Rededicate your life now to God.
- How does your self-image change when you are mindful of being always in the presence of God?

PRAYER

Be with us, Mary,
As we dedicate our lives in fidelity
To the worship and service of God,
The same God you bore in your womb,
And who dwells within us.
Amen.

 *November 22*

SAINT CECILIA

Martyr · Rome (Italy) · 2nd century

SCRIPTURE THEME

Music

"Then I heard every creature in heaven and on earth and under the earth and in the sea, and all that is in them, singing."

— *Revelation 5:13*

QUOTATION

"It is extraordinary how music sends one back into memories of the past."

— *George Sand*, The Quotable Woman: 1800–On, *page 10*

VERY LITTLE IS KNOWN OF SAINT CECILIA. Tradition says she was a Roman girl of a noble Christian family. Her father arranged her marriage with a pagan named Valerian who was baptized at Cecilia's request. Valerian and his brother became active in promoting the Christian faith. It seems that her home was used as a church where more than four hundred of her converts were baptized. It was probably during the persecution of Diocletian that she was martyred, along with her husband.

By the middle of the sixth century, she was honored as Saint Cecilia. The story of her death and life, called *The Passion of Saint Cecilia*, tells how she was sentenced to death because she refused idolatry.

By the sixteenth century, she was held in high esteem as the patron of musicians because her story tells of her singing to God "in the heart" while instruments made music at her wedding.

REFLECTIONS

- Read the *Ode to Saint Cecilia* by John Dryden.
- Sit and listen prayerfully to a favorite piece of music.

PRAYER

For those who make music
For our worship services,
For our celebrations,
For our daily lives,
For our inspiration,
We praise you, God,
And ask your blessings.
Amen.

 *November 23*

HARRIET HUBBARD AYER

Businesswoman, journalist • U.S. • 1849–1903

SCRIPTURE THEME

Mother and child

"His mother said to him, 'Child, why have you treated us like this? Look, your father and I have been searching for you in great anxiety.'"

— Luke 2:48

QUOTATION

"She knew how to make virtues out of necessities."

— *Audre Lorde,* The Beacon Book of Quotations by Women, *page 217*

HARRIET WAS BORN JUNE 27, 1849, in Chicago to a well-off family, as the third of four children. Although the family was Episcopalian, Harriet attended Chicago's Convent School of the Sacred Heart and graduated at age fifteen. In 1852, Harriet's father died and her mother became a semi-invalid. At sixteen, Harriet married Herbert Copeland Ayer from a wealthy Chicago family. They had three girls; the second daughter died as an infant in the great Chicago fire of 1871.

While Herbert pursued business and work, Harriet managed the home and involved herself in cultural pursuits—travel, reading, theater. A growing estrangement from her husband led to divorce in 1886.

In order to support her children, Harriet worked as a decorator and furniture salesperson. In 1886, she established a business of her own in facial cream, which she promoted with extensive advertising. In 1889, Harriet was in a serious tangle with a stockbroker (her daughter Harriet's father-in-law) over loans and management practices.

By 1893, after four years of litigation and an illness (neurosthenic disorder), Harriet was forced into a private insane asylum by her divorced husband and her daughter Harriet. She lost custody of her other daughter, and she lost her business.

After fourteen months, she was released and proceeded to give a series of lectures on asylums and treatment of patients.

In 1896, Harriet was invited to write a beauty advice column for a Sunday paper, the *New York World.* Her columns were popular and formed the basis for her book, *Harriet Hubbard Ayer's Book: Complete and Authentic Treatise on the Laws of Health and Beauty.*

Harriet's work contributed to the movement for independence for women and to mass journalism. Much of her advice was common sense about health and hygiene. Even poor girls could read her newspaper column and learn about beauty "secrets" and enterprising work.

Reconciliation with her daughter came in Harriet's later years. She continued to work for the *World* until her death on November 23, 1903, at age fifty-four, of pneumonia and chronic nephritis. She was buried in Chicago.

Harriet's daughter Margaret took Harriet's place on the staff of the *World* and later married Frank Cobb, editor of the *World.*

REFLECTIONS

- What areas of your mother's life would you like to follow?

- What small businesses in your area are owned by women?

PRAYER

Do you not know
That I must be
About my mother's business?
Amen.

 *November 24*

FRANCES HODGSON BURNETT
Novelist · England and U.S. · 1849–1924

SCRIPTURE THEME

Walled garden

"Their life shall become like a watered garden,
and they shall never languish again."

— *Jeremiah 31:12*

QUOTATION

"It is astonishing how short a time it takes for wonderful things to happen."

— *Frances Burnett,* The Quotable Woman: 1800–On, *page 84*

IN HER BOOK *THE SECRET GARDEN*, about an invalid child, Frances shows great insight into a child's point of view. In the story, Mary Lennox, the sickly child living at her guardian's estate, befriends Dickon, a rather free-spirited country lad. Their discovery of the walled garden and the secret gate of entrance into it offers one of the best novels ever written for children. And it offers to any reader a sense of inner and outer freedom and space, a window into wholeness as Mary regains her health.

Frances was born in England on November 24, 1849. Her father, a wholesaler of hardware, died in 1854, and when the family business failed, she moved with her family to Tennessee in 1865.

By seventeen, Frances was writing stories and selling them to local newspapers. She married in 1873, moved with her husband to Europe in 1875 and back to the United States in 1877. They had two sons, one of whom died at sixteen.

By 1883, Frances had written sixteen novels, some for adults, some for children. When *Little Lord Fauntleroy* appeared in 1886, it became one of the best-sellers of the year. Frances turned much of her attention to writing for children. Her life and work saw the tension of balancing artistic talent and the self-sacrifice of wife and mother.

Her best-known, and probably best-quality, book, *The Secret Garden,* came out in 1911. In her later years, Frances was rather eccentric, escaping into her own world, wearing elaborate and frilly costume clothing; she was tyrannical in behavior toward her family and seemed snobbish in her dream-world life. She died in 1924.

REFLECTIONS

- Have you read *The Secret Garden*? What do you remember about it?
- What secret place did you have as a child? How did this place enrich your imagination?
- *The Secret Garden* and *Little Lord Fauntleroy* are wonderful read-aloud books. Share one of these with a special child.

PRAYER

As Mary Magdalene found you,
Christ Jesus, in the garden
That Resurrection morn,
May we find you,
Christ Jesus, in gardens
While we walk and work.
Amen.

November 25

CARRY NATION

Reformer • U.S. • 1846–1911

SCRIPTURE THEME

Reform

"Do not remember the former things,
or consider the things of old.
I am about to do a new thing."

— *Isaiah 43:18-19*

QUOTATION

"When I had company I always directed the conversation so that my friend would teach me something, or I would teach him."

— *Carry Nation,* Give Her This Day, *page 337*

REMEMBERED—CARICATURED—FOR HER HATCHET-SWINGING APPROACH to shutting down taverns and saloons in her temperance campaign, Carry Moore was born November 25, 1846, in Kentucky. Her family's poverty caused frequent moves, and her education was sporadic. Carry had more than the usual enthusiasm for religion.

In 1867, Carry married Charles Gloyd, whom she hoped to cure of alcoholism. When he died leaving her with a small child, she utterly hated liquor and saloons.

After earning her teacher's certificate, Carry set to teaching school in Missouri. In 1877, she married David Nation, a journalist, and they settled in Texas.

By 1890, they had moved to Kansas, and Carry organized a chapter of the Women's Christian Temperance Union. Kansas was a "dry" state, but many ignored the prohibition. It was in Kansas that Carry went around with her hatchet to saloons, including the saloon of the Kansas State Senate.

In 1901, her husband divorced her for desertion.

Carry went on to disturb the U.S. Senate with her "mission" against liquor. Arrested for disturbing the peace, Carry paid her fines out of lecture fees and money she made selling souvenir hatchets. When she gave lectures, she often appeared in the garb of a deaconess carrying her hatchet.

She died after an illness on June 9, 1911.

History has assessed that the later enactment of national prohibition came more from conventional reformers than from Carry's hatchet-wielding.

REFLECTIONS

- Do you carry or use a "hatchet" in promoting causes you believe in? Do you know someone else who does? How do you feel about this kind of an approach?

- How would you (or do you) handle and help someone in situations of chemical (drug or alcohol or medicine) dependency and abuse?

- What approaches do you consider successful in attaining true and lasting reform?

PRAYER

> For a well-formed conscience,
> We pray to you, Jesus,
> So that each of us
> May decide on activities
> Of demonstration and protest
> With your gospel in mind.
> Amen.

November 26

SARAH MOORE GRIMKÉ

Reformer and abolitionist • U.S. • 1792–1873

SCRIPTURE THEME

Sisters and friends

"A friend loves at all times,
and kinsfolk are born to share adversity."

> — *Proverbs 17:17*

QUOTATION

"In this sublime description of the creation of man (which is a generic term including man and woman), there is not a particle of difference intimated as existing between them. They were both made in the image of God; dominion was given to both over every other creature, but not over each other. Created in perfect equality, they were expected to exercise the vice regence intrusted to them by their Maker, in harmony and love…"

> — *Sarah Moore Grimké, The Quotable Woman: From Eve to 1799, page 428*

SARAH WAS NOT QUITE THIRTEEN when her sister, Angelina, was born. With eleven of her fourteen children still living, Mrs. Grimké was glad for Sarah's help with the new baby. Thus began the bonding of the two sisters, a friendship that lasted a lifetime. And there the two, growing up in the South, came to share views against the Black slavery they saw, though they seemed to be the only ones to do so.

Sarah was born November 26, 1792, and Angelina on February 20, 1805. Sarah became acquainted with Quaker beliefs, and on May 29, 1823, Sarah was received as a member. Angelina, like Sarah, was more concerned about spiritual life than social graces. When Angelina began attending Quaker meetings, the Presbyterian church to which she belonged expelled her.

The two sisters fled the South and settled in Philadelphia, amazed and pleased to find free Blacks in that city. Pennsylvania Quakers were active in the abolitionist movement. The Grimké sisters began reading the *Liberator* of William Lloyd Garrison. One of Angelina's letters was published in the *Liberator*, and this set in motion her radical involvement in the issue. Angelina wrote a long essay, *An Appeal to the Christian Women of the South*, in which she called slavery a crime. The essay had far-reaching effects. In Angelina's hometown of Charleston, South Carolina, all copies of it were burned, and the Charleston authorities banned Angelina forever from the city.

Angelina decided to train as a public speaker, a field not really open to women at that time, and Sarah, though reluctant, joined her. The sisters became deeply involved in controversy as they made their lecture tours speaking about the bondage of Blacks and women. They pointed out contradictions between state slave laws and Christian teachings. Many people were angered that women were speaking out, and tensions grew. Some churches forbade their members to listen to the Grimké sisters.

In 1838, Angelina married Theodore Weld. Sarah helped to care for the children as they came along. The three adults taught at a school open to Blacks as well as Whites. Sarah and Angelina formed friendships with leaders of the women's movement and offered inspiration to a new generation seeking justice and truth.

Sarah died on December 23, 1873, and Angelina in 1879. The windows they opened to a better sense of rights for Blacks and for women offered the next generation a vision to set their goals by.

REFLECTIONS

- Do you have a favorite sister or brother with whom it is easy to share ideas, concerns, values?

- Have you ever been expelled or banned from a group or place because you held differing views? How did this affect you?

PRAYER

May we find spiritual strength
In sharing our prayer and dream and work
With our sisters, with our families,
With our neighbors, and with our world.
Amen.

November 27

CHUNDRA LELA

Pilgrim · India · 1840–1907

SCRIPTURE THEME

Pilgrimage

*"Your statutes have been my songs
wherever I make my home."*
— *Psalm 119:54*

QUOTATION

*"Find me the men of earth who care
Enough for faith or creed today
To seek the barren wilderness
For simple liberty to pray."*
— *Helen Fiske Hunt Jackson,* The Quotable Woman: 1800–On, *page 59*

BORN IN 1840 IN NEPAL, Chundra was married at age seven because of the Hindu fear of an unmarried daughter. Chundra was nine when her husband died, and the expectation was that she would spend the rest of her life mourning him.

Chundra's father was somewhat unconventional when he taught her to read Sanskrit and educated her as a Brahmin.

By the time Chundra was thirteen, her father and mother had both died. Chundra decided to visit and worship at the four great shrines of India: Jagannatha at Puri, Ram at Pamban Island, Krishna at Dwarka and Vishnu at Badrinath. This pilgrimage took Chundra seven years, but still she did not find peace.

She continued making pilgrimages and visiting shrines. On a visit to the shrine of Puri, Chundra came to the attention of the king and queen who made her a priestess of the court. Chundra stayed there for seven years.

But Chundra still felt restless for God and set out again on pilgrimages to shrines where she subjected her body to incredible penances and then settled down as a guru. Chundra came in contact with a Christian family and came to read the Christian Scriptures. She read, believed and was baptized.

Chundra continued to wander from shrine to shrine preaching about salvation in God through Jesus Christ. She was much like Francis of Assisi in that she begged for food and freely shared what little she had by way of clothing or provisions.

Chundra's friends wished to provide her with a house, but Chundra would only agree to it if it would be near the road where she could continue to preach to passersby. In her last months, Chundra shared this home with a disgraced Hindu woman and her child. She died in the little house on November 26, 1907.

REFLECTIONS

- Do you have favorite shrines or holy places you like to visit?
- Do you believe that pilgrimages and penances help one to find God and save one's soul?

PRAYER

For young girls—
In every culture and country
We pray to God, our mother,
That the customs of their peoples
May be celebrated to give them
Fullness of life and joy.
Amen.

November 28

CATHERINE LABOURÉ

Religious visionary • France • 1806–1876

SCRIPTURE THEME

Grace

"A woman clothed with the sun, with the moon under her feet, and on her head a crown of twelve stars."

— *Revelation 12:1*

QUOTATION

"O Mary, conceived without sin, pray for us who have recourse to thee."

—*Catherine Labouré*, Lives of the Saints, *page 478*

ZOÉ LABOURÉ WAS BORN IN 1806, the ninth of seventeen children, to a prosperous farm family. When Zoé was eight, her mother died. When her sister entered the convent, Zoé, age twelve, took over the care of the household. She wished to enter the convent with her sister, but her father opposed it and sent her to Paris to work in her brother's café as a waitress.

Eventually, with the help of relatives, she entered the Sisters of Charity in 1830 and was known as Sister Catherine. During her novitiate, a series of visions revealed to her the form and image of what is known as the miraculous medal and gave Sister Catherine directions as to how to spread devotion to the medal.

Catherine explained these visions to her confessor and insisted he never reveal her name. From 1831 until her death in 1876, she lived an ordinary and hidden convent life, caring for the sick and doing other household tasks.

Meanwhile, her confessor and the archbishop of Paris had miraculous medals made and distributed, and much good came from the devotion.

Catherine died December 31 at the age of seventy. Her incorrupt body lies in the Sisters of Charity Motherhouse on Rue du Boc in Paris, the convent she entered in 1830. She was beatified in 1933 and canonized in 1947.

REFLECTIONS

- Many Catholics have worn a miraculous medal at one time or another. When have you worn something of special personal or religious significance?
- Many good ideas come from people who never receive recognition, and some people have no idea of all the good they do. Is it important that people are aware of the impact they have on others? What impact do you have on those you see daily?

PRAYER

We pray,
United with Catherine Labouré,
"O Mary,
Conceived without sin,
Pray for us
Who have recourse to thee."
Amen.

November 29

MADELEINE L'ENGLE

Author • U.S. • 1918 —

SCRIPTURE THEME

Need for quiet

"Better is a handful with quiet
than two handfuls with toil."

— *Ecclesiastes 4:6*

QUOTATION

"Poetry and prayer are synonymous in my life, and because both are a gift, which I accept with joy and sometimes pain, I seldom know whether I have served the gift well or ill. But perhaps that doesn't really matter; the important thing is to be willing—to want to serve the gift whenever it comes, either as verse or prayer."

— *Madeleine L'Engle in* Weather of the Heart, *Foreword*

MADELEINE, THE ONLY CHILD OF A PIANIST MOTHER and a playwright-critic father, was born November 29, 1918, in New York City, where she lived until she was twelve. She spent her free time drawing, writing and playing the piano. Her teen years at a European boarding school gave her more reason to be imaginative and solitary.

After graduation from college, she worked in the theater. After her marriage, she gave up acting for writing. Her family with three children and then several grandchildren enjoyed her Connecticut farmhouse in summer.

Madeleine has written several books for young adults. Her Newbery Medal book, *A Wrinkle in Time*, offers serious ideas and intellectual stimulation to young readers, as do most of her young adult fiction books.

Madeleine's nonfiction, such as *The Circle of Quiet*, *The Summer of the Great-Grandmother* and *The Irrational Season*, offer her experiences and reflections. *Two-Part Invention* tells of her marriage to Hugh Franklin and her life as a "writing woman," to use May Sarton's phrase.

In *Two-Part Invention*, Madeleine tells how her friends do not always understand her work as a writer or her need for books, poetry and music or "the real importance of a view from a window."

Madeleine serves as writer-in-residence and librarian at the New York City Cathedral of St. John the Divine. Some of her recent books are *Glimpses of Grace, Friends for the Journey* and *A Prayerbook of Spiritual Partners.*

REFLECTIONS

- Do you have your own "circle of quiet"—a place to go to regain balance and serenity?
- When have you used a fictional setting as a place of mental retreat? What is your favorite make-believe place?

PRAYER

In balancing our busy lives
Of home and work,
May we always find God
In our circles of quiet.
Amen.

 *November 30*

SHIRLEY ANITA SAINT HILL CHISHOLM

Social reformer, politician • U.S. • 1924—

SCRIPTURE THEME

Righteousness

"Deal courageously, and may the LORD be with the good!"
  — *2 Chronicles 19:11*

QUOTATION

"I am a candidate for the Presidency of the United States. I make that statement proudly, in the full knowledge that, as a black person and as a female person, I do not have a chance of actually gaining that office in this election year."
  — *Shirley Chisholm in a speech given June 4, 1972,* The Quotable Woman:
    1900–Present, *page 280*

IN JANUARY 1969, SHIRLEY CHISHOLM ENTERED THE U.S. CONGRESS as the first Black woman ever to do so. Her special concerns were urban needs and minority rights.

Shirley was born November 30, 1924, in Brooklyn, New York. Part of her childhood was spent in Barbados and the rest in Brooklyn. In 1946, she graduated from Brooklyn College. She studied elementary education at Columbia University while teaching nursery school. In 1949, she married Conrad Q. Chisholm.

In the 1950's, Shirley became the director of a day care center and a consultant to the day care division of the New York City Bureau of Child Welfare. Her interest in neighborhood problems led her to political activity, where her knowledge of Spanish made her popular among the Puerto Rican residents.

She ran for and won seats in the state legislature and was reelected. In 1968, she ran for Congress in the newly created Twelfth District in a poor area of Brooklyn. In 1972, she made an unsuccessful run for the Democratic presidential nomination. Shirley held her congressional seat for six terms before leaving office in 1980. She retired in 1983.

REFLECTIONS

- What do you admire most about Shirley Chisholm?
- What are the advantages of knowing a second language? What are the disadvantages of not knowing the language of the majority?
- Are you fearful of social concerns leading you into the political arena? Why?

PRAYER

We thank you, God,
And praise you,
For those who work in your name
To make better lives for the poor,
The needy, the oppressed, the underdog,
And we call upon you, God,
To hear the cry of the poor
And have mercy on us all.
Amen.

December 1

ROSA PARKS

Civil rights leader • U.S. • 1913—

SCRIPTURE THEME

Resistance

"The LORD *lifts up those who are bowed down;*
the LORD *loves the righteous."*

— *Psalm 146:8*

QUOTATION

"My only concern was to get home after a hard day's work."

— *Rosa Parks,* The Quotable Woman: 1900–Present, *page 181*

ON DECEMBER 1, 1955, ROSA DECIDED TO RIDE THE BUS HOME from work. She sat in the first seat of the Black section. When the White section was full and a White man told Rosa to give up her seat, Rosa quietly said no.

When the driver told Rosa to move or he would call the police, Rosa again said no. The bus driver carried through on his threat, and Rosa was arrested, fingerprinted and photographed. She relied on her religious faith and prayed for strength.

Rosa McCauley was born February 4, 1913, in Tuskegee, Alabama, and grew up on a little farm on the outskirts of Montgomery. She attended the Montgomery Industrial School for girls, where she became quite adept at sewing. She also liked to read.

During her youth, Rosa and her family were often frightened and threatened by the Ku Klux Klan. Rosa disliked the segregation rules. Because of her mother's influence, Rosa grew up proud of being Black and learned to judge people by the respect they had for themselves and others.

Rosa joined the NAACP (National Association for the Advancement of Colored People) and the Montgomery Voters League.

The segregation on public buses was abused and became a source of intense frustration for Blacks. Rosa's refusal to give up her seat heralded a new era of nonviolent protest. By December 5, four days after Rosa's refusal, the Black people of Montgomery refused to ride the buses. They all walked under the leadership of Dr. Martin Luther King, Jr., and they worked out their own transportation to work, to school, to church.

Rosa faced death threats by phone and by letter. About a hundred of the protest leaders, including Rosa, were arrested. They posted bond, and Rosa traveled around the country giving lectures.

A Supreme Court decision in November 1956 ruled that the bus company had to change and allow Blacks to sit anywhere. Other cities began to require the same. People began calling Rosa Parks the "Mother of the Civil Rights Movement." A large mural in Dexter Avenue Baptist Church in Montgomery, Alabama, depicts civil rights history beginning with Rosa's bus ride.

When Rosa was attacked in her home in 1994, she offered her attacker forgiveness. Her book *Quiet Strength* was released in February, 2000.

REFLECTIONS

- What values do you believe in strongly enough to risk arrest?
- Do you look for alternative and creative solutions to problems?
- Watch *The Long Walk Home*, which is based on the bus boycott events.

PRAYER

We pray for
Rosa's kind of courage
To do what we feel is right.
Amen.

December 2

SISTER DOROTHY KAZEL

Martyr • U.S. and El Salvador • 1939–1980
(also martyred the same day: Sister Ita Ford, Sister Maura Clark, Jean Donovan)

SCRIPTURE THEME

Hallelujah

"Hallelujah!
For the Lord our God
The Almighty reigns."

— *Revelation 19:6*

QUOTATION

*"The whole gospel of John is about love and the whole reason for living is love....
If we can extend a little bit of concern to the people down here, I think that's
about all we can really do. We know we are sort of band-aid instruments; we are
not able to participate fully, completely in the culture and politics and everything that is going on around here. We touch on things. But we can only touch
on things in a hopeful way and in a loving way and in this way bring Jesus
Christ to the people."*

— *Sister Dorothy Kazel*, Alleluia Woman, Sister Dorothy Kazel, O.S.U., *page 21*

DOROTHY KAZEL WAS BORN IN CLEVELAND, OHIO, and baptized on August
6, 1939, in St. George Lithuanian Parish. She grew up with the customs,
festivals and devotions of Lithuanian Catholics. Dorothy loved animals
and the natural world. She performed well in music and sports and was
an outstanding student.

When she graduated from Notre Dame Academy in 1957, she trained
as a medical secretary and as a teacher. She was engaged to be married
when she began to discern a call to religious life. In September 1960, she
entered an Ursuline convent in a suburb of Cleveland. She studied religious life and academic subjects.

She was assigned to teach business subjects in a high school. She also
got involved in ecumenical and interracial organizations. When the
Diocese of Cleveland established a mission in El Salvador in 1964,
Dorothy immediately offered her services. Meanwhile, she completed
her master's degree in counseling and studied Spanish. In 1974, Dorothy
and a companion went to the parish of Señora de Guadalupe in
Chirilagra. In 1975, Dorothy moved to the parish of San Carlos Borromeo
and in 1977 to a third parish in the port of La Libertad.

In addition to usual missionary work, Dorothy grew familiar with
death lists and death squads. When Archbishop Oscar Romero was shot
on March 23, 1980, Dorothy prayed about remaining in El Salvador and
chose to do so, even though all church workers were in great danger.

On December 2, 1980, Sister Dorothy along with Jean Donovan, a lay
worker, and Sister Ita Ford and Sister Maura Clark, both Maryknoll sisters, disappeared. The bodies of the four churchwomen were later found
shot.

Dorothy's body was returned to Cleveland with a wake and funeral at
the Ursuline motherhouse.

REFLECTIONS

- See the films *Roses in December* and *Choices of the Heart*, which depict the events surrounding the martyrdom of Dorothy and her companions.
- Find out more about the human rights struggle in El Salvador and other developing countries. How does this knowledge change the way you view your own daily struggles?

PRAYER

May our faith be strengthened
By the blood of martyrs
And our lives enriched
By the witness of their lives.
Amen.

December 3

MARIA CALLAS

Operatic soprano • U.S. and Greece • 1923–1977

SCRIPTURE THEME

Voice

"A bird of the air may carry your voice."

— *Ecclesiastes 10:20*

QUOTATION

"An opera begins long before the curtain goes up and ends long after it has come down. It starts in my imagination, it becomes my life, and it stays part of my life long after I've left the opera house."

— *Maria Callas*, Simpson's Contemporary Quotations, *page 339*

MARIA CALLAS SANG WITH DRAMA AND POWER. She became one of the most popular stars of contemporary opera.

Born on December 3, 1923, Maria Anna Sofia Cecilia Kalogeropoulos was the daughter of immigrant Greek parents living in New York City. As a child, Maria liked singing. At fourteen, she entered the Royal Conservatory of Music in Athens, Greece, and made her operatic debut in Athens.

Maria began her career by appearing in *La Gioconda* in Verona in 1947. She made appearances in other Italian cities and in 1950 traveled to Mexico City. Throughout the 1950's, she sang in the most prestigious opera houses around the world, with an American debut in 1954.

Maria's talents of voice and drama and sense of theater made possible the revival of nineteenth-century opera scores. Recordings of Maria's singing were received with enthusiasm. She was involved in several disputes and feuds with managers and rivals. Her temperament and prima donna role received much publicity.

In 1965, Maria did her last operatic performance. She made a final world concert tour in the mid-1970's.

She died September 16, 1977, in Paris.

REFLECTIONS

- Listen to a recording of Maria Callas's voice, in an opera or a shorter piece.
- Do you think artistic people have an especially sensitive temperament? Why or why not?

PRAYER

You call us, God,
To use our voices
To praise you
And to encourage one another.
Forgive us all the times
We have failed to use our voices
For the common good,
And strengthen us
To use our voices
For love and truth.
Amen.

December 4

SAINT BARBARA

Legendary woman • Europe and Africa • c. 3rd century

SCRIPTURE THEME

Tower

"Come, let us build ourselves a city, and a tower with its top in the heavens."
— Genesis 11:4

QUOTATION

"A woman is a full circle. Within her is the power to create, nurture, and transform. A woman knows that nothing can come to fruition without light. Let us call upon woman's voice and woman's heart to guide us in this age of planetary transformation."
— Diane Mariechild, The Quotable Woman, *page 7*

IN THE 1969 REVISED ROMAN CALENDAR, the twelfth-century memorial of Saint Barbara was abolished for lack of evidence about her real life. The stories about her life are more legend than history, and historians do not even agree about the site of her martyrdom.

The main legend about the beautiful Barbara tells that her pagan father imprisoned her in a tower to protect her from various suitors. During her solitary confinement, she had a workman make a window in the tower. Through this window, she was baptized by a holy man whom she had sent for. When she refused to take part in pagan rituals, her own father killed her, whereupon he was immediately killed by lightning. The dates given for her life vary from A.D. 235 to 315, and the places she was supposed to have lived range from Rome to Egypt to Tuscany.

Her story was probably written as religious fiction around the kernel of truth of her martyrdom for refusing paganism. She was invoked for safety against lightning, and by extension, she became the patron saint of gunners, miners and artillery companies. Her symbol is a tower.

Saint Barbara's Eve was first celebrated in Syria with children dressing in costume and visiting house to house where they would sing and ask for a blessing and a gift. People would give decorated eggs, coins or candies.

Barbara's day remains popular in the Near East and Asia Minor and some parts of Italy. Her symbol is wheat, sign of a bountiful harvest. It is still an Advent custom to plant on her feast grains of wheat, which sprout quickly and can be "harvested" by Christmas as straw for the Christmas crib.

REFLECTIONS

- It is written of Saint Barbara that after her conversion she took up residence in the bathhouse built by her father. She had the workman add a third window in honor of the Holy Trinity. When have you felt confined by the limits of your abilities? How does a sustaining vision empower you to rise above your limits?
- Try to find a reproduction of Jon van Eyck's famous painting of Saint Barbara. It is housed in the Royal Museum at Antwerp.

PRAYER

May we learn ways
To make windows in the walls
As did Barbara,
So that we may come to know the liberating spiritual forces
And inner spiritual resources
That will make us holy.
Amen.

 *December 5*

PHYLLIS WHEATLEY

Poet • Africa and U.S. • d. 1784

SCRIPTURE THEME

Hagar

"What troubles you, Hagar? Do not be afraid.... I will make a great nation of him."

— *Genesis 21:17-18*

QUOTATION

"No more, America, in mournful strains
Of wrongs, and grievance unredress'd complain,
No longer shalt thou dread the iron chain,

Which wanton Tyranny with lawless hand
Had made, and with it mean t'enslave the land."

— *Phyllis Wheatley,* The Quotable Woman: From Eve to 1799, *page 296*

AT AGE EIGHT, PHYLLIS WAS TAKEN FROM AFRICA (probably Senegal) on a slave ship and brought to Boston, where she was bought by John Wheatley. She worked as a servant for John's wife. The family treated her kindly and educated her. She learned both English and Latin and read a great deal of poetry.

In 1773, when Phyllis was about twenty, some friends in Boston published her poems as *Poems on Various Subjects Religious and Moral.* The poems, while mostly didactic, revealed her personal hope and faith.

Also in 1773, Phyllis traveled to England with the Wheatleys' son. She was honored as a poet everywhere she went.

At one point, Phyllis wrote a poem and sent it to George Washington. He responded. In 1776, Phyllis met General George Washington.

After the Wheatleys died, Phyllis married a free Black named John Peters. Two of her three children died, and her marriage was not happy. She also lost touch with her former circle of friends.

Phyllis became ill and died in 1784 when she was about thirty-one years old.

REFLECTIONS

· Read some of Phyllis Wheatley's poems.

· Consider what it means to be "treated well" in the context of slavery. What fundamental changes are needed in the world today for everyone to truly be treated well?

PRAYER

Inspire us, O God,
With the vision
To see what must be changed
And the courage
To make it happen.
Amen.

December 6

EVELYN UNDERHILL

Practical mystic, poet • *England* • *1875–1941*

SCRIPTURE THEME

Mystical prayer

"The prayer of faith will save the sick, and the Lord will raise them up; and anyone who has committed sins will be forgiven. Therefore confess your sins to one another, and pray for one another, so that you may be healed."

— *James 5:15-16*

QUOTATION

"After all it is those who have a deep and real inner life who are best able to deal with the 'irritating details of outer life.'"

— *Evelyn Underhill*, The New Book of Christian Quotations, *page 146*

BORN IN 1875, EVELYN WAS A BRIGHT CHILD. Before she was twenty, she had published a novel called *The Grey World*. Evelyn's parents did not attend church, but Evelyn did. She was confirmed at age fifteen and then spent some years as an agnostic. When she returned to belief in God, she was very much drawn to prayer. She made retreats, and though it was most unusual at that time for a layperson or a woman to do so, she also served as retreat conductor. During the 1920's and early 1930's, Evelyn conducted as many as eight retreats a year. The talks she gave were later published.

What was attractive about Evelyn's personality as well as her retreat talks and spiritual writing was her practical and down-to-earth approach to spirituality.

Evelyn married her childhood sweetheart, a barrister named Herbert Stuart Moore, but they never were able to have children. She devoted her time to prayer, writing and retreat work. She was educated at King's College in London. The University of Aberdeen recognized her scholarliness with an honorary degree of Doctor of Divinity in 1938.

Ill with asthma, Evelyn and her husband left London during the early months of World War II. They returned in 1941, and Evelyn died that year on June 14.

REFLECTIONS

- Evelyn says over and over that artists and poets show us the beauty just beyond our windows and they show us that God is there, too. How do you experience God in the works of poets and artists? In being a poet or artist yourself?

- How do you feel about the diverse gifts of artists and poets and musicians in worship? In other forms of prayer?

- Are you comfortable in artistic/poetic expressions of your own personal relationship with God?

- Can you, do you, affirm a variety of images of God? Do you have some favorite feminine images of God? Favorite masculine images? Favorite images from the natural world?

PRAYER

> May we find you—Creator, Jesus, Spirit—
> > Just beyond the windows of our lives,
> > And find rest in your presence
> As we live the practicalities of the hours
> Of our days and nights.
> Amen.

 *December 7*

WILLA CATHER

Writer · U.S. · 1873–1947

SCRIPTURE THEME

Words

"I have put my words in your mouth,
and hidden you in the shadow of my hand."
— *Isaiah 51:16*

QUOTATION

"There are only two or three human stories, and they go on repeating themselves as fiercely as if they had never happened before."
— *Willa Cather*, Sunbeams, *page 45*

WILLA CATHER HAS LONG BEEN RECOGNIZED in American literature as a religious writer with spiritual values as her single great theme.

In *Death Comes for the Archbishop*, set in the New Mexico Territory, and *Shadows on the Rock*, set in seventeenth-century Quebec, Willa builds both the character and the setting on the Catholic faith of the New World.

Willa searched for many years to find her own true literary voice. Her early works imitate the writings of Henry James. Befriended by Sarah Orne Jewett, the New England author, Willa grew in her skill of portraying her own themes and style. Two of her best books are *My Antonia* and *O Pioneers!*, novels of strong women on the Nebraska frontier. *The Song of the Lark* is as much the story of Willa's emergence as a major artist as it is the fictional story of Thea Kronberg's opera career.

The intimacy and immensity that nourished her imagination transform Willa's best writing into literature that shares the inner lives of wonderful characters through their lived experiences.

As a youth, Willa cut her hair short and called herself William. She wore mannish clothes and preferred the company of other women. Willa never married, preferring to not submit to a man's power or the expected domesticity. Her characters are strong, proud, determined, imaginative, intelligent, likeable and believable—not unlike Willa.

Willa struggled with her work and job as a journalist and her desire to grow as a literary artist. Her searching and finding are well expressed in Sharon O'Brien's analytical biography, *Willa Cather: The Emerging Voice*.

REFLECTIONS

- Read *My Antonia* or *The Song of the Lark.*
- What prejudices might affect someone who dressed and lived as Willa did? Are those prejudices still evident today?

PRAYER

In all that we are and do,
May values of the spirit
Be our single greatest strength.
Amen.

December 8

CONCEPCION CABRERA DE ARMIDA

Mystic, writer • Mexico • 1862–1937

SCRIPTURE THEME

Immaculate Conception

"The virgin's name was Mary."

— Luke 1:27

QUOTATION

"Without your knowing it, I have given you what you desired so much, and much, much more than that: the ability to be a priest, not that of holding me in your hands but in your heart, and the grace of never separating myself from you."

> — the words of Jesus to Concepcion Cabrera de Armida, as noted in her writings, Revelations of Women Mystics, pages 115, 117

A MYSTIC ON NORTH AMERICAN SOIL, Concepcion, called Conchita, was born December 8, 1862, in Mexico. She married in 1884, and when her husband died in 1901, she was a widow with eight young children.

At nineteen, a few years before her marriage, she had deep spiritual desires that led to an experience of spiritual marriage in 1897. She kept a spiritual diary for some forty years in sixty-six handwritten volumes.

The unusual balance and harmony in Conchita's life of living a natural marriage and motherhood simultaneously with the highest mystical experiences has been verified and authenticated by the two religious congregations she founded and by a special commission in Rome.

Some of the main points of Conchita's mystical insights concern the role of suffering as sacrificial priesthood, the presence of the Holy Spirit, the humanity of Christ, the beauty of Mary and the mystery of the Church.

Conchita's mystical conversations with Christ, recorded in her journals, lasted forty years right up until her death on March 3, 1937. The cause for her beatification and canonization has been introduced to the authorities in Rome.

REFLECTIONS

- One of Conchita's regrets was that she never shared the mystical secrets of her soul with her husband. He died before she thought of doing so. What regrets do you have? Which of these can still be remedied?

- If mysticism is explained as intuition or inner awareness of truth (rather than truth through sense experience), do you find that some of your own spiritual experiences are mystical?
- Many spiritual writers say that all are invited to mystical prayer and union with God. How do you feel about this?

PRAYER

Through the intercession
Of this holy mother and grandmother,
May we grow in spiritual values
As we fulfill our duties
In our daily situations.
Amen.

 *December 9*

BETTY STAIN

Missionary · *U.S. and China* · *1906–1934*

SCRIPTURE THEME

Martyrdom

*"Precious in the sight of the LORD
is the death of his faithful ones."*
— *Psalm 116:15*

QUOTATION

"All Jesus' followers have to do, all they can do, is to lift up Jesus before the world, bring him into dingy corners and dark places of the earth where he is unknown, introduce him to strangers, talk about him to everybody, and live so closely with and in him that others may see that there really is such a person as Jesus, because some being proves it by being like him."

— *Betty Stain, in a letter to her brother Kenneth*

BETTY WAS BORN IN THE UNITED STATES IN 1906 and grew up in China, where her missionary parents worked. She met John Stain at the Moody

Bible Institute in Chicago, and they both went to China as missionaries. They were married in 1932 in China.

Their mission on the Yangtze River was caught in the conflict between Chinese Nationalists and Chinese Communists, and they feared for their baby daughter. Betty and John were seized. When no ransom money was paid on their behalf, they were beheaded on December 9, 1934. The baby was spared and given to her maternal grandparents.

Two other martyrs, Margaret Morgan and Minka Hanskamp, were missionary nurses who worked at a leprosy clinic. Margaret was born in Wales in 1934, the same year Betty died. She trained as a nurse and went to Thailand. Minka, a native of the Dutch East Indies, was interned by the Japanese during World War II. Eventually she went to New Zealand and later to Thailand as part of the Overseas Missionary Fellowship. In 1975, Margaret and Minka were kidnapped and killed when a $500,000 ransom was not paid.

All four missionaries are remembered on December 9 by the Overseas Missionary Fellowship, formerly known as the China Inland Mission.

REFLECTIONS

- What is the wisdom of not paying or paying a ransom?
- What is the current situation of human rights in China and Southeast Asia?
- Pray for missionaries who are in high-risk situations.

PRAYER

With compassionate solidarity,
We pray to you, God,
For all held in captivity
Because of service to others,
And for all who die
In service to others.
Amen.

December 10

RUMER GODDEN
Cross-cultural writer • England and India • 1907–1998

SCRIPTURE THEME

Cross-cultural experiences

"I have been an alien residing in a foreign land."

— *Exodus 2:22*

QUOTATION

"There is an Indian proverb or axiom that says that everyone is a house with four rooms, a physical, a mental, an emotional and a spiritual. Most of us tend to live in one room most of the time but, unless we go into every room every day, even if only to keep it aired, we are not a complete person."

— *Rumer Godden,* A House With Four Rooms, *frontispiece*

BORN ON DECEMBER 10, 1909, IN ENGLAND, Rumer spent much of her childhood in India where her father worked as a steamship agent. Rumer and her sisters grew up familiar with India's great rivers as well as the tidal forest called Sunderbans. Rumer always loved to write poems and stories and was always fond of books. She intended to be a writer, though she also considered being a nun or missionary.

She trained for dancing in London and set up a dancing school in Calcutta. She continued to write, and in 1939, her first novel, *Black Narcissus*, was completed. It became well known and was made into a film.

Rumer married and raised two daughters, mostly in India, though she returned to England from time to time. Rumer nurtured a love for Chinese literature, and this also found its way into her writings.

Rumer's openness to other cultures is revealed as well in her autobiographical book, *A Time to Dance, No Time to Weep.* In this book, she writes of *darshan*, a quiet receptivity in a place of beauty and the absorbing of that beauty into the soul.

Over the years, Rumer's interest in religious life sparked and sustained the writing of *In This House of Brede* and *Five for Sorrow, Ten for Joy.* Rumer's art of conveying emotional experiences through the actions of children manifests itself in *The Kitchen Madonna* and *An Episode of Sparrows.*

All in all, Rumer wrote and published more than fifty works, including fiction and nonfiction, poetry and children's books.

In her book describing her childhood years in India, Rumer speaks of the Hindu goddess Saraswati as the patron of art and music and books. On the festival day of Saraswati, students and artists would bring their books or manuscripts or whatever they were working on to the pavilion or pandal where Saraswati's image was enthroned in order to seek her blessing on their projects. This appealed to Rumer and her sister Jon; they did not consider it idolatry but rather a sense of the muse. When filming *The River,* a movie based on a book written by Rumer, Rumer was asked by the Indian filming crew to lay the script at Saraswati's feet.

REFLECTIONS

- How open are you to learning from other cultures? How might you encourage this in yourself and others?

- Do you have a place of quiet where you can absorb the beauty of the natural world? How often do you visit it?

PRAYER

> May we come to wholeness and holiness
> By entering the physical and mental rooms,
> The emotional and spiritual rooms,
> All the rooms in our house of life.
> Amen.

 *December 11*

ANNIE JUMP CANNON

Astronomer · U.S. · 1863–1941

SCRIPTURE THEME

Heavens

"He determines the number of the stars;
he gives to all of them their names."
— Psalm 147:4

QUOTATION

"They aren't just streaks to me, each new spectrum is the gateway to a wonder-

ful new world. It is almost as if the distant stars had really acquired speech and were able to tell of their constitution and physical condition."

— *Annie Cannon,* Give Her This Day, *page 355*

AT THE HARVARD OBSERVATORY IN 1896, Annie devoted herself to the project of recording, classifying and cataloging stars. She developed a system of classification for the spectra of stars by surface temperature. The project was adopted for universal use. Annie worked at the project until 225,000 stars were classified. Her findings were published in nine volumes.

Born December 11, 1863, Annie showed early interest in music and photography. In 1894, she took a year of advanced study in astronomy and then continued her astronomy studies under Professor Pickering at Harvard. It was Professor Pickering's project that Annie made her own.

Annie became curator of astronomical photographs at Harvard Observatory in 1911. In 1938, she was named a professor of astronomy. In the 1920's through the end of her life, she cataloged tens of thousands of additional stars. Two volumes, published in 1925 and 1949, were added to her original nine.

Annie made several discoveries as she worked. Her contributions became a major influence on the theoretical and philosophical aspects of astronomy.

The first honorary doctorate for a woman from Oxford University was awarded to Annie in 1925. She received many other honors and awards. In 1933, the Annie J. Canon Prize of the American Astronomical Society was established. Annie retired from the observatory in 1940 but continued her research until her death on April 13, 1941.

REFLECTIONS

- Annie's work was published as the *Henry Draper Catalogue, 1918–1924, 1925, 1949.* Look for this in a library or conservatory.

- Annie's method of spectral classification by surface temperature became universally used. How do you feel about the inclusion and integration of women's contributions in scientific, educational and cultural media? How aware are you of the exclusion of women from many fields of knowledge?

- Go out on a clear night and ponder the wonder of the stars.

PRAYER

In the multitude
Of the stars of heavens,

May we come to know
The vastness of your love, O God.
Amen.

 ## December 12

JANE FRANCES DE CHANTAL

Founder of Visitation Nuns • France • 1572–1641

SCRIPTURE THEME

Faith

"We walk by faith, not by sight."
> — *2 Corinthians 5:7*

QUOTATION

"One of the holiest people I have ever met on this earth."
> — *said of Jane Frances by Saint Vincent de Paul,* The Penguin Dictionary of Saints, *page 180*

JANE WAS BORN INTO A NOBLE BURGUNDIAN FAMILY of France in 1572. At age twenty, she married Baron Christophe de Chantal, and they had seven children. Three died in infancy. After nine years of marriage, her husband was killed in a shooting accident.

In 1604, she met Francis de Sales, who served as her spiritual guide, advising her to live well her duties as daughter, mother and member of society.

Later, Jane wished to become a nun, and, with Francis de Sales, she founded the Order of the Visitation with its special purpose of including the infirm, the crippled, widows and the elderly as members. At first, the nuns left the enclosure to visit the sick, but the norms of the times soon had them restricted to cloister, where they devoted their lives to contemplative prayer. Church authorities of the time found "unenclosed" nuns not quite proper. (Angela Merici and Mary Ward, who also founded religious communities of women about this same time, ran into the same kind of challenge and opposition.)

Francis de Sales and Jane set up the convent at Annecy in 1610 with Jane and a dozen other nuns. In thirty years, they established nearly ninety convents of Visitation nuns. When a plague broke out, Jane devoted her convent to the ill and encouraged local officials to tend to the sick and bereaved.

In 1641, Jane went to Paris to visit Anne of Austria. She died during her return journey.

REFLECTIONS

- Jane Frances de Chantal and Francis de Sales had a marvelous friendship. He was bishop of Geneva and helped her to live her responsibilities as a widow and mother and later to establish convents. Their meeting was a turning point in Jane's life. Do you have a friend who has greatly influenced your life?

- Jane's convents accepted women who were not fit for more austere convent life. They were encouraged toward interior mortifications rather than physical self-denials. What virtues, such as humility and meekness, are important to you? Who do you think should be encouraged to enter convents?

PRAYER

That the men in our lives
Be good fathers and dear brothers
And wonderful spouses and friends—
For this we pray.
Amen.

December 13

SAINT LUCY

Martyr • Sicily • 3rd century

SCRIPTURE THEME

Lamplight
"Her lamp does not go out at night."
  — *Proverbs 31:18*

QUOTATION

"It is light that counts above everything. Not colored light, but color that gives off light—radiance."
  — *Helen Frankenthaler,* Beacon Book of Quotations by Women, *page 64*

LUCY WAS A MARTYR at Syracuse in Sicily about 304, probably during the persecution of Diocletian.

In the early Church, her feast was associated with the winter solstice and light. Lucia as a name is derived from the Latin word for light, *lux*. She was popularly associated with light and eyes and invoked for protection against diseases of the eyes. Artists have portrayed her with a dish holding two eyes.

In Sicily, the popular song *Santa Lucia* is still sung. In Venice, it is sung by the gondoliers.

Lucy's name was incorporated into the liturgy, and churches were built in her honor.

In Scandinavian countries, especially Sweden, Lucy Fires were lit on her feast day. As lightbringer, she heralded the approach of Christ, the true Light of the World. Also in Sweden, young girls wear wreaths on their heads, sometimes with candles, as they carry breakfast to the family members.

Lucy is also considered the patron saint of lamplighters.

REFLECTIONS

- Who has brought light into your life? How have you kept that light alive?

- It has been said that the eyes are the windows of the soul. Do you believe this? What is the best way to see into someone's soul?

PRAYER

As we light the evening lamps
In the windows of our homes,
May we also keep alive
The light of Christ in our hearts
And in our lives.
Amen.

December 14

MARGARET CHASE SMITH

Politician • U.S. • 1897–1995

SCRIPTURE THEME

Public service

"Only to fear the LORD your God, to walk in all his ways, to love him, to serve the LORD your God with all your heart and with all your soul, and to keep the commandments of the LORD your God and his decrees that I am commanding you today, for your own well-being."

— *Deuteronomy 10:12*

QUOTATION

"I believe that in our constant search for security we can never gain any peace of mind until we secure our own soul. And this I do believe above all, especially in my times of greater discouragement, that I must believe—that I must believe in my fellow men—that I must believe in myself—that I must believe in God— if life is to have any meaning."

— *Margaret Chase Smith,* The Quotable Woman: 1800–1981, *page 259*

MARGARET, BORN DECEMBER 14, 1897, heard political opinions expressed at her father's barbershop during her growing-up years in Maine. During high school, she became manager of the girls' basketball team. She also worked at the five-and-ten and as an evening telephone operator.

She worked as a teacher, a tax payment recorder, a newspaper circulation manager, an advertising copywriter and a woolen mill manager. In 1930, she married Clyde Smith, then a state senator, and her involvement in politics with him became her life, both as gracious hostess and partner in public life.

When Clyde suffered a fatal heart attack in 1940, Margaret was elected to finish out her husband's term in the House of Representatives. This election of a widow to finish out a term had previously happened, twenty or so times. But with Margaret, it was different. She campaigned and in 1941 won a seat on her own merits.

She worked on committees and legislation to benefit women in the armed services and to improve labor conditions. She voted with honesty and courage and not always along party lines.

Every fall, she toured her home state, learning the views of her constituents. She considered herself a working lawmaker and in 1948 won a

Senate seat. Her nationally syndicated column "Washington and You" ran for five years.

In June 1950, Margaret made a clearheaded speech publicly criticizing McCarthyism and the witch-hunt for Communists. She tried to be thorough and impartial in all her observations and investigations. She was honored as Woman of the Year and Most Admired Woman and received other awards.

She made a global tour in 1954, which was seen by television viewers all over the world. She was noted for answering all her letters and for being present whenever a Senate vote was scheduled.

Margaret ventured into politics when it was a man's world, but she believed strongly in a future in politics for women. In 1968, Margaret completed a book called *Gallant Women*, in which she examines the role of women in American public life. She included the lives of Anne Hutchinson, Dolley Madison, Harriet Tubman, Clara Barton, Lucy Stone, Elizabeth Blackwell, Susan B. Anthony, Anne Sullivan, Amelia Earhart, Althea Gibson, Frances Perkins and Eleanor Roosevelt.

REFLECTIONS

- What local politicians in your area are women? How do you view them?
- Do you support (vote for) women at the state and national levels of political activity?
- If one of your daughters, sisters or friends wished to run for a political office, what would your advice be?

PRAYER

May those of us called to public life
Be gallant women, valiant women,
As we serve God and country.
Amen.

December 15

MARIA CROCIFISSA DI ROSA

Religious founder • Italy • 1812–1855

SCRIPTURE THEME

Roses

"The desert shall rejoice and blossom."

— Isaiah 35:1

QUOTATION

"I can't go to bed with a quiet conscience...if during the day I missed any chance, however slight, of preventing wrongdoing or of helping to do some good."

— *Maria Crocifissa di Rosa*, Lives of the Saints, *page 460*

PAOLINA FRANCESCA DI ROSA WAS BORN IN 1812 in Brescia, Italy. Her father was a public official and wealthy landowner. Paolina was educated by the Sisters of the Visitation.

Because her mother was dead, Paolina ran her father's household and also launched many charitable works such as care for the sick during the cholera epidemic of 1836. She was influential in many social concerns and services in Brescia.

In 1840, she founded the Handmaids of Charity, a religious congregation devoted to care of the sick. As Sister Maria Crocifissa, she was an "angel of mercy" for Brescia. When war broke out in northern Italy, her sisters went onto the battlefield and staffed a military hospital.

In 1850, she went to Rome to seek papal approbation for her congregation, and the congregation spread rapidly.

Sister Maria Crocifissa died December 15, 1855, and was buried at the motherhouse of the Handmaids of Charity in Brescia. She was canonized in 1954.

REFLECTIONS

- Does making a spiritual review of the day send you to bed with a quiet conscience?
- How do you feel about the running of a household as satisfying work?

PRAYER

As we make our evening prayer,

We ask God's forgiveness
For any wrongdoings
And for missed chances
Of doing good.
Amen.

 *December 16*

AMY CARMICHAEL

Missionary • Britain and India • 1867–1951

SCRIPTURE THEME

Preach the Gospel

"Go therefore and make disciples of all nations, baptizing them in the name of the Father and of the Son and of the Holy Spirit, and teaching them to obey everything that I have commanded you."

— *Matthew 28:19*

QUOTATION

"I who said I would never do any work but 'preach the gospel.' It takes some of us years to learn what preaching the gospel means."

— *Amy Carmichael,* Mothers of the Saints, *page 197*

AMY EXPERIENCED HER VOCATIONAL CALL from God on January 13, 1892, in which she heard God say, "Go ye." The faith of her full church life as a Presbyterian had already reached out to young Irish working girls in her native land. Born December 16, 1867, Amy was ready to leave the British Isles at God's call.

She sailed first for Japan as a missionary in an Evangelistic Bond and after a time went to Ceylon. In 1895, she went as a missionary to India where she lived for fifty-seven years. Throughout her missionary years, she wrote long letters home each month, and the letters told of the monotony and discouragement of mission life as well as the joys.

While soldiers, administrators and missionaries in India lived as the British, Amy chose to live and dress as much like the natives as possible. In her intense way, Amy wanted to be a radical disciple, zealous and impatient to preach the gospel. She learned the Tamil language and set herself to preaching.

In 1901, a seven-year-old girl ran away from temple prostitution to Amy and began to call her *Amma*, "Mother." As Amy learned more about the sexual slavery of temple girls and women, she longed to save the children from such exploitation. The collection of babies and children grew and hampered Amy's desire to preach and evangelize.

Gradually, Amy came to realize that God's will for her was to care for the large family of children, and she settled into "motherwork." Amy's mother came out to India to help with the work and was lovingly called *Atah*, "grandmother."

In addition to her letters, Amy wrote a great deal of poetry and several books, which reveal, and, indeed, nurtured, her spiritual growth.

She established a monthly prayer day and developed a hospital out of an old henhouse, which they whimsically called Buckingham Palace. Her work with the children flourished. Amy realized that she had made some mistakes and tried to improve. She tried to learn child psychology and better methods of education.

Several health problems plagued her during the 1930's and 1940's. Amy died January 18, 1951, and was buried under a tamarind tree with the one word, *Amma*, marking her grave.

REFLECTIONS

- Are you aware of the problems of the sexual exploitation of children and women? What can you do to establish justice where you live?
- When have you been a mother to someone who was not your natural child? Describe the experience.

PRAYER

May we call you Amma, God—
Mama and Mother and Amma.
Amen.

 *December 17*

SAINT OLYMPIAS

Deaconess • Constantinople • d. 408

SCRIPTURE THEME

Mission of women

"Greet Prisca and Aquila, who work with me in Christ Jesus, and who risked their necks for my life."

— Romans 16:3

QUOTATION

"The especial genius of women I believe to be electrical in movement, intuition in function, spiritual in tendency."

— *Margaret Fuller,* The Quotable Woman, *page 9*

OLYMPIAS WAS BORN to one of the outstanding families of Constantinople. When both of her parents died, she was cared for by Theodosia, a relative of Saints Basil and Gregory Nazianzen.

At eighteen, Olympias married the city prefect. On that occasion, Saint Gregory of Nazianzen wrote to her a letter of advice in verse, one of the earliest "mirrors for women" in the Christian tradition. By age twenty, she was a widow and resolved to not marry again.

Olympias was personally charming and very wealthy and much sought after for marriage, but she turned away all pursuers, preferring instead to give huge sums to charitable purposes. She was consecrated a deaconess of the church, a practice in use in the fourth century. She lived in a convent community with other deaconesses, widows and virgins who spent their time in prayer and service in a hospital and an orphanage.

Olympias was very supportive of the writings of Saint Gregory of Nicea and of Saint John Chrysostom. When John was in conflict with the emperor and the patriarch, she stood by his cause. When John was exiled, Olympias was fined and later exiled for defending his cause. There are seventeen extant letters from John to Olympias in which he sends her news, gratitude and concern.

Olympias was still in exile when she learned of John's death in 407. She died a year later, in her mid-forties. Her body was returned to Constantinople and buried at the convent she founded near the cathedral.

REFLECTIONS

- How do you feel about the role of women in the modern Church?
- In what way do you protect or aid those doing the work of God?

PRAYER

For women devoted to Church service, we pray—
That their hospitality and service,
Their spirituality and values
May be affirmed and strengthened
By the church they love and serve.
Amen.

 *December 18*

BARBARA HAUER FRIETCHIE

Patriot · *U.S.* · *1766–1862*

SCRIPTURE THEME

Old age

"She was of a great age, having lived with her husband seven years after her marriage, then as a widow to the age of eighty-four."

— *Luke 2:37*

QUOTATION

"Each red stripe has blazoned forth
Gospels writ in blood;
Every star has sung the birth
Of some deathless good."

— Lucy Larcom, The Quotable Woman: 1800–On, *page 53*

THIS PATRIOT WAS IMMORTALIZED by John Greenleaf Whittier in his poem "Barbara Frietchie." The story goes that Confederate bullets tore holes in the flag flying from Barbara's house, and she stuck her head and hands out the window and grabbed up the flag with her famous plea to shoot her and spare the flag. The story in verse became very popular and kept alive Barbara's memory long after her death.

Barbara Hauer was born of German immigrant parents. She grew up in Pennsylvania and Maryland and in 1806 married John Frietchie. Not much else is recorded in history of Barbara's ninety-six years of life.

In early September 1862, just before her last birthday, it seems that Barbara waved a Union flag from the second-floor window as Confederate troops came through the town of Fredericksburg. Whether there was an incident or not, the story grew up that Barbara's patriotic spirit had defied the Confederate army.

Barbara died December 18, 1862. The story made its way to Whittier whose now-famous poem appeared in the October 1863 *Atlantic Monthly*.

In 1913, a memorial honoring Barbara was erected in Fredericksburg. In 1926, a replica of Barbara's house was also constructed in Fredericksburg—the original house had been destroyed shortly after Barbara's death.

REFLECTIONS

- Call to mind and pray for countries currently torn apart by civil war.
- What values mean enough to you that you would risk being shot?
- On what days do you display your country's flag? Why?

PRAYER

We pray for strength and courage
To lean far out on windowsills,
To take the necessary risks
In defending the values
We have come to believe in and love.
Amen.

 *December 19*

NELLIE TAYLOE ROSS

Political official • U.S. • 1876–1977

SCRIPTURE THEME

Public office

"The LORD sent me to anoint you king over his people Israel."
— *1 Samuel 15:1*

QUOTATION

"Leadership should be born out of the understanding of the needs of those who would be affected by it."

— Marian Anderson, The New York Public Library Book of Twentieth Century American Quotations, *page 130*

NELLIE TAYLOE WAS BORN NOVEMBER 29, 1876, in Missouri. In 1902, she married William B. Ross, a lawyer. They moved to Cheyenne, Wyoming, where her husband set up his law practice.

Elected governor of Wyoming in 1922, William died in the middle of his term. Nellie was elected to fill out her husband's term of office from January 1925 to January 1927. On the same day that Nellie was elected as governor in Wyoming, Miriam Amanda "Ma" Ferguson was elected as governor of Texas. Nellie was inaugurated two weeks sooner than Ma, so Nellie is considered to be the first woman ever elected as a governor of a U.S. state.

In 1926, Nellie was not reelected. She devoted herself to Democratic politics and was especially active in campaign efforts for President Franklin D. Roosevelt.

In 1933, she became the first woman to hold the office of director of the U.S. Bureau of the Mint. She worked there, improving its economic situation, for twenty years. In 1940, Nellie was appointed to lead the Treasury Assay Committee.

Nellie was the first woman to have her likeness imprinted on a mint medal. Nellie's name was engraved on the cornerstone of the Fort Knox Gold Depository.

Nellie died on December 19, 1977, in Washington, D.C., at age one hundred one.

REFLECTIONS

- How many states currently have women governors?
- What is your own interest and involvement in politics?

PRAYER

With gratitude for the ever-growing numbers
Of women serving in politics,
Let us pray—
That these women may bring
Integrity and charity
To their leadership roles.
Amen.

December 20

SUSANNE LANGER
Philosopher • U.S. • 1895–1985

SCRIPTURE THEME

Seeker of truth

"If you continue in my work, you are truly my disciples; and you will know the truth, and the truth will make you free."

— *John 8:32*

QUOTATION

"Whenever you know that you've broken through a difficult problem it gives you a great feeling of security. The greatest security in this tumultuous world is faith in your own mind."

— *Susanne Langer,* Famous American Women, *page 261*

SUSANNE'S SUMMERS AS A CHILD were spent at Lake George, where she delighted in observing the behavior of animals. Her winters were spent in New York City, where her father's love of music and her mother's love of poetry made deep impressions on her. Her father also encouraged her to read. In college she gained the skills of a philosopher: holding many ideas simultaneously, searching out relationships between ideas, thinking about concepts with neither belief or disbelief, setting aside unsolved problems for future recall.

She received her bachelor's degree from Radcliffe in 1920 and married William Langer, who had a history degree from Harvard. Susanne earned master's and doctoral degrees during the same years her two sons were born.

Susanne pursued the philosophical thesis that symbol making led to human development, and she began to write about this topic. She believed that symbol usage distinguished humans from animals, and she explored the area of nondiscursive symbols, such as music, painting, sculpture and dance.

She extended the boundaries of twentieth-century thinking and philosophy by including nonverbal communication. Her book, *Philosophy in a New Key*, explained how rhythms, rituals and pictures are also human activities of symbol making, just as much as words and codes are.

In the early 1940's, Susanne and her husband were divorced. She added teaching and lecturing to her research and writing. In 1960, she was elected to the American Academy of Arts and Sciences.

Her former workspace in an old Connecticut farmhouse offered clues to her sources of inspiration. Boxes of index cards on a huge desk contained alphabetized notes on everything she read. Light through the window brightened aquariums and jars containing fish, turtles and tadpoles. In the living room she had a music corner, and outdoors she had a canoe to paddle and woods to roam in. Much of her best thinking was done in solitude—with nature and music as companions.

REFLECTIONS

- How do music, painting, sculpture and dancing help you to express your thoughts, feelings and ideas in nonverbal ways?
- How do words and symbols (such as mathematical ones) help you to express yourself?
- In what ways do you consider yourself a philosopher, a seeker of truth?

PRAYER

We seek truth in our knowledge
Of all good things.
May we come to know you,
The one true God of all goodness.
Amen.

 *December 21*

MARIA CADILLA DE MARTINEZ

Folklorist • Puerto Rico • 1886–1951

SCRIPTURE THEME

Folklore

"By the rivers of Babylon—
there we sat down and there we wept
when we remembered Zion."

— *Psalm 137:1*

QUOTATION

"Continue in your desire to learn conquering your fame that justice and knowledge elevate the woman to the respect of man."

— Notable American Women: The Modern Period, *page 130*

BORN IN ARICEBO, PUERTO RICO, on December 21, 1886, Maria (who used the pseudonym Liana) became interested in the indigenous culture of Puerto Rico. She graduated from a Catholic high school in Aricebo and then attended a public school in the United States. She took up both painting and writing, which she combined with a teaching career.

Maria married an architect-painter, and their intellectual interests led to a lifelong interest in learning. Maria was mother to many children, but only two, Maria and Tomasita, lived to adulthood. For her doctoral thesis, Maria wrote *La Poesia Popular en Puerto Rico*, which became a popular textbook.

While she continued her mothering and teaching, Maria also studied painting and piano. Always, she urged the preservation of Hispanic and Puerto Rican culture and literature, with a special focus on Puerto Rican folklore. The celebration of the feasts of patron saints was one of her special studies.

Maria was devoted to feminist causes, which paralleled her cultural interest. She believed equality for women could be secured by education. Her activism in civic and national associations promoted her feminist and cultural dreams. She was honored with many awards, including being named Woman of Puerto Rico posthumously in 1963.

She died of cancer in 1951 in Aricebo, where she and her husband had made their home.

REFLECTIONS

- Read some of Maria's books: *Cuentos a Lillian, Racies de la Tierre, Hitos de La Raza*.

- Are your artistic and creative endeavors an extension of your life and work? An escape from them? How might the two differ?

PRAYER

May the windows
Of learning and understanding
Bring us closer to equality
Of respect for women.
Amen.

December 22

GEORGE ELIOT

Novelist, essayist, poet • *England* • *1819–1880*

SCRIPTURE THEME

Moral integrity

"The integrity of the upright guides them."

— *Proverbs 11:3*

QUOTATION

"It is vain thought to flee from the work that God appoints us, for the sake of finding a greater blessing, instead of seeking it where alone it is to be found—in loving obedience."

— George Eliot, The New Book of Christian Quotations, *page 171*

CONSIDERED ONE OF THE FINEST BRITISH NOVELISTS, George Eliot (Mary Ann Evans) was born in 1819 in England. Even as a child, she evidenced intelligence, musical talent and a religious sense. When her mother died in 1836, the seventeen-year-old took charge of the household. She was also involved with local charities.

She continued to keep house for her father while she translated Strases' *Life of Jesus* and worked on other literary projects. She worked as assistant editor at the *Westminister Review* from 1851 to 1854. In 1856, she started writing fiction.

A false name to disguise identity has been used by women to gain access to schools, military service and publication. Writers such as Mary Ann Evans (George Eliot) and Karen Blixen (Isak Dinesen) used male pseudonyms to gain access to what was then a man's world.

Her seven major novels fixed her place in English literature. The novels depict society but also reveal the author's moral force and intense desire to change society.

She died in 1880.

REFLECTIONS

- *Silas Marner* and *The Mill on the Floss* are two of George Eliot's best-known novels. If you've never read them, try to read one or both.
- What kind of social values and social criticism do you like to read about in fiction? How do you express your own sense of social concern?

PRAYER

> We sing in our hearts
> To you, O God.
> In quiet prayer,
> May we hear your voice,
> And develop that strong moral sense
> That expresses itself
> In simple human pity
> And a hunger for goodness.
> Amen.

 *December 23*

SARAH WALKER

Inventor, businesswoman • U.S. • 1867–1917

SCRIPTURE THEME

Wisdom in business

"The kingdom of heaven is like a merchant in search of fine pearls; on finding one pearl of great value, he went and sold all that he had and bought it."
— *Matthew 5:45*

QUOTATION

"Men always try to keep women out of business so they won't find out how much fun it really is."
— *Vivien Kellems*, The Quotable Woman: 1800–On, *page 253*

IN 1905, SARAH WALKER CAME UP WITH A FORMULA that transformed the kinky hair of Black women into something smooth and shining. Known as the Walker Method or Walker System, her idea caught on. The Madame C. J. Walker Manufacturing Company became a major enterprise in the city of Indianapolis, and the largest Black-owned business in the United States.

Born on December 23, 1867, of poor farmers, Sarah was orphaned at six. At fourteen she married, and at twenty she was a widow. She took up work as a washerwoman and during those years experimented with various hair dressings.

As sole proprietor and president of the business and with her picture on the product, Madame Walker became a well-known figure. She gave lectures and demonstrations to church groups and women's groups and was generous by way of philanthropy to various groups.

In her employ were more than three thousand people, and she encouraged cleanliness and personal virtues as well as community service among them.

She had a luxurious townhouse in New York City, where she was hostess to leading intellectuals and artists. When she died on May 25, 1917, her estate was valued at more than a million dollars.

The Madame Walker Urban Life Center in Indianapolis, Indiana, serves as a cultural center for the Black community. Displays on local history, cultural events and theatrical productions in the Walker Theater keep alive the memory of Madame Walker. The Walker Theater was designed and built in an African-Egyptian style.

REFLECTIONS

- Look for old advertisements of Walker products when you visit historical museums.
- How do you feel about altering your God-given features? Is it vanity? Struggling for perfection? Wasteful?

PRAYER

May we make wise and prudent use
Of materials and processes
For the well-being of humanity
And the environment.
Amen.

 *December 24*

MARGARET STADLER

Virgin, Second Order Franciscan • *Germany* • *d. 1521*

SCRIPTURE THEME

Child

"Whoever welcomes one such child in my name welcomes me."

— *Matthew 18:3*

QUOTATION

"The Brethren did not believe in celebrating any special days or festivals. The Incarnation was to be borne in mind at all times, but never one time."

— *Anne Arnott,* Harper Religious and Inspirational Quotation Companion, *page 319*

MARGARET, A POOR CLARE NUN at the convent in Sefflingen near Ulin in Swabia, was devoted to contemplation.

The story is told that one day she was so absorbed in contemplating the love of God who came into the world as a child that she missed her turn at kitchen duty. Meanwhile, a beautiful young boy was seen preparing the food in the kitchen. The meal was declared the best the sisters ever ate, but the wonderful little cook was nowhere to be found.

Margaret died in 1521.

REFLECTIONS

• What is your view of the Incarnation? Does your devotion include aspects of Christ's childhood?

• How can you become more childlike in your daily life?

PRAYER

We thank You, O Bread of Heaven,
For all the persons who
Prepare our daily meals.
Amen.

 *December 25*

DOROTHY WORDSWORTH

Nature diarist • England • 1771–1855

SCRIPTURE THEME

Flowers

"They flourish like a flower of the field."

— *Psalm 103:15*

QUOTATION

"I never saw daffodils so beautiful. They grew among the mossy stones around

and about them, some rested their heads upon these stones as on a pillow for weariness and the rest tossed and reeled and danced and seemed as if they verily laughed with the wind."

— Dorothy Wordsworth, Women of Achievement, *page 157*

DOROTHY, THE ONLY GIRL OF FIVE CHILDREN, was born December 25, 1771, in Westmoreland, England. She was six when her mother died. She was sent to live with relatives in Halifax.

In her twenties, she was reunited with her brother, William, eighteen months older than she. She became devoted to him. They met Samuel Taylor Coleridge and moved to live near him in the Lake District.

Dorothy kept journals, recording every sight and sound of their walks about the Lake District and of their trips to Germany and Scotland. Her intention was to help her brother with source material for his poems. These journals (which were published thirty years after her death) also tell beautifully of Dorothy's response to country life, the natural world and her own inner thoughts.

Dorothy never married but stayed on after William's marriage to help care for his children. An illness affecting her brain afflicted the last twenty years of her life. William and his wife looked after her. After William's death, his wife continued to care for Dorothy until her death in 1855.

REFLECTIONS

- What poetry might Dorothy have written had she been encouraged to do so? What latent talents do you have that need encouragement?
- How do you balance service to others with expression of your own gifts and talents?

PRAYER

Let us absorb the healing powers
Of the natural world
So we may be of service to others,
At the services of God.
Amen.

December 26

VINCENTA MARIA LOPEZ

Founder of religious congregation • Spain • 1847–1890

SCRIPTURE THEME

Home for girls

"See, I have inscribed you on the palms of my hands;
your walls are continually before me."

— Isaiah 49:16

QUOTATION

"The girls won out."

— Vincenta Maria Lopez

VINCENTA'S LIFELONG DREAM was to provide a home or hospice to young girls in need. This desire began when, as a teenager, she assisted her aunt in running a home for orphans and a hospice for working girls.

Born in Navarre, Vincenta attended school in Madrid, where her aunt encouraged the idea of a religious vocation. Concerned about the future of the orphans and working girls, Vincenta was torn between their needs and her desire for a contemplative vocation. Vincenta's father, on the other hand, urged her to marry, but she refused.

After prayerful consideration, Vincenta decided in favor of the girls. Her father remained opposed to this and ordered her home. Once there, she became ill. At the doctor's order, Vincenta returned to Madrid for better climate.

In time, she and her aunt gathered women interested in living a religious life and serving the needs of orphans and working girls. Her spiritual and practical strengths helped establish a flourishing community. The sisters begged to get what they needed for new homes.

The new community, called the Daughters of Mary Immaculate for the Protection of Working Girls of Spain, spread throughout Europe. After Vincenta's death in 1890, the sisters spread to Latin America and South Africa. These sisters continued to teach domestic arts and provide hospices in the spirit of their motto, "Steady employment is the safeguard of virtue."

REFLECTIONS

- What does your church do for young working adults? How can you help?
- What are the special needs of working women? How can these needs be met?

PRAYER

Behind the windows of many city apartments
Live single working women.
We pray for them and for their well-being,
And we promise to help them
In their spiritual and social needs.
Amen.

 *December 27*

AMY MARY CHENEY BEACH

Composer, pianist • U.S. • 1867–1944

SCRIPTURE THEME

Music

*"Sing aloud to God our strength;
shout for joy to the God of Jacob."*

— Psalm 81:1

QUOTATION

"You see I am a staunch believer in the possibilities offered for a musical education in our own country, for I have studied only in America; indeed, since I am a very bad sailor, I have never quite summoned the requisite courage until this year to attempt a voyage across the ocean."

— Amy Beach, Give Her This Day, *page 256*

AMY WAS BORN SEPTEMBER 5, 1867, in New Hampshire, an only child. By age four, she was creating melodies on the keyboard, and at six she began serious piano lessons from her mother. During her school years, she studied with other teachers in the Boston area, and at age fourteen she studied harmony, the only formal instruction in music theory she received. She was mostly self-taught in counterpoint, fugue and orchestration. By age sixteen, she was giving public recitals, including performances with the Boston Symphony Orchestra, and again in 1885, she played with the Boston Symphony, at age eighteen.

Her marriage in 1885 to Dr. Henry Harris Aubrey Beach, a surgeon, found her concentrating on composition, instead of performance, with his encouragement. Their marriage was childless, and Amy devoted her time to music. Her *Mass in E-flat Major* was performed in February 1892 by the Boston Symphony and the Handel and Haydn Society.

Amy composed "Festival Jubilate" for the dedication of the women's building at the 1893 World's Fair in Chicago. She became the preeminent composer among American women with more than 150 numbered works.

After her husband's death in 1910, Amy spent several years in Europe doing performances and continuing with compositions. After 1914, she settled in New York City. In the 1920's and 1930's, Amy composed anthem motets and cantatas on religious themes drawn from her devout Episcopalian practice of religion. In her sixties, she composed *Canticle of the Sun, opus 123*, and her only opera, *Cabildo*. At seventy, she composed her *Piano Trio in A Minor, opus 150*. The Chicago International Exposition honored her in 1933 for creative work in music.

Her last work, "Though I Take Wings of Morning," based on the text of Psalm 139, was composed in 1941, when she was seventy-three. She died December 27, 1944, in New York City.

REFLECTIONS

- What part does music play in your life? Are you a composer, performer, conductor, listener?
- Try to affirm and encourage another in whom you see the gift of music.
- What creative work might you do during your sixties and seventies?

PRAYER

May we always remember
In the composing of our lives
That God is the conductor
Of our symphony.
Amen.

December 28

MOTHERS OF THE HOLY INNOCENTS

Martyrs • Israel • 1st century

SCRIPTURE THEME

Rachel weeping for her children

"Rachel is weeping for her children;
she refuses to be comforted for her children,
because they are no more."

— *Jeremiah 31:15*

QUOTATION

"So long as little children are allowed to suffer, there is no true love in the world."

— *Isadora Duncan,* Beyond Bartlett, *page 22*

THE MATTHEAN ACCOUNT OF HEROD'S VIOLENCE against the babies of Israel and their mothers forms the starting point of prayer and pondering about child abuse. All the innocents in all the centuries who have suffered, who today are suffering, from abuse—physical, mental, sexual— cause the Rachel in each of us to weep.

This feast is not so much a glory feast of the martyrdom of babes as it is a heartrending memorial of mothers' hearts aching, weeping, sorrowing forever.

The plight of children worldwide offers sad commentary of the cruelty and neglect of the world at large. Infants, born and unborn, are at great risk from abortion, malnutrition, disease and homelessness. There are babies born with AIDS or drug addictions—how innocent they are! And mothers would do better for their babes if only they could. But poverty and power abuses work against their maternal instincts.

REFLECTIONS

- Hold a baby; hug a child.
- Reach out to a mother who has lost a child.
- What can you do to protect the innocent?

PRAYER

For all who hold responsibility

For killing innocents,
We pray to you, God of life,
That they may be led by grace and by witness
To value life;
And we thank you, God,
For giving us life
Even before we understand it.
Amen.

 *December 29*

SISTER THEA BOWMAN

Woman of faith and joy • U.S. • *1937–1990*

SCRIPTURE THEME

Joy

"I will greatly rejoice in the LORD
my whole being shall exult in my God."

— *Isaiah 61:10*

QUOTATION

"My prayer has been, 'Lord, let me live until I die.' I want to live fully, to love fully."

— *Thea Bowman,* Almost Home

WHEN SISTER THEA BOWMAN DIED ON MARCH 30, 1990, many felt they had lost a personal friend. Some had seen her profiled on the *60 Minutes* television show and were enlivened by her vitality. Bishops had been inspired by her presentation at their 1989 meeting, a message about her experiences of being Black and being Catholic in the United States in the twentieth century.

Also in 1989, Sister Thea Bowman was selected as the recipient of the *U.S. Catholic* (a magazine published by the Claretians) Award because of her work in furthering the cause of women in the Church.

Thea, granddaughter of a slave, converted to Catholicism at age twelve because she witnessed in a group of Franciscan sisters a deep sense of faith. The sisters opened a school for Black children in Thea's hometown of Canton, Mississippi. The sisters brought food, clothing and medical care. In deed, as well as in word, they challenged racist attitudes.

Thea chose to share the faith of these sisters and in due time their very way of life. Thea became a Franciscan Sister of Perpetual Adoration, the only Black woman in an all-White community.

With a special interest in cultural awareness, Thea traveled and lectured on the gifts African-Americans bring to the Church. She did singing performances of Black music and writing on self-appreciation.

Thea helped to organize the National Black Catholic Congress held in Washington in 1987. In 1989, she made a special presentation on the tenth anniversary of *Brothers and Sisters to Us*, the 1979 pastoral letter of the National Conference of Catholic Bishops.

Cancer came in the last years of Thea's life, and even strangers cheered her determination to lecture and sing. She died at home in Canton, Mississippi.

In addition to the *U.S. Catholic* award, Thea received the Laetare Medal of Notre Dame University on March 25, 1990, five days before her death.

REFLECTIONS

- Would your friends describe you as a joyful person? Do we have a duty to be cheerful for one another?
- Do you know someone who has died or is dying from cancer? What strength and joy can you lend that person?

PRAYER

"Lord, let me live until I die."
Amen.

December 30

AMELIA JENKS BLOOMER

Reformer · England and U.S. · 1818–1894

SCRIPTURE THEME

Equal partners

"There is no longer male and female; for all of you are one in Christ Jesus."

— *Galatians 3:28*

QUOTATION

"When woman shall be thus recognized as an equal partner with man in the universe of God—equal in rights and duties—then will she for the first time, in truth, become what her Creator designed her to be, a helpmate for man. With her mind and body fully developed, imbued with a full sense of her responsibilities, and living in the conscientious discharge of each and all of them, she will be fitted to share with her brother in all of the duties of life; to aid and counsel him in his hours of trial; and to rejoice with him in the triumph of every good word and work."

— *Amelia Jenks Bloomer*, American Women Writers, *page 55*

BORN MAY 27, 1818, Amelia Jenks received only a few years of education at a district school in Rhode Island, but by age seventeen, she was teaching school. She married Dexter C. Bloomer in 1840. He was a newspaper editor and encouraged her to contribute articles to his paper.

Amelia attended the women's rights meeting held in Seneca Falls in 1848 more as an observer than a participant. In 1849, she began publication of the *Lily*, the first newspaper devoted to women's interests and the first newspaper owned, edited and controlled by a woman. Through this newspaper, Amelia met Elizabeth Cady Stanton and Susan B. Anthony.

Amelia also worked as assistant editor at the *Western Home Visitor*, a literary weekly. As a woman of strong opinion, Amelia went about giving lectures, especially on employment and education for women. She also spoke on temperance and women's suffrage, key issues of the times in which she lived.

Unfortunately, Amelia's last name is forever associated with the full trousers worn by her and some of her friends: bloomers. The importance of the work Amelia did for society, community and church as writer, editor and lecturer far outweighs that of her experiment in clothing.

REFLECTIONS

- Do you read any magazine or newspaper that is chiefly for women? How does it differ from so-called men's magazines?
- Do you have an equal relationship with a man? Are you comfortable with this? Is he?

PRAYER

We lift up in prayer, O God,
All those women who work in journalism—
The reporters and editors,

The managers and publishers—
That their work may promote
Truth and freedom for all.
Amen.

December 31

ELIZABETH ARDEN

Beauty and cosmetic producer • *Canada and U.S.* • *1884–1966*

SCRIPTURE THEME

Beauty
"Ah, you are beautiful, my love,
ah, you are beautiful."
   — *Song of Solomon 1:15*

QUOTATION

"Character contributes to beauty. It fortifies a woman as her youth fades. A mode of conduct, a standard of courage, discipline, fortitude and integrity can do a great deal to make a woman beautiful."
   — *Jacqueline Bisset*, The New York Public Library Book of Twentieth Century American Quotations, *page 99*

BORN IN CANADA ON THE LAST DAY OF THE CALENDAR YEAR IN 1884 and named Florence Nightingale Graham, Elizabeth briefly pursued nurse's training. Her work as a secretary led her to New York City, where she became an assistant to a beauty specialist. She went into partnership in a Fifth Avenue beauty salon. When the partnership broke up, she continued her work with the corporate name of Elizabeth Arden.

She became an innovator of beauty and cosmetic products and a pioneer in their advertisement. She extended her business to international markets, selling her wares to pharmacies and department stores. She also opened over a hundred beauty salons worldwide where famous and wealthy clientele went for luxury services.

Elizabeth also owned racehorses and operated stables in Kentucky. The 1947 Kentucky Derby winner, Jet Pilot, came from the Arden stables.

Ageless beauty was one of Elizabeth's goals and values, and she successfully hid her age until her death on October 18, 1966.

REFLECTIONS

- What is beauty for you? Do you find that the emphasis on cosmetic beauty is a distraction from true, inner beauty? A complement to it?
- To what degree are you influenced by advertisements?

PRAYER

If beauty is in the eye of the beholder,
May our eyes see beauty
In God's creation
And in creation's God.
Amen.

Bibliography

Alegría, Claribel. *They Won't Take Me Alive: Salvadorean Women in Struggle for National Liberation.* London: The Women's Press, 1987.

Attwater, Donald. *Penguin Dictionary of Saints.* New York: Penguin, 1983.

Armstrong, Regis. *Clare of Assisi: The Early Documents.* New York: Paulist Press, 1989.

Ball, Ann. *Modern Saints: Their Lives and Faces*, Books 1 and 2. Rockford, Ill.: Tan Books, 1983.

____. *Faces of Holiness: Modern Saints in Photos and Words.* Huntington, Ind.: Our Sunday Visitor, 1998.

Barth, Sister M. Aquina, O.S.F. *The Poverello's Round Table.* Joliet, Ill.: Sisters of St. Francis of Mary Immaculate, 1939.

Bartlett, John. *Familiar Quotations*, 14th ed. Boston: Little, Brown and Company, 1968.

Beilenson, Evelyn. *Women.* White Plains, N.Y.: Peter Pauper Press, 1991.

____ and Ann Tenenbaum, eds. *Wit and Wisdom of Famous American Women.* White Plains, N.Y. Peter Pauper Press, 1986.

____ and Sharon Melnick, eds. *Words of Women: Quotes by Famous Americans.* White Plains, N.Y.: Peter Pauper Press, 1987.

Berlin, Irving. "God Bless America." New York: Irving Berlin Music Corporation, 1939.

Burden, Jean. *Journey Toward Poetry.* New York: October House, 1967.

Castle, Tony, ed. *The New Book of Christian Quotations.* New York: Crossroad, 1982.

Chervin, Ronda De Sola. *Quotable Saints.* Ann Arbor Servant Publications, 1992.

Chicago, Judy. *The Dinner Party: A Symbol of Our Heritage.* Garden City, N.Y.: Anchor Books, 1979.

Cooper, Jilly and Tom Hartman. *Beyond Bartlett: Quotations by and About Women*. New York: Stein and Day, 1983.

Cowart, John W. *People Whose Faith Got Them Into Trouble: Stories of Costly Discipleship*.

Creider, Jane Tapsubei. *Two Lives: My Spirit and I*. New York: Interlink Publishing Group, Inc., 1992.

Dash, Joan. *The Triumph of Discovery: Women Scientists Who Won the Nobel Prize*. Englewood Cliffs N.J.: Julian Messner, 1991.

Davidson, Caroline. *Women's Best: The Art and Life of Mary Ellen Best, 1809-1891*. New York: Crown Publishing, 1985.

Deloria, Ella Cara. *Waterlily*. Lincoln, Neb.: University of Nebraska Press, 1990.

De Vinck, Jose. *Revelations of Women Mystics: From the Middle Ages to Modern Times*. New York: Alba House, 1985.

Dickinson, Emily. *Selected Poems and Letters of Emily Dickinson*. New York: Anchor Books, 1959.

Dollen, Charles. *Prayer Book of the Saints*. Huntington, Ind.: Our Sunday Visitor, 1984.

Donadio, Stephen, et al. *The New York Public Library Book of Twentieth Century American Quotations*. New York: Warner Books, Inc., 1992.

Edgerly, Lois Stiles. *Give Her This Day: A Daybook of Women's Words*. New York: Tilbury House Publishers, 1991.

Faber, Doris. *Margaret Thatcher: Britain's "Iron Lady."* Women of Our Time series. New York: Puffin Books, 1985.

Farmer, David Hugh. *The Oxford Dictionary of Saints*, 2nd ed. New York: Oxford University Press, 1987.

Gareffa, Peter M., ed. *Contemporary Newsmakers*, Issue 3. New York: Gale Research, Inc., 1989.

____. *Newsmakers: The People Behind Today's Headlines*, Issue 2. New York: Gale Research, Inc., 1989.

Gilbert, Sandra M., and Susan Gubar. *The Norton Anthology of Literature by Women: The Tradition in English.* New York: W.W. Norton and Company, 1985.

Godden, Rumer. *A House With Four Rooms.* New York: William Morrow and Company, 1985.

Goodall, Jane. *Through a Window: My Thirty Years With the Chimpanzees of Gombe.* Boston: Houghton Mifflin, 1990.

Goodman, Susan. *Gertrude Bell.* Dover, N.H.: Berg, 1985.

Habig, Marion A., O.F.M. *The Franciscan Book of Saints.* Chicago: Franciscan Herald Press, 1959.

Hanley, Mary Laurence. *A Song of Pilgrimage and Exile: The Life and Spirit of Mother Marianne of Molokai.* New York: Harvest Books, 1980.

Harrison, Eric. "Lakota's Lost Bird is laid to rest near her kin at Wounded Knee," *The Buffalo News,* July 14, 1991.

Hoew, James and Robert Masheris. *Carol Burnett: The Sound of Laughter.* New York: Penguin Putnam, 1987.

Houselander, Caryll. *The Reed of God.* New York: Sheed and Ward, 1944.

Jezic, Diane Peacock. *Women Composers: The Lost Tradition Found.* New York: The Feminist Press at the City University of New York, 1988.

Kalberer, Augustine, O.S.B. *Lives of the Saints: Daily Readings.* Chicago: Franciscan Herald Press, 1983.

Kazel, Dorothy Chapon. *Alleluia Woman: Sister Dorothy Kazel, O.S.U.* Cleveland: Chapel Publications, 1987

Kenneally, James J. *The History of American Catholic Women.* New York: Crossroad Publishing Co., 1990.

Kenneth, Brother, C.G.A. *Saints of the Twentieth Century.* London: Mowbray, 1987.

Kollwitz, Hans. *The Diary and Letters of Kathe Kollwitz.* Cleveland: Northwestern University Press, 1988.

Kudlinsky, Kathleen V. *Juliette Gordon Low: America's First Girl Scout,* Women of Our Time series. New York: Puffin Books, 1988.

Kunitz, Stanley J., and Howard Haycraft. *Twentieth Century Authors: A Biographical Dictionary of Modern Literature.* New York: H.W. Wilson Company, 1942.

Lane, Rose Wilder. *Young Pioneers*. New York: Bantam Books, 1933.

Lannon, Maria M. *Mother Mary Elizabeth Lange: Life of Love and Service*. Washington, D.C.: The Josephite Pastoral Center, 1992.

Leifeld, Wendy. *Mothers of the Saints: Portraits of Ten Mothers of the Saints and Three Saints Who Were Mothers*. Ann Arbor, Mich.: Servant Publications, 1991.

L'Engle, Madeleine. *The Weather of the Heart*. Wheaton, Ill.: Harold Shaw Publishers, 1978.

Maggio, Rosalie. *The Beacon Book of Quotations by Women*. Boston: Beacon Press, 1992.

Mandela, Winnie. *Part of My Soul Went With Him*. New York: W.W. Norton and Company, 1984.

Meltzer, Milton. *Dorothea Lange: Life Through the Camera*, Women of Our Time series. New York: Puffin Books, 1985.

Mervin, Sabrina and Carol Prunhuber. *Women: Around the World and Through the Ages*. Wilmington, Del.: Atomium Books, 1990.

Mooney, Louise, ed. *Contemporary Newsmakers*. Detroit, Mich.: Gale Research, Inc., 1987.

Morgan, Robin, ed. *Sisterhood Is Global: The International Women's Movement Anthology*. New York: Anchor Books, 1984.

Nyabongo, Elizabeth. *Elizabeth of Toro: The Odyssey of an African Princess*. New York: Simon and Schuster, 1989.

Oates, Joyce Carol. *(Woman) Writer: Occasions and Opportunities*. New York: Dutton, 1989.

O'Brien, Felicity. *Saints in the Making*. Dublin: Veritas, 1988.

Olsen, Kirstin. *Remember the Ladies: A Woman's Book of Days*. Pittstown, N.J.: The Main Street Press, 1988.

Partnow, Elaine. *The Quotable Woman: From Eve to 1799*. New York: Facts on File, 1985.

_____. *The Quotable Woman: From 1800-On*. Garden City, N.Y.: Anchor Books, 1978.

_____. *The Quotable Woman: 1800-1981*. New York: Facts on File, 1985.

_____. *The New Quotable Woman*. New York: Facts on File, 1992.

Pepper, Margaret, ed. *The Harper Religious and Inspirational Quotation Companion*. New York: Harper and Row, 1989.

Powers, Jessica. "Escape," *The Selected Poetry of Jessica Powers*. New York: Sheed and Ward, 1989.

Quackenbush, Robert. *Stop the Presses, Nellie's Got a Scoop!: A Story of Nellie Bly*. New York: Simon and Schuster, 1992.

Ramsgat St. Augustine's Abbey. *The Book of Saints: A Dictionary of the Servants of God*. New York: Morehouse Publishing, 1993.

Raven, Susan and Alison Weir. *Women of Achievement: Thirty-five Centuries of History*. New York: Harmony Books, 1981.

Ruether, Rosemary Radford and Rosemary Skinner Keller, eds. *Women and Religion in America, vol. 2. The Colonial and Revolutionary Periods: A Documentary History*. San Francisco; Harper and Row, 1983.

Running Press Books. *The Quotable Woman: Witty Poignant and Insightful Observations from Notable Women*. New York: Running Press Books, 1991.

Rupp, Joyce. *The Star in My Heart: Experiencing Sophia, Inner Wisdom*. San Diego: LuraMedia, 1990.

Safransky, Sy, ed. *Sunbeams: A Book of Quotations*. Berkeley, Calif.: North Atlantic Books, 1990.

Sansevere-Dreherr, Diane. *Benazir Bhutto*. New York: Bantam Books, 1991.

Scariano, Margaret M. *The Picture Life of Corazon Aquino*. New York: Franklin Watts, 1987.

Seldes, George. *The Great Thoughts*. New York: Ballantine, 1985.

Sicherman, Barbara. *Notable American Women: The Modern Period*. Cambridge, Mass.: Harvard University Press, 1983.

Simpson, James B., ed. *Simpson's Contemporary Quotations*. Boston: Houghton Mifflin, 1988.

Sister Miriam of Jesus, trans. *Fascinated by God: The Spiritual Adventure of a Hippie*, unpublished.

Sisters of Social Service. *The Spirit of Margaret Slachta Lives On.* Buffalo, N.Y.: Sisters of Social Service, 1984.

Snyder, Robert. *Anäis Nin Observed: From a Film Portrait of a Woman as Artist.* Chicago: Swallow Press, 1976.

Sprague, Rosamond Kent, ed. *A Matter of Eternity: Selections from the Writings of Dorothy L. Sayers.* Grand Rapids, Mich.: Eerdmans Publishing Company, 1973.

Stein, Edith. *Essays on Woman, Collected Works of Edith Stein.* Washington, D.C.: ICS Publications, 1987.

Stevens, Clifford. *The One Year Book of Saints.* Huntington, Ind.: Our Sunday Visitor, Inc., 1987.

Stoddard, Hope. *Famous American Women.* New York: Thomas Y. Crowell, 1970.

Tobais, Tobi. *Maria Tallchief.* New York: Thomas Y. Crowell, 1970.

Von Trapp, Maria. *Los Angeles Times*, March 30, 1987.

Warner, Carolyn. *The Last Word: A Treasury of Women's Quotes.* New York: Prentice Hall, 1994.

Warner, Mary Alice, and Dayna Beilenson. *Women of Faith and Spirit: Their Words and Thoughts.* White Plains, N.Y.: Peter Pauper Press, Inc., 1987.

Whitney, Phyllis A. *Rainbow in the Mist.* New York: Doubleday, 1989.

Wilson, Robert. *Mother Angela and the Felician Sisters.* The Congregation of the Sisters of Saint Felix, 1980.

Zahniser, J.D., ed. *And Then She Said: Quotations by Women for Every Occasion.* Port Murray, N.J.: Caillech Press, 1989

_____. *And Then She Said...: More Quotations by Women for Every Occasion.* St. Paul: Calliech Press, 1990.

INDEX